Cyril Ramaphosa

by Anthony Butler

Jacana / Johannesburg
James Currey / Oxford

First published

in southern Africa in 2007
by Jacana Media (Pty) Ltd
10 Orange Street
Sunnyside
Auckland Park 2092
South Africa
+2711 628 3200
www.jacana.co.za

and in Britain in 2008
by James Currey Ltd
73 Botley Road
Oxford OX2 0BS
www.jamescurrey.co.uk

ISBN 978-1-77009-530-4 (Jacana, hardback)
ISBN 978-1-77009-370-6 (Jacana, paperback)
ISBN 978-1-84701-315-6 (James Currey, paperback)

British Library Cataloguing in Publication Data available ʼpon request

Cover design by miss sweden
Set in Garamond
Printed by Paarl Print
Job No. 000574

See a complete list of Jacana titles at www.jacana.co.za

The author and publisher would like to acknowledge with thanks the permission granted by the following copyright-holders to quote from the works cited:
Jonathan Ball Publishers for Oswald Mtshali, 'Just a passerby' from *Sounds of a Cowhide Drum* (Ad Donker, 1982), Wally Serote, 'Anonymous throbs and a dream' from *Selected Poems* (Ad Donker, 1982); Chris van Wyk, for 'Beware of white ladies when spring is here' from *It Is Time to Go Home* (Ad Donker, 1979); James Matthews for an untitled poem from *Poisoned Wells and Other Delights* (Blac Publishers, 1990); Dennis Brutus, 'Remembering June 16, 1976' from *Remembering Soweto 1976* (Whirlwind Books, 1992); the *Journal of Law and Religion* for Dean Tshenuwani Simon Farisani, 'South Africa: Unasked questions and unquestionable answers', *Journal of Law and Religion*, 5, 1987, pp. 263–73; and Eerdmans Publishing Co. for Tshenuwani Simon Farisani, *In Transit* (1990), pp. 84, 87, 91.

For Anne

CONTENTS

Preface ix

PART ONE: FORMATION

1 No place to rest 1

2 High school 19

3 Turfloop 43

4 Detention 59

5 June '76 71

6 Behind enemy lines 90

PART TWO: WORKING FOR THE WORKERS

7 The emergence of black union power 113

8 NUM: Small beginnings 130

9 The great negotiator 146

10 Entrenching union power 160

11 August 1987 182

PART THREE: THE DOMESTIC STRUGGLE

12 Cosatu and domestic opposition 209

13 Becoming ANC 222

14 By Mandela's side 242

15 ANC secretary-general 252

Contents

PART FOUR: NEGOTIATING TRANSITION

16 B.C.: Negotiations, 1984–1991 267

17 Return of the great negotiator 289

18 Triumph and despair 313

PART FIVE: TREADING WATER

19 Chairman Cyril 333

20 Philosopher and statesman 351

PART SIX: HORIZONS

21 A deepening national crisis 373

22 Visionary pragmatist 382

Notes 397

Index 433

PREFACE

I first considered writing about Ramaphosa more than a decade ago. My interest was less in the man himself than in the National Union of Mineworkers (NUM), which he had helped to create. Ramaphosa is not an easy subject for a biographer. He has written little. His speeches are rarely memorable. He is personally reticent and he gives few interviews. When he does talk, he is invariably unrevealing about his beliefs and opinions. As one of the few successful profilers of Ramaphosa observes, the interviewer is confronted with 'that smile that wraps itself around his face, that conspiratorial baritone chuckle, [and] that constant engagement masking profound reserve'.[1]

Ramaphosa's attitude towards prospective biographers does not help. When I returned to the idea of writing the book three or four years ago, I went to visit him at his Sandton offices to ask if he would consider assisting me. He professed to be gratified by my interest, but claimed to be far too busy to help. If only I could wait five years, he sighed, the burden of work on his shoulders would be less of an obstacle. He would be an older subject, the story of his life less incomplete. By then, he would be only too happy to assist. This has been Ramaphosa's stock promise to previous aspirant biographers, and I indicated that I was not persuaded by it.

Without a pause Ramaphosa changed tack. He frowned with concern, and told me that writing political biography is a perilous occupation. Immediately I felt alarmed. What were these hidden dangers? With worried eyes, he began to relate the cautionary tale of a South African writer of his acquaintance. The young author, hurrying to arrive punctually for an interview with an extremely high-ranking

ANC leader, did not have time to visit the toilet. A few minutes into the interview he realised that he desperately needed to relieve himself. But his subject had embarked on a seemingly endless narrative about his bold bureaucratic exploits in Lusaka in the 1980s. For many hours, despite a bursting bladder, the biographer was afraid to ask to leave the room. His subject was simply too wrapped up in his own historical importance.

Suddenly Ramaphosa was grinning. But just as quickly the smile disappeared and he was touching my sleeve conspiratorially: 'I am an enigma, you know.' He had read this description in a profile and he liked it. You can't write much about an enigma, he observed, unless it lets you into its secrets. He made it clear I would get nothing from him: no introductions, no personal papers, no documents, and no access to police files.

Changing direction once again, he floated the idea that he had always wanted to write an autobiography. Now I was going to ruin it all. He adopted a sorrowful expression to indicate that he was invoking my pity.

At this point, he raised an eyebrow and asked what would happen if he refused to cooperate. Would I write the book anyway?

A faintly sardonic expression lingered on his face. If I answered no, he could safely refuse to assist me and send me packing. Since I would be silly to answer no in such circumstances, his faint smile conveyed that I must not take offence at his question. 'I'm just asking in case you are not very bright,' his expression seemed to imply. As one of Cyril's political associates observes, he is 'an actor who becomes the part he's playing. But he always has a smirk in the corner of his face, as if to say, "I know I'm playing a role, and I want you to know it too."'[2]

When I later secured research leave from my university to write this book, I contacted Ramaphosa again in the hope that he might have changed his mind about assisting me. This time, in a Cape Town hotel, Ramaphosa was not so friendly. The temperature in the bar suddenly dropped to a cold chill. Looking up, I noticed with some disquiet that Ramaphosa's face loomed very large. His hitherto friendly eyes were now hostile. Why, he asked me, why do you have so little respect for me?

Why are you doing this to me? Eyes now blazing, he continued: Why are you letting me down? I will sue you. Yes. I'll have your house.[3]

Quickly, stumbling for words, I told him I did not own a house. Suddenly he looked deflated. For reasons I could not fathom, I felt ashamed of my behaviour. How could I treat him so unkindly? But then he returned to charming equilibrium once again, smiling cheerfully. Instantly my spirits were raised. (Why?) Then, as he got up to go, he cuttingly commented that I had every right to write the book. 'It is *your* right. It is a right that *we* fought for, so that *you* could exercise it.'

In retrospect, I am sure Ramaphosa experienced none of the emotions that his words and expressions led me to attribute to him. I was later to learn that he could induce emotions – happiness or sadness, relief or fear, guilt or shame – almost at will. Like an experienced animal-trainer assessing the temperament of a dog or horse presented to him for the first time, he scolded me one minute and patted me on the head the next, primarily in order to observe my reactions. I was lucky he didn't give me a lump of sugar.

When I next came across Ramaphosa, at a Johannesburg workshop on black economic empowerment, he was back to his habitual and impenetrable charm. He wished me well with my writing and complimented me on my presentation to the workshop but he remained implacable in his unwillingness to help me.

One journalist has described Ramaphosa's 'almost awe-inspiring sense of self-confidence, the fact that his game-playing doesn't come from a place of weakness or insecurity'.[4] Yet any subject of a political biography in South Africa today must feel some degree of vulnerability.

Post-apartheid political biography has mostly presented a procession of saints. Nelson Mandela, Oliver Tambo and Walter Sisulu, great and tough-minded political leaders, have been rendered as cuddly as teddy bears. Even a biographer writing in this sympathetic tradition has little to offer an ANC leader. Indeed, a favourable biography might be regarded as 'touting' for office in a manner contrary to ANC convention. The most incompetent biographer, moreover, can stumble across a skeleton in a closet. Even a competent one can serve as the unknowing instrument of professional character assassins.

A nervous politician always has the power to shut up shop. Given that a book of this kind relies heavily on personal recollection, the subject can quietly ask friends and acquaintances to refuse requests for interviews. Some hesitant interviewees – and more often their personal assistants – confessed to me that they were waiting for assent from Ramaphosa's office to my request for a meeting. In the end, however, almost all of those I contacted were willing to talk to me. In so far as I was able to ascertain, Ramaphosa told those who asked him that it was entirely a matter for them to decide whether or not they wanted to talk to me.

I have persuaded my interviewees to allow me to identify them as my sources, in part because of the cautionary lesson provided by William Gumede's recent fascinating portrait of Thabo Mbeki's ANC. Gumede's book advanced all manner of intriguing propositions on the basis of information from anonymous sources.[5] When critics alleged that errors were present, this anonymity made it hard for the author to rebut them persuasively. If readers have doubts about the truth of claims made in my book I hope in most instances at least, that they will be able to identify the sources I have used.

Critics sometimes observe that biographical and fictional writing share common literary devices.[6] The biography, like the modern novel that emerged alongside it, assumes that a life in the world can be ordered as a chronological plot; that the character of the subject is both knowable and autonomous; and that the biographer (or author) is a reliable and dispassionate informant (or narrator). A biography is a story, they claim, albeit one in which the author is, or should be, quite strongly constrained by the facts and opinions he assembles in preparing it.

I do not think there are any satisfactory remedies for these alleged weaknesses of the biographical form. Constant reminders from purportedly 'post-modern' biographers about the 'unknowability' and 'relational character' of their subjects serve only to irritate their readers, while books that escape entirely the confining assumptions of chronology are simply incomprehensible. My old-fashioned approach is influenced by a saying whose source I have not been able to trace: 'Always try to do things in chronological order; it's less confusing that way.'

I also agree with CA Latimer that a biography should record banal dates and facts: "'Anthony Trollope was born on 24 April 1815 at 16 Keppel Street, Russell Square, London.' That's how a biography should start.'[7] Even facts about a subject's birth, of course, can be few and far between in South Africa. The general secretary of South Africa's largest trade union federation, Zwelinzima Vavi, to take one example, does not know when he was born. Presidency director-general Frank Chikane likewise observed in his 1988 autobiography that he did not know the place of his birth.[8] His birth certificate states 'Soweto', but possibly with the intention to secure him rights to live in the township under Section 10 (1) (a) of the Black (Urban Areas) Consolidation Act of 1945. If he was born in Buckbushridge in the Eastern Transvaal – which he thought he might well have been – his birth certificate would never have said so.

One further convention of biographical writing that has come under post-modern fire is the pretence that the biographer himself is an objective and detached narrator, no more a part of the story than the novelist is a part of the novel. (Once the reader has finished this preface, I will disappear in just this way.)

You cannot have Ramaphosa's life 'as it has been', but only as it has been interpreted by the writer. However, interpretation is the prerogative not only of the author, but also of informants, critics and readers themselves. The recollections of those who intimately know the subject, if they are available, can be the most revealing source for a biographer. The subject's relationships with others, as those others perceive or recall them, allow a refractory human being to emerge.[9]

Recollections and interviews are dangerous, of course. The interviewer is both participant and interpreter. Some interviewees – quite a few for political biographies – spread malicious rumours designed to denigrate the subject. Others offer testimonials to a subject's good character. Selective recollection, whether deliberate or otherwise, is a general and inescapable reality rather than merely a potential danger.

I have unexpectedly received instruction on research methodology from politicians I had not previously regarded as experts in the philosophical underpinnings of truth. Penuell Maduna, for example, told me you only get the right answers if you ask the right questions – but then predictably refused to answer almost all of those I did ask. Mac Maharaj disparaged interviews – while granting one – and insisted that a reliable biography must draw primarily on solid documentary evidence. Maharaj illustrated his point by suggesting I peruse the historical minutes of meetings of the South African Communist Party (SACP).

SACP documents, of course, even when you can get hold of them, cannot be taken at face value any more than can the words of an interviewee. Facts do not become innocent and reliable simply because they are written down. Indeed, a cynic might observe that the SACP has usually written things down only when, and because, they have not been true.

More than one acquaintance of mine has commented that the subject of this biography is an African born in Johannesburg's Western Native Township and raised in Soweto. The author, by contrast, is a white European who knows little about South Africa and her people. The precise significance of this contrast is difficult to pinpoint. It is true, and a matter for concern, that historically advantaged writers and scholars have time and resources to dominate interpretations of events that they may not very much understand.

It is a severe limitation of this book that I write in substantial ignorance of the circumstances in which Ramaphosa grew up, the world from which his family came, and the languages and concepts through which he has interpreted his own experiences and actions.

None of this, however, amounts to a reason for not writing a biography. It is not true, presumably, that a white person can never write a valuable book about a black person or vice versa. To which more competent authority should one assign the preparation of a more 'authentic' portrait of Ramaphosa?

I have tried to allow Ramaphosa's friends and foes the space to explain him in their own, often inconsistent, terms. I have correspondingly been sceptical about any overarching narrative that uniquely 'makes sense' of his life. Perhaps fancifully, I hope that the diversity of opinions

I present will allow readers some imaginative space in which to make a judgement of their own about the kind of political leader and man they believe Ramaphosa to be.

Although the book started out as a political biography, it was soon clear that Ramaphosa's early childhood, family life and religious upbringing decisively shaped his politics.

I am grateful to the many people who have let me share their recollections of Ramaphosa, primarily in time-consuming personal interviews, and for the assistance I have received in locating and understanding written sources. In particular, I would like to thank Peter Alexander, Vic Allen, Kader Asmal, Diamond Atong, Andeya Baleni, Frans Baleni, Denis Beckett, Paul Benjamin, Ann Bernstein, Peter Bruce, Simon Cairns, Phiroshaw Camay, Kate Carey, Irene Charnley, Frank Chikane, Donne Cooney, Saths Cooper, FW de Klerk, Godfried Dederen, Tertius Delport, Henry Dolowitz, Theuns Eloff, Gareth Evans, Tshenuwani Farisani, Don Foster, Sidney Frankel, Frene Ginwala, Bobby Godsell, Marcel Golding, Duma Gqubule, Pippa Green, Bantu Holomisa, Gillian Hutchings, Bheki Jacobs, Reuel Khoza, Johann Liebenberg, Oyama Mabandla, Lybon Mabasa, Saki Macozoma, Ndoda Madalane, Penuell Maduna, Mac Maharaj, Tom Manthatha, Irene Menell, Rick Menell, Roelf Meyer, Ishmael Mkhabela, Caesar Molebatsi, Nthato Motlana, James Motlatsi, Lufuno Mulaudzi, Jay Naidoo, Simphiwe Nanise, Don Ncube, Duma Ndlovu, Pandelani Nefolovhodwe, Christo Nel, Bernard Ngoepe, Martin Nicol, TS Ntsandeni, Percy SF Ntshingila, Padraig O'Malley, Fred Phaswana, Peter Phaswani, Kuben Pillay, Barney Pityana, Douglas Ramaphosa, Rams Ramashia, TA Ramutumbu, Christine Randall, Jabulani Sikhakhane, Michael Spicer, Hassan Solomon, Allister Sparks, Dave Steward, Jan Steyn, Jill Strelitz, Raymond Suttner, Strike Thokoane, Clive Thompson, MS Tshikovhele, Bob Tucker, Nigel Unwin, Fanie van der Merwe, Frederik van Zyl Slabbert, Helbron Vilakazi, Tony van Ryneveld, Patti Waldmeir, and Griffith Zabala.

Vic Allen and Kate Carey were especially generous hosts. Allen's moving book on African mineworkers is a model of intelligence, and the third volume is indispensable for those wanting to understand contemporary South Africa.[10] Without this volume, I would not have been able to make any sense of Ramaphosa's role in the story of the NUM.[11] I am very grateful to Thenjiwe Mlabatheki at the NUM resources centre for all her assistance, especially in finding photographs, and to NUM for giving permission for their use in the book.

I am also grateful to the Department of Historical Papers at the University of the Witwatersrand, the outpost of the National Archives in Cape Town, and the Mayibuye Centre at the University of the Western Cape, all of which offered a highly professional and efficient service. Per Strand's penetrating analysis of the constitution-making process[12] provided me with an introduction to a subject about which initially I knew little. I made extensive use of interviews conducted by Patti Waldmeir, Julie Frederikse and Padraig O'Malley. O'Malley's materials, in particular, are a treasure trove for students of the negotiations leading to the country's post-apartheid settlement. His efforts to make his materials available to other researchers on the Internet have been heroic. The insights he provided me from his biography of Mac Maharaj, then in press, were also valuable for this study.

I am indebted to Cyril Ramaphosa for not actively obstructing the biography. I am also very pleased that he relented at a late stage to my requests for him to read the manuscript and that he was able to identify certain errors of fact.

In my own department at the University of Cape Town, I am grateful to Thiven Reddy and Zweli Jolobe for inspiring me with their knowledge about, and passion for, ANC politics. My thanks also go to Annette Seegers and André du Toit for their historical recollections, and to Robert Cameron, Mary Simons and Sagree Naidoo for so kindly protecting my sabbatical from administration and teaching. I have enjoyed fascinating discussions with Ronald Suresh Roberts, Howard Smith and James Sanders. Colin Bundy, Rupert Taylor, Lungisile Ntsebeza and Chris Saunders looked at drafts of particular chapters and gave me the benefit of their insight and wisdom. Bridget Impey was an exceptional publisher and Russell Martin has been the very model of a patient and encouraging editor.

I am grateful to my family for their patience in the face of what they clearly consider a very eccentric project.

Behold, I give unto you power to tread on serpents and scorpions, and over all the powers of the enemy: and nothing shall by any means hurt you.

– Luke 10. 19

PART ONE
FORMATION

CHAPTER 1

NO PLACE TO REST

Thou shalt not commit adultery, Thou shalt not kill, Thou shalt not steal, Thou shalt not bear false witness, Thou shalt not covet; and if there be any other commandment, it is briefly comprehended in this saying, namely, Thou shalt love thy neighbour as thyself.
– Romans 13. 9

I saw them clobber him with kieries
I heard him scream with pain
like a victim of slaughter;
I smelt fresh blood gush
from his nostrils,
and flow on the street.
I walked into the church,
and knelt in the pew
'Lord! I love you,
I also love my neighbour. Amen.'
– Oswald Mtshali[1]

Matamela Cyril Ramaphosa was born at number 1627 Letanka Street in the Western Native Township close to Johannesburg on 17 November 1952. He was the second of what were to be the three children of Samuel and Erdmuthe Ramaphosa. In the Venda tradition, the names of a newborn child are granted by a senior relative, usually a woman. Ramaphosa's first name, Matamela, was chosen by his mother, and its meaning is 'someone who evokes speechless wonderment'. This choice gives a first clue to the strong shield of love with which Erdmuthe would surround her growing son.[2]

Ramaphosa was born just four years after the National Party (NP) had swept to power under its 'apartheid' slogan. The NP would dominate South African politics for the next four decades, transforming racial segregation into a notorious system of population control and social engineering.[3] It immediately began to enact a body of repugnant legislation. The Population Registration Act enforced the classification of all people into four racial categories – white, coloured, Indian/Asiatic, and native.[4] 'Mixed marriages' were prohibited in 1949, and in 1950 all sexual contact between whites and other South Africans was prohibited in the Immorality Act. The Group Areas Act of 1950 applied residential segregation by race across the entire country, and the Reservation of Separate Amenities Act of 1953 segregated transport, cinemas, restaurants and sporting facilities.

The period was also marked by an upsurge of opposition to racial oppression. Black mineworkers launched a powerful challenge to workplace exploitation in a massive 1946 strike. In 1949, immediately after the NP's rise to power, three radical members of the African National Congress (ANC) Youth League – Nelson Mandela, Walter Sisulu and Oliver Tambo – were elected to the movement's governing National Executive Committee. By the year of Ramaphosa's birth, the ANC and its allies in the South African Indian Congress were able to launch a major passive resistance campaign, and in 1955 the movement and its allies met in Kliptown, close to Johannesburg, and adopted the Freedom Charter. This document, which was to become the central unifying text of the liberation movement, began with a memorable assertion: 'South Africa belongs to all who live in it, black and white, and no government can justly claim authority unless it is based on the will of the people.'[5]

The Nationalists, however, were determined to re-establish control over urban black population growth, and embarked on what they called a 'stabilisation' strategy. They destroyed squatter camps, 'purified' white neighbourhoods, and created new townships far from white residential areas.[6] This programme, like the NP's election victory, was partly a reaction to the growth of the black population in urban areas, itself the result of an extended wartime economic boom.

During the war an export-led economic bonanza had brought about a relaxation of segregation, as rural migrants – Ramaphosa's parents among them – rushed to take up jobs in the booming economy. Between

1936 and 1946, Africans in urban areas multiplied almost threefold to 390,000, black trade unions blossomed, and skilled jobs were no longer the reserve of whites.[7] Johannesburg was at the epicentre of this great industrial and social transformation.

As the black workforce swelled, shanty towns sprang up around the city and existing 'African locations' such as Western Native Township became desperately overcrowded. This township had first been established in 1918 on the site of a brickfield, and in places it had rows of orderly housing. In the boom, it developed a burgeoning and fluid population, much of it living under temporary shelter and in unsanitary conditions.[8] Almost every piece of land was occupied, with backyard shacks squeezed behind brick houses, and the acrid smoke from thousands of wood and coal fires filling the air. Summer storms turned the roads into mud sheets.

The township was also a place of great cultural and political vibrancy, and prominent African families such as the Vundlas and the Motlanas lived there. It was, moreover, immediately adjacent to the legendary neighbourhood of Sophiatown, which was home to many of the country's most powerful black political and business dynasties. Here a cosmopolitan and highly educated elite of doctors, teachers and journalists rubbed shoulders with famous churchmen, artists, and writers – as well as with crooks and gangsters.[9]

For the Ramaphosa family, there were other, more everyday compensations for Western Native Township's economic limitations. A population described officially as 'Non-European' embraced almost every race and ethnicity, living together in a common community. The Ramaphosa family's immediate neighbours, for example, called themselves coloureds and spoke Afrikaans, while other nearby households contained speakers of Zulu, Sesotho and a wide variety of other languages and dialects. Cyril's first education, at Mabitlane Primary School, was conducted in Tswana.

As a small child, Cyril, his older sister (by four years) Ivy, and even his younger brother (by five years) Douglas, were all to learn this great variety of languages from their playmates, and they felt entirely comfortable switching from one tongue to another. It is not simply childhood romanticism to remember, as Douglas Ramaphosa does, that theirs was a happy home in a lively and cosmopolitan neighbourhood.[10]

Soon after Cyril was born, the 1953 Mentz Committee determined that all freehold townships should be cleared of black occupants. The residents of Western Native Township, Sophiatown, Newclare and Martindale were to be relocated, if necessary by force, to new and more distant black residential settlements. Western Native Township was earmarked for development as an industrial area.

In the 'technical' language of one land-use planner, 'the scheme providing for the transfer of Non-Europeans from the Western Native Townships to Meadowlands will clear some of the worst slums of Johannesburg and will concentrate the area of Non-European residence to the south of the mining belt, where industry may be expected to develop as the mines are exhausted and abandoned. A happy relationship between place of work and place of residence for both European and Non-European workers will be achieved by the use of the southern part of the clear area for industry and the northern part for the re-housing of the poorer European workers.'[11]

With Africans concentrated in 'properly laid out townships', the planner continued, 'it will be relatively easy to provide adequate transport facilities to the manufacturing belts'.[12] The parastatal Council for Scientific and Industrial Research (CSIR) and the National Building Research Institute even went so far as to draw up a standard template for the design of low-cost four-roomed houses for relocated Africans. Such four-roomed houses continue to dominate the landscape of Soweto – and much of the rest of the country – to this day.

Alongside the technical demands of town planning, the National Party was elaborating a doctrine of racial differentiation and African 'retribalisation'. The NP's electoral victory in 1948 resulted from whites' dismay at the black influx into formerly white residential areas and jobs. The underlying philosophy of the regime was shifting, however, and no longer rested upon the idea of a hierarchy of races in which whites were at the top and Africans were at the bottom. Instead the notion was emerging that Africans should have their own forms of self-government, their own residential areas, and their own native 'homelands' – and that the African population of the country needed in consequence to be separated into what were viewed as distinct ethnic groups for this purpose. While the immediate motivations for the 'forced removals' of Africans from areas designated as belonging to whites were mostly economic and social, apartheid's emerging second phase represented a change of ideological direction. This would ultimately lead to removals of 'incorrectly' located black people, the creation of Bantustans, and the deliberate 'retribalisation' of Africans.

In its early years in Johannesburg, the NP's project was to have its greatest impact through the creation of what came to be known as Soweto. Many Africans lucky enough to hold rights to live and work in 'white' South Africa – and so in possession of a 'pass' or *dompas* – were settled in newer, racially segregated townships distant from the white residential areas. Initially formed when the city authorities relocated African and Indian workers from the margins of the city to Kliptown, the south-western townships of Pimville and Orlando East were created in the mid-1930s. It was the economic transformation of the 1940s – the demand for homes for Africans manning the booming production lines and factories – as well as a growing tide of refugees dispossessed of their land by racist legislation, that led to the emergence of modern-day Soweto. The area remained a dormitory township rather than a city in its own right, and economic activity was strictly regulated. The main occupations were self-employment in small shops, eating houses, butcheries, and road-side or house-to-house hawking of milk, vegetables and small goods.

As a repository for Africans from all manner of backgrounds and occupations, Soweto was, inevitably, starkly divided by class. Today wealthy suburbs like Diepkloof Zone 5 and Protea Glen rub shoulders with poor formal suburbs and informal settlements such as Power Park and Elias Motsoaledi. This pattern emerged as early as the 1950s with the creation of middle-class enclaves such as Dube.

In the 1950s, Soweto was increasingly marked by a second kind of division that resulted from apartheid policy: strict ethnic segregation. As early as 1954, 10,000 serviced sites were laid out in a segregated pattern. Following a loan of R6 million to the state by Anglo American magnate Ernest Oppenheimer – intended to stimulate the provision of more houses – a housing boom exploded. The 24,000 new housing units constructed in a period of less than five years were set in new townships zoned along ethnic lines, Naledi, Tladi and Phiri for Sesotho and Tswana speakers, and Zola, Zondi, Jabulani and Emdeni for Zulu and Xhosa speakers. Tsonga and Venda speakers were obliged to settle in Tshiawelo (or Chiawelo in the Tsongan spelling).[13] This deliberate 'retribalisation' of African society immediately affected the Ramaphosa family. When forced to leave Western Native Township in 1962, they were obliged to move to Tshiawelo, and the Ramaphosa children had to leave behind the happy multi-cultural milieu of their first home.

Tshiawelo's location and limited services reflected the low priority attached to its inhabitants. More than 35 km from the job opportunities of central Johannesburg, it was grim and unappealing. Tshiawelo – meaning 'place of rest' or 'remaining in harmony' – was built on the 'site-and-service' model: new arrivals were provided with a drained stand, and water and sanitation were made available. The conventional housing model was a four-roomed house in which it was normal to find ten people living at any time.[14] The township as a whole contained perhaps 4,000 houses.[15]

Tshiawelo was to become an increasingly bleak and unprepossessing place as the violence of the apartheid state intensified. Especially after 1976, citizens boycotted the illegitimate apartheid local government and refused to pay local government taxes. In the absence of waste collection, the streets became dirty and rat-infested. A small hillock in the middle of Tshiawelo around which the young Cyril had to negotiate to meet his friends – the 'mountain' or 'koppie' – became a dumping ground for rubbish and a home for criminals, gangs and rapists.

This was a small and bleak world in which to grow up and reach maturity, and until his mid-teens Ramaphosa's experience of the world outside his neighbourhood was limited. Tshiawelo was a marginalised backwater in a Soweto that was itself separated by a gulf of distance and money from the excitement and wealth of Johannesburg.

If Ramaphosa's primary school years were clouded by poverty and apartheid discrimination, there were powerful counteracting forces at work that would allow him to survive and then transcend his circumstances. The most important among these was Cyril's immediate family.

Ramaphosa was born into a widely respected and very stable household, and his parents were renowned in their community for their strength of moral character.[16] Cyril's father Samuel Mundzhedzi Ramaphosa – known universally as Sergeant Ramaphosa – had become a policeman in the year that Cyril was born. He grew up in the Sibasa area of eastern Venda, where he had been schooled in a conservative mission school in Khalavha. In Soweto, he was stationed in the Moroka police station, close to home. A job of this kind provided a reliable and relatively modest salary.

After the political unrest in Soweto in 1976, policemen came to be identified as agents of the oppressor and their lives came under threat. Even in those darker days, however, according to a family friend, 'no one ever dreamt of counting Sergeant Ramaphosa as one of the enemy'.[17] During Cyril's childhood, the sergeant saw himself as a community policeman, and he was evidently a pillar of the local community, widely respected, called upon to resolve conflicts between neighbours, and acknowledged for his wisdom and good judgement.[18] As was often true of Vendas and Shangaans, Samuel Ramaphosa was able to transcend the ethnic tensions that sometimes intruded into township conflicts, because of his ability to speak all of Soweto's languages with such fluency.

Cyril's father also set up a burial society called 'Khalavha' after his area of birth, for his 'home boys'.[19] Such burial societies provided insurance against the unexpected expense of a funeral by covering the exorbitant costs of transporting a body to Venda for burial. They also functioned as social groups through which family problems could be mulled over and community issues might be debated.

While the sergeant was widely admired, he was undoubtedly a conservative man with regard to discipline and respect for the law. Cyril was his father's pride and joy.[20] The streets of Soweto were a tough playground for young men. Gangsterism was rife, and the gangsters were the role models for many of Cyril's school peers. In 1957, for example, more than 50 people were killed in battles between gangsters, the 'Zulus' and the 'Russians', in the nearby and more affluent township of Dube. Yet Cyril had taken a different path, towards decency and Christianity. Not only had he refused to follow these negative role models, but he himself became an inspiration for others.

Cyril later claimed that he had learnt a good deal from his father. 'People would come home, very angry at the injustices, and also pointing fingers at what policemen were doing ... [But] he was one of those policemen who was highly respected in the community where we lived, and people would throng to our home with problems. And later in life, in the trade unions and ... that type of situation, the patience to be able to listen to people and deal with their problems, I think I learnt from my father.'[21]

Samuel Ramaphosa confided in his eldest son from a very young age. For Cyril's younger brother Douglas, the two possessed a mutual respect unusual between different generations. They seemed to share the same outlook, they carried themselves in the same way, and they walked with the same dignified bearing. They even looked exactly alike.[22] Samuel Ramaphosa's pride in his son was palpable, but as the years passed he must have become increasingly concerned about the direction Cyril had chosen. Yes, the young man was a fine and upstanding member of the community who spurned the gangsterism that surrounded them and encouraged others to follow a good Christian path. On the other hand, Cyril was also an activist who moved more and more in the troubled domain where Christianity and politics intersected.[23]

Cyril's father would no doubt have had to explain the behaviour of his sons to his colleagues at the police station in Moroka. Rams Ramashia, who is today chairman of BP Southern Africa, had glimpses of Cyril's father's fears and hopes. Samuel Ramaphosa was a friend of Ramashia's father, and he was a frequent visitor to the small herbalist store that the Ramashia family ran in Tshiawelo. The sergeant was convinced that Cyril could be 'coached', or steered, away from the dangerous world of politics while retaining his commitment to God. Nevertheless, 'his father was torn by a dilemma. His son was morally upright and for this he was proud. But he was also an activist. And the sergeant knew what his colleagues in the police were capable of. He feared for his son's life.'[24]

Cyril's brother Douglas detected a more ambiguous range of feelings in his father. Samuel was not just a policeman, but also a man with a keen interest in politics. He would tell Cyril stories about the words and exploits of Nelson Mandela and the ANC Youth League, and his attitude towards the ANC was broadly positive. In Douglas's eyes,

Samuel understood what Cyril stood for and he respected it. He never discouraged Cyril from political activism for this reason. When his eldest son was detained, Samuel reacted with a quiet stoicism.

Cyril's mother Erdmuthe Muti Ramaphosa was the other key influence on Cyril's young life. Erdmuthe had a very similar background to Samuel, being raised in Tshitasini, a missionary settlement[25] in the west of Venda, about 7 km from Louis Trichardt (now Makhado). She received a missionary education that not only instilled Lutheran values but also equipped her unusually well for formal employment. She was a major community activist, and emerged as a stabilising force in both the family and the local community when Samuel died in the late 1980s.[26] She was also enterprising. In the Western Native Township, Erdmuthe started selling liquor from the house, a common source of income for women of initiative. Indeed Douglas Ramaphosa's very earliest childhood memory is of his mother exchanging liquor for money in the front room of their house. She continued to sell liquor in Tshiawelo, and later became a domestic worker in the then-salubrious suburb of Hillbrow. In later years, she secured work with Arlec Engineering as an administration clerk, employment of a kind that was unusual for a woman of her generation and background.

Erdmuthe adored Cyril almost without qualification and 'surrounded him with a shield of love and protection'.[27] Unlike Samuel, she quite evidently believed that some of Cyril's friends were a bad influence on him, leading him astray into the world of politics. She ran a strict household, and instilled a strong sense of personal discipline in Cyril. The young school boy was always exceptionally well mannered, clean, well groomed and well presented.[28] He never failed in his domestic chores, feeding the dogs punctiliously, cleaning the kitchen thoroughly, and doing whatever other housework was required of him, not grudgingly but with patent enthusiasm. He was, moreover, extremely diligent in his studies, and on his move to high school at the age of 15 he was to go into the top stream of the year.

Until her death in June 2001, Cyril's mother would always keep a watchful eye on his activities. When his friend, the charismatic evangelist Caesar Molebatsi, visited the Ramaphosa home in the late

1970s, Erdmuthe would wait until Cyril left the room before asking, 'Is he behaving?'[29] In later years, as his political career progressed, she became increasingly concerned for his safety and did not like him to be in the political spotlight. In 1993 and 1994, when shots were fired at Ramaphosa on two occasions, and a plot by right-wing extremists to assassinate him was uncovered, she desperately prayed he would abandon politics.[30]

Meanwhile, she loved to watch her Cyril on television, and would comment on, and grade, each of his appearances.[31] At the Lutheran church in Tshiawelo, where the family attended services, she would regularly lead prayers for her son. When they were finished, she would call Cyril on his cellphone, no matter where he was, and tell him that prayers had been made on his behalf.[32] He was always reminded in this way that others were concerned for his well-being and loved him.

Ramaphosa's parents were unusual in their relatively high levels of education, having both reached Standard Six in their missionary schools. They also shared a common approach to religion and to the upbringing of their children, and they sought to find the best for their children in terms of food and clothes. They were sensitive and intelligent parents who understood how to moderate and channel the growing political anger of their children. Their emphasis above all was on education. Like many children whose parents had emerged from poverty, the young Ramaphosa children were always told that their parents would sacrifice anything to ensure them the best possible education.[33] A thorough schooling, they believed, would protect them in increasingly difficult times.

In this home, in contrast to many others, the daughter Ivy was accorded as much respect and opportunity as her brothers, and she became a stable and confident individual. When Ivy became pregnant and had to stop school to have her first child, her parents were profoundly disappointed – but they were not angry. They were saddened that she had not achieved the level of education that would allow her to secure a career or pursue independent opportunities of her own.[34]

Douglas, the youngest of the three children, was to become the most difficult. He was to be the most aggressive and uncompromising in his rebellion against the injustices of the social order. This was in part a matter of generations. The five years that separated Douglas from Cyril were an age in terms of political repression, and Douglas was a product – and instigator – of the student politics of the 1976 uprising. But the difference between the two was also temperamental, with Douglas unable to accommodate and manage his intolerance of the injustice that surrounded them.

The relationship between Douglas and Cyril was never easy.[35] When Douglas would see Samuel and Cyril confiding closely in one another, he must have felt excluded. Erdmuthe doted on her older son. Cyril, moreover, was a leader and a model of perfection not merely in his home but also in his community and school life. Douglas inevitably looked up to Cyril – 'he was my political mentor ... he led by example and I picked up political understanding by seeing what he did and said'.[36] But it was always impossible for Douglas to live up to Cyril's perfect example, and nor was it possible for the younger brother even to bask in the glow of his older brother's success. Cyril was surrounded by admirers who copied his dress and manner of speaking and hung on his every word: they inadvertently formed yet another barrier between the two young brothers. So Douglas loved and admired Cyril but was unable to be as close to him as he might have wished. A sadness lies behind his memory of the two brothers playing football together in the open land opposite their house on Mhlaba Drive.

The distance between the two brothers would grow when Douglas became politically aware at the age of 13 or 14, just at the time Cyril was leaving for boarding school in the north of the country. As Douglas became increasingly politically active, he was openly unhappy about his father's job. When he talked to his friends he would sometimes call his home 'the police station'. Later he would leave the country to take up arms as an ANC liberation fighter and would spend many years in exile in the Soviet Union, Zambia and Tanzania.

Amidst the hardships of everyday life in Western Native Township and the Soweto backwater of Tshiawelo, the pervasive character of the apartheid ideologies of white supremacy and racial separation would initially have been difficult to discern. For the son of a policeman, the signals Cyril did pick up would have been profoundly confusing. In 1960, in the immediate aftermath of the massacre of 69 demonstrators at Sharpeville near Vereeniging, soldiers were stationed close to the

Ramaphosa family home during the imposition of a state of emergency. In an unprovoked and inexplicable assault, a white soldier kicked the 7-year-old Cyril into a ditch when he was on his way to school. 'After being kicked like that, I felt bitter against white people, which took me a long time to overcome.'[37]

As Ramaphosa grew older, as we shall see, he would be exposed to the cruelty of officials in municipal offices, and soldiers and police on pass raids. Pass raids were carried out in the presence of children, resulting in the humiliation of parents in front of their families. It must have been a mixed blessing that such raids could not happen to the Ramaphosa family because of Samuel's position as a policeman.

For Cyril as a young child, the ethnic divisiveness that the NP government was promoting would have been more pervasive and must have left early scars. The character of ethnic difference – or what is pejoratively called 'tribalism' – was very complex in the Soweto of Cyril's boyhood. In the Western Native Township, diversity was experienced as an opportunity and a pleasure. Yet now the government was attempting to enforce a romantic European conception of African tribalism. Like misguided Victorian missionaries, they quite wrongly viewed Zulu, Xhosa or Venda peoples as timeless societies with distinct cultures – whose history and inevitable fate it was to be at war with one another. In the notorious 'separate development' era, Bantustans were justified as political homes for ethnic groups, and a deliberate state project of 'retribalisation' was launched. Soweto's primary schools were segregated by language, and the government funded ethnic youth associations designed to foster ethnic awareness.

The idea of timeless and natural tribes stands in stark contrast to modern scholarly views.[38] For many scholars, tribalism was 'invented' by missionaries and colonial administrators, who created pseudo languages out of dialects, and persuaded the educated African elite to embrace 'invented traditions'. Tribalism, in this view, was an instrument used by colonial administrators and their often inadvertent allies in the churches to divide and rule, maintain law and order, collect taxes, and extract labour.

But while tribalism, like all forms of social identity, is invented, it is not simply imposed by outsiders. Ethnicity in South Africa had to be built out of the real beliefs, interests and experiences of Africans. African intellectuals benefited from tribalism by interpreting tradition for the colonisers and interpreting colonial practice for 'traditional leaders'. Ordinary people, moreover, found in shared dialects and origins a point of reference amid the turmoil of the migrant labour system. For people like Cyril's father, although ethnicity was not a touchstone of good and bad or friendship and enmity, it was natural to form a burial society for his 'home boys' and to meet with them more often and to talk with them more closely as a result of the history and upbringing they shared.

Like most black South Africans, the Ramaphosa children would have developed a nuanced view of ethnicity. Their childhood friendships in Western Native Township, and the mutual comprehensibility of many African languages, were constant reminders of the artificiality of the idea of timeless tribal division advanced by apartheid ideologues. At the same time, there was also pride in the history of their own people, and a search for new ways to recover and develop the pre-colonial treasures of historical, linguistic and cultural diversity.

The supposedly timeless 'homeland' of Venda, the family would have been all too aware, was dominated by the Singo clan, which had invaded the area as recently as the start of the 18th century, subjugating the earlier inhabitants of the Soutpansberg. The pre-Singo ruling clans were sometimes killed and supplanted, but at other times changed their histories by introducing spurious historical allegiances to ingratiate themselves with their new rulers.[39] Samuel and Erdmuthe grew up in a complex political environment in which there were 28 Singo 'chiefdoms', the largest of which possessed 70 'headmen', each of whom represented a different family name. The fluidity and vitality of the politics of the region from which the family came would have been quite naturally imparted to the young children. The reality they experienced was very much at variance with the apartheid government's crude characterisation of the Venda as a timeless ahistorical tribe, and exposed the erroneous character of the apartheid policy, which strictly demarcated one supposed ethnic group from another.

In the wider apartheid state, segregationist doctrine was being supplanted by the notion of 'separate development', which entailed Africans residing in distinct ethnic homelands. The inspiration for this idea was decolonisation in the British protectorates of Botswana, Lesotho and Swaziland. If African nationalists could press for the independence of these artificial and arbitrarily defined states, then why could equally artificial states not then be granted 'independence' within South Africa itself? Separate development implied that every African must be assigned an ethnic group with its own site of self-government. Communities and families were divided by an apartheid bureaucracy that categorised an entire people in accordance with rules of descent. Once classified, 3.5 million 'incorrectly' located people were forcibly removed to their putative homelands or ethnically correct locations between 1960 and 1989.

The homelands never came close to acquiring economic self-sufficiency. As a contribution to their viability, the South African government introduced incentives for business to locate on their borders. The major source of income, however, was always work in the core (now white) economy. Bantustans were justified primarily as political homes for supposedly distinct African peoples. Ethnicity was the principal foundation of homeland self-government, and ethnic affiliation was intended to displace South African nationality as the basis of African political identification.

This policy never secured much legitimacy among Africans, who recognised it as an attempt to deprive them of their land and of the wealth to whose accumulation they had contributed. The poet and evangelist Tshenuwani Farisani, who was later to become a major influence on Cyril's political thought, expressed it in this way:

> You pushed me from the fat of the country to the
>   homelands.
> You fed me a bogus independence.
> You made me a citizen of a banana republic.
> And made babies my rulers.
> You banned me from my country of birth,
> And called me citizen undetermined.[40]

For a member of a small African people from the north of the country, awareness of the sense of ethnic hierarchy possessed by some other Africans would have been sharp. The superiority of some Xhosa political families from the Eastern Cape would not have impinged on Cyril at this stage. More evident would be the special character of Zulu identity, some manifestations of which confronted Cyril in the everyday life of Soweto.

Zulu exceptionalism is partly a result of the celebration of the 'warrior race' descended from Shaka that inflicted a serious defeat on the British army in 1879. Despite a growing pan-Africanist tradition among political elites in the Natal ANC, ordinary Zulus would celebrate their unique monarchy, powerful traditional leaders, and a history of success in warfare – including that against the great colonial enemy of Britain. In Cyril's youth, Mangosuthu Buthelezi's political project would begin to further deepen the ethnic self-consciousness of ordinary Zulus.

Cyril Ramaphosa's family, we have seen, come from the Venda-speaking area of what is today Limpopo Province far to the north of Johannesburg. During Ramaphosa's childhood, there were perhaps 3 million inhabitants of the Xhosa-speaking designated 'homelands', and 4 million people in KwaZulu. Venda contained fewer than 350,000 people in total.[41] The same pattern was reflected in the population of Greater Soweto at the time Cyril went to high school. Compared with around 400,000 Nguni language speakers (Xhosa and Zulu), only around 100,000 were 'Tsonga' speakers, a term that was then officially used to cover both Shangaan and Venda tongues.[42]

It was not the numerical minority of the Venda-speaking population that would have been difficult for Ramaphosa's young mind to embrace, but rather the stigma that attached to this ethnic group. To be Venda, Shangaan or Tsonga in the Soweto of Ramaphosa's youth was all too often to be the object of ridicule and disdain. In part this was because members of these groups were viewed as 'linked to the rural',[43] in a Soweto that was modern and proud to be modern. Zulu speakers, by contrast, possessed an elaborate mythology in which they had vanquished all-comers in the creation of their 19th-century empire. They also had an extended history of urban residence and employment that gave them the confidence to ridicule the 'rural' and 'backward' newcomers. Zulu speakers would typically pretend to be unable to differentiate the minor African languages from one another – or, even more insultingly, on occasion they simply could not do so.

In Cyril's young world, ethnic division was encouraged by the apartheid government within the township as part of its wider retribalisation strategy. As a result of this policy, Cyril was educated in a 'Venda' primary school – Tshilidzi Primary – until the age of 14. Groups of 'promising young leaders' were even selected and taken on character-building camps in which the importance of tribe and culture were instilled by teachers.[44] But white oppressors, who spoke English and Afrikaans, were in most respects invisible. By contrast, when walking through any neighbourhood outside Tshiawelo, Ramaphosa and his friends might be subject to jokes in which it was the Venda or the Shangaan who was always the buffoon or the ugly one.

Among many Africans, moreover, Cyril's home language and his social and historical roots were the objects of disdain. Young people in Tshiawelo, whether Tsonga or Venda speaking, were often eager to learn Zulu or Xhosa – in addition to English and Afrikaans – and in this way they partly disavowed their own ethnic heritage. Yet, even after this act of humiliation, recent arrivals from the north would sometimes be mocked because their accents betrayed them.[45]

At the same time a corresponding capacity of members of the smaller ethnic groups was their ability to move easily between different languages, and to adapt easily to the cultural particularities of others. Like his father, Cyril was able to transcend ethnic divides that sometimes constrained members of the larger Zulu and Xhosa communities.

The stability and strength of Ramaphosa's family were underpinned by the organised religion that his parents embraced enthusiastically. In the 1960s, the churches' importance was magnified because potential competitors for political mobilisation had been driven underground. The churches were partly international in organisation and orientation, and they were important instruments of education and self-education. Cyril's experiences with the church and its teachings were to be decisive in his political and intellectual formation.

Lutheran missionaries had been exceptionally active in the north of South Africa in the colonial era, and the Venda speakers of the former Transvaal were overwhelmingly evangelised by them. Samuel and Erdmuthe, both Lutherans from childhood, became staunch members of the Tshiawelo Lutheran congregation. Cyril's father had been shaped by his own conservative religious upbringing at Khalavha mission station in the far north of the country. His mother remained a bastion of the local Lutheran church until her death in 2001.[46] It was the resolution of conflicts between religious and political imperatives that lay at the heart of the younger Cyril Ramaphosa's political development.

For Lutherans like the Ramaphosa family, it was impossible to compartmentalise the freedom of a human being into separate religious and earthly components.[47] Spiritual liberation and political justice were simply different aspects of the same whole. Moreover, Martin Luther's teachings did not allow a person to acquire righteousness before God through personal striving. Rather, Luther believed that one had to be accounted and then made righteous by God's grace, which believers received only through faith.

Lutheran teachings could potentially carry either radical or conservative implications. It was a conservative reading of his religious duty, however, that left an imprint in Cyril's early years. The Lutheran World Federation to which the Ramaphosa family's congregation belonged was hierarchical and bishop-dominated, and during Cyril's childhood it propagated an intensely conservative theology.

Writing at the beginning of the 16th century, Luther argued that man was unable to understand the will of God but instead idolised his own 'reason' in the kingdom of the world that is also Satan's kingdom. God has created a 'spiritual government' or 'priesthood of believers' for Christians to battle against Satan, but he has also created temporal or secular government to prevent men from tearing one another apart as Satan's influence would otherwise lead them to do. The relationship between God and the government of the world is riven with theological ambiguity. An earthly ruler could never induce inner righteousness, which is purely a gift of God. However, secular government is given by God, and so it must be treated as a divine gift. This imposes an obligation on believers to accept public office, to obey the state, and indeed to go beyond their duties to obey the law.

If rulers violate God's law – a matter that men can determine by reflecting on the Scriptures – believers are obliged not to obey. No earthly person or law has authority over the conscience of a true Christian. But there is no right to use violence against others, not even those who are abusing office. The office of governor is divinely ordained, and the sword is reserved for rulers.

Although Lutheran teachings, as we shall see, are also capable of radical interpretation, the church of Cyril's parents instilled in him respect for the institutions of government. This text from St Paul's Letter to the Romans (13. 1–7) had special power:

'Let every soul be subject unto the higher powers. For there is no power but of God: the powers that be are ordained of God. Whosoever therefore resisteth the power, resisteth the ordinance of God: and they that resist shall receive to themselves damnation. For rulers are not a terror to good works, but to the evil. Wilt thou then not be afraid of the power? Do that which is good, and thou shalt have praise of the same: For he is the minister of God to thee for good. But if thou do that which is evil, be afraid; for he beareth not the sword in vain: for he is the minister of God, a revenger to [execute] wrath upon him that doeth evil. Wherefore [ye] must needs be subject, not only for wrath, but also for conscience sake. For this cause pay ye tribute also: for they are God's ministers, attending continually upon this very thing. Render therefore to all their dues: tribute to whom tribute [is due]; custom to whom custom; fear to whom fear; honour to whom honour.'[48]

Chapter 2

High School

Before I knew the word 'politics', I had already been uprooted with my community three times ... to make room for whites in newly declared white areas. Before I knew the word 'apartheid', I had already been denied timely education and daily bread. Before I learned anything about percentages and equality, I already knew that 'white' meant more food, more land, more money, more cattle, better housing, better schooling, better health facilities. Before I heard the word 'terrorist', I was already being terrorized ... Before I knew the concepts of oppression and exploitation, I knew that our people were killed and buried on the Bethal potato farms ... Before I knew the word 'communist' as defined by Botha and his predecessors, my grandfather had already told me that:
– Whites do not love us; they hate us.
– Hunger among blacks is not a natural disease but an apartheid-created tool of oppression.
– If blacks were edible, whites would have barbecues every day.
– Tshenuwani Farisani[1]

In January 1967, at the age of 14, Cyril advanced from Tshilidzi Primary to Sekano-Ntoane High School. The new school had a wide catchment area, attracting learners from a variety of Soweto neighbourhoods. Sekano-Ntoane lay outside Tshiawelo, on the other side of the Old Potchefstroom Road, and it was a fair trek from his home. Here Cyril found friendship with three other young boys from Tshiawelo who would become his companions each day on the way to and from school: Ishmael Mkhabela, Lybon Mabasa and Griffith Zabala.

These three boys were from Tsonga-speaking families and so had not met Cyril in the ethnically divided primary-school system. Only one of them, Griffith Zabala, remembers the arrival of the Ramaphosa family in 1962 and the building of their house.

Cyril's young friends were to go on to become significant political activists in the black consciousness movement. In their early years, it was Ishmael Mkhabela whose life was most closely to parallel Cyril's.[2] The two began together in Class 1a at Sekano-Ntoane, the reception class for the cream of the students from surrounding primary schools. Their experiences were not immediately happy ones, overshadowed by the ethnic belittlement that the young Venda and Tsonga boys suffered at the hands of their peers. As the children of Soweto were to grow older, the significance of the oppression of black people by white would almost erase these differences of language and culture. And boys from neighbouring suburbs would play football together at weekends without regard to the ethnic composition of the teams. In these early years, however, Mkhabela remembers that the stigma of belonging to what was perceived as a small and rural people was almost overwhelming.[3]

It was nothing new for the Tsonga and Venda boys to be the butt of jokes and victims of ethnic stereotyping on the streets. But now this experience followed them into the classroom in a school that had a substantial Zulu intake. Even more painfully for young children, the teachers in the school – who were middle class and most often themselves came from the established Zulu community – would sanction or even join in this ridiculing behaviour.

Such repeated episodes of belittlement can entrench a sense of inferiority and self-hate among young children, an insight that the black consciousness movement was already exploring in the face of racial discrimination. But it can also provide a motivation to prove oneself. So it was with Cyril and Ishmael, who both found themselves 'under an added burden to prove we were good or better than the rest'.[4] At the high school, the Venda and Shangaan students dominated the first five places in every class, and Cyril and Ishmael were themselves often vying for first and second places – Ishmael because of his shining intelligence, and Cyril, as Ishmael recalls it at least, through sheer determination and hard work. ('I was always that little bit cleverer than Cyril, but he was always even harder-working than me.')[5] Indeed, Cyril was already exhibiting the perfectionist tendencies that were to mark his later career, and he worked tirelessly to polish pieces of work that other students regarded as already complete.

One small Zulu boy who arrived at the school in 1969, two years younger than Cyril and his closest friends, almost immediately became their friend. This had been a school in which Venda and Tsonga speakers were obliged to learn Zulu – never the other way round – but now there came an exception. Duma Ndlovu was a child of strong character and independence of mind, and he was many years later to become a director on Broadway in New York and a major figure in the South African entertainment industry. In 1969, however, he was a small and rather scared little boy, arriving at Sekano-Ntoane school where first years were subjected to painful and cruel initiation processes lasting several weeks.

Ndlovu stood out because he had no time for the ethnic chauvinism of many of his peers. His closest friend in primary school was from Venda, and Ndlovu had travelled there to visit. He loved the people and the language and the place. He stood out on his arrival at school because – uniquely among the young Zulu children – he was determined to speak and learn Venda. He immediately felt at ease with Cyril and Ishmael. 'I felt truly comfortable with these guys and they took me in.'[6] They decided to look after him, and provided a 'protective cloak' against the bullying of the other children that was a part of the initiation process.

Ndlovu remembers Cyril as the best-dressed and neatest boy in the school. 'He was never seen without a Bible. He was the personification of perfection!'[7]

At high school Cyril began to read as widely as the limited book resources allowed. He would also sit for hours on end in the back room on Mhlaba Drive that was his bedroom, reading newspapers and whatever books he could find – of almost any kind. One particular interest was history. Ramaphosa loved to read about episodes of historical upheaval, and in particular the French Revolution. His favourite book, however, was *The Rise and Fall of the Third Reich*. This massive 1,200-page book by American journalist William L Shirer, first published in 1960, is a heavily moralised account of the Nazi era which denounces tyranny in all its guises. It dwells in particular on the evil diaries of Joseph Goebbels, history's most infamous master of the dark arts of propaganda, and explores the culpability of Germany's citizens for the crimes of their leaders. Cyril read this book over and over again, at school and at university, and liked to say to his friends: 'See how the mighty are fallen!'[8]

It would be wrong to categorise Ramaphosa's reading tastes as highbrow: he was mostly exposed to less sophisticated mass cultural products from Britain and the United States. His favourite author was the prolific British writer of American underworld crime stories, James Hadley Chase, who was one of the most widely read writers across the British empire. His titles, indicative of the modest intellectual ambitions of the author, included *A Coffin from Hong Kong*, *The Way the Cookie Crumbles*, *You Have Yourself a Deal*, *The Whiff of Money*, *The Vulture Is a Patient Bird* and *Goldfish Have No Hiding Place*. Such books Cyril would devour rapidly and enthusiastically.

Ramaphosa was also an enthusiast for the movies; they played a very significant role in his development. Among his favourite movies while he was at high school was the 1967 Hollywood hit *The Dirty Dozen*.[9] Ramaphosa also enjoyed the 1968 movie of Alistair MacLean's book *Where Eagles Dare*, starring Clint Eastwood and Richard Burton, and the more leisurely 1963 dramatisation of *The Great Escape* starring Steve McQueen. The celebration of the Allies' wartime triumph over the Axis powers, which these movies exemplify, conceivably appealed to Cyril. He may also have enjoyed the decimation of stereotypical Nazi ogres and SS assassins. According to Ramaphosa's later mentor, Tshenuwani Farisani, the Lutheran Theological College in Natal was staffed in part by German missionaries so conservative in ideology and formal in manner that they appeared to be escapees from a Nazi war movie.[10]

There was no movie-house in Tshiawelo – which then had and still today has quite rudimentary leisure facilities – and the youngsters would walk across to the nearby suburb of Kliptown. As they got older, and as finances allowed, Cyril and his friends would go to the movies accompanied by the girlfriends who were becoming an increasingly important part of their adolescent lives.[11] Cyril was later to become an organiser of film shows, for Christian associations and as a student union chairman. He was even influenced in his choice of his later career as a union organiser by one of the Hollywood movies he watched.

Cyril's life outside school continued to be dominated by religion. With his three best friends, he joined a Christian youth club called the Young Ambassadors, run by one of the growing number of teachers who were infusing their religious teaching with direct and fiery political rhetoric. The four youngsters also joined the Student Christian Movement (SCM), a nation-wide student body that Cyril was quite soon to lead.

In all these actions, Cyril's friends – who were all leaders in their own right – describe him as their leader, someone to whom they naturally deferred and who initiated and drove their activities. Cyril was already an impressive preacher who could deliver a message with real passion and force. His friends still remember him singing with great feeling his favourite song in Venda, which translates as follows:

> For He's coming soon,
> He's coming very soon;
> With joy we'll welcome the returning of the Lord![12]

One teacher at his school was Tom Manthatha, today a commissioner at the South African Human Rights Commission. He remembers Cyril as 'a deeply religious young man' and also as 'a leader'.[13] While Manthatha considered Cyril was at that time 'more religious than political', it was the relationship between politics and religion that increasingly preoccupied Cyril and his fellow Young Ambassadors. In their walks to and from school, the youngsters would debate contemporary political issues. Ishmael Mkhabela remembers how they used to meet for a communal lunch – communal so that those who did not have food could share the meals of the better-off students. They would pray extensively before lunch and then engage in theological reflection, which increasingly turned into a kind of quasi-political debate.

The mechanism through which this debate was initiated was a copy of the *Rand Daily Mail*, the most consistently anti-apartheid of the national newspapers, which the students would borrow from a teacher. They would place it on the table in front of them, and discuss each of the major stories – about political detentions, protests, evictions, and even about police informers. They would ask each other vexing questions: If you were Jesus, what would you say to that judge? If you were Jesus, what would you do to that informer? If you were Jesus, would you testify? These discussions were not politically sophisticated or well informed, but they were ways of reflecting upon the growing tensions between their professed religious beliefs and an encroaching political world characterised by injustice. At the same time as liberation theologians in Latin America were beginning to reconceptualise God's concern for the poor, so South African evangelicals like Cyril were reorienting their conception of Jesus and starting to see him as a friend of the oppressed.[14]

The issue of racial division began to loom increasingly large in Ramaphosa's life. He met few white people in his early childhood. The most memorable of these, for Cyril and his school friends, was 'Miss Brown', a young woman who would tour the schools of Soweto telling stories about Jesus and the path to salvation he offered. When Ramaphosa was 15 or 16, he started to attend Christian camps that she organised, opening his eyes to the world outside Soweto for the first time.[15] Miss Brown was very fond of Cyril and this fondness was apparently reciprocated. The other whites in the everyday life of Tshiawelo were missionaries participating in local church activities – figures of authority but predominantly benign ones.

At this time, new forms of thinking and organisation around 'black consciousness' were emerging as a major force in South Africa's schools, black universities and churches. The exploitation of black South Africans had intensified, and the search for new ways of understanding and responding to this exploitation became increasingly urgent. A new generation of leaders, primarily in the churches and universities, were elaborating a new way of thinking about the nature of black oppression. What emerged as 'black consciousness' towards the end of the 1960s was far from being a political organisation or a social movement. Indeed, the adherents of black consciousness ideas often avoided political organisation in order to evade bannings and arrests, which hampered other political movements. Rather it was a kind of intellectual approach to the position of the black person that asserted pride in blackness, dignity in the face of degradation and oppression, and the humanity of the African.

Some scholars have seen the emergence of black consciousness as a consequence of the political vacuum created by the suppression of the ANC, which had reduced it to what Jeremy Seekings describes as an 'obscure passivity'. By the mid-1960s, Seekings observes, 'overt political activity inside the country had been entirely and brutally suppressed. ANC (and PAC) leaders were either in jail or in exile and the armed struggle had petered to a halt ... It was in this repressive context that new movements emerged in the 1970s that eschewed formal political activity.'[16]

It is true that for Cyril and his friends, and for many like them, the ANC had become almost invisible as a result of banning, detentions and harassment. It was confined to waging an ineffective guerrilla war and launching diplomatic initiatives to isolate the Pretoria regime that were not reported within the country. While Raymond Suttner has recently emphasised that the ANC persisted in an underground form, interacting with black consciousness in areas like Durban and Johannesburg – and we shall see that even Cyril's own brother was to become part of just such underground activity – Cyril had no relationship with or awareness of these ANC structures.[17]

The most famous proponent of black consciousness ideas, Steve Biko, drew on philosophies elaborated across the previous 150 years in the United States,[18] and also upon post-colonial writings that emphasised the need for colonised peoples to reassert pride in their blackness – and sometimes their 'African-ness' – and to restore their own sense of their dignity as human beings after decades of colonial degradation. While black consciousness had an immense ideological impact upon a generation of middle-class black South Africans, the internal psychological transformation it prescribed was both too little and too much. It was too limited in that it did not provide solutions to the immediate practical problems faced by Africans. Black consciousness was found primarily in cultural and educational settings where it was an extension of the traditional generational critique young people were expected to undertake through youth associations.

On the other hand, it went too far where it ran up against the beliefs of those who were committed to a conservative Christian understanding of politics. For many black consciousness thinkers in the United States, Christianity was the imposed religion of the colonisers and should therefore be rejected. Such a position was more unusual in South Africa.

Here, the churches became the incubators of black consciousness thinking, though some of Cyril's contemporaries began to argue that if you were black – embrace and celebrate your blackness – you could not be a Christian.

In the generational tensions characteristic of the period, Cyril and his friends were sometimes regarded as 'hotheads' by their teachers and pastors. In these earlier days, however, they were all equivocal about the tensions between religion and politics. Although he does not himself remember taking such a position, Sekano-Ntoane teacher Tom Manthatha was an influential figure for many students because of his radical message that 'the Bible was poison'.[19] Cyril and his friends rejected any antithesis between Christianity and black consciousness. Their debate was not an ideological battlefield or a contest between dogmas. 'Most of our activities', according to Mkhabela, 'were values-based. We were trying to search for the truth, for justice, and for the purpose of life.'[20]

At the same time, they began to debate the implications of religious belief – its conservative effect and the way it acted (in Marx's words) as the 'opiate of the masses', a formulation of which they were fully aware. Some of them argued that you are a Christian first, but being Christian does not negate your blackness. As they got older, many of them changed their mantra: You are black first, but being black does not negate your Christianity.[21] Mkhabela was increasingly seen by the others as the most 'ecumenically inclined'. Perhaps the most 'worldly' of all the young men, Lybon Mabasa, today the president of the Socialist Party of Azania (Sopa), was to argue in 1972, when the friends were undertaking holiday work together, that 'If I go to heaven and there is a white man in there, I am not going in!'[22] Ramaphosa himself would recount the experiences of the Israelites in Egypt and argue that God was always on the side of the oppressed.

By 1976, when Cyril was in detention, the Student Christian Movement of which he was national chair had moved far enough to declare that 'Apartheid is evil under God'. Any Christian group that wished to share fellowship with the SCM was thereafter obliged to declare apartheid 'anti human, satanic, and demonic'. If they refused to do so, SCM members would refuse to worship with them.[23]

Biko had spoken of two stages of liberation – psychological and physical – but the movement he inspired remained unable to speak coherently about the second stage. However important it may have been as a precursor to effective political action, black consciousness was also a consolatory exercise. For most of the 1960s and 1970s the opportunities for political action were curtailed by a coercive police state at the height of its powers. Discontent remained largely localised, and there were no institutions able to mobilise protest across the country as a whole. There were none of the later powerful agencies – such as a coherent domestic ANC, trade unions, or civil society structures – through which meaningful action against the state could be organised.

Cyril became an extremely popular and successful student at Sekano-Ntoane. Nevertheless, in 1969, his parents took the decision that the young man should continue his schooling at Mphaphuli High School in the small town of Sibasa in Venda, close to where Samuel's family had its roots. Such a decision was not unusual, and many quite ordinary schools in the early 1970s had both day pupils and boarders who would live in hostels on the school grounds.

The motivations behind the move were several. It may have been in part an attempt to insulate Cyril from the growing dangers of township crime and gangsterism. Samuel and Erdmuthe, moreover, may have wanted to separate him from friends they perhaps viewed as hotheads or radicals.[24] Mphaphuli High, they may have calculated, would allow Cyril to follow a properly religious upbringing, rather than facing the politicisation of religion that was confronting students in Soweto's troubled high schools.

The decision that Cyril should study in Sibasa was probably also based on a desire to immerse a young man in his Venda heritage. To grow up with 'proper values', his family would have believed, it was necessary to spend at least some of one's formative years in the north. Cyril was to claim in a 1985 interview that the decision was in fact his and that it was taken on these grounds. 'I am Venda speaking. Having grown up in Soweto myself, I felt a need to go back to my roots, to go and see where my grandfather and my forefathers lived, and that was like an emotional thing for me.'[25]

Mphaphuli High School was set in the sleepy rural town of Sibasa. It was probably one of the three best schools in Venda at the time, and its enrolment included several hundred day pupils and around a hundred boarders, almost all of them boys. The boarders were housed in two hostels – one for boys and a smaller one for girls at the opposite end of the school grounds.

Sibasa was a dramatically different setting from the streets of Soweto. Located in what is today the province of Limpopo, Sibasa is surrounded by an extraordinary natural beauty. At the same time, the region was and remains an economic and educational backwater. Shambolic government authorities – the local Bantustans of Venda, Lebowa and Gazankulu – were the main sources of skilled employment. Harsh agricultural labour on white-owned farms was the norm, and remittances from the cities were an essential supplement to household income.

The school itself had limited resources, and it is described by Cyril's then principal, TS Ntsandeni, as a 'country school'.[26] He elaborates that 'we did not have teaching materials, resources or books. We tried to open the eyes of the students but it was hard without even newspapers to make them aware of the outside world.' At the same time, the school had ambitions. It was one of the first Venda-language schools to offer science in its curriculum, and by the late 1950s it already offered an unusually wide curriculum of Venda, Afrikaans, mathematics, biology, physical science, bookkeeping, agricultural science and religious education.

It was also a school in which the local community had invested some pride. It had its origins in efforts by local chiefs to reduce illiteracy in the earlier decades of the century. The buildings in which the school was housed in Cyril's time were built in 1958 and funded by subscription among 26,000 Venda taxpayers (at the rate of one pound per year for three years). Although the South African government declined to fund the school buildings – excusing itself on grounds of shortage of resources – they were opened by the minister of education, HW Maree, in 1959. Local traditional leader Khosi Raluswielo planted his historic footprint in the entrance lobby to the school, beneath a foundation stone.

In this backwater of high but mostly unmet expectations, Cyril was to make his presence immediately felt. Principal Ntsandeni had been forewarned of his arrival. 'I met one of Ramaphosa's teachers from Sekano-Ntoane here in the street and he told me "you have a very special student starting next year". I had forgotten all about this until the first meeting of the Student Christian Movement at the start of the school year.'[27]

The SCM was the largest student organisation in the school, and attendance at SCM meetings had been compulsory for some years. It was a custom of the organisation that each year's new SCM executive committee would be chosen the previous year by the departing senior students. This year, however, the principal remembers things went awry.

'The teacher in charge of the SCM came to my office flustered. He told me the SCM had met in the normal way in the hall. However, at the end of a long meeting, they had come to him with the news that the chairman had resigned. They unanimously wanted to have a newcomer, Cyril Ramaphosa, as chair of the SCM for that year.'

The principal asked for Cyril to be brought before him and immediately fell under his spell. 'It was the first time I had seen Cyril. And the first time I saw that smile, his special smile.'[28] This smile was to become Cyril's trademark as a negotiator and politician, an irresistibly charming grin behind which almost any emotion could be concealed.

During Cyril's two years at Mphaphuli, the principal became increasingly reliant on Cyril's advice – about school management, student problems and teacher competency. Ramaphosa would stiffen his classmates' resolve, sharpen their discipline, organise their school projects, and hone their class presentations. He would even harangue those whose work was not up to standard, and explain to them what was and was not appropriate and acceptable behaviour.

Even more extraordinarily, Ramaphosa took the same approach with teachers who failed to perform their job to his satisfaction. He was thrown out of classes in mathematics and geography for taking to task teachers who were not properly prepared or whose attendance record was unsatisfactory. As a result he dropped out of maths and wrote his geography exam without attending lessons. It was only because of the protection of Principal Ntsandeni that disgruntled teachers did not achieve their goal of expelling Ramaphosa. Within a year, as we shall see, Cyril was taking the children out of the school with the principal's permission to travel on evangelical missions around the region.

Cyril's academic performance continued to be very good by the limited standards of the school at the time. In his matriculation year, he studied oral and written Venda, Afrikaans and English; physics and chemistry; and geography and history. He was never a strong student of Venda language and culture or of written Afrikaans.[29] Indeed he was always a better student of English than of Venda, perhaps indicating a degree of reticence about embracing his Venda heritage and the Afrikaans language, which was a symbol of oppression for the agricultural labourers of the north.[30]

While Cyril did not shine in the classroom study of Venda culture, the abuse of these traditions ignited the flames of his rage. He was becoming unwilling or unable to maintain the routine deference that was expected of Africans to whites. On one occasion, members of the school were gathered for an event at Mukumbai, the chiefs' kraal in Sibasa. This was a place treated with great veneration even by those, like Cyril, who embraced Christianity and modernity wholeheartedly. At this meeting, there were some white people present. The senior police officer present, Captain Madzena, treated the whites with the then customary exaggerated deference. He gave priority to their needs and accommodated their wishes, leading them to the front of the crowd and ensuring that they were comfortable and well looked after. Such favours would have been accepted by them and others present as quite natural.

Cyril, however, emerged visibly upset from the crowd and began to complain eloquently that this was the chiefs' place. 'Why', he asked, 'must whites be given preference over Africans, even here, at the expense of the true owners of the place?' Madzena did not take kindly to the intervention. He rushed towards Cyril threateningly, and the boy was forced to slip away into the crowd, where he was concealed by his fellow students.[31]

Cyril already knew some of his classmates from Soweto. Among those to whom he became very close was one of the girls, Hope Mukondeleli Mudau, the daughter of a notable Venda politician and Soweto socialite, Baldwin Mudau. Ten years later she was to become Cyril's first wife.

Mudau senior was a flamboyant figure in the Soweto suburb of Dube in the mid-1960s, a businessman and high-liver.[32] His political interest, on the other hand, was in the Bantustan of Venda which the government was hoping to turn into a fully fledged ethnic mini-state, as part of its project to justify the disempowerment of Africans in their own country. This ethnic separatism, as elsewhere in the country, enjoyed a degree of support within Venda, in particular from the local elites – business, official and 'traditional' – who were to benefit most from supposed self-government and the 'independence' that Pretoria promised would soon follow. Mudau became leader of the Venda Independent People's Party – later the Venda Independence Party (VIP) – and he was briefly Chief Minister in 1973. He was also for a long time an official representative of the Venda authority in Johannesburg.

Like most of the local elite involved in homeland politics, he was a conservative broadly in favour of Venda self-government. His party was actively contesting power with the pro-Pretoria chiefs who supported an entrenchment of the 'traditional' authority from which they derived their legitimacy. After the first general election in Venda in late 1973, Chief Mphephu of the Venda National Party (VNP) secured election as Chief Minister.[33] Mudau's VIP was to call a vote of no confidence in the election, accusing Mphephu of bribing MPs by 'ordering R70 suits for parliamentarians' and taking them on a three-day trip to a game reserve in an effort to secure their votes.[34] The VIP was eventually to secure the upper hand over the VNP in 1974 and 1975, as a result of defections of chiefs and headmen. However, Baldwin Mudau himself came under challenge in his own party by middle-ranking chiefs keen to enforce the Venda constitution's demand that only a chief can become Chief Minister. Although Mudau came from a powerful and prestigious lineage, he was not himself a chief.

According to the eccentric British author Douglas Reed – a former London *Times* foreign correspondent who had retired to the Durban coast – Baldwin Mudau was not at all enamoured of African liberation movements. After discussions with fellow black African delegates at a Texas law conference, Mudau reported his new view of 'freedom fighters' as follows: 'They did not want to help their brothers. They meant to take control and they would hit the black man and white man alike; and Vendaland would be the first battleground in the fight against armed insurgents.'[35]

It is unlikely that the political beliefs of Baldwin Mudau had any impact on the independent-minded Cyril. But Mudau was a person of great local political influence as well as a very prominent figure in the black business world of Soweto. He had worked as a public relations manager for Lever Bros – then the most desirable employer for an African in Johannesburg – and much later for McCann Erickson and J Walter Thompson. Mudau would not have welcomed being mixed up with Cyril when he was later in detention. When Cyril eventually married Hope, he was joining a family of considerable wealth and political power tied into the established order in both Venda and Soweto.

The relationship between Hope and Cyril was evidently a complex one, combining affection with what one friend saw as a common spiritual and political journey.[36] She was also by all accounts stunningly beautiful – 'smashingly pretty' says Reuel Khoza – and a person of considerable self-confidence and grace. To this day she remains protective of Cyril.[37]

Cyril also found a new and exceptional role model outside school. If Cyril's father had hoped he might be protected from radical political influences in the far north, he was sorely mistaken. A few months after his arrival, he made the acquaintance of Tshenuwani Farisani, a soon-to-be ordained minister and nationally prominent black consciousness activist who was about to become national convener of the Black People's Convention (BPC).[38] Farisani was four or five years older than Cyril but a world apart from him in terms of political experience. He had been one of the most brilliant students of his generation. When he met Cyril he was enrolled at a theological college in Natal in preparation for a career in the church. He would travel the country, speaking to young people, distributing literature, establishing organisational branches, and articulating his radical and subversive ideas. It was on just such a tour that he met Ramaphosa.

Farisani was a guest at the school's flourishing debating society, in which Cyril was inevitably a star performer, and the house was debating the motion that 'knowledge is more important than money'.[39] Although Cyril was young and inexperienced, Farisani identified something out of the ordinary in his questioning character and moral seriousness. It transpired that Ramaphosa was open to the radical interpretations of the Bible for which Farisani was later to become famous.

Farisani believed that the Lutheran Evangelical Church had to turn away from political conservatism, and instead become an instrument of opposition to oppression. For him, black people were 'in South Africa but not of South Africa, every square inch human but not members of the human race. We have the sense but are not credited with a consciousness of our surroundings. We are present but always very absent! Why?'[40]

The Lutheran Church of Cyril's childhood was a conservative influence on its adherents, charging them to respect the institutions of secular government that God had created. Farisani rebelled against the 'dubious teachings' of the Lutheran Theological College at Umpumulo, from which he would be expelled in March 1972, deriding as nonsense its teaching that 'God created the lion to feed upon the buck. Why should blacks complain about white oppression?' Likewise, he ridiculed the notion that wherever you find yourself 'God has placed you there', so do not complain.[41]

Farisani highlighted for Cyril the contradictions between the professed faith of South African Lutherans and the realities of their practised life. Lutherans confessed Christ, yet almost all of their actions were contrary to Christ's teachings. At the centre of the church, he believed, should be the understanding that God loves everybody, and that His son died for everybody. Yet the Lutheran Church practised apartheid even in its own organisational structures.

'A church must teach if it is to be a living church. The Lutherans' teaching at that time was selective and inconsistent,' he claimed. Leaders of the church turned a blind eye to the circumstances in which the church's members lived – to the pass raids, detentions and killings experienced by ordinary members. For him, the 'inner justice' of the church – its preoccupation with the transformation of the heart – had to be accompanied by an 'outer righteousness' or external justice in the transformation of the social and economic order.[42]

Farisani was a brilliant satirist of the conservatism of the South African church and political establishments, later attributing the following words to PW Botha: 'God is for heaven, and earth is for us. You have no right to take [God] through my country. It's interference in our domestic affairs. Does he have a visa? ... Your application for an entry visa to my country is granted on condition: you come after sunrise on Sunday and leave the same day before sunset; you travel straight from heaven to the Waterkloof Nederduits Gereformeerde Church; [and] only white angels are included in your entourage.'[43]

But Farisani was only incidentally a satirist. His later writings bear witness to a profound anger at the treatment of black people by white, and he was able to give voice to the rage that otherwise lay unspoken in the chests of young men like Ramaphosa:

> Who are we, lord?
> Who will name places after apes?
> No history behind us.
> No future ahead of us.
> No city in our name,
> No park in honour of our heroes.
> No tunnel. No airport. No bay. No cape. No
>   nothing in our name.
> Nothing. Nothing. Nothing![44]

Ramaphosa was more than ready for the radical message Farisani was preaching. Their first collaboration was primarily organisational rather than theological in character. Together they set up the Black Evangelical Youth Organisation (BEYO), an extramural society that evangelised widely and systematically in communities in the region around Sibasa. Their approach was to identify a village and then spend a week there, preaching, praying for the sick and infirm, inviting people to 'come to Jesus', very much in the manner of contemporary Pentecostals.

Cyril was chairman of BEYO, a position that reflected the vast array of other responsibilities that rested on Farisani's shoulders. The older man's travels meant Ramaphosa was largely responsible for the day-to-day running of the organisation, but Farisani took up the position of deputy chairman in order to be able to guide the young Ramaphosa.

Although the organisation initially focused on those of an 'impressionable age', Ramaphosa soon insisted that it should be open to everyone.[45] BEYO was to grow rapidly in size and in the scope of its activities, then mutating into the *Bold* Evangelical Youth Organisation so as to permit the participation of white Lutherans. Later still it became the Bold Evangelical *Christian* Association (BECO), reflecting Cyril's determination that adult members should be admitted too. At the same time, Cyril was rising in the Student Christian Movement. With his perfectionist zeal, he drew up fresh organisational principles of a federal character for the SCM that would allow it to bring together its members in cross-school collaboration.[46]

Like many other politicians, Ramaphosa was a talented youth actor. Most of his performances were religious in character, and he became well known as a driving force behind a production called *The Trial of Trials* which explored the implications of the killing of Jesus. The drama was performed to a variety of local audiences and congregations, and it created great unease. Audiences almost always included highly 'respectable' members of the community, who were in reality the indirect employees of the apartheid government, for example as Bantustan officials. In the conservative manner of the time, they would denounce the acting and preaching of Cyril as 'too worldly', and argue that it was wrong for the 'political' world to be mixed with the Christian project of celebrating Christ.[47]

As Cyril brought his fellow students out to evangelise in poor communities around Sibasa, Farisani was gradually helping him towards a more radical interpretation of the key biblical passages with which he had been raised. For the young evangelicals, these visits to impoverished communities took on an important theological purpose. They came to understand that God was not deaf to the voices of the poor. When a group of evangelicals went out to bring light and hope to a poor rural village, they would read Luke 4 and understand that God was going out with them: 'The Spirit of the Lord [is] upon me, because he hath anointed me to preach the gospel to the poor; he hath sent me to heal the brokenhearted, to preach deliverance to the captives, and recovering of sight to the blind, to set at liberty them that are bruised, To preach the acceptable year of the Lord.'[48]

There was now fresh resonance to the biblical account of Moses' encounter with the Lord in Exodus 3, a chapter Cyril would have learnt by heart as young child, studied, and used as the basis for his adolescent preaching. God was still a forbidding figure for Ramaphosa. But the God of Exodus, he now understood, was not deaf to the cries of the people. Moses brings a flock of sheep to the mountain of God where he encounters an angel who emerges in a flame of fire out of a bush. When Moses turns to look, God calls out to him from the bush: 'I am the God of thy father, the God of Abraham, the God of Isaac, and the God of Jacob. And Moses hid his face; for he was afraid to look upon God. And the Lord said, I have surely seen the affliction of my people which are in Egypt, and have heard their cry by reason of their taskmasters; for I know their sorrows; And I am come down to deliver them out of the hand of the Egyptians, and to bring them up out of that land unto a good land and a large, unto a land flowing with milk and honey ...'

The essence of the religion that now guided Cyril was the recognition of oppression, and the obligation this brought to go out and to evangelise. Not only was God aware of the suffering of his people, but he intended to take decisive action against the oppressors who would attempt to thwart the project of the evangelicals. 'Now therefore, behold, the cry of the children of Israel is come unto me: and I have also seen the oppression wherewith the Egyptians oppress them ... And I have said, I will bring you up out of the affliction of Egypt ... unto a land flowing with milk and honey. And they shall hearken to thy voice: and thou shalt come, thou and the elders of Israel, unto the king of Egypt, and ye shall say unto him, The Lord God of the Hebrews hath met with us: and now let us go, we beseech thee, three days' journey into the wilderness, that we may sacrifice to the Lord our God. And I am sure that the king of Egypt will not let you go, no, not by a mighty hand. And I will stretch out my hand, and smite Egypt with all my wonders which I will do in the midst thereof: and after that he will let you go.'[49]

Under Farisani's guidance Cyril came to understand the Bible's seemingly conservative injunctions about respect for earthly government in a more radical light. The Lutheran Church of Cyril's parents proclaimed that God had created earthly government – even in South Africa – and that God's creations were to be respected by all men. Farisani, however, emphasised that even if God had created government, the system of apartheid which was driving this authority in an evil direction was the creation of men. These men, moreover, could rightly be castigated as selfish, bigoted and racist. Although conservative Lutherans believed one must not fight institutions created by God, for Farisani it was right to fight apartheid because apartheid was an abuse of governing institutions that had been established by God.

As Farisani was to make this point in a later writing, an agent of apartheid was like a baboon that watches its rich master drive a Rolls-Royce car. After a while, the baboon learns a little about how to drive and one day takes his master's key and drives off. The consequences, of course, are dire. The baboon mistakes a road sign with two curves indicating 'sharp bends' for a warning about 'Huge snakes next two miles' and drives off the edge of a cliff. For Farisani it was not the 'Rolls-Royce' that was at fault but the baboon: 'Unlicensed baboons today are driving the institution of government without the mandate of their Creator and of their fellow citizens.'[50]

In evangelising poor villages, Cyril became a celebrated preacher. Already expert in the superficial wordplay of formal debate, and confident enough to preach to a large congregation, he now learnt how to engage very poor rural people in reflection on the very foundations of their theology – and he learnt how to do so with humility.[51] He preached in villages, to the old and to the sick. He preached on trains, on the streets, and in churches of all denominations. He now possessed a kind of quiet magic that he could use to engage audiences of almost any kind on matters of the highest complexity and greatest personal sensitivity.

Beneath his self-assured humility, the fires of political ambition were starting to burn strongly. Denis Beckett, the veteran Johannesburg journalist, remembers meeting Cyril for the first time at an SCM camp in 1969 or 1970 on the banks of the Hartbeespoort Dam, which was then 'camp territory' rather than the tourist playground of today. Beckett had been invited to observe and assist at the camp by the religious activist Steve Truscott. He remembers that Cyril stood out among the humble and reticent black youth at the retreat, youngsters who could hardly meet the eye of a white outsider that they did not know. 'Cyril wasn't like that. He certainly wasn't humble. He was confident like no one else at that camp. I remember that he even said, "I am going to be President one day!"'[52]

For Cyril's young Soweto friends, as we shall see, the greatest change that came over him in his years in Sibasa was not his metamorphosis into a talented and self-assured evangelical, but rather his growing fearlessness in the face of discrimination and racial abuse. Even this change rested on profoundly strong theological foundations. The young men were all familiar with the opening chapter of the Book of Genesis, which includes the following passage: 'And God said, Let us make man in our image, after our likeness: and let them have dominion over the fish of the sea, and over the fowl of the air, and over the cattle, and over all the earth, and over every creeping thing that creepeth upon the earth. So God created man in his *own* image, in the image of God created he him; male and female created he them. And God blessed them, and God said unto them, Be fruitful, and multiply, and replenish the earth, and subdue it: and have dominion over the fish of the sea, and over the fowl of the air, and over every living thing that moveth upon the earth.'[53]

For Ramaphosa, these verses were now among the most important in the Bible.[54] He learnt that God distinguished clearly and deliberately between man and animals. Unlike the scientific racists who were the architects of apartheid, God repudiated a hierarchy in which some men were closer to the animals than others. Man, moreover, was directly instructed by God to subdue the world – rather than to subdue one another. Finally, and most importantly, man was made in the image of God Himself. To be in this sense 'like the Creator' was each human being's gift from God, something that could never be taken away by mere human action. To insult a black man was to insult his Creator too, because every person – whether black or white – was made in the Creator's image.[55]

In the school holidays of 1970 and 1971, Cyril would return from Venda to the family home in Soweto where he spent his time in the company of his old friends from Sekano-Ntoane and engaged in still more evangelical activity. The young friends also worked to earn money for precious luxuries like clothes and movie visits. Cyril had always been preoccupied with the need for financial independence – he did not like to ask his parents for money – and his brother Douglas remembers him returning exhausted after long days working in a bottlestore in Johannesburg. He was almost too tired to spend the money he had earned, but he would rather work than borrow.[56] Cyril recently recalled that 'I've been an entrepreneur from the age of 16. What could have been a business career for me was interrupted by apartheid. I started as a hawker buying and selling things.' Rather theatrically, Cyril went on to explain that his nascent business career was cut short because 'there was a struggle to be prosecuted'.[57]

Cyril and his friends enjoyed quite remunerative part-time work almost every holiday as a result of the helping hand of a sister of Griffith Zabala who worked at the Industrial Council for Clothing Industries (ICCI) in Doornfontein. Here the young men, their friend Frank Chikane from university among them on one occasion, worked as clerks earning the princely sum of R20 per week.[58] The always well-presented Ramaphosa liked to dress up exceptionally smartly as a young gentleman for the train journey to the office, paying special attention to his ties and to the neatness of his suit.[59] He continued to be a voracious reader and enthusiast for movies, and he dressed in the most current fashions that his hard-earned money could buy. At this time, Cyril became fascinated by the politics of the Kennedy dynasty in the United States and sometimes would wear his favourite tie – 'my Kennedy-style tie' – on his way to work.[60]

At the end of 1971, Cyril matriculated with impressive marks. Only one student in his class – a key rival for the teachers' praise named Simon Phaswani – was to receive a first-class matriculation exemption. Cyril, like eight of his classmates, secured a second-class matriculation exemption, sufficient to make possible entry to university. Ramaphosa's academic potential was clear from his B grade in geography, one of only two B grades awarded to the entire class across the entire range of subjects in that year.[61] Cyril's classmates, according to their former principal, 'did very well for themselves'. However, their ambitions were purely local, with the five or six best-performing of them becoming local lawyers, teachers or local government bureaucrats. Cyril's horizons were wider and his ambition fiercer.

Before setting off for university, Cyril had one last summer holiday to spend with his boyhood friends in Soweto. In the long school holiday after matriculation, he returned to Tshiawelo and together they planned an adventure. Travel within South Africa by young black people was highly unusual. A plethora of laws and regulations restricted black people's freedom of movement. Nevertheless, the youngsters had ventured on extended walks and hitch-hikes from Soweto, once reaching Durban and on another occasion Lesotho. Organised with the assistance of their Young Ambassadors Christian Youth Club and the church, these trips had the purported purpose of allowing the youngsters to preach and 'service the community'.

For their late 1971 excursion, the youngsters decided to make their most ambitious trip yet to the city of Cape Town, a place about which they knew almost nothing. The trip was to demonstrate how young and inexperienced Cyril remained. But for Ramaphosa's friends, it was to show him in a new light, as a fearless or even reckless antagonist of white racists.

The youngsters departed on 22 December 1971. Cyril's friends – there were five boys and two girls – collected him last because his house was closest to the Old Potchefstroom Road, which was to be the starting point of their journey. They said a prayer before putting their bags on their backs and saying their farewells. The girls predictably secured lifts almost immediately and arrived in Cape Town within a couple of days. The boys – Griffith, Cyril, Lybon and two friends Eugene 'Chain' Vilakazi and Albert Fela – found the going far harder.[62]

They had chosen the worst time of the year for such a venture. It was the height of summer and the sun beat down mercilessly on their backs as they walked. It was the summer vacation, and most cars and trucks were filled to overflowing with families and friends heading to the sea or to stay with their relatives for the holidays. It was also Christmas holiday time for the truckers, and there were almost none of the expected rides in the back of a lorry available to the youngsters.

They walked for many kilometres down the Potchefstroom Road before they were picked up by a truck. Pointing out that they were heading in the wrong direction for Cape Town, the driver dropped them at the junction with a more promising road. The hot day turned humid and sweltering, and eventually the skies opened in a massive storm that drenched the youngsters' clothes. They had to spend the night sheltering close to a bus stop, the heat of the day transformed into the chill of night. They had decided to limit themselves to half a loaf of bread and a pint of milk per person for each day of the entire journey. Cyril, determined as ever to be the most virtuous of even this virtuous crowd, saved a portion of his bread and shared it with his friends.[63]

What distinguished Cyril on this trip was not this characteristic display of conspicuous selflessness, but his unwillingness to tolerate the casual abuse of whites whom they encountered along the way. On one occasion, the boys were swimming in a small dam cooling off from the hot midday sun. A Zephyr 6 car, pulling a small trailer, slowed to a halt with steam pouring out from under the hood. In the front there sat two young Afrikaners, a boy and a girl. The driver asked their help carrying water to the car. In return he agreed to their request for a ride, and the five of them clambered on to the small trailer with their bags.

After a long ride, they arrived at the home of the young Afrikaner woman's father. They disentangled their limbs and climbed stiffly from the trailer, thanking their driver for the ride. Cyril very politely turned to the older man, and asked, 'Meneer! Could you please give us some bread and water?' The old man turned to him dismissively and said, 'Fuck off! This is not a black man's hotel.' Cyril stood his ground, expressionless, and shouted back, 'Voetsek! You are an arrogant Afrikaner!' before turning coldly on his heel.

A few days later, Cyril and his friends stopped at a small shop to buy their bread loaves and milk for the day ahead. They heard a car coming, and rushed outside in the hope of a lift. The driver, a young Afrikaner, slowed his car, but then rebutted their request by shouting at them in Afrikaans, 'Fuck off, you kaffirs!' Cyril shouted back, also in Afrikaans, 'You fuck off yourself. You are full of the devil!'

Such confrontations could have been a recipe for violence. But on these two occasions, and as was to become commonplace in Cyril's later years, whites who were the victims of his contempt found themselves unable to confront him.

His refusal even to express his disgust with apartheid's indignities was beginning. He would soon walk into a restaurant without concern for the clientele. If there was a 'Whites only' or 'Europeans only' sign, not only would he not look at it, but he would sit directly underneath it – apparently without noticing it was there. In such situations, no one can recall any person daring to confront him.[64] Cyril seemed to radiate a sense of effortless self-confidence and a complete absence of fear. This fearlessness and sense of personal invulnerability further bolstered the respect with which he was viewed by his peers, because he now seemed to offer a shield – almost a force-field – behind which they could safely retreat.[65]

The poet Wally Serote wrote in the 1970s of the retrospective shame that many black people felt for accepting or even embracing those who treated them like dogs.

> I did this world great wrong
> with my kindness of a dog
> my heart like a dog's tongue
> licking too many hands, boots and bums
> even after they kicked my arse
> voetsek voetsek
> shit. I still wagged my tail
> I ran away still looking back
> with eyes saying please[66]

By the time he was 17, Ramaphosa had quite lost the ability to run away.

The friends' journey was to take them nine days in total. Their nights were spent under the stars and their days passed in relentless walking. They rode in trucks and bakkies, and one day all five squeezed with their bags into a tiny Anglia car that already held three occupants. On Boxing Day, 26 December, they trudged all day long without a single lift and slept under a bridge in a small town. Little by little they edged towards their destination, through Uitenhage, Tsitsikamma Forest and Mossel Bay, splitting into twos and threes to take any available lift. Eventually the last of them arrived in Cape Town just before the new year of 1972.

Cyril began to prepare his mind for his studies in law at the quiet backwater of the University of the North. He was about to walk into a political explosion.

CHAPTER 3

TURFLOOP

I babysat you, but now you are baas.
I washed your diapers, but now I must go to hell.
I saved you from a pool, but you shoot my child.
I love you to earn your hate.
I hosted you and lost my home.
I became a human being to you, now I am an animal.
I trusted your God, and it stole my land.

— Tshenuwani Farisani[1]

When Cyril arrived at the Turfloop campus of the University of the North in early 1972, he was joining a small group of black South Africans. To reinforce racial segregation and advance 'retribalisation', the NP government had created universities to cater for the country's ethnic minorities, but they were small institutions with a limited intake.

English- and white Afrikaans-speaking students enjoyed access to large and well-resourced universities on substantial campuses, in which a full arts, science and social science curriculum was taught. In accordance with the twin logics of ethnic separatism and inequitable allocation, the government established five colleges, known as 'tribal colleges' or ironically as 'bush colleges', to cater for non-whites.[2] Students designated Asian or Indian attended the moderately resourced University of Durban-Westville (UDW). Those designated coloured attended the University of the Western Cape (UWC) in Bellville to the north-east of Cape Town. These colleges were smaller, less well-equipped, and narrower in their curriculums than their white counterparts.

At the bottom of the resource ladder were universities for Africans. The University of Fort Hare in the Eastern Cape – *alma mater* of a generation's senior ANC, IFP and PAC leaders, including Nelson Mandela and Govan Mbeki – was the most prestigious African institution, fed by elite missionary schools. Fort Hare managed partly to resist the government's agenda of ethnic homogenisation, and continued to recruit from across the country and beyond. The University of Zululand, by contrast, had an entirely Zulu student body. The University of the North was a more curious creation. At its foundation in 1960 it was designed to cater for the wide variety of ethnic groups – Shangaan, Venda, Tswana, Pedi and Sotho – to be found in the north of the country.[3]

In 1970, the five black colleges were granted 'autonomy' in terms of a series of Acts,[4] mandating them for the first time to grant degrees and diplomas. These Acts of parliament granted a second kind of autonomy, by specifying that they were not the property of, or incorporated into, the Bantustans within which they might be located. Nevertheless, each university was linked to its own Bantu or 'own affairs' department of education, whose purposes included the provision of an education 'appropriate' to the different ethnic groups and their proper expectations.[5]

When Cyril began his education at the University of the North, these universities were still small but in a process of rapid expansion. Turfloop accommodated 810 students in 1970, 901 in 1971 and 1,146 by the time of his arrival in 1972. UWC and Zululand were of similar size, while UDW was already around twice as large.[6] To put this expansion into perspective, however, the University of the North and Zululand awarded less than a hundred degrees each in 1972, and about the same number of diplomas. Fort Hare, UDW and UWC together awarded fewer than 400 degrees to black students.

Like Cyril, most bush college students came from stable, if not affluent, families in which at least one member was in formal employment. Typically, a parent might work for the state or a Bantustan, as a teacher, preacher or nurse. Ramaphosa was quite typical in that his university education was funded not by his parents but by a bursary, one of many for which he applied the previous year, and by a loan from Standard Bank.[7]

These stable backgrounds led the state to anticipate that the new universities' graduates would go on to become productive racial and ethnic elites, staffing the Bantustan governments and own affairs departments. The bush colleges instead profoundly angered most of their student bodies, and produced a new generation of radicalised activists.

In retrospect it is easy to see why. Racial domination was evident in every aspect of the students' lives outside university, and it was reproduced within it, too. The universities were dominated by an Afrikaner bureaucracy at the level of the rectorate, council and senate. The academic staff, especially at senior levels, was overwhelmingly white. Of the 120 professors in the five colleges, 111 were white; likewise 176 out of 188 senior lecturers.[8] In later years, there would be some exceptional teaching staff who chose to work in these colleges out of political commitment, particularly at UWC and UDW. The vast majority of the staff in the 1970s, however, were no-hopers, who had been unable to secure jobs in the more prestigious white universities. Teaching methods were formal and staff–student relations tended to be distant and racialised.

The content and character of the education rankled with students. The campuses were located away from urban centres and white areas. The syllabi were still dominated by University of South Africa (Unisa) study guides.[9] Rote learning and regurgitation were the key teaching methodologies. And the expectations of educators were largely at the low levels set by the 'own affairs' and Bantu education departments. Anything considered 'controversial' or 'political' – for example, any discussion of the ANC – was removed from the teaching programme, which was avowedly 'politically neutral'.

It was unsurprising in such circumstances that many students on the black campuses would become politically radicalised. Yet these black students were not allowed to affiliate to the National Union of South African Students (Nusas) – the council of the University of the North turned down an application by the SRC to affiliate in 1968. Nusas was to remain confined to the white and liberal campuses, and in 1969 the South African Students Organisation (Saso) was formed with a broad black consciousness ideology. This breakaway from the perceived paternalism of Nusas was celebrated.[10] In the famous slogan of the time, 'Black man: You're on your own!' By 1972 Saso was an emerging force in all of the bush colleges, and the primary vehicle for political mobilisation of the students – although there were many other organisations at play, all vying for representation on the Student Representative Council (SRC), the highest representative body in any student community.

Cyril was studying towards a law degree. He may have been drawn to the theatrical aspect of the law, and by the opportunity it offered him to demonstrate his public speaking accomplishments. Study of the law may have held out the prospect of new understanding and leverage in a world dominated by legally institutionalised racism. He may even have been influenced by his keen watching of courtroom scenes in the Hollywood movies he so loved, and by his reading of detective novels.[11]

More prosaically, a legal training offered the possibility of a career, and it was one of the few areas in which a black man could become a successful professional. For Cyril's Mphaphuli classmates, at least, the law was the profession of choice. Cyril's Turfloop contemporary Frank Chikane remembers being encouraged to study law as early as primary school by his father, although he decided instead to read applied mathematics and physics.[12] Cyril's policeman father would likewise have seen a career in the law as a major advance for his son.

Only two months after Cyril's arrival at Turfloop, the university – and very soon politics across the black campuses – was turned upside down by a single speech. At the graduation ceremony of the university on 29 April 1972, Onkgopotse Ramothibi Tiro, a former SRC president who was studying for a diploma at the university, launched a breathtaking attack on the segregated education system. Tiro was a powerful orator and an original thinker. He had preceded Cyril's arrival at Turfloop by three years. The graduating class asked Tiro to represent them at the graduation ceremony.

Tiro was no stranger to politics; indeed his short life was a compressed history of relentless political struggle. He was born on 9 November 1945 in the small village of Dinokana in the north-west of South Africa. When his primary school was closed down by strikes against the imposition of passes for women, Tiro worked as a child labourer on a manganese mine. He began high school in Soweto, but after arrest for failure to produce a pass he was forced to finish his schooling in Mafikeng. His career at the University of the North had been academically sound, but his life was dominated by political debate and organisation.

As he rose to deliver his oration in the hall, he looked down upon an audience that was predominantly white. Towards the front of the hall were members of the council and senate, the white professors and senior lecturers, and other invited guests. At the back of the hall were parents of the graduating students. Some of them were forced to wait outside the hall, unable to see or hear the proceedings properly. Such treatment was conventional at this time – like Captain Madzena's treatment of white visitors at the chiefs' kraal in Sibasa – and would have gone quite unnoticed by the university grandees.

Tiro shattered the illusion that this racial injustice was part of the natural order of things.[13] If there had to be a black university, he asked, why did its council have to be dominated by white outsiders? With building anger, he next complained about the treatment of black parents. 'Our parents have come all the way from their homes only to be locked outside. We are told the hall is full. I do not accept that there is no accommodation for them … Front seats are given to people who cannot even cheer us. My father is seated there at the back. My dear people, shall we ever get a fair deal in this land? The land of our fathers.'[14]

Tiro then told the graduating students not to allow themselves to become instruments for the perpetuation of apartheid. He likened the leaders of Bantustans to 'bolts of the same machine which is crushing us', and argued that whites would never permit true Bantustan autonomy. 'Do you think that the white minority can willingly commit political suicide by creating numerous states which might turn out to be hostile in future? … We black graduates, by virtue of our age and academic standing, are being called upon to greater responsibilities in the liberation of our people.'[15]

With an excusable rhetorical excess, Tiro concluded, 'Let the Lord be praised, for the day shall come when all men shall be free to breathe the air of freedom, and when that day shall come no man, no matter how many tanks he has, shall reverse the course of events …'

The speech shocked and astonished his listeners. The university authorities were outraged. A graduation ceremony is the most formal event in the calendar of a university, and prominent representatives of the establishment were present as guests. Reuel Khoza, today chairman of Nedbank, was present in the hall on that day as a member of the student choral society. He recalls that 'Speakers at graduation were always custodians of the ideology of the time. Black universities would almost always find a speaker such as a homeland leader. Indeed, I remember that either that year, or the year before, the keynote speech was delivered by the leader of the Lebowa homeland, an old school inspector who virtually offered a justification of Bantu education.'[16]

The students, by contrast, were jubilant. Tiro was articulating opinions that were held by most of the student body, opinions they had never dared to voice in a public venue – let alone in the setting of a graduation.

The university responded to this challenge with the immediate expulsion of Tiro from campus. His departing remark to Professor JL Boshoff, rector of the university, as he was driven away from the campus, was another rhetorical flourish: 'For we can do nothing against the truth, but for the truth …'[17]

The rest of what was to be Tiro's short life was devoted to political mobilisation and to the development of new ideas in the black consciousness movement. He escaped the paralysis that gripped those of his peers who were in thrall to the leadership of Steve Biko, and he highlighted the intellectual and political limitations of Biko's idealist philosophy. He toured the black campuses, speaking on one occasion at Fort Hare where black consciousness thinking had been sharpened by its contestation with continuing Congress and Marxist traditions. Tiro advanced a theory of African communalism that tried to release black consciousness from its self-imposed prison of interiority and self-discovery.[18] Drawing on wider streams in African post-liberation thinking, in particular Nyerere's African socialism and Kenneth Kaunda's humanism, he was seeking a uniquely African politics of socialism.

He became a full-time professional organiser for Saso in 1973 and president of the Southern African Students' Movement (SASM). In a message read out at the 5th Saso General Students' Council, Tiro wrote, 'No struggle can come to an end without casualties.' Two weeks later, on 1 February 1974, he was killed by a parcel bomb. Although he had taken refuge in Botswana, he was no longer beyond the reach of apartheid security forces now willing to carry out cross-border assassinations.

The government refused permission for Tiro's body to be buried at his home, and it was only in 1998 that his remains were finally laid to rest in Dinokana Village.[19]

The students' reaction to Tiro's expulsion in 1972 was immediate. SRC president Aubrey Mokoena, today an ANC member of parliament, called a mass meeting at which students resolved to boycott lectures and stage a sit-in. The university responded with the demand that students sign a declaration of orderly behaviour or leave the campus – a demand the students ignored. The university then closed the kitchens and threw the entire student body off the campus, telling them they would have to reapply for admission.[20]

At this stage, the national organisation of Saso began to mobilise. Branches on black campuses across the country organised solidarity protests. Lectures were boycotted at UWC and Natal Medical School, and a resolution was passed by the national Saso executive that all students should escalate the struggle, boycott lectures and even force their universities to close down. Mass meetings of students and their parents took place at Fort Hare, UWC, Zululand and other black colleges, and a consensus emerged that there were common grievances across the black campuses.

The 1972 Saso conference involved heated debate about the implications of the protest and the future direction of student politics. Barney Pityana remembers young firebrand Keith Mokoape shouting the slogan 'Kill the Boer!' as part of a more general expression of discontent with the conservatism that continued to characterise Saso policy.[21] On some campuses, particularly Fort Hare, many students became interested once again in the ANC. Over the coming year, police harassment of student activists was to increase, and Barney Pityana was to be placed under house arrest.

When the University of the North reopened after Tiro's expulsion, combative university authorities banned Saso on campus and excluded more than 20 students. Cyril, who had been too junior to play any significant role in the protests, was readmitted. Yet he was very quickly to become a prominent figure in student politics. When he had arrived in early 1972, there was already no doubt among his friends that he hoped to become president of the SRC.[22] Reuel Khoza, who had been studying psychology, history and African languages for three years when Ramaphosa arrived, remembers Cyril as a 'natural politician' who was 'campaigning from the moment of his arrival'.[23]

Initially, Cyril's political energies were channelled through the Student Christian Movement of which he had been an active member at school. This was a telling choice of vehicle. Here at the university, the SCM was an organisation widely held in contempt. For many of his contemporaries, it was viewed as a 'sell-out' organisation, in part because SCM's emphasis on the gospel of individual salvation seemed disconnected from everyday political and economic struggle. Indeed, the history of the missionary churches was understood by many radical students as a history of exploitation. Europeans had taken Africans' land in exchange for the Bible, a text designed to render them meek and subservient in the face of their exploitation.

Frank Chikane[24] was Cyril's immediate contemporary and colleague in the Turfloop SCM. The year before he arrived at university, he had experienced the growing conflict between critics and defenders of conventional Christian beliefs at his high school in Orlando. Like Cyril, he was a member of his school's SCM and active in evangelical work at school and in the wider community. By 1971, he recalls, 'the clash between Christian students and other students reached a violent level'.[25]

Called upon to help mediate between fighting students, Chikane steered a cautious middle course, very close to that defended by Ramaphosa at the time. Yes, the Bible had no doubt been used to dispossess Africans of their land and to brainwash them to accept their oppression. On the other hand, this use of the Bible was itself an abuse, rather than reflecting the fundamental meaning that it expressed. The task, he explained to his peers, was to re-read the Bible, reclaim it, and then 'turn it against the oppressors'.[26]

But the isolation of the SCM had gone too far at Turfloop for such mediation, and when Chikane and Ramaphosa arrived, it had already been banned from the campus by a decision of the student body. 'The students believed [Christianity] was a religion of the oppressor, of the white man, and therefore worse than irrelevant for them.'[27] SCM members were obliged to worship furtively, gathering together in the fields close by the campus, or hiding 'illegally' in the lecture theatres, after being let in by sympathetic teachers without the knowledge of other students.

Chikane was frustrated by this state of affairs, and by the seeming acquiescence of the SCM leadership in it. Indeed, he found them to have willingly adopted a state of 'persecution', which they viewed as part of their necessary withdrawal from the 'unchristian' political activity elsewhere on campus.[28]

The SCM had also been handicapped by the manner of its creation. It was the general secretary of an established white body called the Student Christian Association, Graham Mackintosh, who while touring the country had organised Christian movements – known as SCM – on all the black campuses as well as in some high schools. The SCA remained an organisation for white students whereas the SCM was the organisation for black campuses. A competing movement, the University Christian Movement (UCM), insisted on racial integration, and for this reason it had the initial support of the Saso leadership and many of the black consciousness radicals. However, university administrators banned UCM and it failed for this reason to gain much of a foothold on any campus.[29]

Rather than adopting the purist position of supporting UCM, and turning his back on SCM, Ramaphosa moved with great speed to control and then transform the more conservative movement's branch. He immediately and eloquently argued for a new role for Christians on campus, and won over enough doubters – together with like-thinking Christians such as Chikane – to secure rapid election as SCM chairman. With the help of Chikane, he then set about restructuring the organisation. He produced a new constitution, and his fellow members were obliged to debate its contents endlessly. In this constitution, Cyril inserted a 'doctrinal basis' section that explicitly repudiated racism and the unjust system of apartheid.[30] Cyril's trademark success in creating a new institution was based on careful drafting of the constitution, careful strategic planning, and relentless persuasiveness in public and private meetings.

While Cyril remade the organisation, Chikane chaired Evangelistic Fellowship, a body responsible for evangelical work in the surrounding communities – an organisation very much along the lines of Ramaphosa's

BECO. In a wide radius around the school, the Fellowship set about systematically visiting one school every week. 'We did not know about management by objectives in those days,' recalls Chikane, 'but the principle was the same. We measured our progress according to a carefully prepared set of targets.'[31]

After the university banned the organisation from the student campus, Cyril was active in the Saso branch that was established in Turfloop. He was not immediately vocal on this wider stage. Barney Pityana, national secretary-general of Saso in 1972, recalls Cyril as 'not a great presence' and 'rather a quiet person ... He did not strike me as someone who would become what he is today.'[32] All the same, Cyril became a powerful actor in the politics of the university, because he was able to bridge two kinds of divide. First, his religious commitment and experience allowed him to retain a religious constituency. It was an inescapable fact forgotten by radicals that almost all of the students on a campus like Turfloop were or had been active members of Christian organisations. There was no future in frontally attacking so fundamental a part of people's intellectual and emotional make-up. National leaders like Pityana – who was later ordained as an Anglican priest – believed that the problem with the churches was that they were 'missing the boat' and 'not reflecting the mood of the people'.[33] For this reason, Saso took upon itself the role of 'conscientising' Christians so as to make them aware of the limits of their movements. The organisation gave special emphasis to working with, rather than against, ministers of religion in order to try to turn them into the instruments of political organisation,[34] and in such activity Cyril was peerlessly effective.

Cyril was also a bridge-builder in that he was able 'to straddle the rural and the urban worlds',[35] carrying conviction with the more conservative students brought up in the north as well as the politically radicalised young people from the south. According to Frank Chikane, this was the most organisationally obstructive division on the campus at the time.[36] On the one hand, students from Soweto tended to be highly politicised and 'conscientised' by the black consciousness movement in their schools. The university authorities perceived these students as political problem-cases. On the other hand, there were students 'from the north', socially and politically conservative, and viewed by the university authorities as 'lovely Christians'.

For Chikane, Ramaphosa was a quintessential Soweto youngster, a sophisticated product of its distinctive social and political environment who could engage in the language of the township youth. Yet as a result of the two years he had passed in Sibasa, his humility, his evangelical experience, and his unwillingness to condemn others as 'backward' or 'rural', Cyril was also able to reach out to a wider constituency of students from the north. Even today, he will first greet an acquaintance who comes from a rural and conservative background in the north quite unaffectedly using local dialects and phrases.[37]

While Cyril built up and politicised the SCM, it nevertheless remained less subject to harassment than non-Christian student organisations, and soon became the largest vehicle for political activity. Other political formations were dominated by the back-stabbing machinations and rhetorical fancies of their student leaderships, whereas Cyril made the SCM genuinely popular, using film shows and informal humour to pack students into social events that would later turn political.

In 1973, a superficial calm prevailed on the campus. Beneath the surface, however, relations between the university authorities and the students quietly deteriorated. Students continued to organise and debate, and the next stage in the confrontation was only a matter of time.

Ramaphosa and his circle of friends studied hard, evangelised, and developed a wider range of interests. Cyril continued with his legal studies, and widened his political understanding by studying the writings of Robert Sobukwe and theorists in the Marxist tradition.[38] His Tshiawelo friends, Ishmael Mkhabela, Griffith Zabala and Lybon Mabasa, all joined him at the university, bolstering his social life and the strength of the SCM at the same time.

Lybon Mabasa worked closely with Frank Chikane on the Evangelistic Fellowship. The two men extended the reach of the evangelical programmes, setting out to visit every school, college, hospital and village within a hundred kilometres of the university.[39] Mabasa was also active as a playwright and director, winning a prestigious Africa Arts Week award for the year's best play.

Mkhabela had been unable to accompany Cyril to Turfloop in 1973, because his family did not have the money to pay for his upkeep. Now he became Cyril's hostel neighbour, and could observe his friend's phenomenal ability to work. A workaholic himself, Mkhabela could get by on very little sleep, but Cyril would always be working when Mkhabela went to bed and was already awake again when he rose a few short hours later. Cyril would spend a good deal of time drafting and redrafting strategy documents and agendas, and inventing draft constitutions for the SCM and other bodies.[40]

Ramaphosa was becoming a gifted manager and administrator, a 'systems person' who could make an organisation function smoothly.[41] Emerging as a major figure in the national SCM, he became adept at meticulous planning which allowed him to wield increasing influence on the policy of the national movement. Through the national SCM, moreover, he began to build a network of religious activists from other parts of the country – SCM members included prominent Eastern Cape activists such as Bantu Holomisa and Makhenkesi Stofile – many of whom were later to play an important role in the struggle against apartheid.

The relationships between SCM and other black consciousness groupings meanwhile became increasingly close, so much so that the university authorities later falsely speculated that Frank Chikane was a Saso leader using 'entryist' techniques to turn the SCM into an instrument of student protest. At this time, almost every activity of the students was politicised. Reuel Khoza, for example, was a member of an a cappella choir and would soon become chairman of the student choral society. The choir's once-innocent songs became increasingly subversive, containing hidden anti-apartheid and anti-university sentiments that the university authorities were unable to pick up. When students began to write these lyrics on the posters they displayed at protest meetings, the choir was castigated by the university for becoming politicised.[42]

Outside his studies and work as a political organiser and Christian, Cyril was also very active in the students' union, the purely social element of student organisation. He still loved Hollywood movies, and his film shows filled the university hall. He was also becoming an enthusiastic entertainer and cook, and had developed growing charm and confidence with women.

Ramaphosa and his friends found it hard to reconcile the pleasures of youth with their belief in an all-seeing and austere God. Lybon Mabasa many years later told a gathering of his contemporaries that having a child had transformed his understanding of God. Gone was the figure of authority and vengeance that had dominated his youth. In its place was a God who forgave, in the way a father forgives the errors of a daughter. Cyril joked that his view of God had changed too. Whenever he went to meet a woman in the female dormitories at Turfloop, he had been sure that an unforgiving God was watching his every move. But later he had come to a realisation about the character of his Maker: The things that God finds important are not the things that we think that God finds important. In Lybon Mabasa's way of putting it, 'God is not petty!'[43]

In the society beyond the black campuses, unseen forces in the international economy were bringing to an end the extended political quiet that had held since 1963. Developing countries like South Africa had been buoyed by a global post-war boom centred on Western Europe, the United States and Japan, which had created a ready market for exports of commodities and finished goods. Three decades of unprecedented economic growth came to an end, however, in 1973, the immediate trigger being a doubling of the oil price by the Organisation of Oil Producing and Exporting (Opec) countries.

The modest gains enjoyed by black workers in South Africa in the 1960s and early 1970s were suddenly reversed. Africans drawn into skilled work in booming manufacturing industries on the Rand, in East London and in Natal, suddenly had to turn to strike action to protect their gains and fight retrenchments. Massive strikes involving more than 200,000 black workers in 1973 secured only limited success because of the narrow and localised organisational bases of the trade unions. All the same, this was the precursor of the growth of a radical labour movement that would transform the prospects of the anti-apartheid movements in the 1980s.[44]

A second set of international events had a more immediate and direct impact on the students at Turfloop. The Front for the Liberation of Mozambique (Frelimo) came to power in neighbouring Mozambique after a ten-year battle against Portuguese colonial rule. The withdrawal of Portugal from Mozambique and Angola had been precipitated by the collapse of authoritarian government in Lisbon, and it brought the 'front line' of international hostility to Pretoria a little bit closer, giving Frelimo's victory wider political significance.

The Black People's Convention (BPC) and Saso decided to hold a series of joint rallies to celebrate Frelimo's triumph and to bring home its significance for the South African struggle. The BPC–Saso initiative was based on a new kind of strategy. Rallies were now to flow out from universities into city centres, and student organisations were keen to engage workers and wider communities in their protests. Demonstrations were planned for Durban, Cape Town, Port Elizabeth and Johannesburg on 25 September 1974.

In Turfloop, despite the lack of a city to which to march, student organisers decided to join in with a rally of their own. Cyril was by now a prominent figure, chairman of the national SCM and also now chairman of the Turfloop Saso branch.[45] This latter appointment was fortuitous, coming as it did after the elevation of then chairman Pandelani Nefolovhodwe to the SRC presidency. Nefolovhodwe had instigated a putsch against a conservative SRC leadership, and in the aftermath he acceded to pressure to relinquish his Saso chairmanship to Cyril.[46] It is perhaps for this reason that Barney Pityana describes Cyril's rise as 'the second level of leadership stepping up' following the rustication or harassment of leaders 'of greater stature'.[47]

In the face of these threatened national protests, the government was not keen to escalate conflict over the rallies. Nevertheless, its hand was forced by an Afrikaner businessman, Cornelius Koekemoer, who threatened that the Durban rally scheduled for the Curries Fountain Stadium would be violently disrupted by right-wing Afrikaner paramilitaries. In response, justice minister Jimmy Kruger announced on the evening of 24 September that all BPC and Saso events were declared illegal for the next calendar month.

This announcement did nothing to discourage the marchers. The event at Turfloop was formally an SRC rally, in any event, and so not covered by the Saso–BPC ban. More than a thousand students gathered peacefully in the main hall of the university on the morning of 25 September. They listened to speeches about the significance of events in Mozambique and debated their implications for the struggle at home.

In the middle of the morning, a convoy of police vans arrived on the campus and parked outside the hall. Police poured from the vans and lined up opposite the entrance. These police were heavily armed, not only with batons and sjamboks (whips) used to control protesters, but also with instruments of war: Sten guns and high-calibre rifles. They brought with them a contingent of savage dogs. Ominously, in an indication of violent intent, an ambulance drove up behind the police vans.

On a signal, the police commander, Major JS Erasmus, marched into the hall flanked by armed policemen. Through a megaphone, he announced that the rally was illegal and that the students had 15 minutes to disperse. Confronted with the show of force, the student leaders wisely instructed the students to leave and to gather in a field outside the hall. There they sang freedom songs, and prepared to disperse for their hostels.[48]

As they were leaving, a contingent of male students was attacked by a wave of baton-wielding policemen. The students backed away but then retaliated by throwing stones at the police. As the violence seemed about to intensify, women students ran back to the scene and demanded that the police desist from attacking the men. At this point events took a radical turn for the worse. Some policemen assaulted the women students, knocking one of them to the ground with a baton blow. Dogs were released and seriously mauled a student. Previously dispersing students now turned around and massed together once again in a dangerous face-off with the armed police. So volatile was the atmosphere that it seemed the police might decide to shoot their way out of the campus. However, Major Erasmus instead released students who had been detained, before making an orderly retreat.[49]

Elsewhere around the country, violence also broke out at rallies. In Durban, whip-wielding police and dogs savaged dozens of student protesters. Behind the scenes, government was preparing to take decisive action. A country-wide sweep was unleashed, in which dozens of activists were detained by security police under the Riotous Assembly Act, and under the General Laws Amendment Act which allowed extended detention without trial. More than 200 people were detained across the country in total, and the police netted almost the entire leadership core of the black consciousness movement in this single fell swoop. Many of those arrested were later to become household names: Aubrey Mokoape, Jackie Selebi, Saths Cooper, Strini Moodley, 'Solly' Ismael, Barney Pityana and Mosiuoa 'Terror' Lekota. These leaders were to be prosecuted in what was to become known as the 'Black Consciousness Trial' or the 'Saso Trial', which commenced in February 1975.[50]

At the University of the North, the university vacation was extended in the hope that tempers would cool. On the return of the students, however, the security police arrested the remaining political heavyweights on the campus, SRC president Gabriel 'Kaunda' Sedibe, and the Turfloop-based national president of Saso, Pandelani Nefolovhodwe (universally known as 'Nef'). These two were part of the leadership core of the black consciousness movement, figures senior to Cyril in years, authority and political experience. Ramaphosa was not at this stage under threat of arrest. Nefolovhodwe observes that Cyril was 'not a big fish' in black consciousness, and 'only the big fishes were arrested initially'.[51]

The vulnerability of the entire leadership to arrest was testimony to the political inexperience of student leaders at this early stage in the political unrest of the 1970s. What followed only confirmed this inexperience. The student body decided to march to the police station and demand the release of Nefolovhodwe and Sedibe. Cyril, as chairman of the Saso branch, was now at the head of the march. Members of the SRC were already inside the station trying to present a memorandum to the station commander.

Very soon, almost the entire student body was assembled outside the police station. Cyril stood in the crowd with Hope Mudau, by now his partner. A hush descended as the most senior policeman, Major Sarel Strydom, emerged from the building with a megaphone. Some witnesses recall Strydom asking if members of the SRC were present. Then he asked, 'Where is Cyril Ramaphosa?'

Cyril's friends gestured to him to keep quiet, but instead he fearlessly stepped forward. He was taken into the police station where he found members of the SRC seated in a circle. Strydom said, 'Cyril Ramaphosa is under arrest,' before turning to the members of the SRC and dismissing them. They scuttled off without protesting at Ramaphosa's arrest.[52]

Ramaphosa was thereby arrested under Section 6 of the Terrorism Act. He was bundled into the back of the police station, and was to spend the next eleven months behind bars in solitary confinement.

CHAPTER 4

DETENTION

When I have protested, you passed legislation against me.
When I have protested the legislation, you detained me.
When I was in detention, you tortured me.
When you could not change my views, you killed me.

— *Tshenuwani Farisani*[1]

Detention without trial was introduced by the National Party in 1961,[2] and before apartheid's end more than 70,000 South Africans were to be detained. Increasingly arbitrary anti-communist legislation culminated in the landmark 1967 Terrorism Act, which mandated indefinite detention without trial by any police officer at or above the rank of Lieutenant-Colonel. All that was required was an intention to elicit information pertaining to offences under the Act. Yet the Act defined 'terrorism' so broadly that the police had effective discretion to detain at will.

In presenting the legislation the minister had persuaded parliament that time limits would undermine the purposes of the Act. Terrorists would be indoctrinated to withstand interrogation for precisely the period legislated.[3] For this reason, the Act allowed detention until detainees had provided 'satisfactory' answers to whatever questions were asked of them. Detainees were entirely at the mercy of their captors.[4]

Detention was used to gather information for specific prosecutions, to collect general intelligence about opposition political movements, or to remove the leadership tier of anti-apartheid organisations. At its heart, it was a blunt instrument of 'psychological violence'. Deaths in detention, rumours of security police torture, and fear of arbitrary arrest created a wider climate of fear that helped to paralyse political opposition.[5] Detention also allowed police to spread malicious rumours about collaboration and the 'turning' of prisoners during interrogation.

For those who were detained, the experience was dominated by fear, confusion and uncertainty. Indeed uncertainty, according to former detainee Raymond Suttner, is the very essence of detention. 'One does not know what is going to happen. One knows it will be terrible, but there is great anxiety because of unawareness of what that entails.' This uncertainty is not ended by the realisation of the detainees' worst fears. 'Even when one has been tortured, one does not know whether it is over, when the torturers will come back and what they will do next time.'[6]

As veteran Soweto activist Ellen Kuzwayo explained, this uncertainty also concerned what was happening to friends and especially family outside prison. During her five months of detention in 1977, she was plagued by worries about what might happen to her children if she were to lose her job and her house. What would become of her son?[7]

Cyril's Mphaphuli mentor Tshenuwani Farisani, who was to suffer several periods of extended detention and torture, described the distorted sense of time in prison. 'Minutes in prison are long. Every hour has three hundred and sixty minutes. Every day seventy-two hours. Every week equals a month outside.'[8] As time dragged slowly by, detainees' experience of fear and uncertainty stretched them on a rack of torment. 'Long morning, long afternoon, long evening, long night. Terrible darkness. Screams. Heavy footsteps in the passage. A round eye through the peephole in the cell door … When would they come for me? When would I join my screaming neighbours? What were they plotting against me? Would I go out alive? Or would I never go out? The present was a painful uncertainty, the future total darkness, the past an irretrievable reality.'[9]

When Ramaphosa had been bundled into Mankweng Police Station in Turfloop, his closest friends were in a state of shock. It now fell to Ishmael Mkhabela, Griffith Zabala and Lybon Mabasa to tell Cyril's parents that they had watched the detention of their 21-year-old son.

They already lived in some fear of Sergeant Ramaphosa and hated to bring such news to Cyril's mother, who they rightly anticipated would be broken-hearted. Like all of those not detained, they felt the guilt of their continuing freedom and the helplessness of having watched the police take their friend away. 'It was almost as if we had handed him over,' Griffith Zabala remembers feeling to this day.[10]

Cyril's friends and family were uncertain how to respond because of the unexpected nature of the arrest, and the turmoil that surrounded the national sweep of black consciousness activists. Experienced community members such as Tshenuwani Farisani and Tom Manthatha tried to counsel the family. Cyril's contemporaries organised a support committee to raise awareness and funds for their friend and for other detained students.[11] Frank Chikane, Griffith Zabala and Ishmael Mkhabela became the leaders of the Turfloop students' Legal Aid Fund, which mobilised resources and took responsibility for supporting both the detained students and their families. Like other friends of detainees, they enlisted the services of Shun Chetty, the brilliant attorney who was to be the key defence lawyer for many black consciousness detainees, and who was later to be driven into exile and struck off the attorneys' roll by the Johannesburg Bar.[12]

Ramaphosa was a detainee at the margins of a major prosecution by the state of its perceived black consciousness enemies, an effort that was to turn from chaos to ultimate farce. The state eventually determined that it would prosecute just 12 accused – the core of the national black consciousness movement, which did not include Cyril – in a trial that was to drag on from January 1975 to April 1976 but would not be fully closed until 1977. Charges were brought under the Terrorism Act, a notorious piece of legislation that placed the onus on the defence to demonstrate that there was no intention on the part of the defendant to commit a terrorist act. Prosecutors also applied the Suppression of Communism Act, legislation that threatened exceptionally long periods of detention but proved exceptionally unwieldy for prosecutors, and other assorted offences such as 'conspiring to revolt', creating hatred, denigrating whites and organising 'subversive' rallies.[13]

In the courtroom, the accused managed to turn proceedings into a circus that embarrassed the authorities. The 'criminals' gave the impression of being relaxed and confident. They gave power salutes to the gallery and sang freedom songs. On one memorable occasion, they came to blows with police guards inside the courtroom.[14]

The weaknesses of the prosecution case were legion, but most damaging was a reliance on testimony that turned out not to be forthcoming. In the event, almost nobody testified against the 12. And those who did give evidence were relatively junior figures who did not know enough to incriminate the accused. They also had to be briefed by the police to give their testimony any credibility.[15] It was the fluid nature of the black consciousness phenomenon that was above all to prove the state's undoing. Black consciousness was not an organisational phenomenon at all, and indeed many BC activists avoided any form of direct affiliation precisely because it would leave them vulnerable to banning. As Nefolovhodwe put it, 'You don't become black consciousness by belonging to an organisation; you become BC because of your response to your experiences.'[16]

Displaying considerable bravery and resilience in the face of isolation and torture, the trialists were to become celebrated heroes in the eyes of their followers; to some degree this bolstered their morale. On the other hand, for the detainees who were not tried, the period of detention and its aftermath led to unrelenting pain. Those who were not charged but simply detained, such as Ramaphosa, became the victims of security police strategies to sow confusion and mistrust.[17]

Though the activists had been arrested all around the country, eventually they made their way into Pretoria prisons. Cyril was held in Pretoria Central Prison, what is today known as C-Max Prison, along with about 40 other prisoners including Saths Cooper, Saso publicity secretary, who had been detained on 25 September at the Durban Frelimo rally. Cooper was to be one of the black consciousness trialists.

Cooper was in a neighbouring block, and did not have direct contact with Ramaphosa, but they were indirectly linked by the prisoners' rudimentary communications system. The prisoners would pass messages from cell to cell, using code names and code words to keep information safe from informers. And they would sing songs to let one another know who had arrived and who had been taken away. In this way, Saths Cooper became aware that Ramaphosa – whom he knew a little of as a younger student activist from a different university – was in a different block of the same prison.[18]

The security police and warders knew there was communication, and tried to make use of it to undermine the trust between prisoners. One tactic was to list detainees as potential state witnesses against the accused. Listed as a potential state witness, a prisoner could not be released on bail, and his detention was likely to drag on for further months. Rather than having the status of the accused in a major trial, he suffered the suspicion that he might be a potential state witness.

A second effect of listing was to drive a wedge between a detainee's family, allies and friends and those of other detainees. Rumour-mongers on the outside, particularly those already antagonistic towards a prisoner, would view his listing as a police witness as a sure sign that he had agreed to testify to save his own skin. Loathing of informers was everywhere – the phrase on everyone's lips was 'Tongues talk!' The paranoia that was to mark the internal struggle of the 1980s – where everyone was a potential spy, subject to denunciation and even the application of 'the necklace' – was rearing its ugly head. To be charged in such circumstances was a relief rather than a burden.[19]

Even today, people do not inquire too deeply into what exactly happened to their friends while they were in detention. Emotions ran so deep around issues of trust and treachery that these questions are almost too sensitive to be raised. At the time, the swirling rounds of rumour and counter-rumour left Cyril's closest friends unsure what to believe or whom to trust. They themselves were becoming victims in this world of double-bluff and suspicion. Venda speakers who disliked them used the opportunity of Cyril's detention to 'play the tribal card' against them. Mabasa, Mkhabela and Zabala were Tsonga speakers, voices whispered to Cyril's family and neighbours. Why exactly then had their Venda-speaking friend been arrested while they remained free?[20]

Of course, even his three closest friends in the world could not have been entirely certain that Cyril would never testify. Such were the disorienting effects of torture and solitary confinement, and so unpredictable was the ability of any individual to resist being 'turned' into an informer or 'askari', that even they could only be sure 'at the eleventh hour' that Cyril would not testify as a witness.[21]

What is more, the cloud of suspicion that an uncharged detainee like Ramaphosa would feel over his own head might easily bear down upon him more than the reality of his friends' beliefs would justify. Locked away and disoriented, a detainee might quickly come to believe that his friends doubted him, when they were merely expressing realistic concerns about the unpredictable effects of detention.

Fortunately, however, political activists in the 1970s learnt very fast that the psychological mind-games of the secret police must not be allowed to destroy the humanity of their victims. As Tom Manthatha remembers, there was a growing feeling that suspicions of treachery and deceit fuelled by the regime's agents should be resisted. 'I never allowed myself unfounded suspicion that people were "sell-outs" or whatnot. You are a sell-out only if you testify.'[22] Saths Cooper confirms that Cyril's fellow detainees destined for trial were likewise sceptical of claims spread by the security police and prison authorities about supposed turncoats. 'Most of us in the leadership were fully aware of who was and who wasn't going to testify. For us it was clear all along that Cyril was not going to testify … The purpose of listing someone as a potential state witness was to prevent any communication between that person and others … Listing was a strategy to help the state case by keeping the lawyers representing different activists from conferring with one another.'[23]

Nevertheless, Cyril was the son of a policeman of 20 years standing, and it was inevitable that there were accusations of 'preferential treatment' and favouritism. The sergeant was a black policeman from a station in Soweto, to be sure, and a very different breed from the security police behind the black consciousness arrests. But which father would not try to help his son to survive imprisonment? Samuel must have tried to find a way to see to it that Cyril was spared some of the worst of the arbitrary violence and suffering that was inflicted upon many prisoners at the time. And surely, voices must inevitably have whispered, a policeman would work to get his son to testify in return for his own release?[24]

Given Cyril's own isolation, the debilitating effects of this sense of distrust must have been very hard to bear. Cyril was held in solitary confinement, unlike his Robben Island contemporaries. 'I never benefited from sitting down and having political discourse with fellow detainees and comrades. It is something I still feel I regret deeply. Those who were in a group with other people were able to strengthen each other, to have discussions on a whole variety of things, and I didn't have that opportunity because I was on my own.'[25] Not able to benefit from the education and political aspects of the Robben Island experience,

Ramaphosa would have suffered from its opposite: an isolation made still more complete by the knowledge that even one's friends might doubt whether one could now be trusted.

For the first three months of solitary confinement Ramaphosa was allowed absolutely no access to reading material. He could hear the opening and closing of doors when others were released but he was denied information on the status of his detention. Every day ended with shattered hopes of freedom. He retained his sanity by observing and naming the insects that crawled across the floor of his cell. When he was allowed a Bible at the end of three months, he fell upon it and read voraciously.[26]

Towards the end of his detention, when Cyril was transferred to the Silverton Police Station near Pretoria, and away from the security police, it was possible for his family to visit him. Here Samuel may have been able to exert some influence over his fellow police officers. It was inevitable, of course, that the rumour mill would grind further: Would this son of a policeman after all turn state witness? Had he been turned?

Cyril was not released until September 1975 after 11 months in solitary confinement. Psychologists today tell us that the way detention affects an individual varies very widely, depending upon the nature of the detention, the 'stressors' to which a detainee is subjected, the support systems on which they could depend upon release, and the personal capacity of each individual to cope. For this reason, it is impossible to generalise about the effects of detention or to gain access into the consciousness of a particular detainee.

Indeed, what has become clear two or three decades later is that most former detainees themselves do not have any real understanding of what their detention had done to them. Raymond Suttner, detained twice by the security police, has written that 'I was tortured more than 20 years ago. I have not spoken much about this episode in my life ... I have written accounts of my abuse, once or twice, in what seems to some people to be a fairly detached style. I am beginning to wonder, now, whether I have ever come to terms with this episode in my life. I wonder whether I have sufficiently "worked it through", and now understand

and acknowledge the character of the violation and the damage it has done.'[27]

Saths Cooper, one of the black consciousness trialists and also a professional psychologist who is today the president of the South African Psychological Association, emphasises the deep-seated consequences of detention for the mental well-being of those who suffered it. 'It came home to me in 1995 during a celebration on Robben Island of an anniversary of Nelson Mandela's release. We had been so joyous when he came out. But now there was a sense of complete bathos. We discovered that the majority of us by far – perhaps two out of three – were unemployed. And we were still struggling with the consequences of our detention.'[28]

Cooper lists the common problems suffered by former detainees – many of them charismatic and energetic leaders: 'Alcoholism; violent behaviour; dysfunctional family lives; dysfunctional love lives; and just an inability to function – in all kinds of situations.'[29] Cooper observes that there was almost no formal support provided for those who suffered in detention to help them rebuild their lives, and a culture that prevailed against admitting to the inner turmoil that would not let them rest.

One activist who helped many families to deal with the effects of detention, Tom Manthatha, confirms this depressing assessment. There was no typical reaction to detention. Some people's character changed and they became withdrawn. Others showed little sign of outward change and soldiered on. Still others had been turned and worked secretly as informers or 'askaris'. All suffered from the suspicion among others that they might have considered in some way 'selling out' their friends. And they, in turn, felt the pain of knowing that even those closest to them had suspected and distrusted them.[30]

One former detainee described the overall effects of his detention in this way: 'It is beyond comprehension how one feels when one is detained. More especially it is solitary confinement, because that is the one that anybody would dread. To feel alone, without anybody to talk to, without anything to do ... There is the constant worry that ... you are liable to be taken further into the location anytime. You are left with no peace of mind even though you are alone ... And you are liable to interrogation and the interrogation may amount to your death.'[31]

When Cyril emerged from detention towards the end of 1975, he appeared outwardly to be his old self. He typically downplayed the effects of his time inside and refused to talk frankly to his closest friends. Indeed, he was always to insist that detention had both negative and positive consequences. Yes, he had been in solitary confinement and so had not enjoyed the camaraderie that those held in common cells could expect. But, even so, it had given him time to reflect on the limitations of his political understanding. 'I suddenly realised', he recalled in 1985, 'that black consciousness was essentially a sectarian type of movement which tried to get black people to be on their own.' He now claimed that he had come to recognise the significance of the Freedom Charter and even developed a devotion to Nelson Mandela.[32]

While this retrospective claim about the intellectually clarifying quality of prison life is greeted with scepticism by his friends, it is nevertheless in parts consistent with a later reflection that he came to non-racialism in detention through realising 'the futility of it all, that the way we were trying to prosecute the struggle was essentially limited in terms of effect because we were a small bunch of people – as Azapo still is today'.[33] The testimony to a sense of helplessness and futility is characteristic of the feelings of a former detainee. Ramaphosa points to an almost unconscious sense that 'we needed to get involved in the armed struggle, and the Black People's Convention and Saso had not taken a decision to go that way'. He remembers that 'one of the things that kept me longer in detention was when they raided my home, they found a diary and a notebook where I had written things, armed struggle this is the option, we will make bombs and things like this ... it was all very innocent, it was just one's thought processes that were operating. I hadn't made contact with the ANC then.'[34]

What Cyril would not discuss was the wider implications of detention for his state of mind. Tshenuwani Farisani was a source of support to the family during Cyril's detention. He noticed a change that had come over the young man. 'He was hurt, angry, and bitter. He almost wished he could have been detained longer. He was frustrated that he had not been charged.' As the son of a policeman he felt that his integrity was open to question. He became withdrawn and less willing to spend time with his friends because he felt that everywhere people were making unspoken accusations against him. 'Sometimes, when I would talk to him for a long time, the old Cyril would emerge. There would be that smile again.'[35]

Farisani himself was to go through a brutal period of detention a year or so later. He explained the terrible loneliness and uncertainty of detention, and its ability to lead one to question one's faith. 'I had to listen to screams like these for almost three months. It was the most terrifying period of my life ... At times the screams came from outside, sometimes drowned out by running car engines or the barking of police dogs. But always, in a mysterious way, the human screams would filter through all the disguises and reach my human ear, breaking my human heart. Then I would fall on my knees and cry softly, at times silently, to the Lord ... "Oh God, you source of justice and love, opponent of oppression and exploitation, enemy of apartheid and torture, where are you?"'[36]

Ramaphosa did tell some of his friends that his faith had been shaken by his experiences, and that he had felt that God had abandoned him. How could a loving and caring God make him go through such an experience as this? He claimed that he was enduring a crisis of faith because of his inability to reconcile his faith with the reality of his experiences in prison, and he spoke of the biblical experiences of Paul and Silas, who had prayed to God and found the doors of their prison swung open. Why had it not been this way for him?[37]

Cyril's friends soon discovered that something had changed forever in their relationship with him. Cyril would not talk to them about detention, other than to say that the security establishment was very efficient in what it did, and to recount some of the mechanisms of interrogation such as the recording of testimony only to play back key passages again and again in the next period of interrogation.

Then one day, as Cyril was walking with his old companions, he said: 'When I was in detention, I came to realise that friends are like teabags. You boil the water. And you use them once.'[38] Twenty years later, the meaning of this remark continues to trouble Ishmael Mkhabela. They had organised tirelessly to raise money for Cyril's legal representation and they had tried hard to give hope to his family. Did his remark mean that if you put your friends in a difficult situation, in hot water, they just lose all their value? Had Cyril himself become victim to the mistrust that marked those times? Did he feel they had in some way 'sold him out'?

Psychologists today would view Ramaphosa's reaction as a typical after-effect of detention. Many of his contemporaries were disoriented in precisely this same way. Released detainees were susceptible to mood swings, fierce temper tantrums, aggressiveness, and episodes of profound depression. They were often withdrawn, and expressed a desire to be left alone. They suffered, moreover, from a sense of insecurity, and from a lack of trust in people, even those who had been their friends.[39] At that time, however, this was all a devastating change for Cyril's friends, and they lacked the experience which was to come in later years that would allow them to place into perspective the psychological effects of his detention. Whatever the precise meaning of Cyril's words, it was clear that the old friendships, if not over, were in some sense dramatically devalued during the period of detention.[40]

In the dark days of late 1975, Cyril applied to return to his studies at Turfloop but he was not readmitted. Indeed, ultimately none of the Young Ambassadors from Tshiawelo was able to graduate from the University of the North. Lybon Mabasa was also permanently excluded. Griffith Zabala was excluded in 1977, three weeks before he was due to graduate. Ishmael Mkhabela left the university in protest.

Among their friends, Frank Chikane suffered a nervous breakdown in the middle of his final examinations as a result of the various pressures of the time. The university refused to make any allowances for this and he was never to graduate – although he rightly felt he had earned, and so in reality possessed as a 'struggle degree', the qualification he had been denied. Reuel Khoza was sacked from his research position after lamenting, in his capacity as president of the university psychological society, the psychological problems caused by the migrant labour system.

Cyril found himself severely upset by his exclusion. He had loved student politics, but now he was cut off from his constituency and from the ambitions he had nurtured.[41] 'The university wouldn't take me back. I was in some sort of academic wilderness.'[42] He was determined that he would become a lawyer, nevertheless, and he decided to enrol with Unisa, the distance-learning university. For now, however, he needed money and he needed work.

By 1976, his situation had started to stabilise. He was attending meetings of the Black People's Convention in Soweto, the umbrella organisation for black consciousness activity. His friend Lybon Mabasa was a member of the Soweto executive. Cyril and Lybon were looking for work together, and finally secured jobs as temporary teachers at Meadowlands High School. Yet as this work was about to begin, a political storm was brewing in Soweto. The unemployed youngsters were to be right in the centre of it.

CHAPTER 5

JUNE '76

They are coming back
through woodsmoke weaving from fires
and swirls of dust from erratic breezes
you will see
ghosts are returning
ghosts of young men, young women
young boys, young girls
students:
and if you look closely
you will see
many of them have torn flesh
have wounds bright with fresh blood
and there is blood in the sands of Soweto
*   – Dennis Brutus[1]*

Cyril's personal troubles were about to be overshadowed by one of the most dramatic and unexpected political upheavals in South Africa's 20th-century history. Soweto's children were to begin an uprising that would mark the end of colonial domination, and the beginning of the end of apartheid rule.

The morning of 16 June 1976 seemed like the beginning of just another normal school day in Soweto. Unbeknown to their parents and to most of their teachers, however, an 'action committee' of the Soweto Students Representative Council had planned a mass rally for this day in protest against the forced learning of Afrikaans.

The schools of Soweto were sites of suppressed anger. Fees of R50 per child, and the additional expense of books, school uniforms and surcharges for new buildings were widely resented. Between 1965 and 1975, moreover, the enrolment of black children in secondary school had increased fivefold. Soweto's eight secondary schools at the start of 1972 had become twenty by 1976. Class sizes averaged 60 and at times reached 100.[2] In overcrowded conditions, poorly trained teachers were quick to resort to corporal punishment, and matriculation rates were low. By 1976, the average age at matriculation had risen to 20. Even matriculants now found employment increasingly scarce in an economy entering a new era of slow growth and periodic recession.

In these conditions, the 1974 introduction of a language code through the Afrikaans Medium Decree was the final straw. It was an imposition made almost casually and against the wishes of the African Teachers' Association. The code obliged all students to study what was widely viewed as the language of the oppressor, and forced more advanced students in the social sciences and mathematics to continue with this language later on in school. The decision was part of the wider philosophy of 'Bantu education' which dictated that Africans should be taught skills appropriate to their position in the apartheid economy – essentially as service workers for English and Afrikaans speakers. In a famous statement, the deputy minister in the Bantu Education department, Punt Janson, commented: 'No, I have not consulted the African people on the language issue and I'm not going to. An African might find that "the big boss" only spoke Afrikaans or only spoke English. It would be to his advantage to know both languages.'[3]

Opposition to the decree was driven in part by the same forces that had led to protest in Turfloop and other black university campuses. An awareness of the character of oppression was shared by school children, the black consciousness ideas of Biko and others having spread from the universities to the peri-urban township schools primarily through radicalised school teachers. Indeed, many of those expelled from the black universities, such as Cyril and Lybon Mabasa, were offered positions as temporary teachers in schools that were growing exceptionally fast.

June '76 was also in part a rebellion organised by Christians. Frank Chikane observes that the leadership of the student movements was mostly built up through Christian youth movements, such as those in which he and Cyril were involved. 'It was only youth movements that gave young people capacity. It was through organisation, learning how to give sermons, writing agendas, taking minutes, and attending workshops that the youth built their capacity to organise.'[4]

The children initially responded to the decree with some restraint despite the fact that, in the words of Ellen Kuzwayo, 'Their only chance of an education had been cruelly snatched from them.'[5] They appealed to the authorities to reconsider and shared their concerns with their parents. At the same time, the children of Soweto's schools, particularly in areas such as Orlando that had a history of political protest reaching back to the 1950s, were organised into potentially effective student representative councils. There was also a wider umbrella body, the South African Students' Movement (SASM), that allowed for the development of campaigns involving schools across many parts of Soweto and that incubated black consciousness thinking.

The children of Orlando West Primary School, a few kilometres from Cyril's home, began a boycott of classes at the end of April 1976, refusing to return until the decree was lifted. As support for their action spread, it was school children themselves who were the primary drivers of the protest action and the planners of the rally on 16 June. As word spread that the march was to take place that day, thousands of children were persuaded by their peers to take part. Somewhere between three and ten thousand students[6] set off on the march, brandishing placards bearing slogans such as 'Down with Afrikaans'.

The police rapidly barricaded the route of the march, and the students took a circuitous path that eventually brought them close to Orlando High School. Along the way the students avoided antagonising the police. However, as police reinforcements arrived, the potential for tragedy grew. The police were not trained or equipped to control large gatherings. Their only strategy was to throw tear gas canisters into the crowd in order to get it to disperse. This simply provoked the children into throwing stones at them, waving their placards harder, and shouting with increased vigour.

There was still hope that the event might pass off without loss of life. But poor training and callousness together precipitated a tragedy. An officer fired a gun shot into the air triggering panic among the students. Children ran in all directions and some police officers started firing at random. Four children were shot, including Hector Pieterson whose photo in the arms of another student was to capture the attention of newspaper audiences around the world. As violence spiralled out of control, youth from across Soweto came out on to the streets and began attacking all manifestations of authority. They torched government offices and vehicles. Beer halls and bottlestores, believed by many youth to encourage acquiescence in oppression, were set alight. Police discipline fell apart and around two dozen children were killed and dozens more wounded.

The fighting escalated the next day. Police reinforcements flooded the townships in armoured cars armed with automatic and semi-automatic weapons. Some policemen drove around taking pot shots, seemingly considering almost anyone on the streets as a legitimate target. Meanwhile, the school children had been joined by the oppressed and dispossessed of Soweto, all of those frustrated by limited economic opportunity and political oppression.

The conflict spread to other townships on the Rand and then made its way to Cape Town and the Eastern Cape. The singular event of the Soweto uprising catalysed a wider 'Soweto revolt' that entrenched school boycotts as a political instrument, saw unrest spread to more than 200 communities across the country, and ultimately resulted in a massive government crackdown against its enemies.

By February 1977, on the minimal official count, 575 people had been killed – 494 African, 75 coloured, 5 white and 1 Indian. Of the victims 134 were under the age of 18.[7] The Cape Town protests were especially notable because of their intensity in the coloured schools of the Cape Flats. The inclusivity of black consciousness thinking – its incorporation of those designated coloured and Indian and its rejection of the non-white label – made it a potent competitor to non-racial thinking as a force in national politics.

Like the industrial unrest of 1973, the Soweto uprising took the state authorities and the political opposition equally by surprise. For Ramaphosa there was one big lesson: the black consciousness movement lacked the intellectual frameworks and political organisation to capitalise on these events.

For the Ramaphosa family as for many others, the uprising was a turning point. Samuel Ramaphosa had been a policeman for almost 20 years, and the police stations of Soweto – such as Moroka where he was stationed – were suddenly key targets for the students and disaffected youth. He was 'a clever and experienced man who managed to keep in touch with Cyril even though he was very, very angry at this time'.[8] Nevertheless, the uprisings left even a respected police officer at risk from politically motivated attack. Cyril and his brother 'couldn't see ourselves in a situation where we'd have to stand outside the house defending our father from our comrades'.[9]

For Douglas Ramaphosa the matter was of special urgency. He had become a prominent student leader and found it hard to live with the contradiction between the things he shouted from the political platform – including the need to 'fight the police' – and the reality of having a policeman as the head of his household, in a home he called 'the police station'.[10]

Douglas was leading something of a double life. The ANC was almost non-existent in the Tshiawelo of Cyril and Douglas's youth. There was known to be an ANC underground, but very few people came across it. Yet in 1974, an ANC exile turned up at the Orlando house of a friend of Douglas. He was a relatively senior man who travelled in and out of the country. For Douglas, this was all 'scary but exciting'. He read the illegal publications the man brought with him, including the journal *Sechaba*, and in the course of 1974 and 1975 he himself became active in the ANC underground. Much of the work was routine, in that it involved distributing pamphlets, for example on political change in Angola and Mozambique and the potential it offered for revolutionaries in South Africa. Yet it was also dangerous work that involved the risk of detention.[11]

Douglas was 17 years old. He did not reveal his activity either to Cyril or to his father. After an unhappy year at boarding school in Venda, he returned in 1976 to Sekano-Ntoane school, where he was elected a member of the student representative council. In the course of the year, he became his school's representative on the Soweto Students Representative Council, which was to be at the centre of the uprising. This conflict was one of Douglas's generation and not Cyril's. While Cyril tried to work to assist the students and to protect them from unnecessary harm, Douglas was at the forefront of organising marches, going from school to school rousing the students to take to the streets in protest.[12]

Douglas's activism made Samuel Ramaphosa's job a source of growing concern. Eventually, it was Cyril who decided that the issue had to be settled. He took Douglas aside and told him he would take care of the matter. He went to his father and explained that his children were children of the liberation movement. According to Cyril's later recollection, his father 'retired in 1976 during the Soweto uprising because we prevailed upon him to resign, my brother and I and the family'.[13] However, in reality, Sergeant Ramaphosa was not immediately persuaded to leave his job by his children. Indeed, he waited for the following year, until 1977, before leaving the force. This allowed him to claim a full pension for 25 years of service. Moreover, the short period before resignation allowed him to make plans for the business that would sustain the family in the absence of a police salary.

Samuel Ramaphosa was to prove as successful a businessman as he was a policeman. He initially owned one truck – a most unusual possession in Tshiawelo at the time – and he used this vehicle to transport women such as Ishmael Mkhabela's mother to nearby farms as early as four in the morning. The women would pick mealies, which they would take back on the truck and later hawk on the streets of Tshiawelo. The sergeant also used the vehicle to run a coal delivery business, which initially had supplemented his police salary. With his skill and tenacity, his network of contacts, and the money he received for his pension, he was soon able to build a very successful business based around a veritable fleet of two trucks and a bakkie. Douglas Ramaphosa would help with this business when he was expelled from high school, driving women in the small bakkie to the cornfields.[14]

Cyril and his friends were sought out for advice by the youth during the 1976 uprising. They were already part of networks of activists, primarily religious contacts from the SCM and black consciousness political groups. In Mkhabela's words, 'come 1976, we were much more conscientised than students who had been to just one meeting or just one conference'. Among their mentors were Beyers Naudé and the Rev. Morris Ngakane, the national secretary-general of the SCM. Yet while Ramaphosa later described himself as 'well connected', he was not an active participant. He was both captivated and concerned. 'I saw a lot of the destruction ... The thing that captivated most of us was the terrible blunder they [the government] had made in terms of forcing the teaching of Afrikaans and that they were paying for the terrible blunder that they had made.'[15]

Given the tender age and inexperience of so many of those involved in the uprising, much of the role of activists from Cyril's generation was protective – trying to prevent children and youth from exposing themselves to the increasingly uncontrolled violence of the security police and the more or less unaccountable police forces drafted into the townships. The government had little idea how to respond to the uprising except with more violence, in this way exposing its moral bankruptcy even to those who had been its supporters. As Ellen Kuzwayo lamented, 'What other government would meet with bullets the grievances of school children?'[16] Detentions of those suspected of involvement in oppositional politics intensified. Inevitably, it was only a matter of time before Cyril was detained once again. The security police picked him up early in August.

Ramaphosa was arrested at 3 a.m. together with a very close Christian friend from Venda, Tshifhiwa Muofhe, who had come to visit him. Muofhe was not sought by the police, but he was mistaken for the 16 June student leader Tsietsi Mashinini to whom he bore an uncanny resemblance. Although released the next morning, Muofhe was so radicalised by his encounter with the police that he was reborn as a political activist on his return to Venda. A few months later he was arrested by Bantustan police and beaten so severely while in detention that he died of his injuries.[17]

After his arrest Cyril was taken to the notorious headquarters of the Johannesburg police at John Vorster Square. There had been many tragedies and horrors in police custody in this building. Detainees had been thrown and pushed from the windows to their deaths. In a case that would have been well known to Cyril, a young man called Ahmed Timol died in police custody on 27 October 1971 after 'committing suicide' by 'jumping' from the tenth floor of John Vorster Square. His death was hardly singular: he was the 22nd person to die in police custody since detention without trial had been introduced.[18] The security police, however, coined the phrase 'Indians can't fly' in mockery of Timol's death, and used it as part of their campaign of public terror.[19]

A young man called Gerald Sizani from Orlando East, who was detained at about the same time as Cyril, was tormented with accounts of Timol's fate. He remembers being taken to the tenth floor of the building in the early hours of the morning by English-speaking policemen. 'They asked me if I heard of Ahmed Timol … They then took me to the window and I was told that this was called "Timol Heights". I was held by my feet and dangled outside the window. I closed my eyes, sure that I was dead.'[20]

After he was taken in, Cyril's mother was distraught, and she would sit and cry during these periods of detention, desperate with fear about the fate of her oldest son.[21] But this time, things were only to get worse. In August, Douglas was also picked up by the security police and taken to John Vorster Square.

The cells were designed to keep prisoners in isolation. Most of the rooms had no view of the sky outside, and their inward-facing perspex windows were opaque and fitted with small ventilation holes. Food would be pushed through a gap in the perspex as if feeding a laboratory animal. Detainees were not permitted to talk. Nevertheless, the prisoners had developed an elementary communication system that allowed them to notify one another of arrivals and departures. Messages were written on pieces of toilet paper and smuggled between cells by the orderlies who brought the food.[22] Cyril very quickly learnt that his little brother had arrived in a different part of the prison. He was able to send a message to Douglas, asking whether he had been tortured and offering him what little emotional support could be conveyed on a small piece of toilet paper hidden under a food tray.

Towards the end of Cyril's six months in detention, the two brothers were transferred to Norwood Police Station. Once again, they were held in solitary confinement, but at the very end of Cyril's period in the station the two brothers were placed in opposite cells. 'We could see each other through the grille gate.'[23] Cyril was released in February 1977, but Douglas was to remain in detention until July after almost a full year behind bars.

Soon after Cyril's release, the black consciousness movement was struck a painful blow. Steve Biko, the former medical student who had become almost synonymous with black consciousness, died on 12 September 1977 in Pretoria after having been beaten and tortured in detention in Port Elizabeth.

Cyril's reaction to this traumatic event, and to the political fallout that followed, demonstrated that he had moved beyond the reactive politics of his early years and into a more reflective phase. He knew all too well that the death was certain to bring a fresh round of protest and violence, and to unleash yet another murderous killing spree by the poorly trained police. He was also aware that there was no effective political organisation in place to harness the energies of Biko's mourners, and to channel it to any productive political purpose. He immediately acted to minimise the human cost that was sure to be on its way. One of his chosen venues for this action was his old university.

At Turfloop, still one of the key centres of black consciousness activism, Biko's death had been greeted with sorrow and anger. The police occupied the campus, disrupting student meetings and detaining student leaders with a heavy hand. In October, after the immediate period of protest was over, the SRC arranged for a requiem mass to be held on the campus. They asked a young pastor, Diamond Atong, to address the students. Atong had recently returned from the United States where he had been studying a variant of radical black theology. He was now teaching theology as the employee of an American-funded foundation called the Campus Crusade, which was based in a small compound close to the campus.[24]

Atong spoke thoughtfully and with moderation at the early morning memorial service, only to discover to his horror that the police had an agenda all of their own. Armed officers stormed the service without reason, and the university authorities used this as a pretext for closing the residences and expelling the students. Atong found himself suddenly playing host to dozens of young students who lived too far from Turfloop to simply go home. Atong feared for their safety in the explosive environment the police had created and was uncertain what to do.[25]

Later that afternoon, Ramaphosa arrived with some friends from Johannesburg. He was still a highly regarded figure for the local student leaders, and he immediately set about minimising what he recognised as the primary danger: that students would drift off the campus, without money or transportation, in an effort to make their way home. Out on the back roads they would be vulnerable to the vengeance of the marauding police.

Having established that Atong was of like mind, Ramaphosa collected money from the students until sufficient had been pooled for his purposes. Together with Atong, he drove to Pietersburg (now Pholokwane), where the two men rented a film projector and a number of films, just as Cyril had done many times before as chairman of the student union and the SCM. On their return, they showed films to the students on campus until late into the evening, encouraging them to remain on campus and out of harm's way until the following morning when tempers had cooled. In time, Ramaphosa and Atong were to become firm friends. As we shall see, they were also soon to become business partners in Soweto.

In Johannesburg, Ramaphosa managed to secure work as an articled clerk in the offices of a small-time lawyer, Henry Dolowitz, in Harley Chambers on Jeppe Street. Dolowitz is a small and energetic man whose practice today, in a run-down block of flats on Louis Botha Avenue in Orange Grove, deals with the same variety of domestic and criminal cases as then: assaults, family violence, divorce, traffic accidents. Dolowitz is a mildly conservative spokesman for 'common sense', and a critic of the new constitution, which he believes gives away too many rights to criminals. 'The victim rots in a public hospital in Soweto while the criminal is put up in a private ward with a television to watch. This country is too kind to the criminals.'[26]

Dolowitz possessed an unusually clear sense of the absurdity of apartheid. 'Any thinking person could see it didn't work and that its end was just a question of time.'[27] He also had an ability to identify talent, an ability that was blind to the colour of a person's skin. The clerk who preceded Cyril was George Maluleke, who was to go on to become a widely respected judge after 1994.

Dolowitz was also highly tolerant of Cyril's politics and the frequent absences this imposed on him. Cyril would disappear for extended periods, claiming that the Special Branch was looking for him. On occasion, a laid-back character was a necessary requirement for employing Ramaphosa. Dolowitz would receive accusatory calls from the police, telling him for example that they had identified him by his registration number as the driver of a speeding car that had created an accident in Soweto (an early instance, in fact, of Cyril's legendarily dangerous driving).

Possessor of a mischievous sense of humour, Dolowitz enjoyed sharing terrible jokes with Cyril. He advised the about-to-be married Ramaphosa in 1978 that he must take out 'an ANC' – an ante-nuptial contract. He also endured Cyril's bad jokes with good grace. 'When I am President,' Cyril would jest, 'you will be made minister of white affairs.' (Observe Ramaphosa's ambition once again, partly concealed beneath a cloak of humour.)

The two men never had a single argument in the two years Cyril worked at the firm. The young clerk rarely spoke seriously about politics, although when he did so with passion one day, quite unexpectedly, Dolowitz was never able to forget his words. 'We won't live with this chain around our necks. I don't care if we have to wipe things out and start from the beginning and it takes a hundred years, we'll do it. We won't live with this chain.'[28]

Cyril was a scrupulous employee, showing attention to detail and demonstrating compassion for the clients. He was also a hard worker who stayed in the office late, often well after the other occupants had left for the night. Dolowitz remembers that he could never be quite sure what Cyril was doing in the late evening hours, and his suspicions were soon to be confirmed. Dolowitz was a cool customer, unconcerned about the attentions of the Special Branch. Yet Cyril's political activity was to bring his employer to the attention of the Special Branch, in a way that, to his credit, he does not seem in the least to regret.

Dolowitz had been offered a position as part-time private security guard for the Israeli airline, El Al. These much-coveted positions were passed between members of the Johannesburg Jewish community, and they entailed few responsibilities: to oversee aspects of the ground security of the periodic flights between South Africa and Israel. In exchange, those chosen received four free tickets per year on the airline, the equivalent of a very considerable stipend. Security clearance was required at both ends, however, and while Dolowitz was cleared by Israeli security, he waited in vain for the South African Special Branch to clear him.[29]

It was many years before he was able to get to the bottom of the decision. In his file, recovered after 1994, it was recorded that he had taken into his employment one Cyril Ramaphosa, who had access to the offices of Dolowitz on Jeppe Street. Ramaphosa had been seen entering these offices in the evenings 'in the company of communists and agitators' and was known to have had meetings in the building with them.[30]

Dolowitz was struck by Ramaphosa's utter disdain for the regulatory minutiae of apartheid. He remembers the absurdity of the two lifts in the Jeppe Street chambers. One was marked 'Whites only' and the other 'Whites/Blacks'. Cyril never gave any indication that he had even noticed the signs. Every single day he rode in the 'Whites only' lift. The building superintendent would watch him, fuming and outraged, but could never confront him. Complained Dolowitz: 'The superintendent used to give me hell all the time about it, asking me to put a stop to it. But he never said a word to Cyril.'[31]

While he clerked in Jeppe Street, and continued to save souls in Soweto, Ramaphosa was confronted with a question with which all his peers also grappled. Should he stay in South Africa and continue the struggle for change from within? Or should he leave for the uncertainty of exile? In the years that followed, a mythology of heroism and military struggle developed around the exile liberation movement, and on their return some exiles even came to believe that they really were liberating heroes. This portrayal could not but cast a negative light on those who had stayed behind, whose lives involved necessary accommodations and compromises with the powerful forces of the white state and with the Bantustan system.

Whether an individual chose exile was in part a matter of generation, temperament, personal circumstances and luck. The factors pushing Cyril towards exile were growing in the late 1970s. The conflict between apartheid and its enemies was escalating. The regime was using its power to ban and harass its opponents, making everyday life ever more intolerable, and dashing any hope of political change. The prospect of another period of detention was always in the minds of those who had been detained before. Many former prisoners had yet to come to terms with their experiences, estranged from friends, constantly reliving the trauma of torture, and enduring nightmares, depression and unfocused anxiety. Many would also suffer from unexplained symptoms: stomach pains, headaches, sweating, and trembling, shivering and uncontrollable crying. Fear of death – one's own or that of friends and family – unsurprisingly haunted many activists.[32] Between 1976 and 1978, many of Cyril's friends and associates left the country.

Griffith Zabala's younger brother, for example, went into exile with the black consciousness movement (BCM). While the majority of exiles would join the ANC, if they had relatives or strong political affiliations with the PAC or the BCM they would choose these as their exile homes. In 1977 Ishmael Mkhabela's younger brother – a friend of Douglas Ramaphosa – also left to join the exile BCM. Ishmael still remembers his brother's words: 'I am not as strong as you are.' He would rather meet his fate holding a gun than become another powerless victim of the security police.[33]

Tshenuwani Farisani was driven into exile only after four periods of detention. 'Like Mandela before me, they kicked me on my black mouth. I lost two black teeth in the process. I wanted a room in my own house, a site in my own country, and like Oliver Tambo before me, they are trying now to force me into exile. I am refusing to accept exile. I have not asked for exile status. I am a South African.'[34]

Older siblings like Cyril were especially unwilling to leave despite the hazards they faced, unless banning orders and restrictions on freedom of movement made it simply impossible for them to function. Eldest children were more likely to have work, and so their parents and younger siblings were more likely to depend on them for material security. They would feel this sense of responsibility keenly. For Cyril, 'one of the things that held me back was a family situation. My father and my mother were getting old and I wanted to be around, to be there for them. And it turned out my brother left, and I was rather pleased … when I joined the trade union movement that I had stayed to make a meaningful contribution.'[35]

Another eldest son was Caesar Molebatsi, soon to become Cyril's friend and later to achieve fame as a television evangelist. Molebatsi's younger brothers, George and Leftie, left for exile in the 1970s, whereas Caesar's journey took place in reverse. He was in the United States studying between 1969 and 1976, and graduated on the very day the uprisings began, 16 June 1976. 'The choice was simple. I packed up and went back home. Those who could stay during what followed did so. They felt they had to give leadership, to create parallel structures to oppose the regime, to support and lead the churches and trade unions without which opposition to apartheid would simply crumble.'[36]

It was probably only a matter of time before Douglas Ramaphosa went into exile. Temperamentally he was not suited to the accommodations of domestic struggle.[37] Cyril, on the other hand, was tireless in exploiting the loopholes of the apartheid system to make advances and protect the vulnerable, 'using his knowledge and compassion to make things better than they would have been'.[38] Douglas was always more aggressive and confrontational, less crafty and cunning in his operations. He was more vulnerable to being detained once again, and probably more susceptible to further psychological scarring should this occur.

Although Douglas's parents also sent him away for a period of education in Sibasa, he had returned to study at Sekano-Ntoane for his matriculation. But he had been forced out of high school by security police harassment after the uprising, and had been obliged to write his matric examinations as a private candidate through Damelin College. There was no prospect of him remaining in a university, or out of the hands of the security police, for long. Moreover, he had a desire to fight using force of arms – his decision to leave was very explicitly one to 'take up arms' against the enemy. According to his friend Rams Ramashia, he was 'a very angry man indeed'.[39]

In 1980 events forced his hand. An ANC exile contacted him to warn him that some of his underground ANC associates had been arrested in possession of firearms. There was evidence directly incriminating Douglas, he was led to believe, and if he did not leave the country he was likely to be detained for a very long time. The exile suggested that Douglas would be able to work at the Solomon Mahlangu Freedom College in Tanzania, a school at which the children of ANC exiles were educated – a possibility that appealed to Douglas. He left the country suddenly, telling almost no one – certainly neither Cyril nor his parents – about his intended departure. He left behind him a very young son; Londani was never to see his father again – such were the almost everyday tragedies of the time. Although he was met over the border by friends, including Ishmael Mkhabela's brother, he was resolute in his determination to remain with the ANC. After two years of teaching in Tanzania, he was sent to study in the Soviet Union, and would not return to South Africa until the ANC was unbanned more than a decade later.

It is conceivable that Douglas was recruited by the ANC precisely to be able to put pressure on his older brother at a later date. On some accounts, at least, the younger brother of Frank Chikane was recruited for just this reason.[40] Cyril was in fact obliged in later years to reach Douglas through the ANC. He was able to meet up with Douglas in Moscow in 1985, on a trip that was to bring him in contact with Joe Slovo and Mac Maharaj for the first time. He was also to see his brother again in the early 1990s in Tanzania, when Douglas had returned from the Soviet Union to teach at Solomon Mahlangu Freedom College.[41]

There was no good to come from either exile or remaining in Soweto. For those who left 'exile was Hell!'[42] For those who remained, everyday life was a dangerous struggle. The most pressing question for those who remained was how to advance the condition of the people while struggling to secure political power. Whereas Cyril's friends continued trying to build black consciousness organisations, Cyril's mind began to take him in a different and more practical direction. He was determined, in the words of his friend Tshenuwani Farisani, 'not to land exactly the same set of punches again'.[43] For their part, his friends were not to be altogether impressed with Cyril's new turn of mind.

Indeed, there was some discussion among them about whether Cyril had become a quite different kind of political animal to them, in part, as we will see, because of new circles in which he was moving. Ishmael Mkhabela and Lybon Mabasa had continued in a straight line after Soweto, organising and agitating in black consciousness politics. Cyril, however, while always acknowledged by them as a leader, found less time for black consciousness, even if he still attended weekend meetings of the Black People's Convention in Soweto.

Ramaphosa was rumoured to be drinking heavily.[44] Perhaps he was coming to terms with the after-effects of detention. It was quite common for detainees to step back in order to take stock and recover their perspective and sense of purpose. The disenchantment Cyril later described with the limitations of black consciousness thinking may have reduced his enthusiasm for the fray. In an interview many years later, he observed that his feelings about black consciousness were changing in the late 1970s: 'Whites were clearly the enemy, they were responsible for the hardships our people were going through. They were not to be trusted, they were not to be worked with in any way whatsoever. So after the '76 uprising, after my detention, I outgrew that, because I realised that we needed to move away from this parochial way of assessing the situation in our country and see that non-racialism, going beyond just blackness, was important to further our objectives and there were whites we could actually work with, who could make a contribution in our struggle. So from '77 when I got out of prison, I started charting a different path.'⁴⁵

Cyril was increasingly practical in his response to the problems of the community. On the one hand, he intensified his work in Christian youth movements. There were at that time three large Christian youth clubs operating across Soweto, a troika sharing a degree of camaraderie but also manifesting a measure of competitiveness. While Cyril had for some time been involved with Life Bearers, he was to join and rapidly become chair of Youth Alive Interdenominational Christian Association, which was being run by his friend Caesar Molebatsi.

Molebatsi had met Cyril at a Christian movement conference for university students in June 1974 in Lesotho, where Cyril was representing the SCM. Molebatsi, meanwhile, was studying in the United States, and was drafted in at the last minute to act as keynote speaker. In the discussion around violence and the struggle that Molebatsi facilitated, he could not help noticing the impressive and measured contributions of Cyril Ramaphosa and his colleague Frank Chikane. As was common in the Christian movement of the time, the general thrust of the conference was that the struggle should proceed by means of non-violent but forceful actions undergirded by a well-developed social conscience.

When Molebatsi returned to Soweto in 1976 he was keen to link up with 'robust thinkers' willing to question orthodoxy and to act constructively. They would meet on Saturday mornings and work out how to develop the youth organisation and, above all, to 'keep people safe'.⁴⁶ The activity of the association was austere and informed by conservative morality. Part of the intention was to keep young people occupied and upright. Intense motivational sessions encouraged participants to adhere strictly to their demanding set of moral principles, forswearing alcohol and cigarettes, and treating all other people, regardless of station, with respect. On Molebatsi's account, Cyril's concerns went further. He was keen to 'see the development of a cadre of leaders who appreciated not just the operation of democracy but also the mechanisms that would make it work'.[47]

Cyril characteristically drew up a new constitution for the organisation. As was his way, he did not try to impose it directly – even though he had devised it alone – but rather insisted on a laborious process, lasting several months, in which the senior members of the youth association worked through and agreed the contents of the constitution together. The document showed a new maturity of thought, including several democratic mechanisms hitherto absent, such as annual elections to leadership positions, and organisational innovations such as the concept of 'team leaders' borrowed from the trade union movement.[48]

Youth Alive filled a desperate need in a Soweto full of angry and fearful young minds. Diamond Atong remembers Ramaphosa working primarily with students and young people, organising camps, retreats and conferences, in an attempt to mitigate the worst effects of the violence that was sweeping across the communities of Soweto. The youth mission worked to alleviate the consequences of abnormal levels of violence and what we would now call the 'post-traumatic stress' associated with it.[49]

Meanwhile, Cyril and his Christian friend Diamond Atong set up a building business called Atorama Construction, Atorama being an amalgam of their two surnames. This was Cyril's first real venture into business, albeit with the charitable mission to improve living conditions in the community and to put unemployed youth to work so as to keep them out of mischief. The firm mostly undertook small-scale building work, typically upgrading four-room houses that might contain ten or more occupants, by adding garages, additional rooms and bathrooms to the side or rear of a property.

Much of Atorama's work was meeting needs identified in a survey of the community, with money going only towards building materials. Besides using Youth Alive volunteers, Atong and Cyril drew on students of building construction from the vocational training college in Dube, Soweto, who honed their skills in the programme. Some of the work was profit-making, and Ramaphosa began to accumulate wealth on a small scale for the first time.

Cyril was very busy with his part-time legal clerking, Youth Alive and Atorama – as well as with the discovery of new social and political circles. His political activity was taking something of a back seat. Then, on 1 July 1978, Cyril and Hope Mudau got married. This union was not a surprise because they had been close for almost a decade. Their friend Peter Phaswani was struck at Mphaphuli High by their common commitment to the same union between politics and Christianity.[50] For respectable Christians like Cyril and Hope, marriage was 'among other things, a way to escape from sin and to be committed to a person – and to have a relationship blessed by the church'.[51] There had been bad news just a week before the wedding – Lybon Mabasa had been detained again by the security police. Nevertheless, the long traditional wedding went ahead and was celebrated with dancing in the streets of Tshiawelo.

Cyril also bought his first car at about this time, a small white and cream BMW, plainly an impractical vehicle for a person of his needs and finances.[52] It was characteristic of his approach to both cars and to expenditure to prefer an unreliable BMW to any more sensible alternative. Cyril's father, now made financially comfortable by his business ventures, agreed to contribute half of the total R4,000 cost of the vehicle.[53]

From the day of its purchase, Cyril was a very proud owner, maintaining the car scrupulously, and performing tricks such as driving hundreds of metres very fast in reverse gear.[54] The car needed a good deal of attention, and Ramaphosa had to learn the skills to service and repair it himself. This vehicle was later to become the victim of Cyril's casual attitude to the rules of the road, and to the long mileages that union business would demand of him. Eventually the battered vehicle could only be refuelled while the engine was still running.[55] Although he claims to be a careful driver, others have always seen him as reckless behind the wheel, on one occasion careering so fast that Hope believed they were going to die.[56]

Cyril and Hope moved into a back room of the Ramaphosa family house on Mhlaba Drive, a room that Atorama added to the building for the purpose.[57] They were to live there for about a year. Hope was working for a controversial organisation that had been created in 1976 called the Urban Foundation (UF). She had completed her BA degree in social work at the University of the North, and was employed as a public relations officer and community liaison worker in the Transvaal region of the Foundation.[58]

With the help of a housing subsidy from the UF,[59] the couple then moved briefly into an area of 'model housing' laid down by the Foundation in Pimville. Their house was still small, however, and Ramaphosa began construction of a new residence, built under his own hand, in Rockville, close to Moroka police station where his father had been a police officer.

When Western Native Township had been bulldozed, and Venda and Shangaan residents had been forcibly removed to Tshiawelo, many of Cyril's childhood friends from the township were relocated to Rockville instead on ethnic grounds. In his choice of Rockville for his new home, Ramaphosa was consciously deciding to rejoin old friends and striking a personal blow against the tribalist logic of apartheid.

CHAPTER 6

BEHIND ENEMY LINES

Beware of white ladies
in chemise dresses
and pretty sandals
that show their toes.
Beware of these ladies
when spring is here.
They have strange habits
Of infesting our townships
with seeds of:
geraniums pansies poppies carnations.
They plant their seeds in our eroded slums
cultivating charity in our eroded hearts
making our slums look like floral Utopias.
Beware!
Beware of seeds and plants.
They take up your oxygen
and they take up your time
and let you wait for blossoms
and let you pray for rain
and you forget about equality
and blooming liberation

– Chris van Wyk [1]

At five o'clock in the early evening of 25 September 1978, the chairman of the Anglo Transvaal Mines Consolidated (Anglovaal) mining house, Clive Menell, took the chair at the regular monthly meeting of the Transvaal regional board of the Urban Foundation (UF). The Foundation was funded by the biggest names in South African business, including the giant Anglo American Corporation controlled by mining magnate Harry Oppenheimer. Around the table in the boardroom on the ninth floor of the NBS Building on Rissik Street sat many of Johannesburg's most powerful business leaders, together with the executive director of the UF, former judge Jan Steyn. Menell's first task was a pleasant one – to welcome a new member of the board: Cyril Ramaphosa.

How did this 25-year-old black man from Soweto find himself in the company of this group of powerful businessmen? And what exactly was the significance of his presence? In order to answer these questions, it is necessary to trace the response of the Soweto community and the world of white business to the events of June 1976.

The 1976 uprising of the children and youth was as much of a shock to the parents of Soweto as to the authorities. In the rebellion's immediate aftermath, community leaders gathered together, on one account at the behest of Percy Qoboza, editor of *The World;* on another account, at the suggestion of Denis Beckett and Aggrey Klaaste.[2] Around 200 Sowetans – the self-selected elite of Soweto society – turned up at the meeting held at the offices of *The World*.[3] Along with dozens of professionals and small business people – teachers, nurses and shopkeepers – there were a few younger people such as Cyril, Frank Chikane and student leader Eddie Siala. Among the more prominent speakers were Dr Nthato Motlana, a pillar of the local community who would play a major role later on in Cyril's life, and Winnie Mandela, whose presence was at that stage always welcome. Wherever Winnie went, journalists were likely to follow, and the security police would be deterred from harassment and arbitrary arrest.

The prevailing view at the meeting was very much at variance with Ramaphosa's own assessment.[4] For Cyril, 'the uprising was the beginning of the revolution, and while [we were] at university we had always thought the real revolution was coming – where there would be mayhem and total destruction … At a political level we thought that this was it, and we needed to exploit it and make maximum use of it.'[5]

The Soweto establishment which dominated the meeting understood the uprising in narrower and less historical terms. As ANC veteran and community activist Ellen Kuzwayo explained, the key to 1976 for them was that the youth attacked and closed down the Urban Bantu Council – they were trying to destroy an illegitimate local government system.[6] Kuzwayo epitomised the conservative approach to the struggle against apartheid within Soweto. A 62-year-old political veteran, she was the child of a relatively privileged family who had been dispossessed of their 1,500-acre Free State farm in her youth. She had been educated in private colleges in Durban and at the prestigious Lovedale teacher training college in the Eastern Cape. Introduced to ANC politics as early as the 1936 Bloemfontein conference, she had gone on in 1944 to be part of the radical cohort of the Youth League that included Nelson Mandela, Walter Sisulu and Oliver Tambo. Initially a teacher, Kuzwayo was disgusted by the Bantu Education legislation and retrained as a social worker. She then became a prominent member of the Soweto community, running classic ameliorative projects and self-help programmes around literacy and the rights of women.[7]

Under the guidance of senior figures like Kuzwayo and Motlana, the meeting determined that a detailed study of the Soweto local authority was required, to better understand its funding and functioning. A 'Committee of Ten' was mandated to complete this study within six months. The committee included newspaper editor Qoboza, shopkeeper Vella Kraai, student activist Eddie Siala, and teacher Tom Manthatha, as well as prominent local notables such as Motlana and Kuzwayo. Curiously, some people who were not present believe that Cyril was one of the members of the committee,[8] whereas this is contradicted by, among others, Nthato Motlana, who was its leading figure. The probable reason for this confusion is that the label 'Committee of Ten' in later years became shorthand for whoever happened to be the current set of prominent Soweto leaders, and Cyril was to become very prominent in the 1980s.[9]

The Committee of Ten was not as conservative as it is sometimes made out to be. Its members were determined to overthrow the widely despised system of Soweto local government and to replace it with a broadly democratic leadership (which they would have conceived as themselves). The report the committee produced ended with demands for a new community-based board with control over the council, the power to levy taxes, oversight over the police forces, and the right to hold local elections. These proposals were vehemently rejected by the minister of justice. When the committee tried to bring them to the attention of the Soweto community, their meetings were banned. On 19 October 1977, almost all the members of the committee were detained by the security police as part of a renewed assault on black political organisations. Kuzwayo was held for five months in the Fort, the grim prison that nestles beside the new Constitutional Court building in Braamfontein. Percy Qoboza was arrested on the same day, and his newspaper, *The World*, was banned.[10]

For its part, the white business community was also concerned by the events of June 1976. Apartheid was charting an unpredictable course that was running increasingly counter to the interests of business. Some companies, to be sure, continued to derive great benefit from apartheid, in particular from the cheap labour that it allowed them to exploit. The economy was now a complex creature, however. Just as manufacturing had outstripped mining in the 1940s, South Africa was now becoming increasingly centred around new technologies and a burgeoning service sector. Even within the manufacturing sector, the demand for a permanent urbanised workforce was strong, and many producers bewailed the lack of a black middle class to bolster domestic demand.

After 1976, business now feared that apartheid could end in ruin and it wanted action to cement black political stability. A memorandum from the Transvaal Chamber of Industries to the prime minister, five weeks after the uprisings began, captured this new sense of urgency. 'The thought most basic to our submission is the need to ensure a stable, contented urbanized black community in our metropolitan areas ... The emergence of a "middle class" with Western-type materialistic needs and ambitions has already occurred in these areas. The mature family-oriented urban black already places the stability of his household uppermost, and is more interested in his pay-packet than in politics. Our prime point of departure should be that this "middle class" is not weakened by frustration and indignity. Only by having this most respectable section of the urban black on our side can the whites of South Africa be assured of containing on a long-term basis the irresponsible economic and political ambitions of those blacks who are influenced against their own real interests from within and without our borders.'[11]

Through an unexpected set of coincidences, the young couple – the stunningly beautiful Hope and the charismatic Cyril – had meanwhile been propelled into the orbit of one of South Africa's most prominent business families. Cyril had been profoundly depressed after his first detention and subsequent exclusion from university. One of the few positive aspects of the experience had been the unexpected discovery that people outside South Africa were protesting against the arbitrary detention imposed by the regime. A British woman called Sarah Woodhouse, living in the English midlands, had energetically campaigned through the organisation Amnesty International for Cyril's release. Along with dozens of other Amnesty activists, she had sent protest letters to Pretoria and collected money to help Cyril's family with legal expenses. She was keen to meet with the Ramaphosas and to do everything she could to make Cyril's life after detention more tolerable.

Sarah's husband, John Woodhouse, was the headmaster of Rugby School, one of England's most famous private boarding schools, at which, according to legend, the game of rugby was invented.[12] He was acquainted with the powerful South African mining magnate Clive Menell, who was an 'old boy' of Rugby, and whose son Rick had just finished his own studies there as a boarder. Menell's wife Irene was a prominent politician in the Progressive Party, a patron of good causes, an assiduous networker, and a performer of virtuous liberal deeds. When the Woodhouses came to meet the Ramaphosa family in 1975, soon after Cyril's release, they introduced the Menells to Hope and Cyril and in effect asked them if they could 'care for' the two of them – a request that did not simply come out of the blue but rather reflected Clive and Irene's own project of 'collecting bright people'.[13]

Cyril and Hope were striking figures at that time – in their intelligence and beauty as much as in the injustices they had endured – and they must have represented an appealing addition to the Menells' collection. These wealthy patrons were to open many doors in the years to follow, providing advice, resources and access to a powerful circle of acquaintances. When Hope and Cyril were finally married three years later, Irene was there to celebrate, walking in a long human snake along the streets of Tshiawelo.[14]

Ramaphosa also began to spend time with the couple's son, Rick, who was exactly Cyril's age and was finishing his studies in England. Rick was cosmopolitan and felt stifled in South African society. He was educated at Rugby and then at Trinity College, Cambridge, and he would later leave South Africa for Stanford University and a period of work in New York. He had imbibed the cautious politics of 1970s English liberalism, and he wanted to befriend South Africans from 'outside the establishment'.[15] The segregation of public places in Johannesburg meant that the two had few places where they could meet. Rick still remembers drinking coffee with Cyril in the basement of the Methodist Central Church in Johannesburg, one of the very few cross-racial venues available at the time.[16] In what must have been a revelation for both men at that time, the two were to become friends.

Cyril's acquaintance with the Menells brought him into giddy social and political circles. Irene Menell was a very grand lady indeed, and like her friend Helen Suzman she has since 1990 effortlessly gravitated from the old establishment into the new. ('Sorry to be a little late – I have just come from lunch with Nelson [Mandela] and Helen [Suzman].')[17] In the mid-1970s, however, she was an activist and sometime chair of the Johannesburg Progressive Party whose leader and sole MP, Helen Suzman, was her very close friend.

The source of the family's great wealth was Anglovaal, a mining house founded in 1933 by Slip Menell and Bob Hersov. The two families have maintained their controlling stake in the business, sons Clive Menell and Basil Hersov taking executive control in the 1960s, and Rick Menell becoming chief executive in 1992. Basil Hersov was a significant power-broker in his own right, working on the margins between money and politics. He was to become chairman of Barclays Bank South Africa and then First National Bank (of which we will hear more later), and was also to become a member of PW Botha's defence council. Hersov, like the Menells, was later to move seamlessly between the old establishment and the new, but controversially so because of his involvement with the

ANC's first minister of defence, Joe Modise, in the British company BAE's component of the strategic arms procurement process.[18]

The Menells divided (and still divide) their time between their mansion in the mining magnate belt of Parktown and a beautiful and historic family farm that nestles in the Constantia valley, a country farm almost impossibly close to Cape Town. In South African terms, this family is 'old money'. To borrow Kenneth Clarke's put-down of British arriviste politician Michael Heseltine, they do not have to buy their own furniture.

The couple recognised that they were 'a powerful establishment family with a high level of immunity from harassment by the security police'.[19] On Irene's account, they were determined to use the space and freedom they possessed to advance a project of 'bridge-building' between South Africa's divided races. On the more jaded reading of the veteran politician and one-time Progressive Party leader, Frederik van Zyl Slabbert, Irene 'did not like to be left behind' in politics, and she was keen to help shape the emerging black elite.[20]

Cynics might indeed dismiss the Menells' politics as self-indulgent. Clive was an aficionado of jazz, and he would hold elaborate jazz evenings in their home on Third Avenue, Parktown. The Menells' white acquaintances included more or less every liberal of significance in the Johannesburg of the time. They celebrated the 'almost unprecedented' opportunity they provided for 'black to mix with white', and their social whirl was dominated by lively friends from the 'performing arts' world. Yet their circle of acquaintance also spanned the business elites of Johannesburg, and they made efforts to engage corporate leaders with the small number of black South Africans they assiduously cultivated.

Visitors at their home included Mangosuthu Buthelezi, darling of white business in the 1970s because of his embrace of market capitalism; Dr Nthato Motlana, Soweto's most prominent ANC activist turned businessman; and Anglican churchman Desmond Tutu, arch-moralist of the anti-apartheid forces. In later years, they would cultivate Africans whose self-conception was somewhat more radical. Irene remembers 'I once had Barney Pityana out there on the stoep [*pointing*] and he was telling me that what we are doing is just a band aid [*incredulous expression*].' She also recollects Sydney Mufamadi sitting on her couch [*she pats a cushion*] 'right where I am sitting now. He was telling me that all of the role models in the Alexandra of his youth were gangsters!'[21]

The Menells' social planning was not always impeccable. At one dinner party, they contrived to invite Nthato Motlana and Motlana's ex-wife – who were not on good terms – to sit at the same table. This error was compounded by the presence of Mangosuthu Buthelezi, with whom Motlana had just engaged in a vituperative series of public exchanges in the press. Fortunately, Buthelezi and Motlana embraced and decided to put the past behind them.[22]

Buthelezi was already a controversial presence for other black South Africans because of his equivocal treatment of the issue of Bantustan autonomy. Irene recollects Desmond Tutu's son, on another occasion when Buthelezi was present, remarking (no doubt with subtle irony) 'What's that nigger [nigga?] doing here?' loud enough for the Inkatha leader to hear. Buthelezi remained impassive.[23]

Along with the jazz evenings and social functions, each of the Menells hosted a more serious forum. For Clive, it was 'Synthesis', a discussion group that had been running since the 1960s. Before Menell took the helm, it was chaired by Frederik van Zyl Slabbert, who believed it should be a small and focused forum for intense debate. Menell's understanding of what Synthesis should be was, however, quite different, and his first decision was to vastly increase the scale of the undertaking – quite ruining the forum in the process, in the view of Slabbert.[24]

Synthesis met on Saturday mornings. It was hosted by Clive at his Parktown house or sometimes on the family farm in Constantia. If circumstances demanded, for example if they wished to meet in Durban where the Menells had neglected to buy a property, the event was hosted by friends. Each session involved perhaps 30 people, selected by Menell, and they would discuss a theme relevant to the 'problems of the day'. Most of those attending regularly would be whites from the Menells' business and social circles, for example powerful Afrikaans and English-speaking businessmen such as Rudolf Gouws, Anton Rupert and Derek Keys – the last of whom was later to bridge differences between ANC and business over economic policy, and to become finance minister in the government of national unity after 1994.

Also prominent were members of what Irene deliciously calls the 'do-gooder wing' of Anglo American Corporation[25] – the likes of Zach de Beer and Bobby Godsell. Clive Menell was also sure to invite Anglo's key strategists, such as Gavin Relly and Julian Ogilvie Thompson, who were to become Anglo chairmen in their turn in the 1980s. Other white invitees included assorted liberal journalists and social policy entrepreneurs – for example Ann Bernstein, Denis Beckett, Raymond Louw and Shaun Johnson – the sort of people who certainly had to buy their own furniture.

Representatives of the liberal Afrikaner intellectual elite were also regular attendees – Van Zyl Slabbert himself, the brilliantly counter-suggestible Stellenbosch political theorist André du Toit, and Du Toit's less-gifted colleague Willie Esterhuyse, who was nevertheless to play a significant role in the thawing of relations between Afrikaner intellectuals and the exile ANC in years to come. Representatives of Afrikaner state power were thinner on the ground, not enjoying the company of men who viewed themselves, with some self-satisfaction, as questioning the established order to which they belonged.

André du Toit, who attended Synthesis meetings in Cape Town and Johannesburg across the late 1970s and 1980s, remembers one occasion in September 1985 when General Johann Coetzee, the head of the South African Police, was invited to present an account at the Menells' Parktown home of the township violence that was sweeping the country. Almost the entire Anglo contingent was present, including Gavin Relly, who had recently taken over as chairman from an ageing Harry Oppenheimer. Coetzee's talk was wooden and largely uninformative – not, in Du Toit's view, atypically for a Synthesis presentation – and the general left rather abruptly after the lunch break, claiming that an urgent mission called him away. It transpired that the mission to which he referred was a Currie Cup rugby match between Northern Transvaal and Western Cape.[26]

Equally tellingly, the very next day Gavin Relly was to fly to Lusaka for a highly controversial meeting with the ANC leadership. Rather than providing a venue in which breathtaking initiatives might stir passionate debate and profound reflection, Synthesis could be a setting in which significant events were brushed under the carpet despite, or perhaps because of, the presence of the key role-players.[27]

Much of the force that Synthesis meetings did possess came from the presence at every session of a small number of black South Africans. The creation of an atmosphere in which interaction at an intellectual and social level between black and white might be possible was still extremely unusual. In the Cape, regulars included Franklin and Julian Sonn. In Johannesburg, alongside Buthelezi, Synthesis attracted members of the Soweto community leadership who were active in the Committee of Ten – for example, Ellen Kuzwayo and Nthato Motlana – and figures such as Fikile Bam, the lawyer who had known Mandela and Tambo in the 1950s, had spent ten years on Robben Island, and along with Madiba and Mac Maharaj had offered prisoners legal advice on the Island when being called before the prison disciplinary committee.

Ramaphosa was a belated and occasional addition to this company and some regulars cannot even recall whether or not he was ever in attendance. Although the Menells would no doubt have liked him to play a prominent part, Ramaphosa was not well disposed towards talking-shops of this kind. His access to the liberal elite, however, gave him a unique insight, for a black man of his age, into the thought patterns of his soon-to-be adversaries in business and government.

The Menells played a major role in the creation and the operation of the Urban Foundation, a body that was to have an important influence on the lives of Cyril and Hope. The events of 1976 created space for the philosophy of constructive engagement that the Menells embraced, and Irene was fired up by the uprising to 'mobilise resources, existing resources, that were simply going to waste, and use them to address practical problems'.[28] Her inspiration was the 'New Detroit' project from late 1960s Michigan, illustrating not only the imaginative hold of American racial politics for her class but also the prevailing misconception that systematic majority exploitation and oppression was not the issue.[29]

In July 1976, Clive and Irene floated their ideas to the Institute of Race Relations director Freddie van Wyk and *Financial Mail* editor George Palmer. Together they hatched a plan. Anglo's 'do-gooders' had a conference on urban housing planned for later that year, and Irene and Clive decided to hijack it. Through Harry Oppenheimer's personal assistant, Nick Dermont, they sold the idea to Zach de Beer, the political strategist in the Oppenheimer inner circle, and then to the old man himself.[30]

Harry Frederick Oppenheimer was the most famous businessman of his day and by far the richest man in Africa. Only marginally in his shadow was Anton Rupert, the self-made giant of Afrikaner business. Oppenheimer and Rupert already partly embraced the Menells' idea that high levels of poverty and limited social provision in peri-urban townships were ameliorable causes of social unrest. They decided together to convene a 'businessmen's conference on the quality of life of urban communities' in place of the scheduled urban housing conference in Johannesburg's Carlton Hotel, on 29 and 30 November 1976.

More than 200 prominent business people attended, representing almost every sector of the economy. Alongside figures like Gavin Relly and Raymond Ackerman, there were also a number of black invitees: members of the Committee of Ten such as Ellen Kuzwayo; familiar faces from the Menells' circle such as Franklin Sonn; and also two Lutheran churchmen, one of whom was Tshenuwani Farisani, Cyril's mentor from Mphaphuli High School. He had no fear of being branded a collaborator, he recalls, because his 'credibility was simply too great'.[31]

The conference was not an exciting affair. As is conventional at such events, the final resolutions were already drafted at the beginning, and the outcome of deliberations was carefully fore-planned. The set speeches, however, offer a hilarious window on the white elite's limited understanding of the character and scale of the challenges it faced. One participant, for example, observed that 'Soweto has got a beautiful stretch that runs from New Canada right up to the end of Kliptown'. Alluding to the famous lake in the elegant white suburb of Parkview, this speaker suggested the Soweto stretch could become 'the second Zoo Lake of South Africa'.[32]

The highlight of the event was a breathtaking closing speech by Anton Rupert. The sage and businessman adopted an especially wide historical perspective on the Soweto uprising. He warned of an alarming deterioration in the overall trajectory of Western civilisation, before lamenting the corrupting force of money in a West 'seduced by wealth'. He then peered sagaciously into the future, condemned 'burying one's head in the sand', and castigated those who hoped to hide from gathering storm clouds that were both around the corner and over the horizon. 'This', he sternly warned, 'is how Knossos, the rich and civilized capital of ancient Crete, fell in a night to the invading Mycenaeans!' With a degree of insensitivity to the black members of his audience, he continued,

'This is how Rome fell to the Barbarians!' Whites must refuse to be cowed by fear, he cautioned, 'the fear of survival as a separate entity, the fear of being overrun by numbers, the fear of possible tyranny by an unenlightened majority resulting in one man, one vote once'.[33]

Turning to the practical implications of his analysis, Rupert observed that 'We cannot survive unless we have a free market economy, a stable black middle class with the necessary security of tenure, personal security and a feeling of hope for betterment in the heart of all our peoples.' He then spelt out the seven dimensions of the practical challenge: job creation, training, a living wage, greater commercial opportunities, extended home ownership, improved housing, and the provision of sporting and other amenities.

The way forward, he concluded, was 'to establish an urban development foundation to accommodate and coordinate, on an ongoing basis, the private sector's endeavours at improving the quality of life in the urban black townships ... to encourage and assist as a catalyst the transformation of South Africa's urban black communities into stable, essentially middle-class societies subscribing to the values of a free enterprise society and having a vested interest in their own survival.'[34] These inspirational ideas were met with acclaim, and the Urban Foundation was born.[35]

Oppenheimer and Rupert chose as chief executive of the Foundation a judge, Jan Steyn, from a famous family of Afrikaner leaders. Steyn coveted the position, writing a flattering letter to Harry Oppenheimer on 8 December that praised the old man for his 'tactful yet courageous' chairmanship of proceedings and making it clear he wanted to work with the Foundation in future.[36] Whether Steyn was the right man for the task was unclear. Rupert's biographer describes how Steyn endured an 'eye-opening' visit to Soweto, discovering to his consternation that there was only one cinema and one sports field, and so inadvertently revealing his unfamiliarity with the lives of most of his fellow South Africans.[37]

At the first meeting of the board of directors in the Pretoria Room of the Carlton Hotel, on 3 February 1977, the triumvirate of Oppenheimer, Rupert and Steyn were joined by representatives from a variety of important business sectors, including mining, banking and retailing. It was decided that regional boards would be created in the Transvaal, the Western and Eastern Cape, and Durban to oversee developmental initiatives. The national board delegated its powers to an executive board, where real power would be exercised. This was to comprise Rupert, Oppenheimer, Steyn and the directors of the regional boards.

Clive Menell, a member of the national board, immediately agreed to become chair of the Transvaal regional board, so taking responsibility for operations in Soweto and Greater Johannesburg. He inevitably invited some of his Soweto acquaintances, including members of the Committee of Ten such as Percy Qoboza and Ellen Kuzwayo, on to his regional board. Menell planned to increase black representation systematically from 7 out of 28 members in 1977 to 13 out of 31 by 1979.[38] Very soon, he had invited Cyril to join them, in what Irene Menell describes as a 'charitable gesture'.[39] Ramaphosa was very young but there was speculation about his potential. Fred Phaswana, who was also a member of the Transvaal regional board, remembers that Cyril was evidently picked out as a future leader.[40] In another episode of patronage, meanwhile, Hope was taken on by the region as a staff member.

The budget of the region for the year when Cyril joined the board was a little over R2 million – about a quarter of the total national budget of the UF. There were 25 or 30 projects on the go at any one time. These included the provision of local 'essential services' such as schools and crèches, the electrification of schools, home improvement projects, housing developments, other construction works, and often very small initiatives to enhance community life.

There were inevitable tensions between long-term development and short-term amelioration, but these were debated openly and thoughtfully by Menell's board. They mostly expected communities to initiate, 'own' and partially finance projects. To take a typical example, in 1978 the board agreed to the provision of a fence for Hilekani School in Tshiawelo. The school had been suffering from vandalism and the destruction of property. The school committee itself initiated the request for funds, and the board approved a payment of R1,330 – of which R890 was a grant and R440 was an interest-free loan.

After joining the regional board in September 1978, Cyril initially attended board meetings regularly on the first Monday of every month. He was an active contributor to discussion, supporting the Foundation's philosophy and critical of the paternalist approach to development embraced by Afrikaner bureaucrats.[41] On occasion he sharply interrogated the assumptions of fellow board members about the character of Soweto community life.[42]

Despite early capacity problems that made it hard to spend the funds they had raised,[43] the UF did have major achievements to its name. It championed a 99-year leasehold for South Africans entitled to live and work in urban areas, and allowed them to buy and sell property or to bequeath it in a will. The leasehold remained controversial among black residents – why a leasehold rather than freehold? – and the rationale for the legislation was intellectually crude. Home ownership, according to Jan Steyn, brings about social stability, 'capital formation among blacks', and an impetus towards 'the rapid development of a stable [black] middle class'.[44] Continuing pressure by the UF led quite rapidly to the introduction of full freehold rights for Africans. In effect, the government's argument that Africans were only temporarily resident in the white cities had been abandoned, and the UF could claim much of the credit.

The developmental initiatives of the UF to some degree started to build intellectual and policy bridges between liberal whites and pragmatic blacks. One regular correspondent of Jan Steyn was Bobby Godsell, who was rapidly making his way up the hierarchy of Anglo's corporate office. A 'Prog' recruited into Anglo by Harry Oppenheimer himself – 'Harry had a very low opinion of almost all human beings but had a lot of time for Bobby'[45] – Godsell was now tramping around some of the same practical and intellectual spaces as Cyril: lamenting the failures of the administration board of Soweto; advancing sensible ideas for the reform of tenure; and identifying government actions that needlessly caused political conflict.[46] Cyril's increasingly erratic board attendance over his second year may, nevertheless, indicate growing disillusion with the acts the national board was carrying out in the Foundation's name.[47]

The concentration of power and information in the national executive board often left ordinary regional board members in the dark. Fundraising was driven at national board level by Jan Steyn, and within five years the Foundation was receiving funds from more than 150 businesses. Anglo American and De Beers, the great mining giants associated with Oppenheimer, were the biggest donors, but Anton Rupert's Rembrandt group also contributed handsomely. Mining houses Gencor and Barlow Rand, retailers Pick 'n Pay and Woolworths, and financial houses Nedbank and Standard Bank were major long-term donors.[48]

South African subsidiaries of foreign companies were also major contributors, Ford giving R1 million over four years, British Petroleum and Shell donating almost as much, and Unilever and Barclays Bank making smaller but significant payments.[49] Steyn soon widened the search for funds, first making regular trips to London and New York in which the Foundation's achievements and needs could be showcased. In 1979, the executive committee decided to establish an outpost of the Foundation in London – 'the Urban Foundation (London) Limited' – and then a further office in New York. This initiative allowed tax advantages to accrue to donor companies in the UK, and was also purportedly designed to allow the UF to exert external leverage on Pretoria.[50] The reality was predictably quite different.

The London and New York offices were never effective fundraising centres. Indeed, the UF continued to be dependent on local donors – and particularly on Anglo – throughout its existence. In fact the overseas offices were primarily lobbying instruments, and it was foreign companies and governments rather than Pretoria that were their target. The Anglo-funded big-business lobby group, the South Africa Foundation (SAF), was already campaigning hard to deflect calls for economic sanctions to be imposed on Pretoria. Although it was not an official policy of the UF, what they lobbied for was increasingly indistinguishable from the SAF campaign. The London and New York UF outposts became instruments in a quiet attempt to discourage forced and voluntary disinvestment in South Africa by international big business. Correspondence with Steyn from British business leaders confirms that this was their central preoccupation.[51]

While the proponents of economic sanctions believed they

could help change hearts and minds in South Africa, business was inevitably opposed on the grounds that sanctions would cost jobs, so damaging black rather than white interests. Irene Menell observes that 'engagement'[52] was always rightly a cornerstone policy for dealing with Pretoria. This chimed with Oppenheimer's own belief that engagement with capitalism, by its own devices, would ultimately unwind the scourge of apartheid.

Steyn used fund-raising trips to visit Conservative politicians in the UK who were strident campaigners for 'constructive engagement' and cheerleaders of Mangosuthu Buthelezi. He overwhelmingly lobbied Conservative rather than Labour politicians, even when Labour was in government. In 1978, for example, he met leader of the opposition Margaret Thatcher and Dennis Thatcher's right-wing journalist friend Bill Deedes, as well as a number of far right-wing Conservative members of parliament.[53] In the 1980s, moreover, long after Ramaphosa's departure, the UF surpassed even the South Africa Foundation in promoting sanctions-busting. In 1986, it proposed a way for companies to retain control of South African assets despite a facade of disinvestment. For critics of the Urban Foundation, it was the sanctions issue that ultimately rankled most.

It is hard to avoid the conclusion that the UF was essentially another appendage of Anglo rather than an independent foundation. On 11 September 1980, Jan Steyn wrote to Colonel FAJ van Zyl, the head of security at Anglo American. A friend of Steyn's, Val Macfarlane, was expecting visitors from the UK: a group of senior British police officers. They had expressed an interest in visiting a diamond mine. In his letter Steyn *instructed* Van Zyl to arrange a trip to the giant De Beers-owned Oranjemund diamond mine on the Namibian coast on 12 November, very much a peremptory demand in an Anglo chain of command rather than a polite request from an independent foundation.[54]

Before Cyril became disillusioned with the UF, it helped him to find a new home for his legal studies, after two years of fitful progress at Dolowitz's chambers on Jeppe Street. In early 1979, he attended a three-day 'strategy discussion' at the Fourways Hotel.[55] In attendance were Jan Steyn, Clive Menell, Rick Menell, other members of the regional board, staff members (including Hope), planning and development experts such as Ann Bernstein and Jill Strelitz, and the UF's legal adviser Bob Tucker.

They considered the implications of a background study of demographic and town-planning challenges in Soweto that the UF had commissioned, and explored potential 'constructive responses'. There were also some genuine moments of human connection. Bob Tucker, for example, was reduced to tears by Margaret Motumi's description of 'how black people live'.[56] Tucker meanwhile warmed to Cyril's character and intellect – and Rick Menell may have mentioned Cyril's search for somewhere new to complete his articles.[57] After later discussing the matter with the other partners at EFK Tucker, Tucker offered Cyril the opportunity to complete his articles at this prestigious firm. The arrangement was slightly problematic. EFK Tucker was the Urban Foundation's lawyer, meaning Cyril was both an articled clerk at the firm and a board member of one of its biggest clients.

This law firm was a very different species from Dolowitz and offered more substantial intellectual challenges. Tucker meanwhile set out a route for Cyril to qualify. He could continue with articles, complete a diploma with Unisa, and finally take an exam that would allow him to practise as an attorney. The move from Henry Dolowitz's seedy offices to the plush world of EFK Tucker did not, however, dramatically improve Cyril's progress with his studies. He failed the exam that he had to pass in order to practise – a common enough event for the first or second attempt – and he never went back to retake the exam.[58]

At no stage did Ramaphosa give any indication of wanting to join this world by becoming a corporate lawyer. Indeed, he became increasingly disdainful of the law, arguing that it had impacted largely negatively on black South Africans. There was no reason, he would tell Tucker, why 'his people' should place trust in lawyers.[59] He was later to describe the law as 'one of those professions ... that tend to promote bourgeois tendencies'.[60]

Although Ramaphosa was never comfortable in these institutions, the Urban Foundation and EFK Tucker provided Ramaphosa with experiences and skills that he could not easily have acquired elsewhere.

At UF he developed a sophisticated understanding of project, financial and strategic management, as well as a grasp of the depth and character of the country's developmental challenges. The relationship between regional and national boards, and the use of externally commissioned expertise, were both to find echoes in the organisation of the National Union of Mineworkers in the 1980s.

At Tucker he experienced the power of the law in business, and developed a sense of the protection that the rule of law might conceivably provide to organised workers. In what was a dynamic and fast-changing environment for industrial relations and labour law, Cyril saw not just a legal minefield but also a world of opportunities for those who knew how to seize them. At the same time, in both institutions Cyril further expanded his now exceptionally wide range of contacts and relationships in business and politics, and developed a wider sense of the range and nature of opinion within South Africa's white elites.

Involvement with the Urban Foundation was later to become controversial, and some leftist intellectuals were hostile to the UF from the start.[61] Barney Pityana recalls criticising the UF for 'tinkering with reform' and helping the Boers to 'find handles from among us', incurring the wrath of Nthato Motlana in the process.[62] Even the Foundation's own 1979 research demonstrated that it was widely despised by young black activists and believed to be promoting influx control. Youth at Diepkloof Community Centre concluded that the Foundation's black staff needed to 'explain themselves'.[63]

Ramaphosa did not fear criticism and the fact that the UF was not fashionable would hardly have registered with him. But there were also differences of substance. What distinguished Cyril from his peers was that he was not a naïve anti-capitalist. Frank Chikane describes anti-Urban Foundation sentiment as part of a wider hostility towards capitalism in post-1976 Soweto. 'Even the corner shop was viewed as exploitative and so was viewed as a target.'[64] Yet Ramaphosa had grown up with a more positive conception of business – his father's businesses, Atorama Construction, and his relentless vacation work taught him to value entrepreneurial activity. Moreover, the Menells gave Ramaphosa a panoramic overview of the tensions between business and state. He knew that the economic liberals of Anglo American saw the National Party as an interventionist dinosaur.[65]

In retrospect, it is easy to see that the UF could never have brought about radical policy change. It was too conservative to threaten economic stability. Yet its underlying philosophy was too much at variance with the government's for the two to engage. As Saki Macozoma recently reflected, it was always under fire from two sides. Government was unwilling to cooperate even where they shared objectives. And the liberation movement felt that 'enfranchisement tended to be ignored by the Foundation in favour of improving socioeconomic conditions ... The sceptical even argued that this was deliberately done to quench the anger on which the struggle fed and to perpetuate the status quo.'[66]

In the end the struggle not to be 'co-opted' by apartheid institutions or by 'capital' was almost farcical. It is something that only SACP activists with large houses and substantial bank balances, Anglican clerics and trade union officials with elastic expense accounts have ever been able to sustain. Middle-class black professionals could not avoid the inherently compromising association with Bantustan, state and business institutions.

As Frank Chikane explains, both the apartheid state and capital were simply inescapable. One of his projects, the Kagiso self-help scheme, brought relief to the poor. However, it simply could not have functioned without a donation of machines from South African Breweries and money from Anglo American. Should these gifts have been rejected? When Soweto leaders wanting to erect a community meeting hall decided to reject the UF as a funder, they approached Anglo American instead. Yet Anglo told them that the Foundation was mostly sponsored by them anyhow, so they had better approach it after all! The community leaders had to satisfy themselves with a ludicrous compromise: the Urban Foundation supplied a tent but removed from it the UF logo.

The purity of exile disengagement was simply impossible for 'inziles'. Chikane observes that domestic activists knew all about this problem of inescapable compromise from their black consciousness days. 'BC could not have been about black self-isolation from whites,' he observes. 'At black consciousness conferences, whites would drop the participants off in their cars ... and they would often be paying their salaries too. Steve Biko had a lot of white friends. There was no possibility of a clear-cut or a tight separation between black and white. What mattered about black consciousness was that black people took the decisions, and that white people did not control their thinking.'[67]

Did white people control Cyril Ramaphosa's thinking? Fred Phaswana was a fellow member of the Transvaal board of the Urban Foundation. He was obliged to serve on the board by his employer, British Petroleum, very much against his wishes. He does not think that Cyril could have had any illusions about the nature of the Foundation. 'At the beginning, the Urban Foundation held some superficial promise,' he observes. 'Clive Menell and Jan Steyn were perfectly nice men. But they were just quite different to black people. At that time white people were quite unable to deal with race relations on anything like a basis of equality. White people were quite unable to understand or relate to the concerns of black people. In fact they still are.'[68]

Phaswana quickly realised that 'the Foundation had nothing to say to the real problem facing the country. White people sitting on such a board at that time were unable to visualise a time when whites were no longer running the country. This was a future they were simply unable to see.' How could Ramaphosa possibly have missed a fact as obvious to any black man as this?[69]

Cyril's white acquaintances were also left in no doubt about his position. His second legal employer, Bob Tucker, observes that Ramaphosa always spoke with his own constituency in mind – and for this reason his move into the trade union movement was very much a natural one. 'Cyril never had any ambition to move into corporate law … It was always very clear that he was going to take the skills he had acquired and use them to best effect to advance the interests of the black community.'[70]

Even Ramaphosa's relationship with the Menells was circumscribed by wider forces than mere friendship could overcome. The Menells' mining house, Anglovaal, was to remain an implacable opponent of the interests of black mineworkers in the 1980s. When Cyril visited the company offices on Main Street in the early 1980s, the doorman told him that blacks had to enter through a door at the rear of the building.[71]

As a thinker, Ramaphosa was a 'visionary pragmatist'[72] who would relentlessly seek incremental reform today but never at the cost of entrenching an unjust social order tomorrow. Fred Phaswana observes that his position was incompatible with the philosophy of the UF. 'Jan Steyn and Menell believed that the system was wrong. But, having said that, they believed if you allow the system to be destroyed then you would in effect destroy the country. Their first goal was therefore to preserve the system. The system has to be sustained and amended before one could even consider handing it over.'[73]

It is worth recalling Cyril's unguarded comment about politics to his previous employer, the small-time lawyer Henry Dolowitz: 'We won't live with this chain around our necks. I don't care if we have to wipe things out and start from the beginning and it takes a hundred years. We'll do it.'[74]

PART TWO
WORKING FOR
THE WORKERS

CHAPTER 7

THE EMERGENCE OF BLACK UNION POWER

You have to know a black. He wants someone to be his
boss. They can't think quickly. You can take a baboon and
learn him to play a tune on the piano, but it's impossible
for himself to use his own mind to go on to the next step.
                        – Arrie Paulus, general secretary
                        of the Mineworkers' Union[1]

While 1970s politics were dominated by June '76 and the ideology of black consciousness, the 1980s were to see the rise of a new scale and intensity of domestic opposition. At the heart of this new struggle was organised labour. In order to understand the rise of black trade unions, it is necessary to look beneath the everyday politics of appearances to deeper changes in the character of the South African economy.

The first major period of black trade union activism had been the economic boom between the mid-1930s and the end of the Second World War which brought black workers into the cities and factories. The power of black labour, however, was severely constrained by racial legislation that denied them recognition agreements and collective bargaining rights. In the 1950s, an ANC-aligned South African Confederation of Trade Unions (Sactu) emerged to fight simultaneously for higher wages and for political freedom.[2] Sactu unions, plagued by weak shop-floor organisation, were successfully repressed in the 1960s.

That decade also saw structural changes in the economy which would create the conditions for a more sustainable wave of union organisation.

South Africa grew at unprecedented rates, and the 1960s brought a concentration of capital, the emergence of new monopoly industries, and the rise of powerful new parastatals (or state-owned enterprises). These developments inevitably brought in their wake a growing black working class. This period also saw organisational innovation in the unions. Many activists focused on organisation itself as the key to successful unionisation, and they built resilient shop-floor structures of representation and mobilisation.[3] This new culture of accountability, in which union officials were not allowed to act without the mandate of their workers, bolstered the resilience of unions in the hard times ahead. They were far less vulnerable than their 1950s predecessors to intimidation and harassment, or to the co-opting or repression of a small number of union leaders.

When the post-war boom came to an abrupt end in the early 1970s – after massive oil-price increases by the Opec countries precipitated a global economic crisis – newly powerful black workers confronted businesses that were looking to cut employment and costs. The outcome was a dangerously volatile labour environment, exemplified by an unprecedented series of strikes in Durban in 1973.

In such circumstances, government and business alike began to consider controversial reforms to the country's outmoded labour relations machinery. Business was increasingly dependent on a stable and skilled black workforce. Until black unions were allowed recognition by employers, they would be unable to enter into formal and binding negotiations with bosses in an orderly manner. Industry after industry would continue to be dogged by unofficial or 'wildcat' strikes that were disruptive of production and costly for business.

Business leaders, moreover, saw black labour as a potential ally in the battle against white unions. A highly organised white working class had over decades used collective bargaining to cement its advantages over black co-workers. Organised whites had benefited historically from legislation that protected them against skill and wage competition from blacks. In the harsher business climate of the 1970s, companies lobbied government to dismantle job reservation mechanisms that excluded black workers. By recognising black labour and removing job reservation for whites, business could hope to see both a more orderly process of negotiation of working conditions and wages, and a sharp downward pressure on the wages of skilled white workers, who had been insulated against competition from their black peers.

For all these reasons, black union recognition was a necessity that government could postpone but not avoid. As in every other industrial society, government had to act to bring order and rationality to conflict-ridden relations between business and labour in what sociologists sometimes describe as 'the institutionalisation of class conflict'. Rather than allowing latent antagonisms between workers and bosses to break out into frenzied wildcat strikes, precipitating violence and worker resistance on the shop floor, a new labour regime was needed to create a more orderly and efficient process for resolving disputes.

Only once black workers were brought into such a coherent framework of industrial relations could the economy be protected against further unnecessary losses. The pay-off from a stable system of industrial relations would eventually make such a settlement worthwhile for almost all parties. Business would enjoy good relationships with a skilled, flexible and productive workforce. Black workers would secure higher wages and better working conditions. And the state would benefit from a buoyant economy and a stable society not racked by violence and disruption. The only losers would be organised white labour.

The mining industry exemplified the new challenges of labour relations. Even in the 1970s, a high degree of violence and disruption characterised the mines, with one strike at Western Deep Levels in 1973 resulting in 38 miners being shot, 12 of them fatally. By the late 1970s, disorganised worker discontent was reaching crisis proportions, and employers were becoming divided over how to respond. The Gold Producers' Committee (GPC) of the Chamber of Mines was finding it hard to reach consensus on appropriate wage increases for the industry: Anglo American and JCI were willing and able to pay higher wages than mining houses like Gold Fields, Gencor and Clive Menell's Anglovaal.

In 1982, Gold Fields and Gencor were to suffer two waves of damaging strikes, involving tens of thousands of workers, in the worst industrial unrest on the mines since the great strike of 1946.[4] The issue of unionisation was on everyone's mind, and it was no longer rejected out of hand. The reasons were both apparent and convincing. Workers had no channel for their many grievances. Resultant explosions of discontent were hard to predict and costly to clean up. Strikes had an amorphous and spontaneous character that frustrated mine managers. According to the historian Vic Allen, 'there was no evidence [in the 1982 unrest] of even the semblance of a strike organisation and no sign of any leaders'. Nevertheless, the workers themselves exhibited 'a high degree of solidarity in pursuit of a clear industrial objective'.[5]

It was Anglo American that took the initiative in creating a new system of industrial relations. Some Anglo executives already strongly supported modernisation of its labour relations. As technologies advanced, the company's mine workforce was becoming increasingly skilled and stable, and Anglo wanted to retain these skilled workers within the company. It wanted wage negotiations to proceed amicably and settlements to be implemented reliably without unexpected and costly industrial disputes. Some Anglo executives believed there was the prospect of a 'win-win' solution: a better-trained, well-motivated and cooperative workforce that negotiated with the employers – rather than fighting the bosses – would pay dividends for the company. (In the economic conditions of the time, of course – with falling gold and diamond prices – bargaining power would anyway remain overwhelmingly with the bosses.)[6]

Anglo American therefore felt confident in pursuing a strategy of engagement with and encouragement of worker organisation. Some mining houses on the other hand – notably Gencor and Gold Fields – did not favour union recognition, and preferred to continue with the old repressive approach. The confidence of Anglo American also flowed from careful planning behind its industrial relations vision. Though this strategy was later to become associated especially with one man, Bobby Godsell, it followed from a commitment on the part of Harry Oppenheimer to address the industrial relations crisis.

Anglo American was a dominant force in the industry. It was directly responsible for 40 per cent of all gold mining – and for perhaps 70 per cent if all Anglo-controlled and -administered companies are included.[7] Anglo was also responsible for more than 70 per cent of uranium mining, and through its sister company De Beers it was the leading player in the international diamond business. And so it was that 'Anglo', as this complex business entity was and still is commonly known in South Africa, would become the decisive actor in the unionisation of the mining industry.

Anglo American was established by Ernest Oppenheimer in 1917. Over the next fifty years, under Ernest, and then his son 'King of Diamonds' Harry Oppenheimer, Anglo was to establish an unprecedented dominance in the mining of gold, diamonds and platinum. By the mid-1980s, Anglo employed more than a quarter of a million people in gold mines, 25,000 in the diamonds industry, and perhaps 100,000 others in other mining sectors such as platinum and coal.[8]

Anglo introduced a vertical integration that slashed across the mining sector, taking over or controlling mine finance houses, manufacturers of explosives, steel product producers, the plantations on which mine pit props were grown, and even the chemicals and munitions industries that provided a market for the mines' outputs. In the involuted economy of apartheid South Africa, moreover, Anglo spread its control and influence horizontally across a range of other sectors: car sales (McCarthy), insurance (Eagle), department stores (Edgars), brewers (SAB), liquor stores (Solly Kramer), peanut butter (Yum Yum), viniculture (Vergelegen and Boschendal), sugar (Huletts) and mushrooms (Denny's). All fell effectively within the Anglo stable.[9] In sectors where Anglo became dominant – such as in paper where Anglo's Mondi became a near-monopoly – the company integrated production vertically, controlling the whole sectoral product cycle from forestry plantations at one end to publishers and newspapers at the other.

By the mid-1980s, Anglo had 1,350 subsidiaries and associated companies with a variety of relationships to the parent.[10] It employed 140,000 workers in the food, beverage and retail industries and around 50,000 others in assorted enterprises within South Africa. Overseas the Anglo empire extended as far away as the Americas and employed perhaps 30,000 people outside South Africa.[11]

The consequence of the emergence of this giant was an economy with a curious structure. The broader Anglo empire was responsible for as much as a quarter of South Africa's economic activity. It was therefore of almost equal economic stature to the state itself – to the sum of government departments, provincial administrations, state arms manufacturers, railways, the iron and steel industry, chemicals giant Sasol, the post office, and the energy parastatal Eskom.

Beyond these two great behemoths of state and Anglo, there were just three other substantial business groupings, each connected to a financial house – Old Mutual, Liberty Life and the heartland of Afrikaner finance, Sanlam – but none of these relative minnows came close to the economic power and scope of Anglo.[12]

At the heart of the Anglo empire were two technically separate companies, Anglo American Corporation (AAC) and De Beers, together with a third family investment vehicle called E Oppenheimer & Son. While formally distinct enterprises, AAC and De Beers fell under the effective control of E Oppenheimer & Son as a result of a system that combined cross-ownership with cross-directorships. In the mid-1980s, the giant AAC owned almost 40 per cent of publicly tradable shares in De Beers, giving it effective control over the diamond trader. De Beers, for its part, owned almost 35 per cent of AAC, and Oppenheimer & Son owned another 8 per cent. Together, De Beers and Oppenheimer could therefore be confident of control of Anglo. So long as the boards of the two companies supported the Oppenheimer family's dominance, it was the family's own vehicle – Oppenheimer & Son – that in effect controlled the entire empire.[13]

A pattern of cross-directorships between De Beers and AAC sustained this system of family control. The chairman of AAC after 1982 was Gavin Relly, an Anglo 'lifer' and former personal assistant to Harry Oppenheimer. The chairman of De Beers was Julian Ogilvie Thompson, who had likewise once been Oppenheimer's PA. Relly was also a director of De Beers, and Ogilvie Thompson was also a director of AAC – indeed the latter would succeed Relly as AAC chairman in 1990. Both men were on the board of Oppenheimer & Son. This pattern of cross-directorships was repeated across the boards' memberships. Nicky Oppenheimer, Harry's son, was deputy chair of both AAC and De Beers, and a director of Oppenheimer. HR ('Hank') Slack, third husband of Harry's daughter Mary, sat on all three boards, as did GC Fletcher and Harry's English cousin Sir Philip Oppenheimer.[14]

In 1982, an ageing Harry Oppenheimer retired as AAC chairman, and in 1984 he also left De Beers. Though he continued to follow the empire's key strategic decisions, he could no longer control the actions of the board. Nor, given his various limitations, could his son Nicky hope to do so. Indeed, the Anglo empire was now so large that it would have been foolish to attempt to replicate the personal power of the two great Oppenheimers. Instead Harry put in place a system of quasi 'family control', stabilised through the system of cross-directorships. 'Family' was understood in a broad sense to include Hank Slack, cousin Philip, and the cream of the Anglo 'lifers' – people like Relly and Ogilvie Thompson, who were 'as good as family'.[15] At a lower lever in the pantheon of Anglo management, the Oppenheimers also enjoyed the loyalty of lifers such as EP Gush, a mine engineer who rose through the ranks to become head of AAC's gold and uranium division and later the managing director of De Beers. Peter Gush would be one of Cyril Ramaphosa's key adversaries in its conflicts on the mines.

Anglo was not just an economic giant. It was also a major political presence, although not one offering any very clear sense of moral purpose or coherent national direction. What purportedly united the occupants of 44 Main Street, where Anglo's corporate offices were located, was a belief that social modernisation and economic development went hand in hand. A thriving market economy, on this view, would break down the racial divisiveness of apartheid, create a black middle class, establish permanently settled urban black labour, and destroy restrictive practices such as the colour bar. The modernisation of industrial relations was just one example of the supposedly benevolent historical power of a developing market economy.

A distinctive political culture evolved within Anglo's Johannesburg offices. The Main Street 'lifers' were white men who imbibed the tacit knowledge of what is and what is not good practice – in business and politics – from the everyday deliberations around them. This entire culture was implacably antagonistic to the ruling philosophy of the National Party (NP) while remaining ambivalent about the character or reality of the exploitation of black South Africans. The NP, viewed through Anglo lenses, was committed to something close to national socialist economics, and suspicious of a private economy dominated by 'English' capital.

The natural economic home of the Afrikaner-dominated NP was indeed the state and the giant state-owned parastatals. It used these instruments to soak up the Afrikaner unemployed and ultimately to propel them into the middle-class life that their English-speaking peers had long enjoyed. The NP's economic philosophy was curiously close to that of the ANC, with both favouring public ownership of the commanding heights of the economy, widespread state interventionism, and exercises in grand social engineering.[16]

The primary focus of Anglo political engagement was to support the 'free enterprise system' against its detractors among Afrikaner ideologues. Of course, the market economy in which Anglo actually operated more closely resembled a system of privately owned cartels and consumer-exploitative monopoly producers than the free market utopias beloved of classical economists. What the Anglo establishment feared above all was the nationalisation and social engineering that the NP often seemed on the verge of unleashing. In 1963, Oppenheimer became sufficiently fearful of the intentions of Prime Minister Verwoerd that he allowed Federale Mynbou – a part of the Afrikaner Sanlam group – to buy General Mining and Finance Group (later Gencor) in order to stave off a perceived threat of nationalisation.[17] Through this action he also achieved an important symbolic advance in the Afrikaner economic empowerment that he was keen to foster.

The NP establishment, moreover, was culturally quite alien to the Anglo elite. Harry Oppenheimer received a classical English education (rugger plus long division) at Charterhouse and Christ Church, Oxford, and Nicky followed a similar path from Harrow to 'the House'.[18] Although most wealthy English speakers went to local equivalents of English public schools, and took their first degrees at the white universities of Rhodes, Natal, Cape Town or Witwatersrand, Anglo high-flyers were more often than not Oxford men.[19] Taking advantage of the Rhodes Scholarships established by mining giant Cecil Rhodes, Anglo's best and brightest became associated with rowing and rugby 'blues', and came home with second-class degrees – or occasionally mediocre first-class degrees – from Oxford's intellectually less demanding degree schools, such as Geography, or Philosophy, Politics and Economics ('PPE').[20]

Intellectually and culturally, the National Party that governed without break or serious opposition after 1948 was formed through the Afrikaans-medium school system, and in universities such as Stellenbosch, Pretoria and Potchefstroom that offered their own distinctive version of elite education. The analysis of 'power elites' in other societies has often stressed the shared intuitions and backgrounds of leaders in different parts of a society. C Wright Mills famously argued of 1950s America that its three seemingly antagonistic military, business and political elites were in fact brought together by commonalities of background, education and culture.[21] In contemporary France, likewise, it is purportedly the networks and commonalities of understanding generated within the elite educational institutions that create a unity among diverse elites. And in Britain, it is the 'public', i.e. private, schools and old universities that generate shared perspectives and values.[22]

If such networks do in reality exist and bring benefit to their members, South Africa's whites were perhaps disadvantaged by their absence. The networks that one would commonly expect to find between business people and their peers in government, the military and politics were fragile and thin. Afrikaner and English elites did not attend the same schools and clubs, gather at the same social functions, worship in the same churches, or holiday in the same resorts.

The Oppenheimers were powerful and rich enough to project their political fancies and fantasies on to the world. Harry Oppenheimer committed substantial resources to the Progressive Party, formed in 1959, whose members became known as 'Progs'. The party was initially dominated by Cape liberals and professionals, but soon it garnered a curious constituency in the wealthy northern suburbs of Johannesburg under the guidance of quasi-liberal opinion-formers such as Irene Menell and Helen Suzman. It went on to develop a robust form of parliamentary opposition to certain apartheid doctrines. The party's members could not, however, conceive of the abolition of separation between racial groups. The notion of one person one vote in a unitary state remained an abstract and distant fantasy.

Anglo was also a driving force behind the South Africa Foundation (SAF), created at the end of 1959 to shape foreigners' perceptions of South Africa as an investment destination and place to do business. Here Anglo showed its willingness to work hand in hand with Afrikaner capital where common interests were at stake. The Oppenheimers, as we have seen, were also behind the Urban Foundation, an organisation dedicated to lobbying and advocacy as well as to developmental interventions, and ostensibly somewhat to the left of the SAF. In later years, Anglo was to complete its do-gooder portfolio with a vaguely leftist Consultative Business Movement, and thereby cover almost the entire ideological and intellectual spectrum.

At the highest levels, the estrangement between Anglo and the National Party continued. It was manifested in the limited interaction between the most powerful businessmen and politicians in the land. Harry Oppenheimer was chair of the South African Institute of International Relations (SAIIA), which the Oppenheimers (inevitably) had founded in 1934. In this capacity, he invited legendary US politician Henry Kissinger to attend a conference in Johannesburg in the early 1980s. He also invited President PW Botha to deliver a speech. When the three men had a private discussion afterwards, Oppenheimer's aides remarked that this was the first time that Harry Oppenheimer had met a South African head of government just to sit down and talk.[23]

Anglo's social philosophy detailing the benevolent relationship between capitalism and social development was, of course, vulnerable to criticism or even ridicule. The Oppenheimers sometimes presented their companies as enemies of apartheid. Ernest and Harry each served as opposition members of parliament protesting against the evils of segregation. At the same time, Anglo was at heart a mining house, whose profits were built out of the exploitation of migrant workers from across the southern African subcontinent. In reality, Anglo mines were just as cruel in their operation as those of supposedly less salubrious mining houses, serving up the same fare of tuberculosis, crippling injury and racist brutality.

The Oppenheimers and their senior managers therefore remained open to charges of bad faith and hypocrisy. Nelson Mandela captured the bitterness that Anglo's seeming hypocrisy provoked very well in this 1953 comment: 'Rather than attempt the costly, dubious and dangerous task of crushing the non-European mass movement by force, [the Oppenheimers] would seek to divert it with fine words and promises and divide it by giving concessions and bribes to a privileged minority.'[24]

Main Street's intellectual elite has, however, proved impervious to insult and ridicule, perhaps because its membership is so selective and its self-confidence based on decades of business success. While it would be a mistake to accept Anglo at its own moral self-estimation, it would be equally wrong to underestimate the corporate office's sheer intellectual verve and muscle. Even before the 1976 uprising sent shock waves down Main Street, Anglo turned its institutional mind energetically to the causes and significance of the 1973 wave of strikes, and to the increasing militancy on the mines that they threatened to prefigure.

Oppenheimer himself began to focus attention on the reform of industrial relations, and on the wider but related project of 'modernising' the economy. Anglo and its associated companies needed permanent and skilled workers, the replacement of at least some hostels with family houses, and the removal of colour bars which drove up the price of skilled labour. Modernised industrial relations, it was quickly hypothesised, might curtail wildcat strikes, improve workforce productivity, and protect the mines against any upsurge in labour unrest.

These were complex and untested suppositions, but Anglo always recruited the best and the brightest from the white English-language universities to take forward its ever-changing project. Few 1970s executives at 44 Main Street in Johannesburg were ever going to become political liberals in the contemporary European sense. Fewer still could conceive that black South Africans would be running their country, through an ANC government, well within their lifetimes. All the same, in the aftermath of the 1973 strike wave, Anglo recruited some young executives with exceptional political skills and vision.

Three recruits, in particular, were to make a big mark on the political side of the company. First, liberal activist Alex Boraine was hired in 1973 as a labour consultant, to think in fresh ways about industrial relations challenges, and how to avert impending international investment codes and economic sanctions.[25] Second, Anglo recruited Zach de Beer, a career politician from the Progressive Party who identified weaknesses in the political profile of the company, and brought greater political sensitivity to its actions. He was soon to gravitate into the inner circle around Oppenheimer.

A third figure who joined the company in January 1974 was to have the longest-lasting effect on Anglo's industrial relations culture. The 21-

year-old Bobby Godsell did not have a conventional Anglo background, coming from a working-class family and having studied philosophy at the University of Natal. He had also completed an ambitious master's dissertation on liberal ethics at the University of Cape Town.[26] Among his roles at Anglo was to consider how the corporation should respond to growing calls for the recognition of black unions.

Godsell and Boraine conducted a comparative study of labour organisation – primarily in developed countries rather than in genuinely comparable cases – and produced an 'Orange Book' that concluded that black union recognition was now a necessity.[27] Although he was to remain hesitant about wider political reforms, Harry Oppenheimer was already disposed towards industrial relations 'modernisation' and he received the report favourably.

By 1975, in a speech to the Institute of Public Management, Oppenheimer had committed himself publicly to black labour organisation on grounds that Godsell considers are self-evident today. 'You took them away from the whites or you extended them to the blacks; because it was completely illogical to say unions were good for white workers but not good for black workers.'[28] Godsell and his boss Christiaan du Toit lobbied compellingly for the creation of a commission of inquiry into labour relations, something the department of labour established in 1977 as the 'Wiehahn Commission' after its chair, Professor Nic Wiehahn.

This was a time of grand commissions. Also reporting for the first time in 1979, the Riekert Commission was established to explore responses to the country's manpower planning crisis. Riekert argued that a permanent black presence in the white cities had to be accepted, but nevertheless he reaffirmed a case for influx control. With a clear distinction between permanent and temporary residents, those qualified for residence could be given workplace rights and limited political representation (for example in township government), and job reservation for whites could be scrapped.

The Wiehahn Commission offered a more forward-thinking and cogent analysis. Wiehahn was a lawyer and labour relations expert and a key adviser to labour minister Fanie Botha. In 1977, in the aftermath of intrusive US interventions in the behaviour of its South African-based multinationals, he persuaded the minister that the entire system required overhaul.

As it happened, Godsell's boss Du Toit was a member of the commission and ensured that Anglo's analysis found its way into the final reports. Wiehahn rejected the longer-term viability of racial labour regulation, and recommended biting the bullet of legal registration of black trade unions. He was to go on to make specific recommendations about the mining industry in the commission's sixth report in 1981. These recommendations forced the hand of the mine owners, and created the prospect of systematic and large-scale organisation of black mineworkers.

Legislation rapidly followed which transformed the labour relations terrain. A 'representative' National Manpower Commission was established, and a new Labour Relations Act passed that made possible the recognition of black trade unions. It seemed that the disorderly world of unofficial strikes was soon to be replaced by an orderly process of bargaining and negotiation, characterised by compliant trade unions and obedient labour bosses.

Sadly for Anglo, this outcome was not to be. Oppenheimer suspected that if Anglo unionised first, its unions might become surrogate political parties given the absence of representative democracy.[29] Godsell confesses that they 'did not fully anticipate the intensity of the clash that would result' from politics being channelled through unions. 'There was a degree of naiveté in my thinking and that of my colleagues.'[30]

While Anglo sought forlornly to depoliticise the 'modernisation' of industrial relations, black consciousness activists were simultaneously turning to unions precisely as agents of political mobilisation. Cyril Ramaphosa once claimed that detention had opened his eyes to the limitations of black consciousness and encouraged him to consider the merits of armed struggle. He was now, however, turning to the more promising alternative of trade union action. In this, he was far from alone. A whole generation of educated activists, frustrated by the lack of a black consciousness political strategy, was working its way towards the black union movement. Even within Saso and the Black People's Convention themselves, debate was turning to class analysis and to the analytic power of the classic Marxist texts.[31]

Harassment and bannings from 1977 had undercut the claims of student activists that they could act as the 'vanguard' of the struggle. For those educated in Durban, the early 1970s labour unrest focused minds on organised workers, who seemed to be potential agents of political unrest. Intellectuals like Jay Naidoo, who had been nurtured in the black consciousness philosophy, decided that the priority was to organise the workers. In 1979, he volunteered to work for the recently established Federation of South African Trade Unions (Fosatu), an umbrella organisation for unions that were concerned primarily with shop-floor issues.

Naidoo was guided by a formidable mentor called Pravin Gordhan[32] – known to the Indian political elite that passed through the University of Durban-Westville as 'the Guru'. Gordhan told Naidoo to conceal his political ideology, and adopt Fosatu's philosophy of shop-floor organisation. At that time, Fosatu was known as a 'workerist' federation, one in which the organisation of workers at shop-floor level was given priority over the attempt to deploy organised workers in political protests. This was 'collective bargaining' unionism, in which the focus was on issues in the workplace, and wider political engagement was left to other organisations.

Such unionism was contrasted with political or social movement unionism, which sought alliances with outside social forces in civil society or to advance the project of the exile liberation movement. Such social movement unions tried to link workplace issues with wider anti-state protest.

This contrast between two kinds of union was in fact exaggerated. The wider social order of apartheid impinged on the workplace, and shop-floor issues could never be addressed in isolation from wider political change. Fosatu's view that sound shop-floor organisation was a necessary foundation for wider political engagement was in fact cogent, and many large unions managed to steer a path between 'workerism' and what was labelled by its critics as 'populism'. Nevertheless, these differences and the complex philosophies that lay behind them made the process of building unity between workers' organisations extremely hard.

Ishmael Mkhabela, Cyril's long-time friend from Tshiawelo and Turfloop, remembers discussing the prospects of the union movement with Cyril in 1978. The two men met on Commissioner Street in downtown Johannesburg, next to the Urban Foundation offices where Hope Ramaphosa was then working. Ishmael observed to Cyril that they knew too little about the unions, and that it was unfortunate how few black university graduates were involved in union activity. Cyril agreed – 'Yes, somehow we all avoid that' – and observed that the unions are 'where our people are'.[33]

Ishmael was later to approach Phiroshaw Camay, the general secretary of the Council of Unions of South Africa (Cusa), to ask if he might work as an organiser. Camay simply laughed. Ishmael was annoyed at the time, and his annoyance grew still more intense two years later when Camay recruited Ramaphosa into the union federation.

Ramaphosa's interest in union organisation was therefore part of a wider rethinking of the limitations of black consciousness and a search for new instruments for political opposition to the apartheid regime. This broader change of perspective was catalysed by his personal experiences into a decision to commit himself to union work. The key, he recalled in a January 1995 interview, was 'a deep concern about the plight of mineworkers'.[34] As a young man he had often seen mineworkers herded together on the platforms at Johannesburg railway station as they travelled between the mines and their distant rural homes. After Ramaphosa had been arrested for a pass offence in Tshiawelo when he was 17 or 18, the sight of the mineworkers being 'herded like cattle' always brought back his anger at the way he himself had been treated. These workers, he came to realise, were never free of their chains.

Ramaphosa's interest in trade union power even began to extend to popular culture. One of his favourite movie performances was Sylvester Stallone's portrayal of a union boss in the 1978 film *Fist*.[35] The Norman Jewison-directed film traces the rise to power of 'Johnny Kovak' – played by Stallone – who rises to the head of the Federation of Inter-State Truckers (Fist). The film is evidently based on the career of the legendary Teamsters union boss, Jimmy Hoffa, whose organisation ultimately turned into an instrument of despotic personal power. Hoffa was surrounded by rumours of Mafia relationships, convicted in 1967 of fraud and corruption, and ultimately vanished without trace in 1975.

Fist traces the role of this hero with a dark side, exploring how he organised ordinary workers, learnt the dark arts of mass persuasion, and ultimately used the power of organised labour in industrial action. The film also addresses with some sensitivity the human cost of industrial action: one scene dwells on the death of colleagues in strikes that Kovak has himself ordered. Towards its end, the movie reflects on the more broadly corrupt nature of the relationship between bosses and union leaders. It is the system that is sick and not merely the bosses, and the corruption of that relationship reaches down through the union itself.

It is not clear whether the subtleties of Jewison's direction were primary factors in capturing Ramaphosa's imagination. According to Cyril himself, what interested him most was 'the negotiations process they were involved in – when Sylvester Stallone was leading the negotiating team on the Union side and they were pushing for a five and a half [per cent] wage increase and they offered them five – and for that half a margin they decided to go on strike. And he stands up, and he says to the bosses, do you know what a strike can do to you, we are going to squash you. And he stands up dramatically and he walks out. The following day everybody is on strike. That was the drama that really attracted me.'[36]

The film was unusual for the Hollywood of its time in exploring the moral ambiguities facing the key role-players. It dwells on the symmetry of instrumental violence between bosses and union members, a matter that was to become a central preoccupation in Ramaphosa's later union and ANC careers. In Jewison's portrayal of industrial conflict, the workers start out fighting the evil of 'Consolidated Trucking', but it is in the nature of their struggle that the union comes to resemble its enemy.

Cyril took a clear decision to work in the trade union sector, and upon his departure from EFK Tucker he combined legal study with the completion of a brief diploma in industrial relations, taken at Damelin College. The twin facts that he found himself in a so-called 'black consciousness' union federation and that he became involved in organising mineworkers were each partly fortuitous.

In 1981 Cyril applied for a job with the Furniture and Allied Workers' Union, an affiliate of the controversial white Tucsa federation.

A majority of Tucsa members repeatedly affirmed that the federation should act only on behalf of white worker unions – or on behalf of black workers only when this would also be to the benefit of whites. It had an NGO offshoot, the Urban Training Project (UTP), designed to increase awareness among African unionists about industrial relations law, and to build management systems and infrastructure – a kind of service organisation for nascent black unions funded primarily by external donors. Unions supported by Tucsa and UTP worked largely within the widely despised system of industrial relations based on 'works committees'.

Fortunately, perhaps, there was either no job available for Cyril at UTP or he decided he did not like the look of the organisation on interview. In the close-knit world of union politics his application was passed on to Phiroshaw Camay, the general secretary of Cusa. Camay immediately recognised the potential of Ramaphosa. In particular, his work at EFK Tucker, dealing with complex legal issues around land tenure, made him unusually experienced for a black lawyer at that time.[37] Camay put Cyril to work in Cusa's small legal resources centre, little realising how quickly the new recruit was going to transform the labour federation.

CHAPTER 8

NUM: SMALL BEGINNINGS

Why is it that we rip gold from the stubborn womb of mother earth, several miles underground, but cannot afford a gold ring on our wives' fingers?

– Tshenuwani Farisani[1]

Ramaphosa began work as legal adviser at the Council of Unions of South Africa (Cusa) at the beginning of 1982. At the time unions were in upheaval as a result of a raft of post-Wiehahn legislation that was transforming the legal and political character of industrial relations. Like other union federations at the time, Cusa had a 'talking relationship'[2] with business, and particularly with progressive managers like Bobby Godsell, who had become Anglo American's head of industrial relations in the late 1970s. High-level deliberation between labour and progressive business was a natural consequence of a shared desire to 'normalise' industrial relations – a process whose conclusion, however, the two parties understood in very different terms.

Cusa was often wrongly characterised as a black consciousness organisation. It was in fact a loose federation of unions lacking any common ideology or programme. Cusa leaders included supporters of the ANC – for example Amos Masondo, who was to go on to become mayor of Johannesburg – and a number of Pan Africanist Congress (PAC) activists. Cusa's supposed 'black consciousness' orientation simply reflected its membership: young and black urbanised workers, few of whom were ANC or PAC cadres but almost all of whom subscribed to the central tenets of black consciousness. A BC orientation was, however, reflected in Cusa's distinctive attitude to whites in leadership roles. Unlike its key competitor, the Federation of South African Trade Unions (Fosatu), Cusa reserved leadership positions for black activists.

Wiehahn created an environment in which black unions could grow very fast. In looking for new opportunities to organise, Cusa did not want to create too much conflict with competitors like Fosatu. The two federations paid lip service to the principle 'one sector, one union', and they had already clashed because of an overlap in the metalworking trades. All the same, Camay identified the mines as an area into which Cusa must move, especially after Wiehahn's 1981 recommendation that recognition agreements should be reached on the mines and an orderly industrial relations process set in motion there.

Mineworkers, after all, were the most exploited workers in the South African economy. They were incarcerated in single-sex hostels, suffered high rates of illness, and were separated from their families for many months at a time.[3] Underground work was arduous and dangerous, and miners suffered from unprecedented incidences of death and disability. Physical violence and racial abuse were everywhere, down the shafts and in the compounds.[4] What is more, there were in excess of 750,000 workers on the mines, a potential membership that every union federation was desperate to tap.

Yet, at the same time, nobody was sure how to go about organising mineworkers. Around half of the workers were migrant labourers from neighbouring countries, divided by language from one another, and subdued by their fear of deportation. The rest of the workforce comprised poor South Africans desperate to earn the wages that might make rural or Bantustan life more tolerable. Deliberate ethnic compartmentalisation of the workforce, using segregated hostels and *de facto* ethnic job reservation, made union organising even harder. Miners lacked even a shared language, communicating instead in Fanagalo, a grammar-free combination of Zulu, Afrikaans, Sesotho and Shangaan nouns and verbs.

In addition, the mines presented a challenge of physical access. The compounds were massive and self-contained encampments, cut off from surrounding communities by razor-wire fences, and quasi-militaristic in their organisation. Worker hostels were organised like military barracks, they could easily be made impenetrable to union organisers, and mine managers had conventionally refused outsiders access to them.

Workers had also been routinely denied permission to gather for union meetings.

Despite the post-Wiehahn ethos of modernisation projected by the progressive mining houses, the mine managers remained an untamed force, beyond the control of their own head offices. Even though he had the personal backing of Harry Oppenheimer, Bobby Godsell spent many years as a virtual pariah even in Anglo's corporate offices in Main Street, before he was able to 'mainstream' modern industrial relations practices and resentment of his demands gradually faded. Yet it was a quite different proposition to bring about change at the level of the mines themselves.[5]

English-speaking Main Street executives were often recruited directly from university and spent their besuited lives in offices and boardrooms. The mines themselves, however, were run by managers who had worked their way up through local management hierarchies. They were usually locals and almost all Afrikaners. They viewed Anglo's regional managers as 'wankers' and the company's Johannesburg executives as 'super-wankers'.[6] When Bobby Godsell tried to sell the benefits of unionisation to Anglo mine managers in the Orange Free State in 1982, a colleague recalls, he was jeered and barracked by every mine manager present.[7]

The then gold division executive Michael Spicer remembers finding on visiting an Anglo mine during the late 1980s that the managers were building brand-new hostels on precisely the pattern 45 Main Street had condemned almost a decade earlier. Outwardly deferring to their Johannesburg superiors, mine managers kept duplicate financial records that allowed them to create slush funds. 'They would pretend to show us the books and we would pretend to look at them,' comments Spicer. 'There was always enough money somehow for country club memberships ... for swimming pools and helicopters for the mine manager.'[8]

The mine managers were preoccupied with the challenge of 'getting the gold out of the ground',[9] and their disdain for their seniors was in some respects understandable. Extracting gold, uranium and coal demanded a bewildering range of engineering, managerial and human skills. The complexity of deep-level mining is brought out well in this 1920s description of the five-kilometre-long Crown Mines. 'Envisage a line of buildings from here to Hyde Park Corner [5 km away], not 80 or 100 feet high but, say, 2,000 feet high. The stopes in the mine may be looked upon as rooms in a house. Work of course is not going on in all the rooms at the same time but in most of the big mines ore is being extracted from various rooms at all sorts of floor levels over the lateral distance [of three and a half miles] from here to Hyde Park Corner. If we take the position we are standing in this room as the central level above and below which work is proceeding we should have to look 1,000 feet below our feet and 1,000 feet above our heads over a distance of three miles in length, with thousands of men distributed all over the area. Imagine the organisation involved in lowering, in raising and in distributing them to their various stations and in conveying the ore from these scattered points of attack to given central points for elevation to the surface!'[10]

Accessing the gold-bearing ore required high-level planning and technical skills. Immensely deep vertical shafts were sunk in some mines more than three kilometres into the earth. From these shafts horizontal tunnels were driven outwards so as to intersect with the thin slanting seams of gold-bearing rock from below. The Chamber of Mines described the challenges this raised as follows: 'Imagine a solid mass of rock tilted ... like a fat, 1,200-page dictionary lying at an angle. The gold-bearing reef would be thinner than a single page, and the amounts of gold contained therein would hardly cover a couple of commas in the entire book. It is the miner's job to bring out that single page – but his job is made harder because the "page" has been twisted and torn by nature's forces, and pieces of it may have been thrust between other leaves of the book.'[11]

The low quality of South African ore meant that many tons of rock ore had to be brought to the surface to extract just a few ounces of gold. The ore had to be blasted out of the earth using explosives pushed into hand- or jackhammer-drilled holes, hauled along horizontal tunnels, and then lifted up vertical shafts. In these frankly terrifying conditions mineworker management was a heady mix of coercion, racial violence and incentives.

Confronting vast technological and geological challenges, and the need to drive down the costs of extracting ore to maintain viability, mine managers had absolutely no wish to hear from the 'super-wankers' of Main Street that their 'worker relations' were in need of an overhaul. The capacity of Godsell and his like to enforce their will on local managers who felt this way was consequently limited. Anglo might sign access or recognition agreements, but local mine managers could almost always ignore or distort them.

Despite the obvious difficulties the mines presented to union organisers, the prize of hundreds of thousands of workers in a classically exploitative industry was too great to resist. Mineworkers themselves were informally pleading for unions to make themselves available.

The ANC-aligned South African Workers and Allied Workers' Union (Saawu) had been the first major union to respond to these demands in the late 1970s. Led by Sydney Mufamadi and the late Thozamile Gwetha, Saawu tried to recruit in a clandestine manner inside the hostels. Its failure to make headway was almost absolute.

Fosatu was also quicker off the mark than Cusa in its attempt to organise the industry, launching a miners' union in 1981, a full year in advance of Cusa.[12] Fosatu had delegated this challenge to an able and charismatic organiser, Moses 'Moss' Mayekiso of the Metal and Allied Workers' Union (Mawu), and created a metal and mineworkers' union as the vehicle for its efforts. Mawu had its own philosophy of labour organisation, believing that clandestine organisation should proceed relentlessly and systematically at all levels, until a critical mass of members had been assembled. At this point, the union would launch a 'recognition strike', which would combine a wage claim with a demand that the union be recognised by the employers.[13] This is the approach Mayekiso decided to apply to the mines.

Funds for Fosatu's initiative were sourced from Scandinavian trade unions, and the new union secured legal representation through Halton Cheadle, a regular Fosatu adviser.[14] Despite Mayekiso's talents and the organisational muscle of his union federation, the approach very quickly ran into insuperable obstacles. Physically impenetrable hostels proved resistant to this organising strategy. The control of mineworkers' movements and the intelligence gathered by traditional mine organisers allowed hostile mine managers to curtail the growth of new union members. Attempts to recruit mineworkers at home, or on the buses that took them there, also failed. It proved impossible to build up a critical mass of members in any of the substantial mines.[15]

Cusa's head, Phiroshaw Camay, was not deterred by his floundering rivals' inability to make headway. As strikes broke out across the industry in 1982, the need for organisation remained obvious. Camay used the unrest to justify Cusa's move into direct competition with Fosatu. At Kloof, a Gold Fields mine, 9,000 miners went on strike out of dissatisfaction with a proposed pay rise. On 4 July, they refused to go underground. The mine management responded by threatening to dismiss the entire workforce. The dispute escalated into a pitched battle, with police and mine security using heavy-handed violence to crush worker protests. The informal leaders of the protest were eventually arrested and 2,000 of the workers were ultimately dismissed.[16]

It so happened that Cusa's national conference was scheduled for 14 July. This made it possible for a group of the Kloof strikers to appeal directly to the Cusa conference floor, and to make an impassioned plea for the help of the federation in forming a new trade union.[17] This approach could scarcely have been the spontaneous initiative Camay made it out to be. Neither was it mineworkers' first such appeal to Cusa. As Ramaphosa remembered in 1984, Cusa unions had been twice approached by mineworkers looking for representation, at the end of 1981 and the start of 1982, but the federation 'did not have the know-how to cater for them'. While Cusa enrolled some of them, they soon realised 'they were just not geared up for this type of industry. So the whole thing started being discussed in Cusa and … the unions within Cusa committed themselves to assist with the organisation of a mine workers' union.'[18]

In a wave of emotion, Cusa delegates resolved unanimously to respond to the Kloof workers' request. But Cusa's decision faced numerous practical obstacles, the first of which was financial. International trade unions played a key and largely unacknowledged role in fostering and financing South Africa's black trade unions. Despite having a mandate from his conference, Camay's initial approaches to Scandinavian unions for finance were turned down – primarily because they had already sunk substantial resources into Fosatu's initiative.[19] Camay could only muster R28,000, a large chunk of Cusa's modest overall budget of R150,000, to launch the union. Fortunately Cusa was later able to secure $250,000 from the Industrial Workers' Union (FNV) of the Netherlands.

A second obstacle was political. Fosatu's leadership was extremely upset that its own initiative was in danger of being undercut by Cusa. Fosatu leaders were able to assemble an alliance with the ANC-aligned

Sactu federation on this issue, and together they tried to persuade the liberation movement to condemn Cusa's plan. Camay met with the ANC in London in 1982 and held a frosty and unproductive discussion. In the end, however, the ANC decided not to support Fosatu's demand that Cusa's initiative should be torpedoed, probably out of respect for the ANC's wider strategic goal of building a unified trade union movement that could one day become a thorn in the side of the regime.[20] The field was now clear for Cusa. The question then became, Could Cusa succeed where others had failed, and organise the turbulent workforces on the mines?

Ramaphosa had impressed his colleagues in his short time as a legal adviser. When Cusa took its decision to launch a union, Phiroshaw Camay had no doubt whom to hand this problem over to. It was not a job that Cyril sought out: he was chosen by the Cusa executive as the person most likely to get the job done.[21] The task facing the 29-year-old was daunting.

Although he was acquainted with various mining-house bosses from the late 1970s and through Cusa's talking relationship with business, Ramaphosa knew absolutely nothing about mining. So unfamiliar was he with the industry that his first action on learning of his appointment was to visit a mine compound (where he bribed his way in) to see what a mine looked like. Next he went to the Public Library in Johannesburg to read about the representative body of the mine employers, the Chamber of Mines, and get an idea of the nature of the industry and its organisation.[22] Cyril then went for a round of meetings at the mining houses, including Clive Menell's Anglovaal, where he was told that a black man could only enter at the rear of the building.[23]

Most importantly, he entered into discussions with Anglo's industrial relations head, Bobby Godsell, who was on a personal crusade to modernise the giant's industrial relations.[24] Ramaphosa identified a window of opportunity. He presented himself as a person of reason and moderation, who recognised that worker organisation could benefit both bosses and union members. He expressed an interest in recruiting team leaders – the most skilled black mineworkers who were excluded on racial grounds from holding 'blasting certificates' – and in this way seemed to promise to ease Anglo's perennial problem of white wage inflation.

Anglo was more than happy to see a competitor emerging to the white mineworkers' unions, and much keener to recognise an elite union than the mass organisational monster they believed Moss Mayekiso was openly trying to create.[25] Godsell was inclined to make life easy for NUM, readily conceding access to Anglo mines and later agreeing to recognise the union even when its very small membership did not really justify this action. Cyril had managed to get the union's foot in the door. Anglo would never get it out again.

Anglo required that access should first be granted by the Chamber of Mines before the company would allow union organisation to take place on its mines. Ramaphosa went initially to talk to the industrial relations head of the Chamber of Mines, Johann Liebenberg, who was to sit across the table from Cyril in the negotiating chamber for almost a decade. Liebenberg had been at the Chamber since 1975, and had become chief industrial relations adviser in 1976. He was therefore a coordinator of the mining industry's contributions to the Wiehahn and Riekert reforms, and a key manager of industry players' responses to the wave of legislation and union organisation that followed.[26]

Liebenberg was a pragmatist and a 'fixer', qualities that were sometimes confused with profound cynicism.[27] A chief negotiator's first challenge was always to hammer out an agreement on his own side. He needed to build consensus between a wide variety of fractious constituencies – mining houses with distinct interests, cost structures and assets – so that he could negotiate with a clear mandate towards a set of agreed goals. Then he needed to wield a second set of instruments, bullying and deceiving his union counterparts, and deploying a capacity to 'read' an adversary's reactions across the bargaining table.

When a fresh-faced Cusa representative arrived for their first meeting – Cyril was still 29 years old – the young man adopted an open and good-natured countenance. Liebenberg had become accustomed to talking to representatives of what he called 'Mickey Mouse unions' filing for recognition agreements. Turning them down very gently,[28] Liebenberg would adopt a patronising manner, addressing the workers' representatives very slowly and deliberately.

Confronted with the fresh-faced and attentive-looking youngster, Liebenberg assumed a benign expression of his own and began slowly: 'When the workers are wanting to be recognised by the Chamber of Mines, it does not happen in a hurry. It is a slow and serious matter. It is like a marriage. When a man wants to marry another man's daughter, he does not just go to her house. His uncles must first make a proper approach to her family.'

Cyril furrowed his brow, adopting the perplexed look of a rural simpleton. Liebenberg continued, if anything more slowly: 'Now, what happens next? The two families must discuss the lobola [bride-price] and how it is to be divided. They may talk for many, many hours, or even days. The man cannot just get straight into bed with the young lady!' Finally this was too much for Cyril. Unable to contain himself any longer, he smiled. 'Do you think we can talk about mining?'[29]

The Chamber represented the largest 139 of the country's 800 mines, accounting for around 80 per cent of all mineworkers. All the big gold-mining companies and most of the larger coal miners were members. Through technical committees for each mine type, the Chamber would hammer out a negotiating position. The gold technical committee, for example, brought together the six major gold-mining houses to an agreed mandate. The coal committee did the same with ten representatives of the biggest miners. The negotiations between mining houses were always longer and more difficult than those with the unions. Their purpose was to establish a strategy for the Chamber in its union negotiations, setting out in very clear terms the mandate of the negotiators. Men like Liebenberg worked within very tight limits and could not exceed the agreed floors and ceilings of the pre-negotiation phase without consulting their principals.[30]

Once the annual negotiations with unions got under way, the Chamber's team faced off against the 11 recognised unions, primarily for white workers. The Chamber and the white unions were bitter adversaries engaged in a decades-long class conflict for their share of the wealth of the mines. Among the central demands of the most powerful union, the Mineworkers' Union led by the irascible Arrie Paulus, was an insistence that black unions must never be given recognition. The goal was to avoid competition between skilled black and white labour, because the monopoly over some kinds of jobs enjoyed by whites allowed them to earn inflated salaries. Ramaphosa recognised a window of opportunity once again. His union would pretend to be the black competitor to white union power that many of the Chamber's members had long hoped to see.

The historian of the NUM, Vic Allen, believes that Ramaphosa was in two minds about approaching the Chamber of Mines to sign an access agreement. In his view, Cyril did not want to compromise the independence of the union, and feared that the Chamber would set conditions for being granted access. But Cyril was also convinced that an access agreement would completely change the prospects of the union and he formally applied to the Chamber of Mines.[31] He was right. When the first recognition agreements were signed, the union numbered a little over 20,000 members. Within two years, membership was more than a quarter of a million.[32]

While Ramaphosa was sweet-talking the representatives of the mining houses, he was also organising. The funds Cusa allocated to him were sufficient to buy a small kombi van and to print leaflets encouraging unionisation. Cyril had an assistant, a former mineworker from Lesotho, Puseletso Salae, and they were joined by dismissed mineworkers willing to act as volunteers. Salae had been a fingerprint expert working for the mines' recruitment agency, who had been trained as a computer technologist and was then told to train white workers in these skills. After that his bosses told him he must now report to those whites he had just trained, and he came calling on Ramaphosa.

Cyril gave him illicit NUM pamphlets to distribute, but Salae and some of his friends were caught and summarily dismissed. When they went to tell Cyril at the Cusa offices, Ramaphosa smiled. 'Gentlemen, let us start working together. You are now the organisers of the union.'[33]

Their initial strategy was crude, consisting mostly of throwing bundles of leaflets over mine compound fences. Direct contacts were at first very difficult. Workers were suspicious of Ramaphosa. He was from Soweto, he was not a mineworker, and he was neither Sotho nor Xhosa. Inevitably they suspected him of being one of the detested salesmen who travelled between the mines trying to sell insurance to the mineworkers.

After one month, however, fate intervened in the form of Alfred Mphahlele, a personnel assistant at Western Deep Levels mine. Mphahlele's family lived in Soweto, and he would visit them whenever he could. Vic Allen tells the story: 'He invariably walked from his hostel in Carletonville to the main Klerksdorp-to-Johannesburg road where he would flag down a car for a lift to Soweto. He did that on Friday evening towards the end of August and as he climbed in he recognised the driver as Cyril Ramaphosa, whose picture he had seen in a Northern Transvaal newspaper during the student protest in the mid-1970s. A conversation began and Ramaphosa asked who he was and where he worked. When Ramaphosa learnt that he was a mineworker, he told him that he was trying to organise a union for black mineworkers. Mphahlele said he was interested and told him about the course he was attending, where 30 men had recently discussed that very same topic.'[34]

Mphahlele was attending a training course for black personnel assistants, and they had discussed together how to form a union. Cyril sent him on his way with a bundle of union application forms, having agreed to meet up with him again in Soweto. The first person Mphahlele met on his return to his mine was James Motlatsi, a fellow personnel assistant, who was very excited to hear about Ramaphosa's initiative. Motlatsi and Ramaphosa met up a few weeks later, and formed one of the most important partnerships in South African politics in the 1980s.

James Motlatsi was an unlikely partner for Cyril Ramaphosa. He came from Lesotho, where he had been radicalised as a child by opposition to the injustices meted out by chiefs. At the age of 12 he rejected the practice of presenting tribute to local chiefs. 'If one wished to build a house, one would have to cut eight to ten bundles of the special grass, and present the same amount again to the chiefs ... They were blood-suckers.' Relishing the memory of his first protest action, he comments, 'I still remember burning the reed bundles at night.'[35]

He left Lesotho during its 1970 state of emergency, when the anti-chief party for whom he was an organiser was 'cheated out of its election victory'. Like many other subjects of Lesotho, Motlatsi went to work underground on the South African mines. He described his experiences as 'going from the frying pan into the fire. I realised the problem was here even worse than it was there.'[36]

Motlatsi was not especially impressed with Cyril in their first meeting. 'He was young – I could see he was even younger than me – although he spoke very well. He seemed nothing special.' Like other mineworkers, Motlatsi could not understand why Cyril was interested in looking after the interests of miners. 'There were no mineworkers from the townships. They were from Lesotho or rural Transkei or from Mozambique. There was nobody interested in looking after them. I asked myself, Why is he so interested in finding solutions to the problems of mineworkers?'[37]

Motlatsi credits himself with inventing the tactic that he and Cyril were to deploy to such effect: they concentrated all their early energies on the mines' own training centres. Anglo American's gold and uranium division had a divisional training unit at Western Deep through which senior black workers regularly passed. Motlatsi's insight was that he and Cyril could extend their influence across the whole of the gold division through a relatively small number of senior workers who passed through this unit. The personnel organisers possessed the organisational skills and relative freedom of movement that would allow them to spread the word about the union.

The union was formally launched at the end of August 1982 in Hammanskraal, north of Pretoria. Much of its constitution was simply copied from that of the high-profile British National Union of Mineworkers. None of those present at the meeting was aware that there had been a great 1946 strike led by the African Mine Workers' Union – whose name they might otherwise have resurrected. Instead, after five hours of deliberation, they provisionally chose the name National Union of Mineworkers (NUM), rebutting Cusa's insistence that the black character of the union be reflected in its title.[38]

This dispute exacerbated tensions between Ramaphosa and Cusa's national executive committee. NUM rapidly outstripped other Cusa affiliates in size, and Cyril's flair for publicity made him better known than the federation of which NUM was a part. Jealous of NUM's success, his comrades tried unsuccessfully to rein Ramaphosa in – although at one stage that year he formally tendered his resignation – and Phiroshaw Camay had to protect him against the sniping of Cusa's old guard. Cyril was especially stung by one barb: 'You are an intellectual, and you intellectuals always want to have positions so that you can have power.'[39]

Soon after the launch, on 13 October 1982, an access agreement with the Chamber of Mines was signed. While this was a significant step, committing employers to allow the union access to potential recruits, many mine managers remained combative opponents of the union. These managers continued to prohibit mass meetings, to intimidate organisers, and to spy on activists, and they banned the distribution of union literature. Such restrictions placed a premium on organisation through close personal networks. A recruited miner would be set a recruitment target of his own, bringing on board friends and acquaintances who would then be set targets in their turn.

Access agreements included tight controls on times of access and barred entry to hostels, distribution of non-approved pamphlets, and singing of organisational songs. However, access was vital to remove what Ramaphosa saw as primarily psychological barriers to recruitment. Mineworkers were conditioned by overarching systems of control on the mines not to engage in any activity not explicitly sanctioned by the mine bosses. The first question mineworkers invariably asked NUM organisers was, 'Do you have permission to do what you are doing?' Access agreements broke the psychology of deference by allowing workers to sign up without putting their jobs on the line. An office in the hostel was an enormous advantage, even if it was near to the hostel manager's office, because workers believed they had some measure of protection from victimisation and arbitrary dismissal.

The union received a further big boost in October when 58 Kloof miners arrested during a strike were released after NUM intervened with a lawyer. This simple step exposed the sloppiness and arbitrary character of mine managers' dismissals, and opened the eyes of many ordinary workers to the potential power of a union. Pressing home his gain, Ramaphosa hired kombis to take the workers back to their mine, where he demanded that the management reinstate them. A surprised management team complied. Cyril played the media to leverage this success further in advance of the inaugural congress of the union, set for Klerksdorp on 4 December.[40]

When more than a thousand delegates assembled for the congress, they had some tangible achievements behind them. NUM had 14,000 members in nine branches, and more than 25 active organisers bringing in new recruits. However, the branches were concentrated in Anglo mines, in the Orange Free State and the West Rand, and the membership of 14,000 had to be seen in the context of a 1982 total mine workforce of 766,000.[41]

Ramaphosa characteristically devoted much of the congress's time to the constitution. Clauses were translated into Xhosa and Sesotho so that delegates could debate its provisions. The meeting ratified the name 'NUM', and decided upon a structure of shaft stewards' councils and committees to promote accountability in the branches. In elections that were to shape the union across the following decade, the delegates chose a national executive committee (NEC) to run the union between conferences. The NEC nominated Cyril Ramaphosa as general secretary – the only full-time official in the union.

Once Cyril was installed, elections were held for the part-time positions of president, vice-president and treasurer. The little-known Ishmaele Thulo was elected treasurer and James Motlatsi was unsurprisingly elected president – although he claims today that his nomination was a great surprise. He was well known to many delegates from his travels around the country as a hawker selling blankets – and militant ideas – to Sotho miners from the back of his van.[42]

The big surprise of the congress was the election of the unknown Elijah Barayi as vice-president. Barayi was a Xhosa speaker from Cradock in the Eastern Cape and brought an ethnic balance to the leadership that reflected the growing proportion of the workforce made up of contract workers from Transkei. Equally important, Barayi was a long-time ANC supporter. While the ANC had a deep presence in Cradock and was not destroyed by government repression, Barayi was probably the first ANC member Cyril Ramaphosa had knowingly met. The union was on its way. On 1 January 1983, NUM was formally established.

Ramaphosa immediately sought out links with wealthy trade unions in Scandinavia, Britain and the United States, primarily to establish the financial independence of NUM.

During a brief visit to the United States in 1982, he also visited Stanford University in California, where he made a major impression on Professor William B Gould IV, a scholar of labour relations. 'Cyril Ramaphosa, NUM's leader, visited Stanford University in 1982 and talked with me about his vision and goal of organizing the workers who live under this migrant labour system. He spoke of workers who are separated from their families, who are alone, who exist under a policy where separation on the basis of tribe is supported and divisiveness among workers is promoted. He spoke of a system where the worst criminality can flourish, where people by definition are degraded. He said his people are not accorded the right of free association, even the right to live with one's family. He had a vision of working with this new union. He was a young, fully educated lawyer. Listening to him speak at Stanford in 1982, one could not be criticized for thinking to one's self: "What a fine man; what a worthy goal. Too bad that it simply cannot succeed."'[43]

On 9 June 1983, NUM signed a memorandum of agreement with the Chamber of Mines that allowed the union to negotiate on mines where it was recognised. For the Chamber's chief negotiator, Johann Liebenberg, this formal recognition agreement marked the 'real start of the NUM'.[44] Ramaphosa's strategy of quiet negotiation was succeeding. There was no obligation on the Chamber to recognise NUM. Yet most of the mining houses, led by Anglo, now accepted that it made sense to establish a sound relationship with NUM at the outset. If the union grew a little faster in consequence of recognition, they were willing to bear this cost.[45]

The mining houses also believed they could destroy the union if it got out of hand. At this stage, NUM could not survive a frontal confrontation with the mining houses. It lacked the organisational and financial resources to last out a strike of any length.

The 1983 wage negotiations that soon got under way had a largely ritual significance. The bargaining strength of the Chamber was such that it was certain to get its own way on the headline wage increases. It could just impose whatever figure it had decided. Ramaphosa understood NUM's weakness. 'At that time, unions were not sophisticated in their approach to negotiation. We used to go more on gut feeling than [on] the force of the arguments we had to put forward at an intellectual level. At times we would be caught with our pants down because they had the facts, they were smooth, they were sophisticated and they had the resources. All we had then was just a sense of injustice and a mission to improve the lot of the workers, and raw power in the sense that the workers were there. So intellectual persuasion was not one of the key factors that we built into the way we did things ... At times in negotiations we would make serious mistakes and they would point this out and they would in a way be sort of laughing at us, be gleeful and all that.'[46]

For the mining houses, NUM seemed to be everything that they had hoped. But Ramaphosa and Motlatsi were gradually building the organisational and financial strength of the union. Meanwhile, NUM's tentacles were spreading largely unseen. The union was growing quietly but spectacularly.

CHAPTER 9

THE GREAT NEGOTIATOR

It's not all over yet if you're still talking.
— Cyril Ramaphosa[1]

NUM's growth was staggering. At the time of its inaugural congress in December 1982, it had just 14,000 members in nine branches. By the end of 1983, it claimed 53,000 members on 48 mines. In January 1985, there were 120,000 workers on 85 mines, and by the middle of 1986 an astonishing 344,000 mineworkers had signed up to the union. Of these, 228,000 were also paid up, bringing substantial internal funding to the union for the first time, and the union could boast more than 5,000 shaft stewards.[2]

Mine organisation had defeated every other union that had attempted it. Yet NUM's growth continued even after 1985, when Anglo American finally realised, with a shock, that NUM was not the sweetheart union it had made itself out to be.[3] There are a number of explanations for the union's success, the most important of which is also the most obvious. Conditions on the mines were so appalling that workers rushed to sign up once the chance was offered to them.

Vic Allen's history of black mineworkers unforgettably describes the systematic destruction of minds, lives and families in the pursuit of mine profit.[4] In a terrifying working environment, miners laboured with jack-hammer drills and pushed heavy ore-moving trucks. Routine use of explosives, the movement of large machines in confined spaces, and 'rock bursts' at high pressure, all had the potential to tear off limbs and crush bodies. Accidents underground killed and maimed thousands every year, and historical mortality rates on South Africa's mines were exceeded only by labourers building the Panama Canal.[5] Mine managers treated workers as disposable objects, and would 'medically repatriate' men killed or crippled in rock falls or blasts, paying them off with a nominal sum before sending them home.

Mineworkers also endured the psychological scarring of incarceration, almost like prisoners, in single-sex hostels. The hostel system exposed workers – and their rural families and communities – to diseases of urbanisation such as tuberculosis, which grew rapidly in the crowded, stress-filled and fatiguing mine compounds. Migrancy meant that families were often broken. There was virtually no family accommodation on the mines and the hostels were desperate places for workers to live. On one account, they were 'miserable almost beyond imagining … quartered in long, brick-walled structures with corrugated iron roofs. They live twenty to a room that measures 18 by 25 feet. Each man has a concrete cubicle, the slab floor of which is his bed. The most privacy a man can get is to hang a blanket in front of his bunk.'[6]

Compound culture was brutal and denied miners social and cultural outlets. Anglo's own 1970s research identified the 'foci of compound culture' as alcohol, dagga (cannabis), 'town women' and homosexuality.[7] An induna system of discipline used ethnic division and patronage to control workers. Apartheid logic was also applied relentlessly on the mines, with white separated from black, Xhosa workers segregated from Sotho, and so on.

Racial abuse and arbitrary violence were commonplace, with Anglo research concluding that 'the major source of tension underground, apart from the dangers of the job itself, is the White miner'.[8] The industry remained 'essentially repressive' in character,[9] and workers were routinely humiliated, for example through forced stripping, homosexual abuse on the part of indunas, and demands for bribes from corrupt personnel officers.

Mineworkers had always faced the threat of arbitrary dismissal, and a computerised system of blacklisting introduced in the early 1980s meant a dismissed worker might never find mine work again.[10] Grounds for dismissal were capricious – arriving a few minutes late, not seeing eye to eye with an induna – and there was no appeal mechanism.

In most countries miners have enjoyed relatively high salaries, partially to compensate for the arduous and dangerous nature of the work. Francis Wilson's influential 1972 study of the condition of South African mineworkers showed that their wages had actually fallen in real terms between 1910 and 1970.[11] Despite increases in the second half of the 1970s, black miners were still paid a pittance. They had few career prospects, moreover, with 'Category 8' over-ground work an absolute racial ceiling. The racial bars on promotion above ground, and blasting certificates under ground, made the upper skill echelon of black workers frustrated and ripe for organisation.

Mineworkers were acutely aware that the indignities of apartheid society were being expressed on the mines. Black workers would carry whites' bags, stand in long queues, squeeze into crowded lifts, and be forced to accept the casual violence and racist language of their white overseers. As violence in the wider society dramatically escalated in the middle of the 1980s, and the townships entered the period of 'ungovernability', the repressive mines became a new 'front line'. Unions also became channels through which deeper political aspirations about the end of the apartheid system could flow. In the face of appalling circumstances, an 'impatient collective consciousness among ordinary mineworkers'[12] fuelled the NUM's rapid growth.

At the same time, NUM's recruitment drive was helped by wider changes in the labour relations environment. In most countries, union membership had reached a plateau or had even gone into decline, but in South Africa post-Wiehahn labour reforms opened the floodgates to union organisation. 'The growth of trade unions in South Africa from the 1970s to 1996', economist Ian Macun observes, was 'nothing short of phenomenal.'[13] Industrial workforces were just 30 per cent unionised in 1977, but by 1990 70 per cent were signed up. The mining data – 7 per cent unionised in 1977 and more than 55 per cent in 1990 – are not out of line with these trends. Across the non-agricultural economy as a whole, there were 800,000 union members in 1980,[14] 1,250,000 in 1983, and more than 2 million by 1988.

For NUM, with its especially difficult organising environment, cooperation with the biggest mining house – Anglo American – was decisive. By opening up its mines to organisation, Anglo allowed NUM to establish a bridgehead. By 1986 more than eight in every ten members were employees on Anglo mines. Around one in ten, however, were employees of Gold Fields, the most conservative of the mining houses. Ramaphosa explains that Anglo American 'itself developed a lot of structures allowing workers to air their views and so forth … Their industrial relations policies were actually fairly good … On the other hand, Gold Fields mines were probably the worst in terms of the treatment at work and the residential places … and the pay.'[15] As Dunbar Moodie reflects, 'The union found most of its support from workers at either end of the spectrum of treatment – at Anglo American, where workers were already accustomed to speaking their minds, and at Gold Fields, where conditions were really bad.'[16]

NUM was also bolstered by a recruiting strategy that initially favoured clerks, team leaders and personnel assistants, and then machine drillers, rather than ordinary underground workers.[17] Once the senior black workforce was on board, it proved easy to extend the reach of the union downwards to lower grades, with whom the senior grades regularly interacted. The disproportionate representation of higher grades was anyhow to be expected, because these workers had better access to information, greater powers of organisation, freedom of movement, and clear differentials between themselves and lower-paid workers to protect.[18] NUM's growth balanced out rapidly when less-organised regions and occupations discovered the power of the union.

The mining houses faced one additional difficulty that was largely of their own making. The proportion of difficult-to-organise foreign workers, drawn from a wider subcontinental labour empire, had been dramatically curtailed by the mining houses just before NUM came into being. In 1974, between 72 per cent (at Anglo) and 88 per cent (at JCI) of workers were foreign. By 1980, after deliberate efforts to reduce dependence on foreign workers – so as to decrease vulnerability to political risk and to build permanent local skills – Anglo's workforce was 60 per cent domestic and JCI's 55 per cent.[19]

This shift from foreign to domestic workers necessitated quite substantial real increases in mineworkers' wages, which occurred largely before the arrival of the union. An expectation that real wages would continue to grow helped NUM to capitalise on the mine bosses' difficulties in the tougher economic and mining conditions of the 1980s.[20]

Lastly, NUM's growth depended on a careful strategic plan developed by Ramaphosa and Motlatsi. They pragmatically signed access and recognition agreements, avoided the frontal confrontations with mining houses that might have destroyed them, and built the union's mass base in an exhausting and relentless drive for new members.

Ramaphosa appeared quite transformed by the sense of responsibility that he now felt for improving the mineworkers' condition. He had known almost nothing about the suffering on the mines when he first took on responsibility for NUM, but he quickly came to recognise the wider significance of their exploitation. 'My biggest regret is ... that I have never been a miner ... The miners represented to me the utter degradation of man, [his] utter exploitation, and I wanted to experience that so that I can be able to do something about it.'[21] As mineworkers came to trust Cyril as their advocate, his popularity soared. But it was above all his performances at the negotiating table that were celebrated by the regional organisers and officials who were able to watch them.

At the centre of any union is the practice of collective bargaining. The annual wage cycle at the heart of mine industry bargaining was managed by the Chamber of Mines. Mining houses would first reach a consensus among themselves about wages and working conditions, and the employers' body would then seek to impose its preferences on its union adversaries in an extended process of deliberation and negotiation.

The NUM, like other unions, would make various wage and non-wage demands, usually with a focus on the headline wage figure. Their goal was to secure concessions from the Chamber, and to push its negotiators as far as their mandate would allow them to go, ideally dividing the mining houses along the way.

When union met employer, the two teams would sit facing one another in the Chamber's grand boardroom in downtown Johannesburg. At the heart of the process was a battle between the two chief negotiators, Ramaphosa and Johann Liebenberg, who spoke on behalf of their respective teams. Liebenberg was flanked by representatives of the major mining houses, collectively bound by the prior negotiation of a 'mandate' in laborious pre-negotiations. On the other side of the table was Ramaphosa, flanked by his key lieutenant, James Motlatsi, and other officials. Behind NUM's negotiators sat 30 or 40 representatives of regions and branches, on hand to observe the negotiations for themselves and to report back to ordinary mineworkers.

The Chamber's negotiators were initially unsettled by the presence of so many NUM representatives. The mineworkers themselves were enthralled by the opulence of their surroundings. On NUM's first visit to the boardroom, the visitors were served tea in china cups and delicate sandwiches, and there were sugar bowls with silver spoons. Arrayed along the length of the boardroom table were ornate boxes brimming with cigarettes, next to which lay matches in special holders. When the mining-house negotiators stepped outside for a brief caucus meeting, the initially reticent mineworkers began to enjoy the hospitality. Encouraged by Ramaphosa – 'Help yourselves to what is yours!' – they stripped the table within minutes. On their next visit they were greeted with paper cups and empty cigarette boxes.[22]

Cyril instinctively understood what industrial relations negotiators usually learn through long experience: discussions with your own people are always tougher than negotiations with the other side.[23] NUM's branch representatives were carefully briefed in advance of meetings with the Chamber, and the NUM negotiators would regularly break off to 'caucus' with them. In this way, concessions could be more easily sold to members, and regular feedback ensured that expectations were constantly tempered by reality.

Negotiations were often complex and laborious. Each side would look for signs of weakness and compromise in the other, NUM delegates even observing the body language of mining house representatives. James Motlatsi recalls of one Anglo executive with whom NUM often interacted, 'If he began tapping his foot, we knew that that was it – there was no way he had a mandate to concede on that issue. We would just move on to the next thing.'[24]

For their part the Chamber's team would rotate the job of observing NUM delegates' body language, but with the same intention of finding signs of weakness or indecision.[25] Most negotiators were smokers, and the pressure was high. As the day wore on, the chamber would fill up with acrid cigarette smoke.

In this ritualistic and formal battle, almost no tactic was seen as illegitimate. The Chamber's negotiators would sometimes attend in full suits, and turn down the air-conditioning in the negotiating chamber to discomfort the NUM delegates.[26] The union team used their charm to play on the sympathies of the secretaries – who were white women on the receiving end of their own bosses' patronising sexism[27] – and sometimes obtained information on the Chamber's strategy in this way. On one occasion, the Chamber was even obliged to fire its secretarial assistants.[28]

NUM's leaders worked as a team. Cyril used his gifts as an orator to modulate his voice and to tease and threaten his opposite numbers. Even his body language would change in response to the demands a situation presented – for example, to maintain pressure on an indecisive Chamber negotiator. His ability to out-talk his opposite numbers, and always to find the right form of words, was a great source of satisfaction and pride for the observing union representatives. They were equally delighted by his seeming disdain for his adversaries, and his complete immunity to browbeating by mining executives.

Over time, Cyril became increasingly devious and unreadable, but also increasingly systematic in preparation. 'We learnt to present our case very very well, to do research ... We paid [them] back once we had the power.'[29] Ramaphosa almost always negotiated with a calm demeanour. Despite the high pressure built up during negotiations, he almost never showed any stress. Liebenberg, an immensely experienced professional negotiator, was eventually able to recognise when Cyril was getting angry, but not by any outward change in his demeanour. 'It was like something was filling up to the brim behind his eyes – but it would never break through. On the outside Cyril always remained calm.'[30]

There were very occasional exceptions. In 1987, Cyril made the mistake of giving up smoking shortly before the negotiations began. The Chamber team that year sprang a surprise, by presenting their revised pay increases in percentage terms, rather than in the rand money terms that had hitherto been conventional in the industry. The large NUM caucus behind the union's negotiating team was thrown into confusion by this move. Cyril was 'visibly rattled'. Irritated and agitated, he turned behind him and shouted, 'Someone give me a cigarette.' After a few puffs, his conventional external demeanour returned.[31]

Ramaphosa increasingly became a master at manipulating the feelings of his opponents and at changing the atmosphere of a meeting. He could 'turn the temperature in the room up and down by sheer force of will', and he could shift the mood in an instant.[32] One strategy he employed when dealing with a fresh opponent was to 'play ignorant', furrowing his brow and pretending not to be able to understand his white interlocutor.[33] Early on in a negotiation with Cyril, unknowing mine negotiators would often feel sorry for him, believing him to be out of his depth. Many naïve human relations executives made early concessions to Cyril that they would later regret.[34]

As negotiations advanced, Cyril read the body language and expressions of the employers' entire team. He knew instinctively who would make concessions and who was determined to hold the line. And he had an uncanny ability to distinguish the real power-brokers from managers who merely made a lot of noise. He would often drive a wedge between his adversaries, heaping praise on some individuals for their wisdom and intelligence, while pouring scorn on others.

Cyril and his immediate deputies made up a formidable team. Despite his diminutive stature, Marcel Golding would rise confidently to present detailed arguments on technical issues and to set out the union's analysis of data. He was to prove a highly competent negotiator in his own right when Ramaphosa was unable to attend negotiations. Kuben Pillay, the union's legal adviser, would calmly lob legal hand-grenades at the Chamber's team.

The heart of the NUM negotiating team, however, was the very special double-act between Ramaphosa and James Motlatsi. Motlatsi maintained a stony silence throughout the negotiations, his face – 'my ugly face' – locked in a frown that the Chamber's representatives found very difficult to read.[35] Behind Motlatsi's motionless countenance, he was thinking hard. Listening to the evolving character of the negotiations, his role was to manage the emotions of the NUM caucus, and to gauge the likely reactions of the union's wider constituency to concessions Cyril was making or extracting.

Motlatsi was relentlessly calculating and recalculating, in the light of the way the negotiations were progressing, how to whip the caucus into agitation and, equally, how to ameliorate its anger. Canadian sociologist Chuck Sabel once argued that union bosses need a 'domestic policy' for their own members and a 'foreign policy' for their employer counterparts.[36] In order to extract concessions, a domestic policy must stoke up members' anger so as to scare the bosses into backing down. At the same time, once there is nothing more that the other side can concede, a compromise has to be 'sold' to one's own side as a victory.

Ramaphosa controlled the 'foreign policy' engagement with the enemy. Motlatsi, on the other hand, was the master of 'domestic policy', agitating and soothing NUM's representatives by turn. His hardest tasks took place before the negotiations began, in reading the mood of the members, and after they had concluded, when he had to go out with the regional organisers to the mines and sweeten the bitter pill of ordinary mineworkers' disappointment. In Motlatsi's rather grand way of summarising his own position, 'Cyril was the chief negotiator; I was the Field Marshal!'[37]

Ramaphosa rarely lost his temper, but during a 1985 negotiation at the South African Nuclear Fuels Corporation (Nufcor), he became livid with anger. The circumstances say a lot about the nature of collective bargaining. Nufcor was notorious for driving a very hard bargain on wage issues. Its management had succeeded in suppressing wage increases to such an extent that skilled nuclear industry technicians earned less than their counterparts in conventional mines. In a surprise move designed to retain scarce skills at the plant, Nufcor's human relations team decided to make a substantial improvement in levels of pay.

Meanwhile, Cyril had been gathered with the local union organisers discussing what kind of pay rise was realistic. Given their low wage levels, they had pushed him hard and wanted him to demand very substantial rises. Cyril eventually persuaded them that they must be 'realistic' or else have a very unfavourable figure simply imposed on them. He advised them to ask for 19 per cent.

When the two parties sat down to negotiate, Johann Liebenberg allowed Ramaphosa to present his full case for a 19 per cent increase

– with representatives of the workforce looking on. At the end of the presentation, the employers held a ten-minute caucus in which they appeared to be deliberating the merits of Ramaphosa's case. Then Liebenberg announced that management proposed a wage increase of 27 per cent! Liebenberg rubbed in Cyril's embarrassment by insisting that Nufcor would not let the workers take away anything less.[38]

Ramaphosa was furious and his Nufcor members were outraged. He had to spend more than an hour calming them down. The next day Liebenberg and Ramaphosa met for a cup of coffee. Ramaphosa was still fuming: 'Don't ever do that again.' His anger was understandable. When worker representatives are sold a lower offer by their own leader than the management is willing to make, it might seem that the leader was on the management's payroll.[39]

When Cyril met up with Motlatsi to conduct their usual post-mortem on the negotiations, the two men seriously considered whether this might be part of an attempt to destroy the union's presence at Nufcor.[40] They wondered if Liebenberg was trying to drive a wedge between the union and its members, and to discredit NUM in the eyes of other workforces. The camaraderie that was sometimes established between the opposing negotiators fell away at such times, and the fundamental chasm of mistrust between the two sides was revealed.

Ramaphosa later made much of his unwillingness to humiliate his opponents. The 'real lessons' he learned from NUM negotiations were 'sitting down with the bosses, learning to cut deals, but also in the end being courteous, not being brash and not being disrespectful and not seeking to humiliate them – that was an important lesson for me, to also respect your adversaries. I did have a great deal of respect for quite a number of people that I negotiated with.'[41]

The true source of this supposed insight is, however, quickly revealed. 'This lesson was more than confirmed for me when I read Madiba's book, where he says even when you deal with your adversaries you have got to deal with them with great courtesy and not try to humiliate them. In a way that to me has been an important lesson in life.'[42]

In reality, Motlatsi observes, Ramaphosa could be a vicious negotiator, and humiliation was part of his regular negotiating armoury, ready to be unleashed 'at the right moment – to paralyse his opponents'.[43] Ramaphosa does concede that 'tactful humiliation' can be useful. Humiliation is tactful, he explains, when 'you don't go all out of your way to rub their noses in the mud. You know when it's the time to pull back and give them time to withdraw or accept the humiliation with dignity.'[44]

When provoked, he sometimes took his opposite numbers apart and inflicted prolonged and deliberate humiliation. At the end of one particularly arduous 1985 negotiation concerning the reinstatement of dismissed Witbank mineworkers, an agreement was finally ground out. The union's position had been weak, and Cyril had been compelled almost to plead for the reinstatement of the workers for more than four hours. When copies of the deal had been signed, the general manager of the mine waved his copy in the air and said to Cyril: 'Now, you had better tell those members of yours to stick to this agreement.'

Ramaphosa's response was immediate and explosive. 'Who the fuck do you think you are? You can't give me instructions. None of you can give me instructions. Don't you ever dare tell me what I have to do.'[45]

An instant later, Cyril turned on an avuncular smile which he directed at one of the mine manager's juniors, and the youngster could not help reciprocating. The young man blushed as Cyril commented that at least there was one capable negotiator in their team. The general manager went red in the face, and though his lips were moving slowly he was incapable of uttering a word. He got up and left the building. James Motlatsi later learnt from the manager's driver that he sat in stony silence for the whole drive back to Witbank and then exploded. 'He just shitted all over me.'[46]

There were strict limits to what negotiations could achieve for either side. Wage increases are constrained by a mine's need to be profitable. Downward pressure on wages and conditions is likewise contained by a mine's need to retain scarce skills. While the union fostered expectations on the part of the workers that could never be satisfied, the mining houses could do little to change the wider social and political problems of late apartheid.

Cyril saw organising mineworkers not, as he had once been told, as 'the art of the possible' but rather as 'the art of the impossible …

trying to make a fundamental change in a system by using structures and instruments that were designed to perpetuate that system'. For Ramaphosa, this was like trying 'to make a revolution with moderate tools that were invented to prevent a revolution'.[47] His own shop stewards were constantly pushing for new kinds of intervention and action, and insisting that a new issue – such as 'resistance to the system' – be added to the union's objectives.

In fact, the mines were part of a wider pattern of exploitation of black by white that could not be ameliorated by the industry alone. Vic Allen observed, for example, that the town of Welkom was 'a modern white conservative town with a population of 65,000, of whom 80 per cent were directly or indirectly dependent on mining'.[48] Distributed across this town, but not part of it, were mine compounds accommodating 150,000 black mineworkers. The nearby township of Thabong, built by Anglo American, had a population of 450,000, and no water or electricity. Welkom was known as the 'white by night' town because black people were banned from its streets after dark by law and later by convention.[49] To meet mineworkers' grievances like these required a wider political and social change than negotiation could hope to bring about.

Even in the narrow realm of wage negotiations, there were strict limits on what the union could achieve. While they were the beneficiaries of state privileges – such as the right to import workers from outside South Africa – the mines were private enterprises in a market economy. Wages were ultimately driven by factors other than the relative bargaining power of workers and bosses. Prior to the formation of the union, workers had in fact enjoyed a decade of wage rises on the mines, primarily as a result of the mining houses' decision to reduce dependency on the subcontinental migrant labour system, and their growing dependence on more skilled employees. If NUM had been founded in the mid-1970s, it would have been celebrated for bringing unprecedented gains in real wages. Instead, NUM's formation coincided with the emergence of a pool of excess labour for the first time, and the union battled to secure wage gains.

Ramaphosa never tired of improving the capacity of the union to negotiate, eventually using outside consultants, funded by international donors, to produce new tools to strengthen the negotiating case of the union. This might involve analysis of the differentials between mineworkers and comparable workers in other industries, international comparative studies of mineworkers' wages, and adjustments of demands for anticipated changes in rates of inflation. Yet, as one of the union's later innovators points out, 'while the union developed many fact-based resources, "the facts" were often one of the least important things in the negotiation'.[50]

On one occasion, NUM was drawn into torrid negotiations at the Durnacol coking coal mine in Newcastle in Natal. Durnacol had been taken over by the national steel giant Iscor, which wanted vertical security of coking coal supply to its local steelworks. The local management, which had a reputation for poor labour practices, found itself drawn into a complex dispute with the workforce that it was now unable to end. Mineworkers were staging an underground sit-in and production at the mine was at a standstill. Ramaphosa and NUM industrial relations head Martin Nicol went down to Newcastle to engage in negotiation with the local managers and union organisers.

The management representatives were under severe pressure. Their new bosses in Iscor had evidently told them to settle the dispute as a matter of urgency. Cyril, meanwhile, was at the peak of his form, provoking, teasing and confusing the management by turns. He exploited the situation to the full, toying with an increasingly desperate management whom he pressured into making one concession after another. Eventually they gave away everything Ramaphosa could have wished for and more.

On the face of it a victory for the workforce, it proved to be a defeat. A negotiator as tough and skilled as Ramaphosa needs an opposite number who knows what he is doing. The Durnacol bosses unwittingly made concessions they could not afford, promising wage increases and new working practices that were simply beyond the means of the mine. Durnacol had a weak seam of coal that was difficult and costly to extract. Within two or three years of the agreement being reached, these economic realities made themselves felt. It had become cheaper for Iscor to import coking coal from abroad than to dig it out of the ground at Durnacol. A wave of retrenchments began in which thousands of workers were ultimately to lose their jobs.[51]

For a brilliant negotiator like Ramaphosa, his own powers of persuasion carried with them a hidden danger. He always remembered afterwards that one should never force the other side to make a concession they simply cannot live with.[52]

CHAPTER 10

ENTRENCHING UNION POWER

Workers' skeletons litter the mines of this land. Many of those killed underground were never retrieved; their families never had the opportunity to bury them decently, according to African rituals and tradition.

– Frans Baleni[1]

In addition to wage bargaining, NUM relentlessly pursued non-wage grievances using innovative methods. The most important of these was the law. For decades the mining houses had grown accustomed to the arbitrary exercise of legal and administrative dominance over the workers. The post-Wiehahn environment, however, provided opportunities that Ramaphosa was quick to seize.

Soon after his arrival at Cusa in 1982, Cyril met some of the sharpest labour lawyers practising in South Africa. The Centre for Applied Legal Studies at Wits organised a training workshop on labour law for Cusa officials at Wilgespruit. The conference was set up by Halton Cheadle and another young lawyer, Paul Benjamin, in liaison with the two Cusa legal officers, Zoli Kunene and Cyril.[2] At the workshop, Ramaphosa met the three members of what was to become Cheadle, Thompson & Haysom, the most prominent pro-labour legal practice of the 1980s.

Cusa was still committed to the promotion of blacks in leadership positions, and this made it difficult for Ramaphosa to create a substantial in-house legal capacity. Labour law was in post-Wiehahn upheaval, and NUM could exploit the opportunities this presented only by drawing on high-level legal skills at that time monopolised by whites. For Fosatu, this was no problem because the federation was happy to employ whites in high-profile positions. While Ramaphosa respected Cusa's position on black officials, he pragmatically contracted out work to external white practitioners. In this way, he was able to draw on the very best of the progressive labour lawyers then practising, including Halton Cheadle, Martin Brassey, Paul Benjamin, Arthur Chaskalson and Gilbert Marcus. The lawyer with whom NUM developed its closest relationship in the early years was Clive Thompson.

Thompson observes that when Cyril approached him in 1983 to act for NUM, it was 'odd on the face of it in that he was very much aware of my association with Halton Cheadle and was equally aware that Halton had very established links with Fosatu'.[3] While Thompson was advising NUM, Cheadle was just two offices down the corridor working for Fosatu's competitor union.

Thompson's advice to NUM was crucial, he himself observes, because 'it was a time of huge churn and innovation in South African labour law, and difficult for anyone not entirely immersed in the discipline to attempt to call the shots'. The availability of some of the country's finest legal minds was to give the union a decisive edge in a fast-changing terrain that bewildered the mine managers.[4] Thompson describes Cyril's overall approach in this way: 'His key concern was not so much to argue the merits of a legal strategy but to make certain that it supported or did not undermine his broader organisational goals, which were set pretty much exclusively by his union leadership team. He would make the large calls – on whether to underwrite a legal plan – but generally concurred with specific advice.'[5]

Ramaphosa's overall legal strategy had four key components. Firstly, the union clarified and enforced its access rights in its early and formative months. Access agreements detailed the obligations of mine managers to allow workers to meet and hold ballots, and they specified that organisers should be free from harassment in the mine compounds.[6] By drawing up these agreements with care, and then acting swiftly against any breaches, the union's lawyers overcame the resistance of recalcitrant mine managers, whose presumption had been that they could continue to act without regard to the law.

Secondly, careful pre-planning before disputes broke out allowed a number of defences against the abuse of 'scab' labour. In fact, the law offered some protection, subtle but meaningful, against the use of strike breakers where a strike had been called in a procedurally correct way. Thirdly, in the bulk of the everyday work of the legal team, the lawyers dealt with the constant stream of dismissals, which were one of the workers' greatest fears and grievances. The arbitrary and often vicious nature of the sackings, and the brutish refusal of mine managers to countenance the notion of fair process, allowed the lawyers to make substantial inroads into this problem very rapidly.

Finally, Cyril's 'hired guns' turned the law into a powerful instrument for advancing the cause of health and safety. The union was still unable to act against silent killers such as tuberculosis that decimated mineworkers and their rural families. But the legal mercenaries developed strategies to discourage the waste of human life in tragic and unnecessary accidents. At Hlobane Colliery almost 70 mineworkers had died in 1983, soon after the union was established; 177 died at Kinross in 1986; 62 at St Helena in 1987; 53 at Middelbult Colliery in 1993.

The union's new health and safety strategy took a complacent industry by surprise. Till then civil claims had not been allowed in the event of mine accidents and injuries. The widows of dead miners, and workers disabled by accidents or rock bursts, had been paid trifling statutory payments. In so-called medical repatriation, crippled miners had been given minimal payments and then sent home. Soon the union began to respond rapidly and effectively to major tragedies, as well as to the endless stream of smaller accidents. With growing success its lawyers pressed for the full financial losses incurred by mineworkers and their families to be met.[7]

In all these areas, NUM's lawyers initially enjoyed the advantage of a complacent and underskilled adversary battling to keep up with changes in the law. Nevertheless, the odds continued to be heavily stacked against the union. Ordinary workers still enjoyed few tangible rights, and the administration of the justice system continued to work in favour of the mine bosses. In the smaller mining towns of South Africa, such as Klerksdorp, it was all too easy to get the wrong judicial officer – and sometimes it seemed almost impossible to get a fair one. The mine managers and the magistrates were linked by family ties and a culture of Afrikaner solidarity. NUM's lawyers would sometimes enter the courtroom to find the mine managers, their lawyers and the magistrates chatting about the braai they had enjoyed together the previous weekend.[8]

Ramaphosa was viewed by the external legal representatives as a very hard taskmaster.[9] It was something of a cultural peculiarity among the late-apartheid white liberal legal fraternity that some of its members sought not only gratitude from the black people they were representing but also market rates for their services as a 'matter of principle'. Moreover, activists would fear detention in the months of December and January because the contribution of many white lawyers to the struggle was suspended during the summer vacation period.

Ramaphosa did not always enjoy cordial relationships with what Clive Thompson acknowledges were 'headstrong and opinionated lawyers'. Thompson observes of Cyril that 'in the social context', their opinionated character was 'a source of unevenly repressed irritation and occasional resentment for him. But not excessively so, for he knew, and they knew, he disposed over the real power in the relationship.'[10]

For the employment of these external lawyers Cyril sourced funds wherever he could find them, among other places from the International Defence and Aid Fund (Idaf) and from the International Confederation of Free Trade Unions (ICFTU). At the same time, given the great volume of litigation and the increasingly central role of the law in the union's activity, it made sense to create a legal office in the union. Running such an office was not an altogether attractive prospect for an outside legal specialist, because such a lawyer would have to sacrifice a handsome salary for the union's flat-level rate of pay – which was then capped at a few hundred rands per month.

Nevertheless, Paul Benjamin, who had coordinated the union's legal response to the major mine disaster at Hlobane, approached Ramaphosa some time in early 1984 offering to work for the union. He was an idealist with teeth, an accomplished and methodical lawyer, and someone highly committed to the cause of the union. All the same, Ramaphosa turned down his offer on the ground that it raised a 'policy problem'. On the historian Vic Allen's reading of the situation, the problem in question was that Benjamin was white, while the union was still reserving senior offices for black people. If this is true, Allen observes, Cyril was 'still influenced by the ideology of the black consciousness movement'.[11]

By 1986, the need for in-house legal capacity was becoming desperate. The union was now a very large organisation with hundreds of thousands of members, and Cyril had moved to a more ambitious management model. He decided to recruit a core of skilled professionals in a new and greatly expanded head office. Marcel Golding, who had been running a radical Western Cape newspaper, was enticed to take charge of the union's communications strategy. Meanwhile, Cyril looked high and low for a lawyer to coordinate the growing deluge of legal work. The delay suggests that Ramaphosa was still determined that a black candidate should be found.

In the event, a highly talented young black lawyer called Kuben Pillay made an approach to Ramaphosa.[12] Pillay had earned a law degree from Wits, and then secured a South African Council of Churches (SACC) scholarship to study civil rights and comparative labour law at Howard University in the United States. In his vacations, he had been working as an intern at the massive American union federation, AFL/CIO, in Washington DC.

One day in 1985, he was sitting in his student residence at Howard University, watching PBS (the public broadcasting channel on television). A programme came on detailing the rise of the NUM in South Africa, featuring footage of strike action and organisational meetings. Pillay watched mesmerised. He remembers Cyril – a man about whom Pillay knew nothing when he left South Africa – appearing on the screen, and talking with extraordinary confidence and calmness about the demands of the workers. At that moment, he recalls clearly, he decided he was going to work for Ramaphosa at NUM.[13]

As soon as he finished his studies in 1986, he sent a beautifully prepared and impressive curriculum vitae to Ramaphosa. Pillay was an attractive proposition for Cyril: a black lawyer with expertise in labour law, excellent academic results, and experience in a union federation. Moreover, he was committed to working for the workers.

Unfortunately, Anglo American's gold division in Main Street was also interested in employing lawyers with just such a profile. One part of Anglo's recruitment strategy was to tap the database of the SACC, and to look for any likely prospects on their scholarships programme. Anglo executives Bobby Godsell and Nigel Unwin – who, as we shall see, were already well known to Cyril – identified Pillay as a likely prospect.

As soon as he was back in the country, Unwin wrote to Pillay inviting him to come for an interview – the following Friday – at Anglo's gold and uranium division. Meanwhile, Ramaphosa had invited Pillay to come for an interview on Wednesday, just two days before he was due to go to Anglo. Pillay was uncomfortable about the 'contradictory work opportunities' – torn between his heart and his head: Anglo was a dream employer.

At his NUM interview, he found a less than ideal work environment. The union was still housed in the dilapidated and unprepossessing Lekton House, in Wanderers Street, Johannesburg. There was an air of confusion – and tension – in the building, as a result of large numbers of retrenched mineworkers camping out on the union's premises (part of a problem to which we shall shortly return). There were piles of papers strewn everywhere, and an overwhelming sense of confusion (although Pillay was soon to find that there was in fact order beneath the seeming chaos).

Pillay recalls his astonishment as a mineworker tipped a huge bag of notes and coins on to a table top. These were the subscriptions from a union branch, he was told, and the local organiser had carried the notes and coins all the way from his mine compound.

Pillay found Cyril in a small and makeshift office towards the back of the building. Despite the surroundings, it took him only a few seconds to confirm that this was where he wanted to work. 'Cyril blew me away. He was humble, gracious, concerned, and he had an incredible ability to make me feel totally at home right away.'[14] Pillay outlined his case for employment at NUM, and Ramaphosa agreed he was the right person for the job. The salary on offer was R800 per month, about R200 more than Cyril himself was taking home. He was told he could start the following Monday.

Pillay decided to tell Ramaphosa about his other interview. Should he just cancel it? he asked. Cyril's response was immediate and mischievous. The young man followed his plan to the letter. Two days later, he went for his interview at the operational offices of Anglo at 45 Main Street. He sat attentively through an extended presentation in which an executive outlined the glamorous profile of the mining giant, the opportunities it offered for career progression, its extremely generous pay scales, and the various benefits that would accrue to anyone who accepted an offer of employment.

Pillay waited until his interview was over. Nigel Unwin smiled indulgently, and welcomed Pillay to the gold and uranium division. As he had been instructed by Cyril, Pillay turned to Unwin and said: 'I'm afraid I'm not interested in your offer. I would rather work for Mr Ramaphosa at the National Union of Mineworkers.' Unwin stared back at Pillay with uncomprehending eyes.[15]

Pillay created what was in effect an in-house law firm for the union, to deal directly with its flood of routine legal actions and to act as a channel through which specialised work could be farmed out to practices such as Cheadle, Thompson & Haysom. The key problem the office faced was a shortage of information: there was almost never enough time and knowledge to take preventive action against employers. Most of their work, for this reason, was reactive. There was litigation every day, as the union dealt with a growing number of mass dismissals, arbitrary sackings, and the fallout from wildcat strikes. They would use a variety of tactics to challenge dismissals on grounds of fairness and incorrect process, using both labour courts and conciliation mechanisms.

In 1986, when Ramaphosa moved NUM from Lekton House to the spacious new offices in Cosatu House on Jeppe Street, the legal and health and safety departments of NUM were able to occupy a whole floor. At last they had the resources, computers, office equipment and space to increase the efficiency of their operation. Pillay now had five people working under him in the legal department, and he began to build up a substantial database.[16]

Cyril did not allow his new 'middle-class' recruits to hide themselves behind their desks. Immediately after his arrival Pillay was exposed to industrial unrest in the turbulent compounds. After just two weeks on the job, he was sent out with one colleague to Kloof gold mine, where his task was to advise workers engaged in a three-day-old strike about their legal rights. The inexperienced Pillay stood up to address the crowd of workers, who were fired up with discontent and had gathered together excitedly to hear what their union's representative had to say. Pillay told them straight out that the legal position was clear: if they did not go back to work immediately, the employers would be able to dismiss them.

After a brief stunned silence, complete chaos broke out among the assembled throng. For the next three hours, angry miners rampaged around the compound, burning down concession stores and stoning mine security police. Pillay had to run and hide in a storm-water drain in fear for his life. He was ignominiously rescued by mine security and escorted off the compound.[17]

Later that year, Ramaphosa sent Pillay to deal with a potentially violent stand-off between miners and mine security during an illegal 'wildcat' strike on a small mine in the Orange Free State. The mineworkers were being held on the compound against their will, and they had massed together in an angry crowd. Less than a hundred metres away, a line of heavily armed mine security faced them. Pillay and his colleague parked their Opel between the two lines. He approached the workers, who explained that they had decided to storm the mine security lines. 'The first wave of us may die,' their spokesman told him, 'but they can't shoot all of us.'[18]

Pillay shuffled across to the mine security line, and informed the mine security commander that he was a lawyer for the union. When he explained that they were legally obliged to let the workers leave the compound, they told him to fuck off. Pillay tried to talk to the mine manager, whose office was on the second floor of a building nearby, but the manager simply shouted down to him from his window, and refused to invite Pillay in.

The tension was now palpable and the potential for tragedy high. In his desperation, Pillay took out his Dictaphone – a large hand-held recording machine of a kind then unfamiliar in South Africa – and waved it about ostentatiously. The head of mine security, a burly Afrikaner, peered at it mystified. Pillay started to talk into the machine, pretending that he was addressing someone on the other end of the line, perhaps on a new kind of field telephone.

In a loud voice, he mentioned a variety of phrases – 'the constitution', 'the BBC' and 'international law' – in his panic scarcely knowing what he was saying. The mine security boss hurried off looking highly agitated, presumably to tell the mine manager that the hotshot Indian lawyer was talking to the international media through some new kind of communications device. A few minutes later, the mine security line was pulled back, and the workers were allowed to leave the compound.[19]

Alongside innovative use of the law, Ramaphosa gradually developed a professional media strategy. NUM's media profile was dominated by Ramaphosa himself, his personal authority, eloquence and clarity of expression making him a perfect television and radio spokesman. He had been preaching since he was a child, and he could talk effortlessly and calmly, in a voice carefully modulated to its audience, in almost any setting.

Cyril was also a natural television performer who stood out among the wooden and inarticulate politicians of the time. He was a young man appearing on a medium dominated by the middle-aged or old, and he retained some of the physical attractiveness of his youth. He projected urgency and controlled anger, and his sense of invulnerability and inner conviction came across strongly on the television screen. He was also a black man radiating confidence, who without hesitation or apology made demands on behalf of the most exploited black workers in the land.

Ramaphosa was careful to manage his own media profile. He had a small set of carefully crafted remarks about his own past that recurred in almost every interview. Reporters would observe that Cyril's 'one real regret in life' was that he had never been an underground miner. He was not averse to corny heart-rending tales about relatives who used to be miners, and he could summon up the image of himself as a small child, being pushed into a ditch by a white policeman: 'I still live with the scars.' For the journalist Mono Badela, this Cyril Ramaphosa was a 'leader with a heart of gold'.[20]

Sheryl Raine, writing in the *Sunday Star*, reflected at length upon the significance of Ramaphosa's media image, in a 1986 piece entitled 'SA mining faces its "Cyril factor."'[21] Raine observed that 'cult figures, particularly those spawned by the commercial press, are anathema to the emergent labour movement. But every now and then, the calibre of a certain leader in the movement pushes through. Workers' democracy, mandated policy statements and organisation-by-committee ... give way to a hero in the making.' For her, Ramaphosa was just such a figure, 'a workers' hero and media celebrity'. (Raine also observes, of course, that 'in fact, Mr Ramaphosa's one regret is that he has never been a miner'.) Her conclusion was that 'since the NUM was born in 1982, the mining industry has been forced to consider the "Cyril factor".'

The power of Cyril's media presence was partly based on the uncomfortable truths that he was rehearsing. When he described the miners' working conditions, the racist abuse to which they were subjected, their deaths in terrible and preventable accidents, and the callousness of the mine managers, he was speaking truths to which his audiences could not easily close their minds. Ordinary mineworkers, in particular, found it a revelation that their anger could be articulated in normally hostile news media.

For Ramaphosa, of course, the white press was not simply an alien force. At Sekano-Ntoane High School, when he and his friends would scan the columns of the *Rand Daily Mail,* they were already conceiving the readership of a newspaper as a moral community. The *Rand Daily Mail* was the only staunchly anti-apartheid white newspaper in the country, and in April 1985 it closed down – an event celebrated by PW Botha as indicating that a new spirit of national unity was emerging.

Black papers, meanwhile, were harassed and sometimes banned. The newspapers that remained were increasingly self-censoring publications, and one Rhodes journalism professor lamented in 1984 that 'Few editors in the past 15 years have fulfilled their editorial responsibility of ensuring adequate reporting of news which is of real importance to the total population'.[22]

Building communications capacity was a priority for Ramaphosa. When, in late 1985 and early 1986, he came across three articles on the NUM written by a young leftist on a short-term contract with the *South African Labour Bulletin (SALB),* he did not hesitate to recruit him. Marcel Golding was a radical, labouring under a heavy weight of theoretical Marxist education, but he remained a clear thinker and a direct writer. *SALB* was a mouthpiece of the 'workerist' worldview of the Fosatu labour federation, and it had hitherto criticised the NUM as an ill-formed and undisciplined mass union, lacking the necessary shop-floor organisation to advance the longer-term class interests of the mineworkers.

Golding attacked this received notion, and implicitly expressed scepticism about the dualistic view of union organisation it assumed. For him, NUM did have a 'mass character'. However, it also possessed 'a very strong organisational coherence. The shaft steward structures of the union were in most respects as robust as the shop steward structures favoured by Fosatu.'[23] Ramaphosa enjoyed the articles – the first sympathetic pieces written by the intellectual left on his union – and he asked Golding to join NUM to develop its in-house information sheet, *NUM News*, into a proper union newspaper.[24]

In the event, Golding rapidly became the union's *de facto* press officer, establishing a network of relationships with journalists that greatly enhanced its media impact. Suddenly NUM policy positions were expressed widely and clearly. As in the past, the amateurish and arrogant mining houses often depended on sloppy or even gratuitously hostile media relations, leading journalists to source stories from NUM instead. Soon many hacks became accustomed to accepting media releases from the union as the foundations for their stories.[25]

In the tumultuous wave of strikes that broke out in 1986 and 1987, Golding was increasingly drawn into organisational work and conflict resolution, and had less and less time for the editorial and press work for which he had been hired.[26] The media profile of the union, nevertheless, was established.

The NUM's pragmatic approach to improving the conditions and opportunities of black mineworkers was highlighted in late 1986 by the union's decision to accept an invitation from a parliamentary committee to make a submission about the removal of racial job reservation. The political context was a difficult one for such an engagement with the parliament. Government had imposed a national state of emergency just months earlier in a clamp-down that re-emphasised the apartheid sympathies of the legislature.

Parliament was preparing to amend the 1956 Mines and Works Act which governed the operation of the mines. In August a bill had been tabled to delete parts of Section 12 of the Act, the notorious section that enshrined in law the colour bar governing skilled work in the mines. There was a broad agreement between the Chamber of Mines and the NUM that the colour bar should be removed. The mining houses were keen to alleviate their skills shortage and consequent upward wage pressure by allowing black mineworkers hitherto forbidden blasting certificates.[27] For the union, the colour bar entrenched in Section 12 was one of the most offensive aspects of the apartheid mining workplace.

The NUM's national executive committee determined that the union should present a case to parliament notwithstanding the fact that a state of emergency was in place and that the 'apartheid parliament' lacked popular legitimacy. Ramaphosa, Elijah Barayi and James Motlatsi, together with a strong legal team that included Paul Benjamin and representatives of Cheadle, Thompson & Haysom, travelled to Cape Town to make their case. The committee was on the face of it receptive to their demands, although the outcome was in many respects an ambiguous victory for the miners. Although a new clause tabled early the following year no longer included a colour bar, it still made possible the abuse of language and educational criteria to block the advance of black mineworkers to skilled positions.

By 1989, there were still just 100 black mineworkers in possession of blasting certificates, around one per cent of the total with such qualifications.[28] As Ramaphosa's response demonstrated, his pragmatic approach did not imply that matters would be allowed to rest. He observed that 'the Chamber has been devious in substituting educational standards for racial segregation ... It knows that the standards it demands for skilled positions are unobtainable for the vast majority of the black miners because of the inadequacies of the system of black education.'[29]

As the membership numbers mushroomed, Ramaphosa had to cope with the managerial challenges of a rapidly growing union. According to the historian of the union, 'the rate of recruitment outpaced the growth of the union's administrative infrastructure so that it was incapable of servicing them effectively'.[30] In the early days, Cyril's controlling and perfectionist character ensured a tight ship. He was a hands-on manager who personally maintained control over office resources – down to the paper clips and the stationery.

He soon grudgingly had to learn how to delegate effectively, and to make use of whatever skills could be found in the office. The staff and organisers, who were mostly drawn from the mines themselves, were for the most part poorly educated and lacking in experience. NUM 'was so persistently short of staff that Ramaphosa had to accept almost anyone who offered to work for the union'.[31] Posts that were already funded by foreign donors – for example, an education unit and a health and safety department – could not be staffed. For several years the union operated without a bookkeeper, accounts were not properly kept, and members' subscriptions were spent without adequate records or controls. The abuse of office resources – and especially cars – led to the union incurring unnecessary costs that detracted from its effectiveness.[32]

Ramaphosa was a demanding manager. He has always been an exceptionally, even obsessively, punctual person, and he required the same from his employees. He paid close attention to the detail of his subordinates' work, and was critical of what he perceived to be failures of attention or effort. Simphiwe Nanise, a young organiser recruited from the General and Allied Workers' Union, was one of many exceptional talents who flourished in Ramaphosa's NUM. He found Ramaphosa to be 'a perfectionist – he wanted people to do things right. He didn't like people who were lax in their jobs.'[33] But Cyril was also supportive and capable of considerable kindness. His approach was always to challenge subordinates with problems as well as to support them. His first question, when a NUM worker approached him with a problem, was 'What steps have *you* taken?' If he was convinced they had exhausted the avenues available to them, only then would he step in and take action.[34]

Ramaphosa continued to be preoccupied with the always parlous financial state of the union. For most of the decade, the NUM was to remain heavily dependent on external funding. In its early days it drew upon support from the Industrial Workers' Union (FNV) of the Netherlands. However, as the NUM became a runaway success in 1984 and 1985, it began to attract the interest of Swedish unions, who soon became the key funding sources.

The Scandinavians were generous and benevolent partners. They drove important focused initiatives such as shop-steward education as well as providing core institutional funding, and the disciplines they imposed helped the union to develop systematic and credible organisational and financial reporting. The NUM became the darling of the Scandinavians because of Ramaphosa's personal commitment to

The former Ramaphosa family house on Mhlaba Drive, Tshiawelo, Soweto, as it appears today. (Photo: the author)

The courtyard at Mphaphuli High School, Sibasa, Venda. (Photo: the author)

Cyril Ramaphosa in Stockholm, Sweden, on a fundraising visit for the NUM, October 1983. (Photo: NUM)

Cyril Ramaphosa and Harry Oppenheimer at a debate to mark the first anniversary of the Weekly Mail, *June 1986. (Photo: Johncom)*

Elijah Barayi, vice-president of the NUM from 1982 to 1994 and president of Cosatu between 1985 and 1991. (Photo: NUM)

NUM press conference at the Carlton Hotel during the great strike of August 1987. From left to right: Kuben Pillay, James Motlatsi, Cyril Ramaphosa and Marcel Golding. (Photo: NUM)

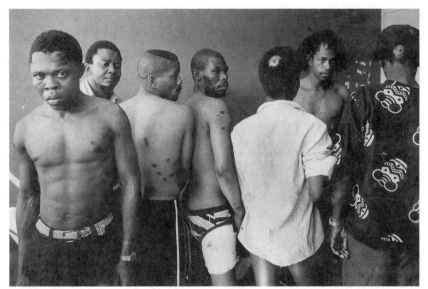

Rubber bullet injuries. Aftermath of a clash between mine security and mineworkers, Western Deep Levels, August 1987. (Photo: NUM)

Joe Slovo and Cyril Ramaphosa at a march to the Chamber of Mines, September 1990. (Photo: NUM)

March to the Chamber of Mines, September 1990. From left to right: Cyril Ramaphosa, Kgalema Motlanthe and Pallo Jordan. (Photo: NUM)

ANC press conference, September 1991. From left to right: Nelson Mandela, Jay Naidoo, and recently elected secretary-general Cyril Ramaphosa. (Photo: Business Day)

Nelson Mandela and Cyril Ramaphosa, August 1993. (Photo: Sunday Times)

The management committee of the Transitional Executive Council, March 1994, celebrates its choice of a new national flag. Centre, standing: Joe Slovo, Mac Maharaj and Fanie van der Merwe. Seated left to right: Cyril Ramaphosa, Mathews Phosa, Pravin Gordhan, Colin Eglin, Roelf Meyer. (Photo: Gillian Hutchings)

The principals and the 'channel' at a press conference near the culmination of constitutional negotiations, 28 April 1996. From left to right: Ramaphosa, Nelson Mandela, FW de Klerk, Roelf Meyer. (Photo: Business Day)

Cyril Ramaphosa and his wife Tshepo Motsepe, at the Sowetan awards ceremony, June 2002. (Photo: Sunday Times)

The Africa Investment Forum, April 2003. From left to right: Commonwealth Business Council CEO Mohan Kaul, trade and industry minister Alec Erwin, and Cyril Ramaphosa. (Photo: Business Day)

Cyril Ramaphosa and Trevor Manuel at the Blue IQ Smart Partnership, October 2003. (Photo: Business Day)

financial accountability and the good relationships he developed with Swedish trade unionists and government officials in the department of international aid (Sida). A similar relationship with the British National Union of Mineworkers probably also helped keep NUM afloat in the second half of the decade.[35]

The politics of international labour solidarity were exceptionally complex during the Cold War. Unions were divided into two hostile camps. A World Trade Union Federation (WTUF) brought together trade unions closely associated with Moscow-aligned national communist parties. Meanwhile, an International Confederation of Free Trade Unions (ICFTU) served as the umbrella for reformist West European trade unions and the anti-communist American Federation of Labour/Congress of International Organisations (AFL/CIO) in the US. Within the mining sector this split was mirrored in a division between the pro-Moscow International Miners' Organisation (IMO) and the reformist Miners' International Federation (MIF).[36]

The NUM was largely successful in avoiding embroilment in the debilitating stand-offs between international federations. While there were political sensitivities about accepting funds from US affiliates of the ICFTU in particular, the Swedes were willing to bypass their own umbrella organisation. Ramaphosa was equally happy to solicit funds, at the opposite extreme, from the All-Union Central Council of Trade Unions of the Soviet Union.[37]

Ramaphosa gradually built up the capacity of the national and regional offices. By 1986, the union had 32 full-time officials, around half of these in the national office. He had created a structure that could survive the death or detention of its leadership. It was still, however, a very imperfect machine.

When Andeya Baleni, the daughter of a worker on the Saaiplaas gold mine in the Orange Free State, arrived for her first day of work in the office in 1986, she found an administration stretched to the point of breaking. The key focus of the national office was on organisation and recruitment, with seven of the staff working full-time in this area. They had no computers and relied on a rudimentary paper card system for recording members' details. The two workers in the finance department who were supposed to manage members' dues were underqualified, and systems for collecting subscriptions were rudimentary. Money was usually still brought into the office in bags and simply tipped on to the table tops.[38]

The national office officials were assigned to departments for collective bargaining, organisation, health and safety, finance, research and publications, and education. Most departments were perennially understaffed, and all of them were overseen by a restless Ramaphosa. In Cyril's 'all-embracing approach to leadership',[39] he also continued to write his own speeches, handle correspondence, prepare press briefings, assemble materials for the negotiations rounds, and liaise regularly with representatives of the regions and branches. He was increasingly drawn away from the office by his wider political commitments.

Cyril was never really successful in managing either his escalating personal workload or the growing organisational overload afflicting the national office. He sacrificed his personal life, and perhaps his second marriage to Baragwanath nurse and aspirant lawyer Nomazizi Mtshotshisa, to absurdly long and relentless hours of work in the union offices.

To relieve the pressure on other national office workers, he introduced a strategy of decentralisation in 1985, designed to bolster the authority and resources in the regional offices of the union. In its intentions, this shift of authority should have increased the accountability of officials to members, improved the management of subscriptions and spending, and reduced the burden on the head office. In reality, the national office continued to be the centre of important decision-making, and representatives of the regions and branches flowed through the national office every day, engaging Cyril personally with their grievances and problems.

Ramaphosa, moreover, refused to decentralise the collection of subscriptions. He was of the opinion that financial federalism would lead to endless conflicts over money and insisted that resources continue to be allocated from the centre according to need.[40]

The other staff members were obliged to perform to Cyril's demanding standards. New recruit Irene Charnley still recalls his first request for her to draft a letter. 'When he handed it back to me, he said "What is this?"' The piece of paper was covered with hand-written corrections. 'I never made that mistake again. We all looked up to Cyril so much that

we were desperate to avoid disappointing him.' Charnley feels this was
a valuable stimulus to self-discipline for a whole generation of NUM
activists. 'Wherever you look at NUM people today, they are successful.
It was Cyril who gave us this opportunity and taught us discipline and
respect, and I will always be grateful to him for it.'[41]

Members of the head office staff were constantly pulled away from their
designated tasks by the more immediate demands of organisation and
negotiation. Irene Charnley's own trajectory illustrates this well. Her
early story bears some striking similarities to Kuben Pillay's. Studying
in England, she had seen Cyril Ramaphosa and James Motlatsi speaking
at a rally organised by the British NUM. She immediately decided that
the R500 salary was no obstacle to working for the union and decided
to join on her return from London. She was to stay for 13 years and
ultimately became the union's chief negotiator in the coal, diamond and
uranium sectors.

Charnley had trained as a graphic designer. Like Marcel Golding,
she was recruited to create a proper union newspaper, but within a few
days Cyril called her over. 'I need someone to go to Dover Coal. I'm
throwing you in at the deep end – you will sink or you will swim. Get
down there and meet the shop stewards.'[42]

In a society dominated by sexist assumptions about the capacity of
women to engage in 'man's work', Charnley's experience was typical of
Ramaphosa's young female employees. Before her first participation in
negotiations with employers, Cyril said to her directly: 'Watch me. You
will only have one opportunity to learn from me. Watch exactly what
I do.' Whenever new recruits lacked skills, Ramaphosa would demand
that they acquire them. Few of the negotiators could drive a car, for
example, creating a dire problem of wasted time and staff duplication.
Cyril insisted that everyone simply had to learn to drive – a major hurdle
at the time – and then to acquire licences.

In the wage determination process, he forced everyone to prepare
rigorously in advance of negotiations – whether they would have to
participate directly or not. 'He would make us study a company's
financial reports until we knew its financial situation better than their
own negotiating team,' remembers Charnley. 'Then they would have to

pull their human resources people from the negotiations and bring in their CEOs.'[43]

Ramaphosa liked to say that the union offices belonged to the members, a position that on one occasion led to a major difference of opinion between him and James Motlatsi. Dismissed workers, and some who had other grievances that had not been satisfied in the regional offices, would come to Johannesburg to appeal for help. In December 1985, a number of workers who had been dismissed from Rustenburg and Western Areas arrived very upset. Some of them, penniless and with nowhere to stay, demanded that the union provide them with travel money so that they could get home.

Ramaphosa discussed this problem with Motlatsi and Elijah Barayi, arguing that they should allow the men to sleep at the union offices and provide them with some money to travel home for Christmas. Ramaphosa proposed an allowance of R300 per man. Motlatsi was utterly opposed to this action, arguing that it would set a precedent. Elijah Barayi grudgingly supported Cyril.[44]

The consequences Motlatsi had feared soon materialised. The retrenched workers returned from their Christmas break in January 1986, but now there were more of them. Word had got around that the union was offering money and accommodation to members with grievances. Quickly, numbers began to get out of hand, with first 50 and then 100 mineworkers sleeping in the building. At Easter they demanded travel money once again – but this time R450 each. When Cyril made them an offer of R320, they turned him down.

It was Ramaphosa's style in such circumstances to defuse tension. Once again he partly accommodated the demands, even though the union's finances were already in a parlous condition. Motlatsi was livid. At times like these, the two men – who had become almost like brothers – would row endlessly and then withdraw into an extended sulk, refusing to talk to one another for days at a time. Both of them were capable of intense stubbornness. Office workers would have to pass messages between the two men because neither was willing to talk until the other apologised for actions they could scarcely remember.[45]

After Easter the situation in the office became untenable. The number of miners continued to grow, and soon there were as many as 400 people sleeping in the building. After appealing to the central committee and other structures for help, Ramaphosa seconded a team of senior regional officials to the head office and tasked them with negotiating the exit of the now thoroughly unwelcome visitors. After 21 days of talks, they came to Motlatsi and told him they had failed.[46]

Members of staff were now being threatened with theft and violence by increasingly unruly miners. The slight but tough Andeya Baleni, who would truck no nonsense, was told she would be thrown out of a window.[47] It was evident that something had to be done, and soon. Motlatsi's view was that intimidation or even force might be essential instruments. Cyril could not countenance premeditated violence. But he was unable to offer any serious alternative. He left the offices and shut himself up in his home in Soweto's Jabulani Flats.[48]

Motlatsi thought of Ramaphosa as a relative political innocent. 'He did not have experience dealing with the mob psychology of a group of mineworkers. He thought they could find a solution through persuasion.' Relentless exposure to violence had hardened Motlatsi and the regional organisers. 'Where there was a faction fight,' Motlatsi comments, 'Cyril would be lost … [whereas] I knew from my experience of dealing with a violent mob that persuasion could not work … They were disruptive, they were paralysing the organisation.'[49]

Motlatsi and two comrades from local branches of the union met in the Victoria Hotel close to Park Station to consider the options. They decided that one of the three, Lebohang Hlaele, should assemble members of his Grootvlei branch to persuade the mineworkers to leave, if necessary using intimidation. In his history, Allen explains that 'The Grootvlei branch had a reputation for providing a heavy-handed security service for the union. Its members travelled around in red combis and were nicknamed "Amabutho" or "the army".'[50]

Hlaele took upwards of 30 Amabutho to the union offices in the middle of the night. En route, he later claimed, he decided that shock tactics would be needed to drive so many people out of the building. He planned a sudden and brutal physical attack, executed by fast-moving Amabutho who stormed through the front of the union offices. Allen continues the story. 'All of the mineworkers were forced into the road and were dispersed. Some ran out without their clothes. Many were badly beaten, in some cases with broken arms or legs; at least one was seriously injured and one allegedly died from his injuries. The members of the Grootvlei branch disappeared into the night immediately after the incident. Hlaele then reported to Motlatsi that the office had been emptied.'[51]

Unfortunately, despite this robust intervention, some of the occupying miners regrouped and made their way back to the offices. Once again they entered the building and threatened staff with violence. Motlatsi decided that the eviction should be repeated, only this time with a contingent of union executive members and some students leading the fray. The siege leader was a union organiser who had come round to support the protest. 'Though he was armed,' reports Allen, 'he was overpowered, forced into the boot of a car and driven away. He was never seen again, but it was rumoured that he was returned to his home in the rural areas.'[52]

Motlatsi drove to Jabulani Flats and told a distressed Ramaphosa that the miners had been evicted. Cyril was not consolable, and stubbornly refused to accept that the action was necessary. In Motlatsi's view, his friend just could not admit he was wrong. Did he ever come round to seeing that Motlatsi had been right? 'It was five years before he would accept this.'[53]

The union kept no record of the events of those two days, and they were not reported in the newspapers. This saved NUM from the embarrassment of being accused of attacking its own members. But talk of the events spread by word of mouth. Although dismissed union members continued to petition the head office for financial support during the day, they would leave the building at 6 p.m. This became known as 'Motlatsi's hour'.[54]

If Cyril often depended on his partner Motlatsi to manage the turbulent internal politics of the union, he was the master of its interaction with the world outside. He had a mandate from the executive that allowed him to talk outside the negotiating chamber and to deal informally with industry bosses whose cooperation was sometimes essential. Although Cyril had this freedom to negotiate outside formal structures, he always reported back in detail to Motlatsi.[55]

Cyril's work at EFK Tucker and his interaction with bosses on the Urban Foundation board gave him a subtler understanding of the mentality of white business people than his comrades. He also had a far wider and quite different network of relationships. Motlatsi was a miner's miner, whose life had revolved around the industry for more than a decade. He never felt it appropriate to question Cyril about his life before the union. For him the man was a genius in his work as a negotiator and an organiser – 'I have never heard a man so able to collect his words'[56] – and his trust in Ramaphosa's fundamental commitment to the interests of the union's members was complete.

Cyril also had to earn the trust of mineworkers themselves, despite his evident compassion and dedication to their cause. Miners often questioned his motivation in the early days. 'Eventually,' Cyril explained, 'I found that I was well accepted ... because looking at my own personal life they found out that I had been in conflict with the state and had been detained.'[57]

Ramaphosa's authority grew as a result of his relentless work rate, his fairness to mineworkers who visited NUM offices, and by tales that began to circulate about his fearlessness, a quality much prized among underground workers who faced down fear every day. Clive Thompson remembers that 'some of the fearlessness took the form of apparent indifference to danger', demonstrated on one occasion when he had been detained unlawfully during industrial conflict at Foskor in Phalaborwa in the mid-1980s. Thompson went to Phalaborwa, and brought urgent proceedings in the Supreme Court for Ramaphosa's release.

'The legal pressure obliged the security forces to release him even before any court determination on the rights of his detention, and I went to the cells to get him out. He emerged barefoot and dusty, but essentially unmoved by everything around him. Phlegmatic about both his arrest and release. All in a day's work, almost matter of fact. No great indignation over his incarceration, no great jubilation or appreciation upon his liberation. No sense of martyrdom either. He was just doing the necessary and wearing the consequences.'[58]

Ramaphosa also showed no fear when he was underground. On one occasion, he was over two kilometres below ground at an accident scene at East Rand Proprietary Mines, one of the country's oldest and deepest mines, where a rock burst had 48 hours earlier killed several mineworkers. Crawling along largely collapsed stopes towards the scene of the rock burst, with half a dozen companions, the group suddenly heard cracking noises in the 'hanging wall' above their heads. A mine safety engineer instructed the party to flee. The scramble to extract themselves from the zone of immediate danger took some 15 terrifying minutes. 'While being just as keen as everyone else to get the hell out of the area, [Cyril] was essentially unshaken by the event. Just another day at the office.'[59]

While respect for Ramaphosa deepened among ordinary members of the NUM, he also had to quietly establish working relationships with the bosses whom mineworkers so profoundly distrusted. He recognised that if the union was to grow, it needed at times to work closely with the mine head offices to overcome the recalcitrance of the most conservative mine managers.

Cyril's key interlocutor was inevitably Bobby Godsell, evangelist for the modernisation of labour relations within Anglo and initially the most acceptable face of the bosses to Cyril and his senior colleagues. Godsell had been in charge of the research division at Anglo, which had tried to predict and manage the consequences of the Wiehahn reforms, and he was instrumental in the creation of a new industrial relations department in Anglo's gold and uranium division.

There were in essence two kinds of communication. A high-level 'channel' between Cyril and Godsell was reserved for unusually intractable disputes or for the high points of the annual wage round. During the yearly negotiations, the two men would sometimes meet for breakfast at the Carlton Hotel, informally to settle differences that might become intractable if left to the negotiating table.[60] Godsell was based at Anglo's corporate offices for most of this period and he was not in daily touch with the gold division.

The second and more routine interlocutor, Nigel Unwin, was head of industrial relations at the gold and uranium division. (He was the same Unwin who later tried unsuccessfully to woo Kuben Pillay to 45 Main Street.) Unwin dealt on a day-to-day basis with the relations between union and management. When NUM had concerns about the actions of particular mine managers or problems at mine level, Cyril would contact Unwin directly. When Anglo was concerned about mineworker violence or indiscipline, Unwin could raise the matter directly with Cyril. This channel was a boon to both sides, allowing the negotiators and deal-makers at the centre to manage their own hardliners – be they conservative mine managers or problematic local union organisers.[61]

Like wage-bargaining itself, the Anglo channels drew the key parties on each side closer together. As we have seen, the toughest and longest battles in the negotiating process are with one's own side and not with the avowed enemy. The mining houses would struggle bitterly to reach a common negotiating position, while the union desperately battled to rally workers. The senior negotiators on both sides naturally came to recognise the constraints under which their opposite numbers laboured, and to understand their difficulties in dealing with their own constituencies.

Indeed, the channels between NUM and Anglo were so vital precisely because neither side could really control its own constituency. The mine managers were a breed apart, rising through the ranks at a mine, proud of their technical prowess, and jealously guarding their autonomy from company head offices. They were mostly implacable defenders of a mine culture in which the induna system, hostel control, ethnic manipulation, and shoot-first mine security were the established instruments for getting ore out of the ground in a demanding technical and financial environment.

A gulf also separated the ordinary mineworkers from their leadership in Lekton House. Bitter divisions between grades of workers sometimes broke out – with skilled workers jealously guarding their privileges and wage differentials. Within the compounds conflicts could flare up that the union leadership had no possibility of controlling. Even Motlatsi was keenly aware of the limits of his influence over aroused workers.

It was hard work for both teams to ensure that the agreements they struck in Johannesburg were enforced in the mine shafts and compounds. The negotiators shared a scepticism about the words and motivations of people who were purportedly on their 'own side'. Moreover, they developed relationships of qualified trust. But these fragile bonds were about to be shattered by the most devastating year in the history of the South African mining industry.

CHAPTER 11

AUGUST 1987

In the early days of the NUM, Ramaphosa sought to avoid a major strike that might destroy the union. The leadership instead focused on building membership and organisational strength. Within two years of the union's creation, this strategy was already bearing fruit. At the same time, Anglo American's project of industrial relations modernisation was turning into a nightmare. Not only was there no end in sight to escalating conflict on the mines, but NUM was also becoming a channel for wider political protest.

Workers, initially awed by their new ability to exercise some kind of control over their living and working conditions, began to raise their sights.[1] In 1984, their potential power began to emerge. The union demanded wage increases of between 30 and 60 per cent for different categories of workers for that year. After a show of negotiation, the Chamber simply imposed its far lower offer on 1 July, sparking an outburst of uncoordinated strikes. NUM carefully exhausted all conciliation avenues, and religiously adhered to Labour Relations Act guidelines in balloting, so that the 75,000-strong strike which began on 16 September was legal.

The limited reach of the new labour relations system was indicated by the violent spillover conflicts that did not involve the union, conflicts that left 16 people dead. In consequence, the Chamber of Mines was forced to make tactical concessions and the official strike ended two days later. As Allen emphasises, 'in the space of two years the NUM had come to symbolize opposition to white management'.[2] Even while it adhered carefully to the letter of the law, the union discovered that strikes have great symbolic and emotional power. 'When we had our first strike,' Ramaphosa observes, 'that was when we thought we were now a real union.'[3]

In 1985, there were numerous fractious and uncoordinated disputes and mass dismissals on many mines. In a new form of political protest, two limpet mines exploded at Anglovaal's offices in Main Street, creating an uproar among white citizens and increasing political pressure on the mining houses to regularise relations with workers.[4] Yet the union now had muscles to flex. Established as a symbol of opposition, NUM attracted further worker interest and its growth continued at a dizzying pace.

In the same year the union was able to prepare to take out on strike some 200,000 members in 18 gold and 11 coal mines. When the Chamber imposed its 'final' offer on 1 July, and the union sought to ballot its members on strike action, Anglo American, JCI and Rand Mines broke ranks and made concessions. These mining houses were partly motivated by tactical considerations, seeking to undercut pressure for strike action, but their decision underlined the questionable solidarity of the Chamber's members. One of Ramaphosa's strategies in the early 1980s was to peel Anglo away from its fellow employers, in effect persuading the giant to trade higher wages and better conditions for industrial peace.[5]

In 1986, there were more than a hundred 'wildcat' strikes in the industry. After the Kinross disaster, in which 177 miners were killed in a preventable accident, a one-day NUM protest in September brought out a quarter of a million mineworkers. The end of the year was marked by a wave of conflict within the mines, much of it 'faction fighting' resulting from the union organisers' challenge to existing systems of induna and tribal authority. More than a hundred mineworkers were killed. The union took out an advertisement in the liberal *Weekly Mail* on 9 January 1987: 'Let it be known once and for all that the source of conflict is rooted in the institutions of oppression and exploitation which exist in the mining industry. The hostel system, migrant labour, and the induna system were pioneered at the turn of the century by the mine owners to ensure maximum exploitation and control over all aspects of mineworkers' lives. It is from this brutal and draconian system that Anglo American Corporation has benefited. Over time these structures have been refined but kept intact. AAC has identified and acknowledged some of the issues which have caused the tensions. But what has it done? AAC wants industrial relations to be sound and orderly yet it is not prepared to remove the archaic structures which are the source of conflict.'[6]

Earlier in 1986, Ramaphosa had an opportunity to confront Harry Oppenheimer directly about mine conditions. At a celebration of the first anniversary of the *Weekly Mail*, Ramaphosa and Oppenheimer were both asked to speak. Ramaphosa was invited as the darling of the media. Oppenheimer had made a R5,000 donation to the paper. Ramaphosa went on the attack. 'The mining industry', he argued, 'provided the furnace in which race discrimination was baked … Today it relies absolutely on the exploitative migrant labour system and on police oppression to operate. It pays black workers the lowest wages of any major mining company in the world, with the exception of India …'[7]

Oppenheimer complained that Ramaphosa was politicising what should be a celebration. 'I differ a little bit from Cyril Ramaphosa in thinking that this ought to be fun. I think it should be rather a cheerful occasion. The fact that Mr Cyril Ramaphosa is here to talk as he did talk tonight – a most touching and moving speech, made all the more touching by the neglect of the facts – the fact that we were both here to talk together is something which gives me very great pleasure.'[8]

In reply, Ramaphosa characterised the difference between the two men in this way: while Oppenheimer 'loves diamonds, I love diamond diggers'.

Meanwhile, a wave of popular discontent was sweeping across the country. Mineworkers were also parents, consumers and political activists, and they inexorably brought the deepening political conflict into the mine compounds. As political unrest intensified, government responded with violence and detentions, and finally imposed a nation-wide state of emergency in 1986. The leadership of the United Democratic Front (UDF), the body that coordinated domestic opposition to apartheid, was decimated by detentions and harassment. Trade unions like NUM, with their more robust organisation, became increasingly central to political struggle. While union leaders differed over the best tactical deployment of union power, most black unions were now vehicles for anti-regime as well as labour relations protest. During 1986, an unprecedented 1.3 million days were lost to strike action.

Most of NUM's officials were sure that there would be a major confrontation on the mines in 1987. Regional organisers believed that mineworkers' discontent made a massive strike simply inevitable.[9] James Motlatsi remembers that mineworkers were so profoundly angry that headline wage increases were almost irrelevant. 'They could have offered 30 per cent, they could have offered 50 per cent. It would have made no difference. If somehow the strike had been put off for a year, the expectations would have been higher in 1988.'[10]

Powerful forces were also propelling Anglo American towards a showdown. These pressures induced subterranean shifts in the complex internal power structure of the Anglo empire. Within the company that had embraced modernised labour relations most wholeheartedly, many operational executives had come to regret the decision bitterly. Anglo had the best labour practices and had willingly signed access and recognition agreements. Yet it was Anglo that was reaping the bitterest harvest in terms of strike action. Its initial openness to union organisation resulted in 80 per cent of striking mineworkers being Anglo employees.

For many mining-house conservatives, battles on the mine compounds were instigated by communists and professional agitators.[11] Within Anglo, reactions tended to be more pragmatic, but executives nonetheless saw the union as a monster of the company's own creation. All mining houses had been left vulnerable to proxy political struggles as a result of their decision in the 1970s to escalate the use of domestic rather than regional labour. Anglo's embrace of the union seemed to have greatly deepened this vulnerability. The failure of Godsell to deliver a tame labour union was just one more failure of his 'modern' labour relations.

Discontent on Main Street about labour modernisation was echoed elsewhere. To the mine managers, it was music to their ears. They had felt that NUM's inroads into the induna system, and the union's drive to take control of the hostels, were leading managers to lose control of 'their mines'. Almost to a man, they were itching to re-establish conventional forms of control and to crush organisational mechanisms introduced by NUM.

In the meantime, the position of Anglo's 'do-gooders' and 'modernisers' was weakening fast. At the start of the decade, the gold price had soared from $234 per ounce to $850, allowing Anglo to reap handsome profits, accommodate real wage increases, and still have resources to respond to the initiatives of industrial relations 'modernisers' such as Godsell.[12] Yet the promised benign consequences of unionisation had not materialised, and the hard economic times were back with a vengeance. Deteriorating business conditions transferred power back from the labour relations empires towards tough-minded finance departments.

The heart of the problem was that the mining houses were running out of mineable gold.[13] Declining ore grades meant digging out more rock to extract less metal, in ever-deeper and more technically demanding mines. A phenomenal 550,000 mineworkers were now employed. Moreover, demand for costly skilled workers such as drillers and winch drivers was growing, while demand for lower-paid lashers and hand trammers was falling.[14] Furthermore, although the gold price is notoriously unpredictable, the consensus was that it was likely to fall sharply in coming years.[15]

NUM emerged just as these economic pressures on an industry in historical decline were starting to bite.[16] Harry Oppenheimer, who had nurtured Godsell's project, was no longer on hand to protect his modernisation brainchild. Since 1983, a more orthodox management committee held sway at Anglo. The new executive chairman was Gavin Relly, the first non-family chair as successor to Ernest and Harry Oppenheimer, who had successively run the company from 1917 to 1983. Relly was almost family, an Anglo 'lifer' selected for the fast track and appointed as Harry Oppenheimer's PA as early as 1949.

Relly was also first and foremost a professional businessman, who would adopt the paternalism and social interventionism of Oppenheimer only if it made business sense. He was certainly a most political animal. It was Relly who saw the need for Anglo to investigate the character of the exile ANC leadership, organising the famous 'businessmen's trip' to Lusaka in late 1985. He took with him Anglo political strategist Zach de Beer, robust business realist Tony Bloom, editors Harald Pakendorf of *Die Vaderland* and Tertius Myburgh of the *Sunday Times*, and the head of the South Africa Foundation. Anton Rupert characteristically withdrew under pressure from PW Botha – pressure to which Harry Oppenheimer also capitulated, resulting in the old man telling Relly not to go. Relly rebutted this suggestion and insisted the trip must go ahead regardless of the hostility of the government of the day.[17]

Relly was building a bridge for an uncertain future. More importantly, he was determined to assess the radicalism of the ANC leadership, and the threat it correspondingly posed to the survival of Anglo in a post-apartheid era. He came back smiling, convinced that the liberation movement leaders were patriotic sheep in Marxist wolves' clothing.[18] While Relly was decisive in relations with the ANC, he also managed Anglo's interactions with government professionally rather than paternally. In March 1985, he recruited Anglo's first full-time public affairs executive, Michael Spicer – just in time for Spicer to report back on PW Botha's 'Rubicon' speech, which dashed the hopes of reformers in South Africa and abroad.[19]

There was no reason to suppose that an executive committee headed by Relly, whose other key members were Julian Ogilvie Thompson, Hank Slack and Nicky Oppenheimer, would risk Anglo assets to defend labour relations initiatives in the absence of a compelling business logic for doing so. Godsell's ideas were compelling in their own way, because chaotic labour relations had proved demonstrably costly and a transition to formalised labour relations had to be brought about at some stage. But NUM, right then in the second half of the 1980s, was a lightning rod for wider grievances and a potential obstacle to the rationalisation that deteriorating economic conditions necessitated. Now was not a good time to lose control of the mines. In the very near future, many mines would have to close and low-grade ore would have to be left in the ground. In such circumstances, a showdown with NUM was not merely about one year's wage increases: NUM had to be decisively defeated in order to set advantageous future patterns of industrial relations. No doubt, there were some Anglo executives who wanted to destroy the union. If a decisive confrontation was coming, moreover, it was better for Anglo that it came soon.

For Ramaphosa, the impending strike was also much more than an industrial relations dispute. He was one of many activists who overestimated what in the language of the time was called 'regime vulnerability'. At the union's fifth annual congress in February 1987, Cyril told the assembled delegates that the apartheid regime had been decisively weakened by mass protest and that a 'dramatic transformation' was on the cards.

The keynote speaker was Winnie Mandela, symbol of ANC struggle. The slogan chosen for 1987 was 'The Year Mineworkers Take Control', a deliberate echo of the ANC's 'Year of Advance to People's Power'. Delegates adopted the Freedom Charter and endorsed the following motion: 'The NUM and the organised working class in general must play their historic role in the struggle for a non-racial and democratic South Africa.'[20] All of this unambiguously committed the union to the wider liberation struggle.

On 20 March, NUM demanded a 'living wage' for all mineworkers, the first step towards which would be a 30 per cent increase for 1987/88. The union also demanded the abolition of the migrant labour system, improved hostel accommodation, and democratic hostels. Unreasonably, Ramaphosa demanded a response by 30 March, clearly aching for a fight.[21]

The union began to make preparations for a major confrontation. NUM had moved in 1986 from the dingy Lekton House to the relative luxury of Cosatu House in Jeppe Street, where it was able to spread out over three floors. In early 1987, the building began to attract security police attention. Adriaan Vlok, the minister of law and order, determined that Cosatu House was fostering a 'revolutionary climate', giving sanctuary to wanted political activists, and hosting undesirable activities such as proscribed meetings. Vlok contacted Johannes van der Merwe, head of the Security Branch, to discuss how these activities could be curtailed. Van der Merwe brought in local Special Branch head Nicholas Erasmus and Willem Frederick Schoon, the head of Unit C1 (Vlakplaas), the operational arm of the police service responsible for covert operations against the ANC and its allies.[22] He briefed them on the sinister character of the building, cautioned them to avoid deaths and serious injuries, but otherwise gave them a free hand to neutralise the problem.

The Security Branch operational team carried out preliminary surveillance operations from a nearby rooftop, and used a hidden camera in a briefcase to determine the internal layout of corridors and rooms. The head of the operational team, Eugene de Kock, purchased torches, stabbing knives, rope and bolt cutters, and sourced 50 kg of explosives of Russian origin – such as hypothetical communist terrorists might be storing in Cosatu House.[23] He then assembled a team of 16 Vlakplaas operatives, and equipped them with firearms, including silenced AK-47 rifles. The men removed all identifying insignia and badges, before preparing drugged cans of beer designed to render guards unconscious.

In an operation that took just four minutes, they approached and entered the building through basement windows after cutting through security bars. Explosives specialists placed charges where they would create the greatest structural damage. The Vlakplaas agents then retreated unobserved to a highway to the east of the city centre. A few minutes later they heard the expected pair of powerful explosions.[24]

The twin blasts had devastating effects. The first three floors of the building were occupied by NUM, and these bore the brunt of the explosion. When NUM workers came to work the following morning, they found that their third-floor desks were in the basement. The legal department and the health and safety department, on the first floor, were more or less completely obliterated. Years of data and records were destroyed.[25] The city council rapidly cordoned off the building after declaring it unsound, and in this way prevented union staff from retrieving sensitive records.

NUM hired rooms in Victoria Hotel and then borrowed office space from the South African Council of Churches. Soon they relocated to NUM's own regional office at Darragh House in Wanderers Street. As the wage negotiations progressed, NUM was crammed into a single floor of the old office building, where tiny working spaces were divided by flimsy partitions. Although the bomb was detrimental to the longer-term development of the union's databases and infrastructure, the inadvertent introduction of a then unfashionable open-plan office – in which everyone could see everyone else simply by looking over their partitions – made this an exceptionally efficient space during the crisis to come.

The turmoil of the national office also bolstered the union's programme of decentralisation, and immensely talented tiers of area and regional organisers made a virtue out of necessity. Most of these officials had worked on the mines, and they had first-hand experience of the grinding war between union and management at the level of the compounds and mine shafts. They were able to develop strike plans tailored to the conditions in which they had to work.

While the union recovered from the bombing, the mining houses were making their own preparations for the strike to come. Johann Liebenberg, Chamber of Mines' head of industrial relations, cautions today against seeing too much rational calculation in the strike. 'We were all acting on gut feel, and we had only been at this process with Cyril and black mineworkers for five or six years – it was still a new process for us all.'[26] Despite this disclaimer, there were many indications that the mining houses had laid their plans carefully that year. The key figure in these plans was the head of Anglo American's gold and uranium division, Peter Gush. He was not one of Anglo's Oxford boys, but rather a mining engineer with a natural sympathy for the difficult tasks confronting mine management. After a strong early career at Anglo, he had spent seven years in the Canadian mining industry where a union-intolerant industrial relations culture prevailed.[27] Gush was not by temperament a negotiator, rather being disposed to take a well-reasoned decision and then stick to it.[28]

As president of the Chamber of Mines from July 1986 to June 1987, Gush prepared the ground for the strike in accordance with this personal style. His philosophical adversary, Bobby Godsell, was away in Boston in the six months preceding the strike, engaged in an episode of personal development. Although Godsell returned just in time to act as Anglo's key strike spokesman, he was to play no role in the negotiations that year.[29] In the lengthy pre-negotiations in the Chamber, Gush secured a mandate among the mining houses for an uncompromising stance on wages: there would be no divisions this year. Johann Liebenberg still recalls adamantly that 'the union got nothing on wages!'[30]

Vic Allen observes that mine owners also had 'ample time to take their usual precautions of building up stockpiles of ore or coal, preparing their security forces for conflict, recruiting vigilantes and ensuring that there were adequate supplies of strike-breakers'.[31] Gold stockpiling on the mines began many months in advance. Even a short strike would cause longer-term disruption to production, and some precautionary stockpiling was essential.[32] This year, however, there would be no interruptions of supply during the strike or its aftermath, and the unprecedented size of stockpiles allowed the mining houses to negotiate from a position of strength. Overall gold production in the year of the great strike would fall only 10 tons short of its prior target of 630 tons. Meanwhile, the Reserve Bank doubled the size of its strategic reserve of gold, which reached 6.2 billion fine ounces by November 1987.[33]

Anglo also had plenty of time to consider a strategy of dismissals. Mass dismissals in 1987 are sometimes viewed as an unprecedented reaction, by a highly pressurised management, to a desperate situation underground. At the time whole shafts were in danger of deteriorating to such an extent that production would be permanently lost. In the words of the gold division's industrial relations head, Nigel Unwin, 'Certainly, the stope collapsing was the primary reason (and defence) for commencing with mass dismissals.'[34]

But Anglo had used dismissals before, and as recently as 1985 had found that they could be a costly weapon. During the torrid 1985 conflicts at Vaal Reefs, Anglo had decided to break the strike by dismissing 14,400 workers and forcefully evicting them from the mine premises. According to Allen, this decision had devastating consequences for No. 8 shaft, probably Anglo's single most productive shaft, which never recovered to its pre-dismissals production trajectory.[35]

The lesson that Anglo learnt was not that mass dismissals must never be used. Indeed, Johann Liebenberg announced on the first day of the strike, in a comment reported in the American press, that if the strike lasted longer than a few days the mining houses might resort to a policy of mass dismissals.[36] Minister of manpower Pietie du Plessis also saw a role for dismissals, telling the BBC on 11 August that they would not disrupt production for long because 'the mines will most probably take on other workers; they have a surplus of workers in the mining industry'.[37] Even Bobby Godsell, a few days after his return from the US, reiterated that 'a business had to defend its financial interests' and could not permit workers to continue striking 'until it was sequestrated.

But no employer wanted mass dismissals of workers in whom a lot of money had been invested.'[38]

Today Godsell says he was fearful of the 'visceral conflict' that he discovered on his return to Johannesburg. His reported comments about dismissals had nothing to do with a premeditated plan to attack or destroy the union. Rather they were intended as a public warning to NUM not to exclude the possibility that such dismissals really could occur. He wanted NUM to understand that this time 'Anglo would not crumble!'[39]

When formal negotiations got under way on 15 May, the atmosphere was poisonous. NUM demanded 40 to 55 per cent wage increases, concessions around holiday leave, danger pay and death benefits, and (mischievously) that 16 June be declared a paid holiday. The Chamber responded with a 12.5 per cent offer. The gulf was wide, and the likelihood of conflict hardened.

NUM declared a dispute under the Labour Relations Act, which in principle should have triggered a complex conciliation process. The Chamber, however, decided in the normal way to impose its offer on 1 July. This act seemed to signal that the mining houses believed the balance of power in the industry 'had been unaffected by the rise of the NUM'.[40] The Chamber then taunted NUM officials for misrepresenting members' opinions and for exaggerating membership figures. Allen believes that this 'policy of trying to sideline the union by repeatedly understating its influence annoyed Ramaphosa, who began to see an all-out national strike as the only way of proving that the Chamber of Mines was wrong'.[41]

A ballot of 210,000 mineworkers soon showed that more than 95 per cent of those eligible to vote supported a strike. The union's executive discussed the results of the ballot on 2 August and decided to call a strike beginning the following Sunday, 9 August. On 3 August, Ramaphosa announced the union's decision to the press: 'We have been in dispute with the Chamber of Mines for some time now. After reaching deadlock at the conciliation board we proposed to the Chamber in the usual reasonable way that the dispute should be referred to mediation and arbitration. The Chamber of Mines rejected both proposals. We then proceeded with the strike ballot which received overwhelming support from our members … The strike ballot was a clear proof that our members are not satisfied. Our national executive committee met yesterday and decided that strike action should proceed this coming Sunday, that the night shift should not proceed underground and the day shift the following day until we have won our demands.'[42]

No one knew how long the strike would last. Experience pointed to a short episode of four or five days at most, but wise heads were concerned that a protracted war of attrition was quite conceivable. The Chamber's Johann Liebenberg publicly predicted a dispute of two to five days, while at the same time threatening mass dismissals if the strike lasted longer.[43] Michael Spicer, already a confidant of chairman Gavin Relly, observes today that 'Cyril's strategic agenda in 1987 was much bigger than just securing a few wage concessions. It would have been naïve to suppose that this strike would be a quick event.'[44]

NUM's organisers and officials were equally uncertain. 'It was a new kind of strike. We were more organised than ever before. But we never thought it would last 21 days.'[45] Marcel Golding agrees that 'there was no certainty about the length of the strike. We knew there was substantial support. There was no clear sense of the time it would last and there was a generally shared view that it would be short. But this was not planned for carefully.'[46]

James Motlatsi, on the other hand, was struck by the fury among ordinary mineworkers. 'I knew there would be a strike, I knew it would be hard to get people back to work, and I knew there would be mass dismissals.' Once the stoppage had begun, he recalls, the anger of the miners was of such great intensity that he would not have dared to suggest they return to work.[47] Even before the strike began, he was preoccupied with the repercussions of mass dismissals. It is on record that at the biggest mass meeting in the run-up to the strike in the Secunda region, he told mineworkers to prepare for a long stay-away.[48]

The action commenced on the evening of 9 August. 'The next day', remembers Johann Liebenberg, 'there were 300,000 workers on strike.'[49]

Ramaphosa felt elated – this was 'the pinnacle really, because you had 340,000 people out on strike on a strike that started on a day that was decided by two people, myself and James Motlatsi'.[50] Over 70 per cent of all black coal and gold miners had come out.

A battle for mineworkers' hearts and minds now commenced, with the hostels as the battlefield. Most mineworkers stayed in their hostels throughout the dispute. 'For 24 hours a day,' Allen observes, 'the mineworkers were exposed to the competitive moral and physical pressures from the local strike leaders, on the one hand, and the managers and security forces on the other.'[51]

Within the limits imposed by the national state of emergency and management repression, union officials tried out new tactics to maintain the strike. Elected strike committees had been put in place immediately before the stoppage began. In Welkom, miners elected by branches wore green T-shirts identifying them as committee members. They took control of hostels and kitchens, and ensured that catering and cleaning services continued. They also closed bars and ensured that strikers could not access smuggled liquor. Strike committee chairs gave regular feedback to miners on strike developments in mass meetings held two or three times every day.[52]

In most Witwatersrand mines, by contrast, management closed canteens and withdrew food from the striking mineworkers, in an attempt to starve them into submission. The union had to arrange for emergency rations to be smuggled into the hostels. Meanwhile, logistical and communications problems escalated when heavily armed mine security sealed compound perimeters.[53]

The union's temporary office in Johannesburg, a hive of round-the-clock activity, tried to coordinate and support local strike committees. Communication was exceptionally difficult, however, with fax and teletext machines working constantly. Even in the heat of battle, the legal department warehoused huge volumes of documentation of violence, intimidation and unfair dismissals. This paper trail was to prove decisive the following year in establishing the brutality of mine security and advancing grounds for the rehiring of dismissed workers.[54]

But more often than not, organisers had to come physically to the union offices to pass on information about developments on particular mines – and also to get updates from the national leadership about changes in strategy and developments in the negotiations.[55]

While the strike unfolded in various ways – no two mines were alike – violence, at least, was everywhere. The worst of the violence was inflicted by NUM's own members. Strikers assaulted non-strikers and strike-breakers with unprecedented viciousness. In some compounds, armed workers set up kangaroo courts and strikers received 'death sentences' for betraying their comrades.[56]

Mine security was also responsible for a 'familiar pattern of provocation and assault'.[57] Managers feared the strike might drag on and tried hard to break it quickly. Their determination to curtail the strike by force was evident in 'the manner in which the intensive and large-scale confrontations conducted by the security forces and the police were synchronized between Wednesday and Saturday in the first week'.[58] On the third day, the police made 177 arrests of shaft stewards and strike committee members in what Ramaphosa described as a 'pattern of repression that is beginning to evolve to try and destroy our strike. It was very well calculated by the Chamber of Mines as well as the government to crush the strike by arresting the leaders and leaving the strikers leaderless.'[59]

To this day mining-house executives remain reticent about the violence of mine and state security police in 1987. After mine unrest in the early 1970s, a confidential Inter-Departmental Committee of Inquiry into Riots on the Mines had identified communist agitators, migrant labour and hostel accommodation as the key sources of tension.[60] It recommended vastly scaled-up security, including a dedicated security unit at every mine, equipped with whips, shotguns, attack dogs, tear gas and armoured cars. The report also indicated that the security police should back up mine security.[61] Mine managers embraced the document wholeheartedly. By 1987, some of the larger mines had armoured cars and surveillance helicopters, and security police supplemented mine security intelligence by using supposedly prohibited paid informers.[62]

Industrial unrest policing was the responsibility of the deputy police minister, whose oversight of the National Security Management System entailed coordinating responses to major episodes of strike action, and ensuring that intelligence, police and private agencies worked together to best effect. The deputy minister between 1986 and 1988 in such a politically sensitive post was inevitably an Afrikaner political insider who could be trusted by PW Botha. This hardline minister was one of the few with direct access to the President at all times. His name was Roelf Meyer.[63]

Meyer liaised continuously with representatives of the mining houses and the Chamber, most frequently with Bobby Godsell and Johann Liebenberg. Godsell continues to defend aggressive policing in more or less the same terms he used at the time. 'Our security forces have only one role to play in a strike situation and that is to simply maintain order and prevent violence.'[64] He admits that boundaries were sometimes overstepped – for example in the use of live ammunition against what were civilian protesters, and in the piping of tear gas into worker hostels (which was undertaken by mine managers without the knowledge of Main Street). In such ways, he concedes, mine security did sometimes use 'inappropriate levels of violence'.

All the same, Godsell counters that 'it is hard to calibrate the level and form of violence to levels of threat'.[65] Given the degree of violence perpetrated by striking miners on non-strikers and strike-breakers, he claims intriguingly, Anglo's heavy-handed policing should be understood as an attempt by the company to 'protect the civil rights' of non-strikers.[66] It was over security, and the devastating use of violence, that the greatest falling out was to occur between Anglo and NUM.

By the end of the first week, there were no signs of an early end to the strike. Indeed both sides were digging in. On all sides there was a sense that the strike was getting out of hand.[67] Anglo called for a meeting with NUM leadership at the Carlton Hotel in downtown Johannesburg, to sound out possibilities for resolving the dispute but also to discuss escalating violence.[68] From the point of view of the NUM, there were two big issues on the table. The first was violence: who was responsible and how could it be curtailed? The second was the route to a settlement: would Anglo make the kinds of concessions that might allow the union to sell an offer to its increasingly entrenched strikers?[69]

The meeting was hastily arranged, and only a small venue was available in the hotel. Ramaphosa arrived first with his team: James Motlatsi, Marcel Golding and Kuben Pillay. Cyril carried a bag full of shotgun cartridges and rubber bullets that had been brought to the NUM headquarters by organisers. The NUM team placed these instruments of violence on the tables.

When Anglo's team arrived, it included Peter Gush, Bobby Godsell, Nigel Unwin and Don Ncube. There was bad blood between Gush and Ramaphosa, the senior negotiators on both sides. They had each come to blame the other for the violent behaviour of their subordinates. In addition, Ramaphosa's pragmatic and restless style of accommodation was anathema to the straightforward boss of the gold division.

The fireworks came when Ramaphosa spoke to Godsell about police violence on the mines. Ramaphosa had already become increasingly frustrated with his Anglo interlocutors. He would be on the phone many times every day with them and the conversations were largely cordial, if angry. On occasion, however, Cyril would simply shout 'Fuck you' and slam the phone down. He could then refuse to talk for days.

In personal meetings, on the other hand, Cyril tended to be calm and collected, making his behaviour on this day all the more extraordinary. He greeted the Anglo team with a blast of invective. With a sweeping arm, he brushed the rubber bullets and cartridges from the tables in front of him on to the floor. He shouted words at Bobby Godsell, the man who he thought had made promises and then failed to keep them. His words are remembered slightly differently by different participants. 'You are no longer Bobby Godsell! From now on you are "Baas Godsell",' recalls Nigel Unwin. For Godsell himself, it was the cartridges that were the focus of Ramaphosa's rage. 'Is this your concept of minimum force, Baas Godsell?'[70] The NUM delegation walked out of the talks once it became clear that Anglo had no concessions to make.

Things were not going entirely against the mining houses. They were not suffering heavy financial losses because of their careful planning, and they seemed to be weathering adverse international media coverage of mine security violence. However, the longer-term deterioration of the mine stopes was becoming a pressing concern. The collapsing of unworked stopes was a problem about which almost everyone in the industry was fully aware. Deep-level mines are like organisms whose survival depends upon constant activity. Without daily maintenance of support systems, the incredible underground pressures relentlessly crush flat mine supports, and rock bursts collapse tunnel roofs and walls. It was inconceivable that Anglo would simply allow its assets to be permanently destroyed in this way. The company now had to decide how to bring the strike to a rapid end.

In reality, Anglo still held most of the cards. At one end of its spectrum of options, it could make substantial concessions, particularly on headline wages, that would allow NUM's leaders to sell a return to work to the membership. At the other end of this spectrum, it could use the often-threatened policy of mass dismissals to force the union to concede.

Peter Gush bore the heaviest responsibility for deciding how the company should proceed. He stuck firmly to his position that there should be no concessions around wages, and he was supported in this decision by the Chamber. NUM's leadership was stranded. There was no way in which a deal without wage concessions could be sold to its members.

In public, Bobby Godsell defended the Chamber's hard-line position. But within Anglo he argued for concessions to be made that would allow a resolution of the strike.[71] The issue would have been deliberated by the inner cabinet at Oppenheimer & Son, as well as more formally in Anglo's boardroom. On one account, Gavin Relly told the board that he was concerned about the domestic and international political implications of mass dismissals. In response Gush told Relly to 'join a political party' if he wanted to play politics. He also brushed aside others arguing for concessions 'with the quip that they knew nothing about the reality of mining'.[72]

From the perspective of the board, Gush had a compelling point. Amelioration and compromise might solve the immediate crisis at the rock face but would not solve the developing crisis of authority on the compounds. There was 'desperation, a sense of rage, a sense of terror' enveloping Main Street. Violence and mayhem was growing, 17 hostels were entirely closed to outsiders, and managers were worried about industrial sabotage.[73] As Godsell sees it today, 'You can't run mines if you don't run the hostels.'[74]

Gush's strategy offered more than the solution to a crisis of collapsing stopes. It offered an opportunity to cut down the authority of NUM's leadership by following dismissals with reprisals against union organisers. Induna power could be reasserted and the traditional authority of the mine managers rebuilt. Some hard-liners doubtless hoped that the union could be completely crushed. If NUM resisted mass dismissals and somehow sustained the strike, one momentous series of dismissals and reprisals could destroy the union for good. At the same time, the dismissal strategy was also compelling to moderates like the gold division's head of industrial relations, Nigel Unwin, who remains convinced that the strike 'probably wasn't capable of amicable resolution. I genuinely believe that dismissal by ourselves, in the knowledge that we would have to take most workers back almost immediately, was the only way.'[75]

From a battle of attrition on the mine compounds, the strike suddenly turned into a relentless programme of mass dismissals. In the strike's second week, Godsell announced that mass dismissals of some 17,000 workers would begin the following Monday. Meanwhile, at Anglo American's annual general meeting, which happened to fall in the middle of the week, a statement was issued that confined concessions to holiday bonuses, death benefits and the nature of a planned provident fund.

Despite the advance warnings about mass dismissals in British and American news media, Godsell – who was responsible for implementing the dismissals – avers that there was simply no strategy for dismissals – 'there was no plan!'[76] The Chamber's chief negotiator claims that 'We were never looking more than two days ahead at most. We kept thinking they would fold tomorrow. And they kept thinking we would fold tomorrow. We should not ascribe too much sophistication to the process.'[77]

By contrast, the sociologist T Dunbar Moodie's interviews with mine managers suggest that a clear strategy was in place. Anglo had learnt from its 1985 experiences at Kloof mine that mass dismissals should occur only on the least profitable shafts. As Moodie observes, 'Anglo's mass dismissals during the [1987] strike were very carefully orchestrated. They dismissed workers from the least profitable shafts first. Managers remembered that process was much less traumatic than the 1985 dismissals. They too had learnt their lessons.'[78] The dismissals were also targeted at those shafts in which support for the strike was strongest.[79]

Dismissals and lock-outs began around 18 August. Within two days, around 40,000 workers on Anglo, Gencor and JCI mines were threatened with dismissal. Godsell was possibly still fighting a rearguard battle for concessions that would make defeat more palatable to the union. Relly made a small cash offer through the Chamber of Mines, which the NUM membership predictably rejected.

By 24 August more than 10,000 workers had been sacked. After 26 August, mass dismissals began on a large scale, and by 27 August more than 30,000 had been retrenched. Godsell was formally in charge of the retrenchment process, and he worked with the union to minimise the violence and disruption it brought. However, on some occasions, when NUM organisers thought they had a verbal agreement with Godsell, they would find his commitments rescinded in telexes sent by Peter Gush.[80] The mining houses meanwhile accelerated their recruitment of substitute 'scab' labour, in particular from Lesotho, where there was a deep pool of experienced mineworkers.

By the third week of the strike, the mineworkers were in desperate straits. Their families had spent almost a month without remittances. Six workers had been killed and more than 600 injured or arrested. When negotiations recommenced on 25 August, the Chamber refused to make concessions except at the margins, around holiday pay and death benefits. The NUM put the offer to a ballot without recommending for or against it. The miners voted not to return.

By 27 August, 9 mineworkers had been killed, 500 injured, and approximately 400 arrested. More than 50,000 had been dismissed.[81] Very late that night, in a phone call from *Newsweek* correspondent Robert Reis, Ramaphosa learnt that Anglo was now ready, if necessary, to dismiss virtually its entire striking workforce. A shaken Ramaphosa woke James Motlatsi and the two men considered the options available to them. Cyril then called Callie van der Colf, a 'straight talker' whom Ramaphosa and Motlatsi knew perhaps better than any other Anglo executive. In negotiations they had found they could 'read him like a book'. Van der Colf confirmed to Cyril that there was indeed now a plan to continue dismissals until the bitter end.[82]

Ramaphosa and Motlatsi were left with no option. The collapsing stopes would force an end to the strike, one way or another, in the next few days. If Anglo continued with mass dismissals, the union would lose more than four-fifths of its membership. Its remaining presence would be in mining houses where it was too small to secure recognition. The union would be destroyed, and there was no telling if it could ever be rebuilt. Cyril was not willing to sacrifice the future of the union to a dispute it could no longer win.

Ramaphosa and Motlatsi then called together representatives of the regional strike committees. The delegates bitterly agreed that the only course was for the strike to end. But the mining houses did not let matters rest. When a NUM delegation met the Chamber negotiators on Sunday 30 August to agree to their offer, it had been rescinded. Ramaphosa had to battle hard to secure something close to the earlier concessions on death benefits and holiday pay. Moreover, he was unable to secure any promises about reinstatement of dismissed workers. On the evening of 30 August the mineworkers returned to work.

Anglo had curbed union power and it was able to manage a major reorganisation on the gold mines over the next decade largely on its own terms. In 1987, there were more than half a million black mineworkers on the goldfields. By 2000, there were just 169,000.[83] These massive retrenchments were driven primarily by economic fundamentals, including exhaustion of mineable ores and falling gold prices. But they were also influenced by a strike which taught managers that most shafts could operate with a reduced workforce.[84]

While bowed and beaten, the union was not destroyed. As NUM was later to gloss the outcome, 'the strike was not a defeat. It was a set-back … The employers were bent on at least curbing if not destroying our union. But they did not achieve this objective even though 50,000 workers were dismissed.' In words that Cyril himself probably penned, the union declared that 'Defeating the bosses' aim of destroying the NUM is clearly a resounding victory'.[85]

The immediate fall-out from the strike seemed nothing short of disastrous for many officials. Their depression was deepened by a devastating mine accident on the day the miners returned to work. Almost 50,000 mineworkers had been dismissed, and there was no enforceable commitment on the part of the mining houses to reinstate them. Dismissed workers had been upbeat and full of defiant songs when they were bused away from their mines. Very quickly, however, their bravado was replaced by dismay and demoralisation, and deepened by the vindictiveness and retaliation of those who had opposed the strike.

The union's legal office was swamped with faxes and teletexts about dismissed workers and engulfed by a sense of 'utter helplessness'. It would be weeks before the union's instructing attorneys for strike litigation could begin to construct paper trails and battle for the rights of dismissed workers. While negotiating reinstatement, the union had to organise programmes to keep unemployed members busy in rural areas in Lesotho and the Eastern Cape.[86]

It was the regional and local organisers of the union who bore the brunt of discontent about the outcome of the strike. They had incited and encouraged the workers to down tools, and now they had to explain the necessity for capitulation and the delay in reinstating sacked miners. Workers who had proudly sustained strike action at great personal cost left the mines with their heads held high. Now they were conscious they could never recoup lost wages.

Although he soon recognised the wisdom of their decision, Frans Baleni remembers his own intense anger with Ramaphosa and Motlatsi.[87] Every day, strike committee members endured taunts from indunas and white mineworkers. Shop stewards were subjected to intensified harassment by the mine managers, union facilities were taken away, and rights to meet and organise were rescinded.[88] Baleni was summarily dismissed after being accused of 'incitement', the evidence for which allegation was captured on now routine tape-recordings of a union meeting.[89]

James Motlatsi, more than anyone, had sustained workers' confidence that they could defeat the bosses. Now many union members saw him as a traitor. Throughout 1988, 'a nightmare year' for him, workers would sing 'James Motlatsi is a killer'. Even today he is sometimes greeted in parts of the Eastern Cape with the song 'James Motlatsi – he is the one who sold us out'.[90]

Peter Gush personally decided that Motlatsi must be fired, an unprecedented attack on the senior leadership of the union. Harry Oppenheimer and Gavin Relly both attempted to intercede on Motlatsi's behalf, but Gush would not be swayed. Incensed at the time,

Motlatsi bears no ill will today, and the two men were later to negotiate constructively when Gush became managing director of De Beers.[91]

Some organisers and ordinary workers, not initially understanding the union's vulnerability, suspected betrayal by their own leaders. Only later did they realise that, as the union's historian puts it, 'There was no collusion over the ending of the strike. It ended because [Anglo American] threatened to destroy the union.'[92] A substantial minority of ANC exiles – themselves of course hardly experts on successfully taking on the power of the apartheid state – also believed the strike should have been continued to its bitter end. The idea that strikers were sold out by their leaders resurfaced several years later, in smear campaigns directed at Ramaphosa when he was challenging for the country's deputy presidency.

Historians like to debate the significance of political leaders in changing the course of history. Some prefer 'structural' explanations that emphasise what was likely to happen in the long run, regardless of the capabilities, intentions and actions of particular individuals. Others focus on the ability of particular individuals – most famously figures like Lenin, Hitler or Mao – to change the trajectory of whole societies through their actions.[93] How can we understand Ramaphosa's relationship to the union of which he was general secretary for so long? Did the union emerge as a result of inexorable social forces, incidentally propelling Ramaphosa to undeserved prominence, as some of his critics claim? Or was the union Cyril's individual creation, the direct product of his restless will and pragmatic genius?

The historian of black mineworkers, Vic Allen, is in no doubt. He observes that 'though there would have been attempts during the 1980s to organise black mineworkers, there would have been no NUM without Cyril Ramaphosa'.[94] For Allen, Ramaphosa formed NUM 'with the materials at hand', taking advantage of Anglo American's enthusiasm before creating 'an organisation that was capable of surviving a major strike defeat and its aftermath ... In a sense Cyril Ramaphosa and NUM are synonymous when discussing their impact on South African society. One could not have been achieved without the other.'[95]

At the same time, the strike and its aftermath also bear testimony to the limitations of trade union power in a capitalist society. Throughout its history the union has been heroic in its spirit and spectacular in its growth, but the character of a market economy still limits the overall capacity of a union to bring about fundamental change.

Unionised mineworkers enjoy higher wages, greater protection against arbitrary dismissal, and larger retirement funds to cushion their old age, than they would possess in the absence of NUM.[96] But the logic of the industry still imposes a migrant labour pattern and dehumanising single-sex hostels. The burden of disease is worse than ever, with HIV/AIDS and a resurgent TB epidemic. The risk of accidental death is virtually the same today as it was when the union was founded. Most importantly, the industry is still in terminal decline. Geology, technological constraints and price volatility lie beyond the reach of organised labour.

Indeed, the cages of capitalism and geology confine the bosses almost as much as the union organisers. On Main Street, and in the diamond-shaped building at 11 Diagonal Street that today houses AngloGold Ashanti,[97] the death, disease and unremitting labour endured by mineworkers make the industry an emotionally difficult one in which to be a boss.[98] In 1985, Cyril was already sensitive to the wider constraints within which employers and workers negotiate, arguing that the mining industry 'is defined by an evil social and economic structure which manufactures two kinds of people, blacks and whites, and which keeps blacks and whites fighting against each other for the benefit of a few capitalists'.[99]

The significance of the union, of course, went far beyond its impact on the working conditions and wages of a particular industry. Allen observes of the wider liberation struggle, 'I doubt whether the outcome would have been reached so quickly and that the ANC and the SACP would have been ready and capable of providing leadership when they did without the NUM's involvement.'[100]

The significance of the union for Ramaphosa, moreover, was human as much as political. He would sometimes say to his NUM confidants that 'the best thing the NUM has ever done is to give mineworkers dignity and pride'.[101] In 1982, mineworkers had been ashamed of their work. According to organiser Simphiwe Nanise, they were 'at the bottom of the ladder. They would have a belt or a strap with a number on it – each worker had a number they would be forced to wear. They had to take that belt off if they went into a township, otherwise they would risk being mugged or assaulted. In those days, if people knew you were a miner, you were looked down on and treated without respect.'[102]

Ramaphosa was adored by NUM's members because he approached them with humility and treated them with respect. He also insisted that the dignity of 'my' mineworkers was respected by others. Even when the union was close to insolvent, Ramaphosa would never economise on their accommodation. As Frans Baleni recalls of his days as an underground worker and organiser, 'Cyril insisted that we would stay in the best hotels, in the same hotels as our counterparts in management … Our finances were in a mess, but Cyril always told ordinary workers like me – workers who had never even seen the inside of a hotel before – that they were staying there because they deserved it. He wanted them to have the things they had been denied in life.'[103]

By the end of the great strike, Ramaphosa was a man recognised and respected in deep rural areas across the mining industry's entire subcontinental labour empire. NUM had taken on the might of the mining industry at the heart of the apartheid economy and it had not been destroyed. Ramaphosa was still just 34 years old.

PART THREE
THE DOMESTIC STRUGGLE

Chapter 12

Cosatu and domestic opposition

The people inside South Africa have recognized that victory will come as a result of their struggle, their own efforts; as a result of their reliance on themselves.
— *OR Tambo, October 1984* [1]

As the 1980s recede into the past, the broad historical forces undermining apartheid and creating conditions for negotiations have been thrown into greater relief.[2] At the time the economy was stagnating with investment barely replacing capital stock for more than two decades. The economic nationalism of the ruling National Party (NP) was incompatible with the political economy of the new era, and government was unable to attract inward investment flows, secure transfers of technology, or access growing global markets. At home, the power of organised labour grew, influx control gradually crumbled, and the urban black population relentlessly increased. The Soviet economic crisis meanwhile undercut South Africa's protected status as a client regime of Western powers.

While these developments suggested that a change of regime would one day become inescapable, organised political opposition was required to close down the NP's avenues for evasion and delay. In this 1980s endgame of the struggle against apartheid, domestic rather than international actors played the decisive role. Within the domestic arena, moreover, it was disorganised local protest and 'ungovernability', rather than the stratagems of opposition political leaders, which posed the greatest challenge to the regime. Nevertheless, when state oppression deepened after 1986, and popular unrest swelled up in response, the trade union movement was to play a crucial role in bringing the regime to the negotiating table.

The Lusaka ANC's interpretation of the end of apartheid tends to view the decisive actor, perhaps unsurprisingly, as the liberation movement itself. Yet, by the 1980s, the exile movement was close to organisational collapse, and Oliver Tambo's much-heralded diplomatic strategy had united the Western powers and the Soviet bloc in condemnation that remained mostly rhetorical. Howard Barrell has shown that most ANC exiles had an anachronistic and unrealistic understanding of how change would come in South Africa. They 'treated armed struggle as the central feature of [ANC] operational strategy, the ultimate aim of which was the forcible overthrow of the South African state'.[3] Yet by the mid-1980s, the armed struggle was 'patently a military failure', remaining at 'a very low level of intensity … and pos[ing] no military threat' to the regime. Indeed, the movement's military adventurism was probably counterproductive because for domestic and Western audiences it justified Pretoria's repression and refusal to negotiate.[4]

The ANC leadership was, however, unable to change strategy, in part because 'it held that fundamental political change necessarily entailed the use of violence', and the 'brutal humiliations of apartheid appeared to require an armed response'. Most importantly, the ANC derived an immense political dividend from armed struggle. 'The authority and popularity that armed struggle gave the ANC explains the paradox in its trajectory: the more it failed, the more it succeeded.'[5]

At home, meanwhile, popular discontent grew in Soweto's aftermath, but young people and students were a poor match for a militarised state. By the end of the 1970s, local political leaders were calling for concerted action by the youth, organised labour, churches, and community groups known as 'civics'. The NP government precipitated just this organisation of political protest in 1983, by introducing a 'tricameral parliament' that promised to exclude Africans permanently from power, and to fob off coloured and Indian demands with greatly circumscribed 'own affairs' privileges.

In his memoirs, FW de Klerk exhibits well the hypocrisy behind these constitutional reforms, explaining that as a junior minister at the time he became concerned about the forced removal and racial segregation of coloureds and Indians. 'The more I got to know the coloureds, the more ambivalent I became and the less enthusiasm I had for our official policy.' As for Indians, De Klerk 'was brought up on the basis that one should never do business with Indians or buy anything from them. But as a young practising attorney ... I had a few Indian clients and quickly established a good relationship with the local Indian community. It soon became clear to me that they were not getting a square deal,' presumably, in De Klerk's eyes, in contrast to Africans.[6]

At a January 1983 Transvaal conference to oppose the new constitution, a brilliant Cape Town orator, the Rev. Allan Boesak, called for a new 'united front' against apartheid. When excited delegates departed at the conference's close, they were determined to create regional structures able to unite civic associations, students, trade unions and churches. The United Democratic Front (UDF) was formally launched in Mitchell's Plain, Cape Town, in August 1983. It adopted the key philosophical underpinning of non-racialism, testifying to the hitherto unsuspected strength of Congress-aligned organisations after a decade of opposition seemingly dominated by black consciousness.[7] While the UDF was never merely a front for the exile ANC, its affiliates mostly adopted the Freedom Charter.[8]

As the decade progressed, it was disorganised rather than organised protest that became of most concern for the regime.[9] The UDF and exile ANC began to articulate a demand that the people make the country 'ungovernable'. But this call was more a reaction than a spur to what were largely autonomous localised protests. In 1984, a progression of small but violent insurrections began in the Vaal Triangle, quickly spreading to the East Rand, Natal, the Eastern Cape and Orange Free State. Neither ANC influence nor UDF leadership had initiated or shaped these events, even if UDF member organisations were often involved in them and ANC symbols played a prominent role in the theatre of violence they unleashed.

The liberation movement's attempt to capitalise on these uprisings was tactically inept. A minority of astute exiles recognised that domestic 'flashpoints' might best be used to attract new cadres and to shape them into the disciplined underground that the ANC so evidently lacked. The dominant view among the exile leadership, however, was that township defence committees could be quickly transformed into 'combat groups' that would challenge the apartheid regime.[10] As a result of this miscalculation, Umkhonto weSizwe (MK) undertook a 'mass' infiltration of 150 poorly equipped and under-trained cadres in 1985–6, an effort that briefly doubled MK's presence on the ground before inevitable capture and death at the hands of state security services restored the status quo.[11]

Meanwhile, the violence of insurrectionary African youth began to drive a wedge between these proponents of 'liberation' discourse and the coloured and Indian activists who had a rights-based understanding of UDF objectives. When the state of emergency was introduced in 1986, experienced leaders were detained across the country. The youth – and sometimes *comtsotsis* or criminals – took control of many UDF affiliates, undermining community control and leading to escalating levels of violence.[12]

The impotence of ANC exiles and UDF moderates alike was brought home by the famous words of Winnie Mandela on 13 April 1986. In Munsieville, near Krugersdorp, she declared that 'together, hand in hand, with that stick of matches, with our necklace, we shall liberate this country'.[13] The previous year's widely publicised necklacings in KwaNobuhle and Duduza had already provoked Desmond Tutu's famous threat to 'pack my bags, collect my family and leave this beautiful country'.[14] For her speech Winnie Mandela was demonised in white South Africa and abroad.

She later claimed to George Bizos that her words were a reaction against a notorious apartheid atrocity. 'I had been to the Goniwe funeral. As is the custom I had to view the burnt bodies. And I became very bitter and this is why I said it.'[15] Yet Murphy Morobe was later to tell the Truth and Reconciliation Commission that 'one of the most probable' interpretations of Mandela's speech was a call to activists to kill police collaborators.[16]

In his biography of Nadine Gordimer, *No Cold Kitchen*, Ronald Suresh Roberts re-examines this troubling episode in South Africa's history by distinguishing between what he terms 'settler' and 'native' understandings of necklacing.[17] The 'settlers', on this view, condemned this act of violence primarily in order to deny the capacity of 'the natives' to be civilised. What kind of human being, such condemnations implied, could commit such a dreadful act?

The 'natives' of the liberation movement, on Roberts's account, were in fact engaged in a painful but necessary debate about the efficacy of the necklace as an instrument of armed struggle. Roberts uncovers evidence of equivocation among the ANC leadership around necklacing in 1985 and 1986. Oliver Tambo, for example, argued that they were 'not happy' with the necklace but would not condemn those 'driven' to use it.

In a coup for Roberts, he quotes notes made by Nelson Mandela's lawyer, Ismail Ayob, during a meeting between Nelson and Winnie Mandela in Pollsmoor Prison on 19 May 1986. 'NM approved of WM's necklace speech. He said that it was a good thing as there had not [since] been one Black person who has attacked WM.' According to Roberts, Ayob's notes were available to Nelson Mandela's official biographer, the late Anthony Sampson, but they were excised from the manuscript of that biography on the instructions of the former President's office.[18]

Mandela himself observed in his autobiography that 'a freedom fighter learns the hard way that it is the oppressor who defines the nature of the struggle, and the oppressed is often left no resource but to use the methods that mirror those of the oppressor'.[19] Such words suggest to Roberts that, rather than being the saint or 'teddy bear' that Gordimer imagines him to be, Mandela is 'a man of profoundly practical moral wisdom' whose reconciliatory achievements were all the greater because he was able to shoulder responsibility for the 'harder chapters' of the 1980s struggle.[20]

There are, of course, reasons to question Roberts's claim that ANC equivocation resulted from strategic and moral deliberation about the role of the necklace in armed insurrection. First, Nelson Mandela's words, at face value at least, are explicitly personal. Roberts does not convincingly link an incarcerated husband's consolatory comments to his embattled wife to any wider political debate within the liberation movement.

Second, Roberts is wrong to view necklacing as a calculated political intervention that could be directed from outside the communities in which it occurred. Burning was not political assassination. The use of fire invoked symbolic purification to destroy evil. It allowed young men to assert fleeting control over their desperate lives. And it demonstrated the determination of communities to enforce their own local moral codes. In fact, necklacing was part of a continuum of violence that preceded and outlived the political turmoil of the mid-1980s. Its victims were mostly not 'collaborators' at all.

Joanna Ball's study for the Centre for the Study of Violence and Reconciliation shows that a wave of burnings began as early as 1976.[21] Initially the victims were described as 'witches', and only later were they labelled 'collaborators' or criminals. Of 65 burnings she studied between 1984 and 1993, Ball found that 39 followed witchcraft accusations. Just 15 were 'political' killings of collaborators, policemen or political enemies. She speculates that these victims shared the same fate because they were each viewed as traitors, who corroded the cohesion and integrity of their communities. More recent studies show that necklacings and other burnings continued after 1994. In the democratic era, however, the 'traitors' have been described in police and media reports not in political terms but rather as 'drug dealers', 'gangsters' or as 'foreigners' fallen foul of 'vigilante killers'.

Third, far from being a potential instigator of 'tactical necklacing', the ANC was an impotent and distant observer. The words of then ANC secretary-general Alfred Nzo, in an interview with the London *Times*, capture the exile leaders' powerlessness perfectly: 'Whatever the people decide to use to eliminate those enemy elements is their decision. If they decide to use necklacing we support it.'[22]

Necklacing remained a 'punishment' primarily meted out within, and by the members of, local communities. The equivocation of ANC leaders testifies to their unwillingness to admit their own impotence, rather than to any earnest but hypothetical moral deliberation that may have occurred among exiles and prisoners. James Matthews captures the horror these events invoked:

> we are living in
> spring's wasteland
> man/woman stumble
> their shoulders necklaced
> with fire transforming them
> into blazing crosses
> their deaths recorded
> by choirs of crows
> mocking their pain

we have turned ourselves
into charnel houses
the reek of blood
heavy on our breath
our quest for freedom
make us night-stalkers
obscening the fields
with charred flesh
stunted souls we are
drinking too deeply
from poisoned wells[23]

While most of the exile leadership remained wedded to a military overthrow of the apartheid state, the ANC also advanced a strategy to develop a mass organisational base within South Africa. This ambitious plan was spelt out in some detail in a 1979 document, of uncertain status in the ANC, known commonly as the Green Book.[24] Its key objectives were to elaborate a 'mass mobilisation' strategy, create a broad national front for liberation, and draw activists 'thrown up in mass struggle' into the ANC's underground machinery. In response to the question 'Which is the principal social force of our revolution?' the Green Book responds that the 'principal and most consistent social force for the achievement of the aims of our national-democratic revolution is the exploited and nationally-oppressed working people in the towns and the landless mass in the country-side'. In recognition of this fact, it determines that 'together with our ally, the SA Congress of Trade Unions, we must work for the strengthening of a Trade Union movement which will genuinely represent the interest of the working class and ensure their organised participation in the struggle for national liberation'.[25]

Notwithstanding the evident deference to Sactu, and the fact that this was just one of many proposed programmes, it does suggest renewed exile interest in organised labour as a vehicle for political opposition. Yet such organisation had to be carried out within South Africa by union activists who seemed to be forever at loggerheads. In the light of the increasingly unstable political environment outside the workplace in the early 1980s, debates raged inside trade unions about the appropriate strategy for political engagement. Were trade unions simply ameliorative in their effects, taking the edge off workers' appetite for fundamental change? Or were they indispensable instruments of political struggle, uniquely able to open workers' eyes to their ability to change the world? In the early 1970s, two main schools of thinking emerged. Some activists believed unions should be instruments for waging war against apartheid, and that workplace issues should be relentlessly linked to community protest. Unions that adopted this approach were often described as 'political' or 'social movement unions' – or as 'populist' unions if the intention of the speaker was critical. Political union organisers, when they expressed allegiance to the ANC and its Freedom Charter, were labelled 'charterists'.[26]

An alternative philosophy, represented primarily in the Federation of South African Trade Unions (Fosatu), favoured 'orthodox' or 'collective bargaining' unionisation. Such unions focused on shop-floor organis-ation and worker control. The shop-floor approach made them resilient in the face of oppression and detention. In the aftermath of the Wiehahn reforms, with their sets of recognition agreements and legal requirements, they were also bound tightly into the industrial relations system. In the eyes of charterists and political unionists, these constraints made them apolitical or even co-opted conservative organisations. However, some Fosatu leaders were radicals keen to link workplace issues with wider community politics.[27] 'Orthodox' organisers could also be 'workerists' who believed that a socialist workers' party would emerge out of rigorous trade union organisation. Such critics of the 'bourgeois' politics of the ANC and its Freedom Charter – most volubly, Moses 'Moss' Mayekiso of the Metal and Allied Workers' Union – were also opponents of the 'Stalinist' politics of the South African Communist Party (SACP).

Union politics were further fragmented by the presence of unions affiliated to homeland parties and others committed to black consciousness approaches. As we have seen, the NUM's initial federation, Cusa, was not a 'black consciousness' organisation – even if it was later to merge into a new BC federation. But it did adhere to the rule that the leadership should be black. By contrast, Fosatu and the charterists adhered to the principle of non-racialism, and this difference was to prove a stumbling block to unity talks.

Ideological and political differences were supplemented by more practical issues of demarcation, as competing unions often fought for control of overlapping aspects of the work process. Sometimes, as with NUM's own competition with other trade unions to organise mineworkers, there were more direct rivalries over unambiguously the same group of workers. Such conflicts made unions unwilling to share information with one another about their respective membership figures and recruiting activities. Perhaps even more importantly, wealthy unions were jealous of their cheque books and foreign sponsors, and felt unhappy about pooling resources with less well-resourced comrades.

Despite these obstacles to unity, the political logic of union rationalisation became increasingly inescapable. How could the workers continue to fight one another when they shared common foes in capitalism and apartheid? 'Unity talks' took place in Langa, Cape Town, in 1981; in Wilgespruit and Port Elizabeth in 1982; in Athlone, Cape Town, in 1983; and in Johannesburg in 1984. There were also endless bilateral meetings, where conflicts over demarcation and organisation were sometimes successfully addressed. Over time, union leaders developed a deeper understanding of what divided them and of the potential that existed for greater unity. Some unions were proponents of a single giant confederation. Others preferred a process of rolling mergers. A third group favoured a 'federation of federations' that would allow leaders to retain control of autonomous philosophies – and of their own cheque books and bank accounts.[28]

In 1985, after exhausting meetings in Soweto between the most tenacious seekers of unity, a critical mass of trade unions – including Fosatu and Ramaphosa's NUM – finally agreed to unite in a federation to be called Cosatu. It was launched on 1 December of that year. The ultimate success of these talks was testimony to the fact that some unions' apparent differences were smaller than they initially seemed. Social movement unions already recognised the need for more robust organisation, and growing political oppression drove this lesson home. Orthodox unions could not prevent community politics leaking on to the shop floor. In 1981, only a small minority of Fosatu activists would countenance any linkage between union and community struggles.[29] By 1984, the federation was able to support a student protest on the ground of members' obligations as parents towards their younger comrades.

The ANC's Sactu ally and many UDF-aligned unions were, however, hostile to unity talks, which they believed would strip them of influence and resources. They feared Fosatu's efficient organisers, such as Alec

Erwin and John Copelyn, and worried that the larger federation would swallow them up.[30] Unity was pushed through against their wishes by the exile ANC, which remained true to its Green Book analysis and sought a single federation broadly under its own sway. The ANC sloganeered for 'One industry, one union, one country, one federation', most exiles arguing that unity would bring power, and gambling that any federation that emerged would fall under their control. In the event, the presence of Ramaphosa as the head of Cosatu's largest and most powerful affiliate was to prove a continuing source of concern for many in the ANC.

At the start of the decade, Ramaphosa was still widely regarded as a Christian brother whose closest political affiliations were with the black consciousness movement. It is quite possible that at the turn of the 1980s, he had still never knowingly met an ANC member.[31] Yet as the NUM grew, Ramaphosa began to recognise the need for wider union unity, and he increasingly despaired of the inability of Cusa to participate constructively in the unity talks.[32]

In the 1970s, moreover, Cyril came to recognise some of the political limitations of black consciousness, and he toyed with alternative instruments such as armed struggle and organised labour. His political and ideological commitment to black consciousness was always qualified, as was his commitment to any overarching philosophy that might obstruct pragmatic calculation. It was in his character to adapt his frames of understanding to changing circumstances only gradually, without fully relinquishing prior principles and beliefs.[33]

By August 1985, when the Cosatu show was more or less on the road, and Cyril was in the driving seat, he firmly disclaimed any genuine commitment to black consciousness in his days at Turfloop. 'At that stage it was the "in thing".'[34] It was in this context that he recalled his sudden conversion to the ideals of the Freedom Charter while in detention, and his discovery that 'black consciousness was essentially a sectarian type of movement which tried to get black people to be on their own'.[35] These convenient retrospective denials of the influence of black consciousness are not fully persuasive. Certainly, some of his friends and contemporaries – who were to go on to play significant roles in the formation and politics of Azapo – had no doubts about Ramaphosa's BC philosophy.[36] Moreover, he respected the key tenet of Cusa, that leadership positions should be held by blacks and that whites should not influence the strategies and decisions of these black leaders.[37]

If Ramaphosa never underwent a sudden conversion to the Freedom Charter, he did nevertheless begin to act according to its premises. He was always a gradualist, embracing new perspectives and ideas while never fully abandoning the old, pragmatically ignoring unwelcome tensions within his complex system of political beliefs. When he turned to worldly politics, he never rejected the church. When he converted to non-racialism, he did not relinquish the hold of black consciousness philosophy on his view of the worth of black leaders. He was soon to embrace certain communist ideas while steering around their political implications, just as he was later able to become a financier and businessman without jettisoning his avowed socialist values.

On some accounts Ramaphosa's strength as a negotiator lay in his ability to act as a processor.[38] He could secure agreement between bewilderingly diverse antagonists, a capacity that drew on his ability at any one time to accommodate and reflect on a wide range of contrary perspectives and beliefs within his own mind. Confronted at any time with the question 'What does Cyril really believe?', his colleagues and comrades would offer wildly differing answers.

At the NUM, Ramaphosa and Motlatsi headed the biggest trade union in the country and their views made a major impression on the character of Cosatu. The NUM was uniquely capable of bridging divides because it had avoided association with either workerist or political ideologies. Although it had initially been derided by Fosatu activists as having a 'mass' character, NUM's high and growing levels of solidarity and shaft organisation demonstrated its organisational power. At the same time, the exceptional exploitation and racism to which its members were subject kept it highly and openly political in all of its activities.

During the unity talks preceding the formation of Cosatu, Ramaphosa became a key broker in dialogue between unionists such as Joe Foster and Chris Dlamini, the general secretary and president of Fosatu, John Gomomo of the Metal and Allied Workers' Union, and Jay Naidoo, the general secretary of the Sweet, Food and Allied Workers' Union. The broad agreement they reached about the nature of a new federation emphasised their points of greatest agreement: a goal of one union, one industry; expanded workers' control; representation in the federation on the basis of membership; 'cooperation' in national-level actions; and non-racialism.

This last issue seemed most problematic for NUM, as a member of Cusa, but Ramaphosa and his lieutenants had already decided that the union's future did not lie with its founding federation. Phiroshaw Camay's Cusa gradually estranged itself from the negotiating process, its demands for black leadership creating an insuperable barrier to unity with its pivotal Fosatu rival. In its January 1985 congress, NUM resolved to join a new federation even if it had to do so without Cusa. Later in the year Cusa withdrew from the unity talks over the issue of black leadership, and Elijah Barayi staged a walkout at the Cusa convention over this same issue.[39]

Ramaphosa chaired the final summit of the decisive June 1985 unity talks in Soweto. His performance was celebrated as tactful but forceful, and he became the 'inevitable' choice as chair of Cosatu's launching conference scheduled for the end of November.[40] At this hastily convened event, Ramaphosa's rhetoric steered a careful line between the demands of different affiliates. He set out the principle that 'the struggle of the workers on the shop floor cannot be separated from the wider political struggle for the liberation of this country', giving support to the views of the political unions. Yet he went on to argue that 'if workers are to lead the struggle for liberation, we have to win the confidence of others sectors of society. But if we are to get into alliances with other progressive organisations, it must be on terms that are favourable to us as workers.' Finally, he soothed orthodox fears – but upped the stakes simultaneously – by arguing that when 'we do plunge into political activity, we must make sure that the unions under Cosatu have a strong shop floor base not only to take on the employers, but the state as well ...'[41]

The leadership of the new federation also reflected its diversity. Jay Naidoo from the Sweet, Food and Allied Workers' Union – a former black consciousness activist who valued Fosatu's organisational doctrines – was elected general secretary. NUM's own Elijah Barayi was elected president, a position NUM 'earned' through being by far the largest union in the federation. Significantly, Barayi was the key ANC advocate in NUM.[42] Radical Fosatu leader Chris Dlamini became deputy president. Office-holders also included the longstanding ANC activist – and by 1985 probably SACP member – Sydney Mufamadi, whose relationship with Ramaphosa, on some accounts at least, was soured by his own failure to organise mineworkers in the early 1980s.[43]

In the middle of Ramaphosa's closing speech to the new federation, he remarked that 'what we have to make clear is that a giant has risen'. Edited by journalists, this was to become the famous slogan that is still recalled today at Cosatu congresses: 'A giant has arisen!' Ramaphosa had helped to create a federation that could serve as a vehicle for the ANC's ambitions. As the historian Vic Allen observes of his inaugural speech, 'it could have been written by the ANC'.[44] But while Cosatu held out great promise for the liberation movement, the prominence of Ramaphosa left many exiles uneasy. In Allen's judicious assessment, 'from 1985 Cyril Ramaphosa was in full support of the ANC, though the ANC was not in full support of him'.[45]

Chapter 13

Becoming ANC

Cosatu was widely and immediately recognised by liberation movement exiles as a triumph.[1] Resolutions adopted at the inaugural congress – including demands for the withdrawal of troops from townships, the release of political prisoners, the unbanning of illegal movements and parties, and the imposition of economic sanctions by other countries – were overtly political and promised to place the federation squarely in the ANC camp. Yet suspicion and misunderstanding clouded Ramaphosa's relationship with the movement's Lusaka headquarters. When exiles returned at the end of the decade, the notion that Cyril 'became ANC too late' or 'was rather slow to become an ANC supporter' became a throwaway insult used to tarnish his reputation – and that of many other trade unionists and UDF activists.

Certain aspects of Ramaphosa's personal history laid him open to this charge. Cusa's Phiroshaw Camay viewed his defection to Cosatu in quite cynical terms, for example, as an effort 'to get on the winning side' by gravitating to the most powerful of the labour union forces.[2] The same charge could easily be levelled at his move to the ANC. Moreover, Cyril was never imprisoned on Robben Island but rather detained in solitary confinement in a variety of prisons and police stations around Johannesburg and Pretoria. A term on Robben Island was not a sure-fire route to becoming an ANC supporter, of course. Current national executive member Saki Macozoma remarks, 'I spent five years on Robben Island and I didn't join the ANC. There were things about the ANC I did not like.'[3] But, for Cyril, his inability to develop relationships and networks with other political prisoners hindered his later acceptance in the movement.

A third, and politically more sensitive, problem was simply an accident of birth. Ramaphosa's family came from a part of South Africa in which the ANC had almost no historical foothold, and he grew up in a Soweto in which the liberation movement had become a shadowy and insubstantial presence. His early adoption of black consciousness ideas – and his much later conversion to the value of the Freedom Charter – were quite unremarkable for someone with this background.

The strongest advocate of the ANC in the NUM, Elijah Barayi, was almost inevitably from Cradock in the Eastern Cape. Barayi's longstanding affiliation demonstrated the historical entrenchment as well as regional character of the ANC. By contrast Ramaphosa's affiliation to black consciousness reflected the geographical spread of black consciousness thinking across elite black schools and university campuses in the early 1970s.

One danger posed by criticism of an activist's 'late conversion' to the ANC is evident in Barney Pityana's assertion that, despite his prominence in black consciousness politics in the 1970s, 'I was never not ANC.'[4] By this, Pityana presumably means to indicate that as a result of the accident of his birth in the Eastern Cape, and his education at the ANC stronghold of the University of Fort Hare, he was always engaged with the ANC's political and intellectual traditions even when he marched under a black consciousness banner. Pityana's statement is, however, just a short step away from the divisive claim that only those who come from an area with an unbroken history of ANC organisation – in effect, selected regions of the Eastern Cape – can be truly or 'deeply' ANC people.

Without an extended history of immersion in ANC ideas, and lacking a substantial network of ANC contacts, Ramaphosa's embrace of the liberation movement was inevitably doctrinal and political rather than emotional. Ishmael Mkhabela met Cyril in early 1986 in Jabulani Flats, Soweto, where Cyril was then living. Ramaphosa said to him, quite unexpectedly, 'Why don't you join the ANC?' Mkhabela had already dismissed this possibility, despite being courted with a Christmas card from Oliver Tambo in Lusaka, and he asked Ramaphosa what he saw in the movement. Referring to the Freedom Charter, Cyril replied, 'They have a progressive document.' 'What else?' demanded Mkhabela. 'That's all.'[5]

In the second half of the 1980s, Ramaphosa's interaction with the ANC began to increase in frequency and intensity. This and the next chapter chart his startling rise to prominence in an ANC whose senior members often continued to resent his growing power. By 1988, he had been recruited to membership of an important underground ANC executive.[6] By 1990, he was the most prominent spokesman for the internal ANC, and head of the reception committee for released political prisoners. In 1991, he was elected by a landslide as secretary-general of the ANC, and chosen to lead the movement's negotiations with the National Party.

Ramaphosa soon discovered that the ANC was no monolith, and that the unifying language of struggle concealed myriad differences over the appropriate strategy to defeat apartheid. There was equally little consensus over the character of the society that was to replace it. Cyril was to engage and befriend one fiery leftist intellectual after another, first Govan Mbeki, then Mac Maharaj, and finally Joe Slovo. These were all significant figures in the Communist Party (SACP), and 'the party' was to become an important factor in Cyril's political rise. Very soon he would also enjoy a close relationship with the man who was to emerge as the ANC's leader, Nelson Mandela.

Cosatu's relationship with the exile movement seemed at first to be blessed by higher powers. A few days after the December 1985 launch of Cosatu, its leadership had the opportunity to meet informally with exile leaders at a World Council of Churches forum being held fortuitously in Harare. The newly elected office-holders of Cosatu – and Cyril, who attended despite not holding any formal position in the federation – met with the two exile power-brokers who were later to become his closest political allies: Mac Maharaj and Joe Slovo. The meeting was cordial and produced a statement committing the parties to working together. It sent a clear signal to remaining sceptics of 'one union, one industry' that the ANC was determined to see Cosatu succeed. Maharaj and Slovo accepted that Cosatu was a specialised vehicle for class politics, and that it should therefore possess organisational autonomy from the ANC.[7]

In February 1986, there was the first official meeting in Lusaka between new Cosatu office-holders and the 'tripartite alliance' of the

ANC, SACP and Sactu. The alliance delegation was heavyweight, including unchallenged ANC exile leader Oliver Tambo, Joe Slovo and the MK firebrand Chris Hani. The Cosatu delegates included not only two ANC loyalists, Sydney Mufamadi and Liz Picker from the Food and Allied Workers' Union, but also supporters of 'orthodox' union autonomy in the persons of Jay Naidoo and Max Shope. Ramaphosa was the wild card – neither a Fosatu workerist nor an office-holder of the federation – and it soon became clear that he was determined to resist certain ANC demands.

The meeting agreed that Cosatu was the legitimate representative of organised workers within South Africa. At the same time, Sactu was fighting a rearguard battle to maintain its existence and 'legacy' in the face of the new federation, and it was agreed that 'contradiction' between the two federations should be avoided. In the course of the negotiations, moreover, deeper underlying differences between Cosatu and the ANC were exposed. The exile leadership had become accustomed to a corrupted form of democratic centralist decision-making, and to the infiltration and control of mass organisations in the service of wider liberation goals. The ANC leadership believed it was in the best position to determine when and in what manner a union federation should act politically, and what its goals should be.

At the meeting, Cosatu's general secretary, Jay Naidoo, reiterated the orthodox understanding of union independence from political control. Cosatu stood for accountability to the shop floor, freedom of debate, and leadership selection through a free ballot.[8] The union had developed codes of conduct to prevent unfair labelling or smearing of participants in debate, and it systematically encouraged worker education so that such debate could include the widest possible range of participants. Such a federation, Naidoo explained with Ramaphosa's support, could not simply be subordinated to the ANC's political project.[9]

Beneath the clash of principles, there was also a more pragmatic struggle over financial autonomy. Sactu would not allow a Cosatu takeover, in part to protect its leaders' bank accounts and cheque books. Ramaphosa had already clashed with Sactu over finances as early as December 1983, while NUM was still part of Cusa, when he refused demands that he channel funds sourced from the British NUM through Sactu offices.[10] By 1986, Cyril had developed a broad and powerful funding base, largely through Scandinavian mineworkers' federations, and he had no intention of ceding these moneys to the ANC. (Neither, indeed, did he intend to let Cosatu control NUM's purse strings.)

Ramaphosa also believed that his key task was to secure the institutional and political power of his sector of organised workers. He did not participate very much in the UDF, except within Soweto, and he did not believe that NUM should become affiliated to it. When the UDF was formed in 1983, 'I was deeply involved in organizing mine workers, and the urban centres and so forth were not my terrain, it was mine compounds. By remote connection, yes, one had links to the UDF but not directly.'[11]

The poor relations between Ramaphosa and the exile ANC also had a personal dimension. He was now the most prominent of the many accomplished trade union leaders who emerged in the post-Wiehahn era. For 1980s exiles in Lusaka, frustrated by their inability to make any difference on the ground in South Africa, Ramaphosa's exploits had an electrifying effect. As NUM's membership soared, and the union began to take on the mining houses in strike action and in the media, 'everybody was giddy' and 'fascinated by Cyril'.[12] He both captivated and unsettled exile leaders more than other talented organisers such as Jay Naidoo and Alec Erwin. He was not just a charismatic and exceptionally accomplished leader of the most powerful trade union South Africa had ever seen; he was also a black African. In consequence, he inevitably became the most pursued 'target' of liberation movement recruiters. The SACP in particular, with its focus on the organisation of workers, saw Ramaphosa as an indispensable ally. Members of the ANC leadership also feared him as a potential rival.

If the ANC and SACP were exceptionally keen to recruit him to their circles of influence, for most of the 1980s the question of actually joining these organisations did not arise. Prominent leaders were not expected to join the underground ANC because this would expose them to harassment and detention. For his part, Ramaphosa was now keen to engage closely with the ANC. He later recalled that 'we would go for briefings to Lusaka … and we would brief them on the situation. And the NEC would discuss the matter and decide this was a new campaign that had to be launched. We were not really the foot soldiers as such but we knew that the movement in exile, its leadership and membership, was playing an important role.'

Ramaphosa captures a growing emotional affiliation to the Lusaka leadership when he observes that 'There was a sense that that is where the heart of the ANC is. Much as we were involved in Cosatu and the unions and the UDF, we knew that we were executing an important task. But we always felt that we wanted to execute that task within the policy guidelines and parameters set out by the movement outside. So in terms of inspiration, in terms of encouragement, the movement outside was very important.'[13]

When later asked by an interviewer if Lusaka issued orders, Cyril replied, 'Ja, there were some. Those were the days we would scrutinize the January 8 [ANC annual] statements very closely and carefully to watch out for calls being made on us ... We always recognized that that was where the leadership of the movement really resided, much as we were leaders in our own organizations and sectors, we recognized and accepted [that] leadership was outside.'[14]

Yet there was widespread scepticism among UDF and Cosatu leaders about the ability of the ANC leadership to plan domestic political action coherently. As UDF leader Valli Moosa reported his own experience, domestic leaders would travel to Lusaka and set out their concerns about the effective stalemate that was developing on the ground. More often than not they were simply sent back with the injunction to just 'Get on with the revolution!'[15] There were substantial elements within the exile leadership trapped within a crude paradigm of military struggle. Others were die-hard communists strongly affiliated to the Soviet model. While some bolder thinkers, such as Thabo Mbeki, were arguing coherently that negotiation with business and the regime now had a place, their initiatives were viewed with great unease by their comrades.

The ANC, moreover, had more than one centre of power. The exile ANC, with its headquarters in Lusaka, was led by Oliver Tambo. On the other hand, the Robben Island leadership contained significant figures such as Nelson Mandela, Govan Mbeki and Walter Sisulu. There was also a fragmentary 'underground ANC' together with what was loosely called the 'internal leadership' – trade union, church and community leaders, who were sometimes but not always affiliated to the UDF.

By 1987, the question 'Who is the ANC inside the country?' was being ferociously contested within the UDF and Cosatu. According to then Cosatu general secretary Jay Naidoo, such argument was becoming so fierce as to be debilitating.[16] Some activists demanded that unions be fully subordinated to the exile ANC. But most Cosatu leaders believed that military and labour struggles should be kept apart. In an attempt to promote reconciliation, the Cosatu executive invited young firebrand populist Peter Mokaba to speak at the federation's 1987 congress. In Naidoo's recollection, Mokaba 'abused his right to speak' by deliberately exacerbating political divisions and threatening the labour movement's hard-won unity.[17]

Meanwhile, the 1987 mineworkers' strike transformed Ramaphosa's position, from being a significant outsider to becoming a central actor in the battle to make the country ungovernable. By electing Nelson Mandela as its honorary life president, the NUM demonstrated clearly where its sympathies lay. It also adopted the Freedom Charter as an adjunct to its constitution, the first union in the country to do so. This was still not enough for Lusaka. Some exiles betrayed their limited understanding of the realities of industrial action by criticising Ramaphosa's 'too-early demobilisation' of the workers that ended the 1987 mineworkers' strike. More astute exiles were excited almost despite themselves by what they saw as a 'phenomenal development'.[18] Concern correspondingly grew that such a 'captivating figure' was not fully under the exile movement's control. As a consequence, the SACP stepped up its use of 'entryist' techniques to infiltrate its own underground activists into the union's leadership.[19]

Cyril's first direct involvement with domestic ANC structures resulted from his bold 1986 decision that NUM would directly support newly released Robben Island prisoners. When young intellectual Kgalema Motlanthe was released, NUM immediately appointed him head of the union's education department. He accomplished little in this role, leaving posts unfilled and funds raised by Cyril for this purpose unspent.[20] His attention, in reality, was focused on fulfilling the instructions his Robben Island mentor Govan Mbeki had given him when he left prison. He was told to create a new underground internal structure of the ANC.

On 5 November 1987, Govan Mbeki was himself released from the Island. He had been sentenced to life imprisonment together with fellow legends Nelson Mandela, Walter Sisulu and Raymond Mhlaba in the 1964 Rivonia trial. Known as 'Oom Gov', Mbeki was an unrelenting advocate of communism and a fierce critic of what he viewed as Mandela's woolly thinking and hazy anti-socialist tendencies. His key project was to deepen the dominance of the SACP over the ANC's political strategy, and to intensify armed struggle. As a major intellectual force on the Island, he spawned protégés and admirers as prolifically as Mandela himself. As the two equally grand and stubborn men aged together over two decades of incarceration, they argued furiously and fruitlessly, and ultimately passed many years of close proximity in stony silence.

His release on 5 November was in some respects a 'trial run' for the release of other political prisoners. When the London *Times* reported in August that 'the South African government is considering the imminent release of an ageing black guerrilla leader from prison', many diplomats believed that President Botha was 'exploring ways of freeing the African National Congress leader Nelson Mandela'.[21] Prior to Mbeki's release, Nelson Mandela demanded that Mbeki should keep a low political profile in order to facilitate the rapid freeing of other prisoners.[22]

This was always wishful thinking given the tireless activist's personality. The Lusaka ANC made a virtue out of necessity, observing hopefully that 'Comrade Mbeki emerged today after 23 years in the racist prisons unbowed and unbroken, a living legend in the minds of our people ... His release will significantly enrich and augment the leadership of the democratic forces as a whole and, as the fight continues till all are released, we say: Let him speak to the people.'[23] Mbeki took up this challenge with predictable alacrity. In his own eyes, and those of many of his followers, he was the most authoritative intellectual in the ANC with the most powerful 'scientific' command of its role and future. His protégé Kgalema Motlanthe had already made preparations for him to begin work. He was soon to be joined by the redoubtable Harry Gwala, ANC leader from the Natal Midlands, who was released from prison in 1988.

Cyril had offered Motlanthe employment at NUM, and now he was among the first people to visit Oom Gov in Port Elizabeth on his release. When Harry Gwala was freed, NUM provided him with a car and money.[24] Mbeki was inevitably a magnet for local activists who were keen to hear the 'authentic' voice of the ANC. Contrary to Mandela's expectations, he did not confine his activity to the Eastern Cape. Soon he expanded into Natal, where he connected with a variety of other underground activists.

The union was in effect bankrolling Govan Mbeki's self-appointed task of creating a new underground structure. Ramaphosa would use every possible opportunity to visit Mbeki, and on Allen's account he soon took up a senior position in the underground ANC network which the old man and Motlanthe were creating. In this capacity, he became a prominent spokesman for what some activists now considered the 'internal leadership' of the struggle. The significance of such designations was, however, quite unclear given that unanswered and perhaps unanswerable questions hung in the air: Where is the real ANC? And who are its true leaders?

Confusion deepened when the exile leadership created a quite distinct alternative underground ANC structure in the country. This secret project went by the name of Operation Vulindlela ('open the way'), but it has become more commonly known as just Operation Vula. Its central rationale, spelt out towards the end of 1986, was that the ANC needed to establish from scratch an internal leadership. Ivan Pillay, who was chosen by Joe Slovo to administer Vula in Lusaka, observed that 'progress inside the country far outstripped our capacity', and that the ANC 'needed to make a qualitative shift to stay on top of the situation'. South Africa faced nothing less than an internal revolution, and 'we were not there to take full advantage of it'.[25] Vula was not an attempt to 'plant' a new leadership, Pillay emphasised, but rather to shape internal leaders' key decisions.

What later made Vula controversial was that it was hatched very much in secret; every effort was made to ensure that its existence was not leaked. Even very senior members of the ANC, such as Thabo Mbeki and MK head Joe Modise, were not informed of its existence. Most senior cadres in Lusaka would have insisted on participating if they had known about it, and this would have left the project vulnerable to the inefficiency and poor security that dogged routine ANC operations.[26]

Equally controversially, Oliver Tambo allowed Vula's directors, Joe Slovo and Mac Maharaj, to hand-pick whichever ANC and MK operatives they thought best equipped for it. [27] Inevitably Vula was dominated by the SACP – because the party recruited the best and brightest ANC cadres. This left it open to later accusations that it was a communist front. Vula recruits were certainly an elite, and members such as Mo Shaik, Pravin Gordhan, Ivan Pillay, Dipak Patel, Siphiwe Nyanda, Ronnie Kasrils and Charles Nqakula were to go on to have illustrious, if sometimes controversial, careers.

The operational head of Vula was the former Robben Islander everyone knew as 'Mac'. Satyandranath Raghunan 'Mac' Maharaj spent 12 years on the Island, from 1964 to 1976, after enduring unimaginable torture ahead of his trial. Whereas Kgalema Motlanthe and Harry Gwala had followed Govan Mbeki on Robben Island, Maharaj was unmistakably Nelson Mandela's protégé.

There is an interesting tale that illuminates something of the character of both men. When Mac was a prisoner on Robben Island, Mandela took him under his wing and determined, in the manner of the Island, that he should be inducted into the wisdom of the ANC. Every day during a rest period, the two men would break from work in the quarry and sit down together among the rocks. Mandela would place himself on a large boulder, and Maharaj would occupy a far smaller rock nearby. The older man would talk about his philosophy of politics and offer up his famous homespun wisdom, advising Maharaj, for example, that the Afrikaner is best talked to in Afrikaans – only if you learn his language will he listen to what you have to say.

Mac eventually tired of sitting always on the smaller stone. One day, when the time came for them to break from work, he ran as fast as he could to their meeting place and planted himself on the larger boulder. A few minutes later Mandela arrived, only to find Mac sitting in his place. He observed the small rock, his face quite expressionless. With an almost imperceptible turning of his head, he scanned the area for another place to sit. Without comment, he then walked over to where Maharaj was sitting, and stood over him. He began to talk in the normal way and remained on his feet for the whole session. The next day, a resigned Mac took up his usual place on the smaller stone.[28]

After his release from the Island, Maharaj escaped from house arrest in 1977, and made his way to London and then to Lusaka. He was a very clever man indeed, and he rose relentlessly through the ranks of the ANC and the SACP. By the early 1980s he was a key thinker in the SACP's Politburo and an important leader of the ANC's senior executive instrument, the Politico-Military Council (PMC).

Among his PMC responsibilities was 'tracking everything that was going on at home'.[29] He saw trade unions as vital vehicles for collective organisation. Through interaction with union leaders, including Phiroshaw Camay at Cusa, he followed the rise of Cyril very closely. Maharaj was unusually sympathetic to the 'orthodox' conception of unionisation, arguing that 'these people should not have been labelled "economistic" – they simply needed space, and beneath the surface they had the right tactical position'.[30] At the same time, he also remained partially persuaded by Sactu's project of building politically affiliated unions. He much appreciated Ramaphosa's finely balanced organisational approach to the dilemma this created.[31]

In late 1988, in the first stage of Vula, Maharaj and Siphiwe Nyanda were infiltrated into South Africa.[32] Within two years, there were 12, mostly middle-ranking, Vula operatives on the ground. The presence of Maharaj had major implications for Ramaphosa, who had already developed strong relations with Govan Mbeki's internal structure. Given the organisational character of the ANC, and the fear that penetration by South African spies would expose agents to capture, there were at any time quite a number of clandestine external units within South Africa unaware of each other's presence. Quite often they 'bumped into each other unexpectedly'.[33] Now, however, there were two substantial parallel structures competing for influence, and their heads, Mac Maharaj and Govan Mbeki, inevitably clashed. Ramaphosa was in regular touch with both of them.

Using secure Vula communications, Maharaj alerted Oliver Tambo in Lusaka to Mbeki's unauthorised, and in his view imprudent, initiatives. Mbeki was in fact behaving properly, in the sense that he was reporting back to Tambo on his activities. But, in Maharaj's view, he was inadvertently creating a security risk. 'There is always a tendency for a centralized structure to emerge, with everyone attracted to a magnet figure like Mbeki. But this was an invitation to another Rivonia. Everyone who went to see Mbeki, everyone surrounding him, was exposed.'[34] Consequently Tambo 'nudged' Mbeki to confine his activities henceforth to the Port Elizabeth area, an instruction he largely ignored.[35]

By this time, Ramaphosa had adopted Govan Mbeki's assumption that apartheid would necessarily be ended by the violent overthrow of the regime. The historian of the NUM reports that Cyril had come to believe 'there would be a major, most probably violent confrontation between the ANC and the SA government followed by a society created according to ANC values ... as late as 1989 he never envisaged a negotiated settlement and he knew no-one that did'.[36] As we shall see, this is not entirely consistent with Ramaphosa's other political actions in 1989, for example in helping to negotiate the end of the Soweto rent and rates boycott. He was not exactly hedging his bets. But he certainly refused to put all his political eggs into the basket of insurrection.

Ramaphosa probably went along with the conventional wisdom that Tambo, and not Mandela, was the natural leader of the ANC. Tambo was certainly the uncontested leader of the exile ANC, and those around him mostly supposed that he should become the movement's leader in a post-struggle era. Ramaphosa observed that 'people spent a long time with OR, they loved him, they adored him, he had led the movement very well and kept them together and was a very compassionate person and very clear, politically, very democratic also in his way of doing things. So that is the president that they loved ... Madiba they had a great feeling for because he was in prison and he was the embodiment of what the movement stood for ... It was only when Madiba came out that some people realized the important role that he could play ... '[37]

Uncertainty about Mandela's suitability for leadership was encouraged by the 1988 revelation that he had been negotiating from his prison rooms with the regime. Now he proposed to meet with the great enemy, President PW Botha. Ramaphosa found out about these initiatives through the media. He could neither understand nor accept Mandela's reasoning. He knew they were a long way from defeating the NP, 'but we also realized that they were in deep crisis and there was a stalemate of sorts ... they couldn't, even with their emergencies, smash us completely ... But that was the time that international sanctions were intensifying as well, so the general and overall approach was that we smash them.'[38]

In such circumstances, Mandela's overtures were alarming. 'At first it was like a bolt from the blue.' In the ANC's democratic culture 'you just dare not go and talk to the other side without getting a mandate ... That for us was not the time when we thought there would be negotiations, we were going to smash the apartheid state to smithereens. The country was being made ungovernable ... there were strikes all over, and on an incremental basis we thought all this was leading up to the hour of decision – and here was Madiba negotiating.'[39]

At the centre of the controversy was a memorandum that Mandela had written in preparation for his meeting with PW Botha. Mandela gave copies of the document to his lawyer and to Dullah Omar during a prison visit. In ever-widening circles, copies spread to incredulous readers including Cosatu boss Jay Naidoo, UDF leader Valli Moosa, NUM's Kgalema Motlanthe and, of course, Govan Mbeki. When Maharaj met up with Valli Moosa in Rosebank, Johannesburg, soon after Moosa had seen the memorandum, the UDF activist greeted Maharaj with the words, 'Did you hear that Madiba is selling out?'[40]

Maharaj sat down patiently with Moosa and together they considered the document Mandela had presented to the State President before their meeting on 5 July 1989. Maharaj took the younger man through it, line by line, until Moosa was persuaded that Mandela was in fact acting properly. The document was a quite masterful statement of the need for a negotiated settlement. Mandela had taken exceptional care to insist that he was not able to negotiate on behalf of the exile ANC:

'I am a loyal and disciplined member of the ANC, my political loyalty is owed, primarily, if not exclusively, to this organisation and particularly to our Lusaka headquarters where the official leadership is stationed and from where our affairs are directed ... In the normal course of events, I would put my views to the organisation first, and if these views were accepted, the organisation would then decide on who were the best qualified members to handle the matter on its behalf and on exactly when to make the move. But in the current circumstances I cannot follow this course, and this is the only reason why I am acting on my own initiative, in the hope that the organisation will, in due course endorse my action. I must stress that no prisoner irrespective of his status or influence can conduct negotiations of this nature from prison. In our special situation negotiation on political matters is literally a matter of life and death which requires to be handled by the organisation itself through its appointed representatives. The step I am taking should, therefore, not be seen as the beginning of actual negotiations between the government and the ANC.'[41]

Once Moosa was persuaded that Mandela had not been seduced into improper collaboration, the two men quickly assessed how to limit the damage. Moosa was a member of the same underground 'committee' as Jay Naidoo, and the next morning he was able to apprise the Cosatu leader of Maharaj's analysis. Meanwhile, the Vula boss contacted Harry Gwala, another potential flashpoint and antagonist of Mandela, and tried to assuage his concerns. The two men also sought to assemble and destroy all copies of the memorandum for fear it might cause wider confusion.

Fortunately, Vula was soon able to establish reliable communications with Mandela, and through its secure link with Lusaka to keep Tambo abreast of his negotiations. Mandela argued that his negotiations were not 'secret' but merely 'confidential'. Through the Vula channel, Tambo was correspondingly able to confirm that Mandela was not breaching the collective decision-making of the movement – so long as he reported back to Lusaka on the content of the 'confidential' deliberations. Ultimately it was the bond of trust and mutual respect between Mandela and Tambo – two men who were in effect also competitors for the presidency of the movement – that allowed this difficult period of interaction with the regime to be managed.

Govan Mbeki, nevertheless, took an uncompromising line: Mandela's contact with the regime was simply unmandated. He was rumoured to have characterised Mandela as a sell-out and he instructed cadres not to talk to him.[42] This position was not altogether unreasonable, given that the South African National Intelligence Service (NIS) was indeed trying to engineer a split between the domestic and exile wings of the ANC. Cyril also remained unconvinced by Maharaj's explanation, recalling that 'We did have quite serious debates with Mac because he has always had this faith in Madiba's visionary approach on issues. At that time I thought it was just blind faith because he didn't know what the hell was happening and he just said, no he thinks Madiba is doing the right thing because he has finally arrived at a conclusion that the only way in which we can take this country forward is for negotiations between the ANC and the government.'[43] It was only when Cyril later met Mandela face to face that his understanding of the prisoner's strategy was transformed.'

Despite his now exhausting range of commitments to the wider struggle movement, Ramaphosa was continually engaged in the battles the NUM was fighting against its mining house adversaries. One of these fights, in the conservative mining town of Welkom, led him into unexpected contact with the notorious mastermind behind the bombing of Cosatu House, law and order minister Adriaan Vlok.

Welkom was a town forever on the verge of racial violence. The town's population of 65,000 whites was segregated from ten times that number of blacks, living in hostels or the nearby township of Thabong, by segregated residential and social spaces and a *de facto* curfew for Africans. In the course of 1989 and 1990, violence across racial lines escalated at a frightening rate. Whites and blacks were attacked and killed in racial assaults on the streets and in the mine compounds. A bomb was exploded at a local NUM office. Thabong residents boycotted white-owned businesses.

After the death of a white mine manager and security guard at the President Steyn mine, right-wing groups including the Afrikaner Weerstandsbeweging (AWB) and the vigilante group Blanke Veiligheid (BV) organised a boycott of wholesalers to prevent food reaching Thabong. 'We will starve the kaffirs into submission,' the BV leader explained.[44]

In an attempt to defuse a situation that was likely to bring production at its mines to a halt, Anglo American called an emergency meeting between the Chamber of Mines, the NUM, Cosatu, the white unions, the defence force and Adriaan Vlok.

Ramaphosa drove down to Welkom from Johannesburg with James Motlatsi and Cosatu general secretary Jay Naidoo. A fourth passenger in the car describes their experience on arriving in Welkom. 'White vigilantes were patrolling the streets of Welkom, but as [we] approached the town Ramaphosa suggested that, instead of going straight to the meeting place, [we] should drive slowly through the centre so as to see the situation for [our]selves. Naidoo said: "OK, but slow down so that

I can have my last cigarette.'"[45]

The drive went off without incident and the union leaders arrived safely at their meeting with the minister of law and order. Free State NUM leaders joined them for the closed-door discussions, and eventually an agreement was hammered out to prevent any further escalation in the violence. The police committed themselves to desist from their campaign of harassment and to refrain from joining mine security in attacks on black mineworkers. NUM agreed to stop further threats of violence against white mineworkers. Vlok's role was primarily one of facilitation.

A few weeks later, Ramaphosa and Motlatsi met Vlok in Pretoria for a follow-up meeting on the state of the truce in the Free State town. On this occasion, Vlok had a large file on the desk in front of him. Flicking through it, he remarked to Ramaphosa, 'I was not aware that your father is a policeman.' After Cyril commented, 'He was a policeman,' Vlok commended the sergeant, Samuel Ramaphosa, on his career. With an incredulous Motlatsi looking on – but with Cyril's faced arranged in its usual dispassionate calm – Vlok handed Ramaphosa a pair of police cufflinks, with the words, 'Your father had an exemplary service record.'

Although he was never a high-profile UDF leader, Ramaphosa was an important political firefighter in Soweto. Two of his many interventions were especially significant – one for its positive impact on the welfare of Soweto's people, and the other for its negative impact on Cyril's own later political fortunes.

His first initiative was in resolving Soweto's longstanding and well-organised rates and rent boycott. This boycott was quite unlike the spontaneous and unsustainable community protests then breaking out across the country. In Soweto, civic activists had started organised payment boycotts in 1986, and they sustained the campaign into the late 1980s. Eventually the finances of Soweto municipalities became critically drained, and provincial resources had to be used to bail them out. By 1989, debt had reached the equivalent of US$100 million and there was no sign of a resolution in sight.

Ramaphosa took up the issue as spokesman for a group of local associations called the Soweto People's Delegation, an ideological descendant of the Committee of Ten.[46] In what was in some respects a continuation of the committee's 1976 battle, the educated and organised members of the Soweto community, seeking fairness and the ability to organise their own affairs, had faced off against the intractable bureaucrats of the Transvaal Administration. For many exiles and non-Soweto activists, this was the Committee of Ten at work once again, but now under the auspices of the UDF.[47]

In 1989, the delegation commissioned watershed research that demonstrated that black Soweto was subsidising white Johannesburg. The white city's commerce depended on black labour, yet the city contributed nothing to the Soweto services those workers consumed. The delegation demanded 'One city, one tax base', a rationale and slogan that 'became the rallying cry of township activists throughout South Africa'.[48] Ramaphosa began 14-hour daily negotiations with provincial government and Soweto's council officials in October 1989, eventually hammering out a settlement. Government agreed to cancel arrears, charge a flat utility service fee, and take steps towards creating a unified city administration. It was also agreed that the houses the people of Soweto had stayed in all their lives would be transferred to them – they would at last receive freehold title. Inferior services, Ramaphosa observed, would have to be addressed through a resolution of the wider problem of racial division. A multi-racial Central Witwatersrand Metropolitan Chamber was formed to take practical steps to solve the city's problems.[49]

In all this, Ramaphosa took a major political risk to achieve concrete results for his own community. He appeared to see the ability to secure a favourable bargain as the consequence of a successful strategy of ungovernability: the representatives of the regime could no longer govern. Exiles campaigning for ungovernability, however, saw the settlement as tantamount to selling out. Many of them were unable at that stage to make a transition from the symbolic politics of opposition to the constructive effort of institution-building. The Metropolitan Chamber's creation contradicted the ANC's demand that local government reform should occur only as part of national transformation. Among other reasonable concerns, the ANC feared that the National Party would be able to make inroads into a potential black electorate by effecting local-level changes in advance of the first democratic elections.[50]

What the Chamber's complex committee system did was to bring together civic associations and government officials in an environment of practical problem-solving. More than a thousand activists, consultants, engineers and councillors were ultimately involved. As one observer noted, 'White bureaucrats typically saw the civic activists as communist-inspired anarchists, hell-bent on overthrowing the government and installing a Stalinist regime. For their part, the activists considered the bureaucrats to be extensions of the apartheid apparatus.'[51]

After months of painful acrimony, the two sides began to better understand the real constraints facing the other side. Frederik van Zyl Slabbert, who became the Chamber's chairman, observed that 'The civic associations came into the chamber with foam in the mouth, and the provincial government came in accustomed to saying "Take it or leave it". After a while the civics began to appreciate the complexities of administration, and the province began to understand that there was a real crisis of legitimacy in township government.'[52] For Slabbert, this solution would have been impossible without Ramaphosa. Cyril was the one negotiator who was 'able to deliver'. [53]

A second high-profile Soweto issue of national significance into which Ramaphosa was drawn was how to contain the human and political damage being done by Winnie Mandela, the increasingly unpredictable wife of Nelson. Winnie's sponsored gangsterism and general disregard for ANC discipline were tolerated because of her special status and popularity within the movement. As ever, the ANC was keen to cover up the misdeeds of its most prominent members. Yet Mandela's 'football club' – an unruly gang of bodyguards and thugs – was so undisciplined and relentless in its violence and intimidation that local community organisations and international journalists were together exposing its actions, with potentially damaging implications for the ANC. Matters came to a head over the murder of a child who was last seen in the hands of Winnie's gangsters.

Saki Macozoma, an organiser with the South African Council of Churches (SACC) in the late 1980s, recalls that 'Winnie was on the rampage. She would not listen to criticism. She would say, "You boys, what do you know? I take my instructions directly from Lusaka."'[54] The SACC was a substantial force within the UDF, and its leadership took upon itself the task of bringing Winnie under control. This was a task the exile leadership seemed too feeble to contemplate. The SACC sent Macozoma on a mission to Lusaka in 1989 to brief Oliver Tambo and the exile leadership on Winnie's behaviour and attitude. Tambo quickly and predictably hit the ball back into the SACC's court, placing upon the Soweto civic establishment the moral duty to limit her actions and safeguard the ANC's international reputation. Frank Chikane and Cyril were both drafted on to the 'Mandela Crisis Committee' created to take this strategy forward.

The committee worked assiduously, and with some success, to isolate Winnie within the UDF, to rein in the worst excesses of her followers, and to discourage the patronage of foreign funders. Winnie herself was never to forgive those who had ostracised and contained her, later describing them as an 'undemocratic cabal' bent on destroying her influence in the movement. She was repeatedly to attack this group over coming years, in the 1991 trial on charges related to kidnapping and murder, and in the following years when her purported lover Dali Mpofu was removed from his ANC position and Nelson Mandela dissolved their marriage. Along with Ramaphosa and Chikane, this so-called cabal contained much of the more moderate and capable national leadership of the UDF, including Murphy Morobe, Azhar Cachalia and Valli Moosa.

For an ambitious politician in the early 1990s, Winnie Mandela was a dangerous enemy. She would never be reconciled to Cyril's rise to leadership, and she probably influenced others, for example in the Youth League, to campaign against him. Yet Cyril's involvement brought him popularity among the wider majority of ordinary Soweto residents who had long since tired of Winnie's arrogance and casual brutality. In addition, it drew him closer to the Mandela family, and later helped to cement his relationship with Nelson Mandela.

At the end of this brutal decade, Cosatu and the UDF became increasingly close. The UDF had survived government harassment in the mid-1980s and weathered the 1985 Delmas treason trial of key leaders Mosiuoa Lekota and Popo Molefe. In February 1988, however, the government massively stepped up its pressure, effectively banning the

UDF and introducing substantial 'restrictions' on the movement and activity of almost all its leaders.

Only Cosatu's organisational and financial resources could fill the vacuum left by banned and restricted UDF campaigners. Activists on both sides began to call for a unified 'mass democratic movement' (MDM), and in 1989 this new formation came into existence. MDM was an amorphous entity that could not be subjected to banning or restrictions. In two major conferences, Conference for a Democratic Future and From Opposing to Governing, members of this new grouping began to look to a post-apartheid future. There was a sense of anticipation in the air, but no one guessed that fundamental change was just around the corner.

CHAPTER 14

BY MANDELA'S SIDE

At the end of the 1980s, popular unrest swept the country. In reaction, the besieged National Party (NP) desperately used state coercion to contain a growing crescendo of protest. Many of its leaders now recognised that a negotiated settlement, on its own terms, was the only way to avert disaster. Indeed, the necessity of reform had been openly recognised by PW Botha as long ago as 1985, in his widely slated 'Rubicon speech' at Durban City Hall. The content of this speech was generally condemned at home and abroad for exemplifying Afrikaner stubbornness. Progressive business people, such as Anglo American chairman Gavin Relly, were 'aghast' at its content.[1] But Afrikaner politicians saw beyond Botha's infelicities of style, and recognised that he had made a major shift in political strategy. He had quietly committed the NP to the principle of one person one vote in a unitary South Africa, overturning decades of intellectual orthodoxy.

Only PW Botha could have made this concession appear to be obduracy of the highest order. Botha's mistake taught a crucial lesson to his party and to the Afrikaner constituency that it served. The party's next leader would be a politician of the new school – a master of presentation whose modernity and sophistication would allow Afrikaners to put behind them the moral opprobrium of apartheid. Despite a growing consensus about the need for change, there were, however, many divergences of strategy in the NP leadership, and a more general unwillingness to relinquish real power. Three factors cut the ground from under those Afrikaners who were still resisting change. First, the intensification of the state of emergency after 1988 had successfully, if brutally, dispelled ANC activists' expectations of revolutionary change. In FW de Klerk's way of explaining it, this reign of state terror had obliged ANC revolutionaries to adopt 'more realistic perceptions of the balance of power'. Such perceptions, De Klerk believes, were 'indispensable' pre-conditions for the start of genuine negotiations.[2]

A second key change was the unravelling of the Soviet empire under reformist president Mikhail Gorbachev. The new USSR seemed to demonstrate that liberalisation and political change could be initiated and managed by a bold leader. More importantly, Gorbachev made life much harder for the opponents of negotiation by removing the 'red peril' that Afrikaner die-hards always identified as the root of their intransigence.

For its part, the ANC was stripped of the funding and support mechanisms that had helped ameliorate the discontent of ordinary recruits in the camps. The doctrines to which SACP members had shown exceptional fealty were rapidly becoming discredited, and there was no longer a 'Moscow line' to which to appeal. ANC leaders had to face up to a sudden and dramatic end to the Soviet financial largesse and political credibility that had buoyed their morale across decades in exile.[3] Most alarmingly for those habituated to exile life, the end of the Cold War ensured that the Western powers, especially the United States, would move to bring about a resolution to southern Africa's last protracted stalemate. Suddenly, the exiles realised they had to get home fast, before a settlement was reached without them.[4]

The third key factor was the stroke to which PW Botha fell victim on 18 January 1989, and the opportunity it provided for the adroit FW de Klerk to manoeuvre himself first into the party and then the state presidency. In his autobiography, De Klerk claims that he was just on the verge of confronting the 'Groot Krokodil'. 'I felt that I could no longer serve under PW Botha and that the time had come to make a stand. His surliness, aggression and poor human relations were doing serious harm to the National Party and to the country ... I told my friend and colleague Dawie de Villiers that I was going to resign from the cabinet.'[5] The reality, of course, is that he did nothing until Botha was partly paralysed and politically isolated.

In this new President, nevertheless, the process of negotiation had found a skilful Afrikaner tactician. De Klerk was born in

Johannesburg on 18 March 1936, the son of Senator Jan de Klerk, who was later a minister in Verwoerd's cabinet. FW graduated in law from Potchefstroom University in 1958, and practised in Vereeniging. A gifted analytical thinker, later offered a professorship of administrative law at Potchefstroom, De Klerk rose rapidly through the Transvaal National Party, becoming member for Vereeniging in the early 1970s. In 1978, Prime Minister Vorster appointed him minister of posts and telecommunications, the first of many ministerial portfolios. Under PW Botha, these included mineral and energy affairs (1980–2), internal affairs (1982–5), and national education and planning (1984–9). As minister of education, he was a supporter of segregated universities but committed to increasing resources for non-whites.

A relative centrist in the party who led moves in 1982 against the extreme right, FW was not a natural reformer. But he was a relatively modern politician who understood political communication, international public opinion and the demands of a market economy. In February 1989, shortly after Botha suffered his debilitating stroke, De Klerk was elected leader of the NP in a carefully planned internal coup. In September 1989, after a protracted struggle to displace an ailing Botha, he became State President.

De Klerk steered a careful course between slowly dismantling a militarised regime and ensuring that a divided Afrikaner elite could be relied upon to accept negotiated change. Sensibly he did not use the military as a bargaining chip in the negotiations, insisting that they were a part of the state, and that the fiction of their impartiality must therefore be respected. There was in fact little likelihood of a coup. The military leadership mostly shared De Klerk's belief that the institutional separation of the armed forces from politics must be enforced. When conservative leader Constand Viljoen, himself a famous general, later asked Defence Force head General Meiring, 'What will you do when the soldiers mutiny?' Meiring coldly replied, 'I will have them shot.' 'You will have them shot?' responded Viljoen incredulously. Meiring: 'The order has already gone out.'[6] Because the means of state coercion remained so overwhelming and so robust, neither a military coup nor state-destabilising civil war in Natal ever posed a credible threat.

One of De Klerk's first actions as State President was to summon to his office the government's head of communications, Dave Steward, and tell him that henceforth he would report directly to the President. This was to be a presidency of managed perceptions, international diplomacy and scientific opinion surveys.[7] Steward was a former diplomat with a glittering career that had culminated in his rise at a young age to the coveted position of ambassador to the United Nations. He had perhaps the sharpest understanding in government of foreign perceptions of the apartheid state, and he had managed South Africa's involvement in Namibian independence. Since 1985, he had been head of government communications, remodelling his department along the lines of the United Kingdom's Central Office of Information – as a supplier of information to government rather than as a propaganda instrument.

Steward pioneered the use of opinion polling within government, commissioning representative national surveys to gauge the mood of black and white South Africans. Steward was able to inform De Klerk – with more confidence than the ANC itself possessed – that the liberation movement had the support of between 60 and 65 per cent of the voting-age population. The NP, meanwhile, could count on only 20 per cent of the vote and the IFP only 10 per cent. From 1990 Steward was to be De Klerk's main speechwriter, and in 1992 he became chief government spokesman and director-general in the presidency – in effect De Klerk's chief of staff. It was characteristic of De Klerk to elevate an English speaker and a diplomat to this prominent role, a man who, like De Klerk, represented the palatable face of reformist South Africa.

In his first speech as party leader in early 1989, De Klerk called for a fresh spirit of reform. His first demonstrable shift on political prisoners came on 10 October, when he announced that Walter Sisulu, Raymond Mhlaba, Ahmed Kathrada and several other Robben Islanders were to be summarily released. Then, on 2 February 1990, De Klerk made his most famous address to parliament, in which he announced that opposition political parties would be unbanned forthwith and that Nelson Mandela would shortly be released from prison.

De Klerk's 10 October 1989 announcement threw the UDF and Cosatu into frenzied action. Walter Sisulu and the other struggle veterans could not be released into a political vacuum. Yet the ANC was still illegal, and most of its formal leadership remained in exile. Above all, there was a sense of uncertainty about the sustainability of the NP's new strategy, and a consequent desire to avoid unnecessary confrontation. The eventuality of prisoner release was one for which Mac Maharaj had already planned. In 1988, Maharaj had set up a 40-person clandestine 'release committee' that represented almost every ANC and UDF constituency within the country. From this 40-person group, a seven-person committee, one of whom was Cyril, was chosen as a decision-making executive. They had all been briefed individually by Maharaj on their roles.[8]

When De Klerk made his announcement on 10 October, this pre-planning provided some basis on which to act. The group was quickly gathered and tasked with making preparations for the impending releases. Cyril was a junior figure in the Mass Democratic Movement (MDM) – in the words of Frank Chikane, 'not on the UDF radar'.[9] Yet he soon emerged as chair of the reception committee. Cyril's rise was prompted perversely by his lack of UDF seniority. In its desire to protect De Klerk's incremental strategy, the MDM was determined to avoid rocking the boat with a politically contentious appointment. Because the UDF was accused of being an 'ANC front' by the government, it created fewer tensions to appoint the non-UDF leader Ramaphosa.[10] It was also important that a black African should head the committee and be seen at the released prisoners' sides.[11] There had been growing tension within the UDF because a disproportionate number of leadership positions were held by white, coloured and Indian activists.

Some contemporaries also believe Cyril was very keen to secure this prize for himself. He had insinuated himself into the network around Mac Maharaj, and had taken every opportunity to demonstrate his suitability for a high-profile public position of just this kind. As Frank Chikane observes, 'others like myself were more deeply involved with release planning for Mandela and others. I was very deeply involved with the Mandelas, although I always stayed in the background and retreated out of photographs. But Cyril assumed a high profile.'[12]

Once Ramaphosa became chair of the reception committee, he began to build upon the profile that it gave him. Saki Macozoma, who was head of media relations on the reception committee, recalls Cyril's adroit strategies for creating publicity without compromising negotiations.

He unobtrusively turned the Sisulu release rally into an ANC event – something that was at that stage not permitted by law – and so brought about a *de facto* legalisation of the party before its actual unbanning in 1990. This made the unbanning itself almost inevitable, and rendered the legalisation politically painless for the government. Through his selection of the slogan 'ANC lives, ANC leads', Ramaphosa meanwhile re-established the ANC in the consciousness of ordinary people who had not directly engaged with it since the 1950s.[13] In January 1990, he took the prisoners released in later 1989 – including the new *de facto* leader of the internal ANC, Walter Sisulu – to Lusaka. There he was a participant in the historic reunion between Robben Islanders and exile leaders, including Joe Slovo and acting ANC president Alfred Nzo.[14]

Ramaphosa had remained sceptical about Mandela's unmandated initiatives to engage the regime in dialogue until 1989, when he was able to meet Mandela for himself for the first time. Only during this face-to-face meeting did he become convinced of the feasibility of negotiated settlement. They met at Victor Verster Prison in late 1989, some weeks before the release of Sisulu, after Mandela had issued a call for MDM activists to visit him. Many UDF and Cosatu leaders shared Ramaphosa's concern about Mandela's negotiations with the regime. Mac Maharaj, still active with Vula, remembers that many of them would make promises on the way to their first visit with the old man, waving their fingers and saying, 'I will tell him to stop talking to the fucking enemy!'[15] When Ramaphosa was scheduled to visit, Maharaj provoked him about his views. 'Go on then,' he laughed. 'Go and make your case to him!' At their next meeting, after Ramaphosa had seen Mandela, Maharaj teased him again: 'Did you tell him to shut up then?'

Ramaphosa was almost breathless with excitement about Mandela. 'He was fantastic. He was on top form. What could I do? ... This old man walks into the room, he comes straight up to me, and he asks me how my wife and my son are doing ... This old man, he knows every fucking thing!'[16] The two men shared a meal with wine, an event that Cyril recalled several years later with still somewhat incoherent delight. 'It was wonderful, it was a really wonderful visit. Madiba is a very striking person and when you meet him for the first time, particularly at the time we did, he was not [physically] known to anyone ... you just see a leader without even questioning, he stands out, [he] just walks very quietly through a doorway, you are not expecting him and there he is. You virtually fall backwards, and he knows every small detail about you, it's amazing. He knew quite a lot of what I had done, he had been reading and had followed my career ... That was very touching and very moving in very many ways.'[17]

Ramaphosa's scepticism about Mandela's position on negotiations immediately turned to agreement. Like other converts, he 'could not really articulate [this] to those we were supposed to report back to in a convincing way ... When you first see him for the first he just disarms you, mesmerizes you completely, takes you in. So in the end there were rumblings, particularly among those who hadn't met him, that he is negotiating, [but] we were convinced he was doing the right thing.'[18]

Through his positions on committees dealing with released prisoners and Winnie Mandela, Cyril had an opportunity to spend considerable time with Mandela, and the two men developed a strong personal rapport. Ramaphosa eventually served in an advisory capacity – as a kind of personal assistant – preparing materials and speeches, and marshalling the information Mandela felt he must absorb before his release.[19]

Mandela was clearly a candidate in his own right for the leadership of the ANC. But he was also a potential foil to the ambitions of the exiles, and in particular the supporters of Oliver Tambo's elevation to the presidency. In such circumstances, Mandela's purported transgression of the morality of the movement by unilaterally engaging the regime in talks could easily be used as a stick with which to beat him. The veteran was soon to recapture the combativeness and guile that had characterised his political dealings before prison. However, in the immediate aftermath of his release, it was the young Ramaphosa who had to be the older man's protector and guide.

Few South Africans will ever forget the release of Nelson Mandela on Sunday, 11 February 1990. A huge crowd met Nelson Mandela and Winnie outside the gates of the Victor Verster prison in Paarl. Ramaphosa had been in overall charge of the logistics of the event, and some of the strain showed on his face. In Tshiawelo, Cyril's mother watched on television as her son walked alongside the Mandelas, on the proudest day of her life.[20]

Later in the day, Mandela spoke to a gigantic crowd outside the City Hall in Cape Town. His speech was a turgid statement of ANC positions, including a reiterated commitment to nationalisation. There was much speculation that Cyril had written the speech himself.[21] Although he almost certainly played a major role in its formulation, numerous internal UDF activists – including Trevor Manuel – were insistent that references to nationalisation be included.[22] In photos of Mandela speaking at the City Hall, Ramaphosa is hanging from the balcony and holding the microphone. Just outside the frame, however, less determined to be seen with Mandela, were leaders of the UDF, including Trevor Manuel and Cheryl Carolus, who were to become Cyril's close allies.[23]

The central point of the speech was not to convey a policy platform. Rather, Mandela was keen to rebut critics of his initiation of talks. 'I am a loyal and disciplined member of the African National Congress. I am therefore in full agreement with all of its objectives, strategies and tactics.' He continued, 'No individual leader is able to take on this enormous task on his own. It is our task as leaders to place our views before our organisation and to allow the democratic structures to decide. On the question of democratic practice, I feel duty bound to make the point that a leader of the movement is a person who has been democratically elected at a national conference. This is a principle which must be upheld without any exceptions.' Mandela then reiterated, 'We have not as yet begun discussing the basic demands of the struggle. I wish to stress that I myself have at no time entered into negotiations about the future of our country except to insist on a meeting between the ANC and the government.'[24]

The exile ANC leadership had in fact already decided on a collective internal leadership to manage this period of change. In September 1989, a new 'inner core' was chosen and it was planned that it should meet for the first time on 14 February 1990. Its members were Walter Sisulu, who was the chairman, Raymond Mhlaba, Mac Maharaj and Govan Mbeki – and a place was held open for Nelson Mandela.[25] Its composition had been ratified in January 1990 by an ailing Oliver Tambo, who was then hospitalised in Stockholm. But this seeming resolution of the leadership issue quickly unravelled when Govan Mbeki introduced new names, including his protégé Kgalema Motlanthe and the controversial Harry Gwala, to shift the balance of the internal leadership in his own favour. Mac Maharaj refused to work with Gwala and stormed out, writing to Joe Slovo that he was leaving for London. It took the intervention of Nelson Mandela to persuade Maharaj to return.[26]

The jostling for position within the leadership of the ANC was only just beginning. Oliver Tambo's illness and the unexpected charismatic force of Nelson Mandela meant that the most senior leadership question began to answer itself – although not without resentment among exiles who had conceived and created a Mandela legend that was now threatening to swallow them. The movement still faced an unprecedented period of upheaval. The exile leadership and the ANC's National Executive Committee were being repatriated to South Africa after decades abroad, with the first major exile cohort arriving in April 1990. At the same time, Robben Islanders were being released in large numbers. The role of the SACP, at a time of collapse of international communism, was uncertain and influential cadres such as Thabo Mbeki were tearing up their party cards. Perhaps most important of all, the exiles' relationship with the domestic leadership of the UDF and Cosatu was fraught with uncertainty.

Matters were further complicated in July 1990 when a number of Operation Vula operatives, including Mac Maharaj, were detained under the Internal Security Act. Maharaj had left the country secretly in May and re-entered legally in June. On one view, the arrests were simply evidence of the regime's determination to isolate the SACP from more moderate ANC leaders, and Vula was characterised by the government as part of an insurrectionary communist conspiracy. Intriguingly, one reporter for the BBC was reportedly briefed by an ANC official that Vula was a maverick operation that the movement did not sanction. It took four months for Maharaj to get released on bail, and many months more for the ANC leadership to mobilise around indemnification of the operation's members. It is quite conceivable that Vula members were hung out to dry by ANC and MK leaders who had been excluded from the operation and were outraged to discover its existence.

Equally plausible is the possibility that Vula posed a real threat to the ambitions of the exile leadership that had developed around Tambo in Lusaka. James Sanders observes that Vula's 'deeply problematic contribution to the struggle was that it had established, in addition to DIS [Department of Internal Security] and MK's Military Intelligence, a third ANC intelligence network'.[27] Even after it was formally disbanded, there were suspicions that the Vula network lived on in sets of informal relationships between exile SACP cadres such as Mac Maharaj and Joe Slovo, and leftist UDF and Cosatu leaders such as Trevor Manuel, Cheryl Carolus, Pravin Gordhan, Valli Moosa and Cyril Ramaphosa.

The ANC was due to hold a conference in the following year, 1991, to elect new office-holders and build an integrated party after the enforced divisions of the struggle. Ramaphosa had the opportunity to secure senior office. And now he possessed some powerful allies.

CHAPTER 15

ANC SECRETARY-GENERAL

As a result of Ramaphosa's skilful management of the release and reception of Robben Island prisoners, he was now something less of an ANC outsider. He was still just a trade union leader with a limited UDF base, regarded as a 'Johnny-come-lately'[1] by many exile and Robben Island grandees. Yet Cyril was also suddenly everywhere, and often at the side of the man, Nelson Mandela, whom everyone wanted to see. With the approach of the ANC's July 1991 conference, at which the organisation was due to remake itself after decades of exile and suppression, Ramaphosa could have contemplated standing for a major office with some confidence. But he was reticent about an open campaign for such a senior position, exhibiting an unchanging aspect of his political character: he did not like to stand if he thought he might lose.

On the eve of the ANC conference, Ramaphosa sat by chance next to black consciousness activist Saths Cooper on a flight to Durban. Cooper recalls, 'He asked me if he should stand. Did I think it was a good idea? Did I think he would win?'[2] Not for nothing do two of Cyril's greatest admirers, James Motlatsi and former cabinet minister Kader Asmal, use almost the same words to describe his reticence to run for office even when he has a good chance of success. Motlatsi laughs that Cyril is 'a coward' when it comes to elections; and Asmal observes that you never really know until the last minute 'whether he has got the balls' to run.[3]

On this occasion, there was some justification for Ramaphosa's reticence. The 48th national conference, held between 2 and 7 July 1991, was the first full assembly of the liberation movement for decades. It provided a first opportunity for members to debate together the character of the movement that would dominate post-apartheid politics. More than two thousand delegates, representing 760,000 members, attended, and they included UDF activists, members of underground structures, foot soldiers from the camps of Umkhonto weSizwe, the Women's and Youth Leagues, and returned exiles from foreign ANC missions.

The first key challenge was electing a new leadership for the movement, and a new National Executive Committee (NEC). UDF and Cosatu convention was to insist on an open contest for leadership positions, whereas the traditional exile practice, forged in different conditions, was to take key decisions behind closed doors and in advance. The conference was therefore held in an atmosphere of uncertainty and sometimes hostility between different factions. Most members of the current NEC were lobbying hard for the 're-election' – in effect, reappointment – of the entire exile slate.[4] On their view, the exile ANC possessed a monopoly of wisdom and political legitimacy.

The most senior available positions, those of president and national chairman of the ANC, were unanimously secured without contest by Nelson Mandela and Oliver Tambo. Since his release, Mandela's rise had continued, and he was now the movement's *de facto* presidential candidate. Controversy, however, surrounded the remaining offices. Delegates were looking to the future, and contemplating the likely successors to the ageing generation of Mandela, Tambo and Sisulu. Two relative youngsters were clearly in the succession frame, at least in the eyes of exiles: Chris Hani, charismatic leftist firebrand and head of the ANC's armed wing; and Thabo Mbeki, protégé of Oliver Tambo, a man with considerable diplomatic experience, and the brave initiator of Lusaka's 1980s negotiations with the regime.

Fearing a divisive contest, the movement's elders characteristically persuaded Thabo Mbeki and Chris Hani not to contest for the senior office of deputy president. The focus of these two men's campaigns shifted to securing as many votes as possible in the 'beauty contest' of the NEC elections, in which they were now vying for first place. Walter Sisulu was meanwhile elected deputy president, and Thomas Nkobi was a non-contentious choice as the movement's treasurer-general.

It is possible that Thabo Mbeki believed he had Ramaphosa's agreement that he would not contest the office of secretary-general.

Mbeki's close ally, Jacob Zuma, was also running for the office. However, Ramaphosa's supporters had planned quite carefully for him to compete, and he enjoyed the advantage of an ageing and uncharismatic incumbent, Alfred Nzo.

Ramaphosa's victory over both Zuma and Nzo turned into a landslide. In the final count, he secured three votes for every one Nzo received. This crushing of Nzo was no fault of Cyril's, but it generated some counter-reaction against his 'humiliation' of an elder. Jacob Zuma, meanwhile, was obliged to retreat licking his wounds, doubtless harbouring a deep resentment against Ramaphosa. He was eventually elected Cyril's junior in the post of deputy secretary-general.

As the dust settled, the forces behind Ramaphosa's election to one of the ANC's key offices became clearer. He had established a strong reputation for competency and organisation-building. Given that the infrastructure of a political party had to be created in time for elections that might be a few short years away, these were strong *prima facie* recommendations for his appointment. Ramaphosa had also established a strong relationship with Nelson Mandela. By the public nature of their interaction, Mandela conferred a legitimacy on Ramaphosa in much the same way as Tambo's aura surrounded Thabo Mbeki. Cyril, moreover, turned out to have a constituency that was unexpectedly broad. He was an acknowledged leader of Cosatu, and the union movement was already emerging as a major breeding ground of political organisers. Many of the most talented and energetic activists at the first conference were union officials, and Ramaphosa was their natural choice as secretary-general. In the economic heartland of the country around Johannesburg, then known as the PWV, Ramaphosa was especially well known among trade unionists. He also had the support of much of the powerful civic establishment from his home town of Soweto.

Less well understood was the fact that Ramaphosa enjoyed a massive and influential constituency among working and retired mineworkers in the ANC's heartland of the Eastern Cape, in the Orange Free State, and in the northern Cape. Ramaphosa had been general secretary of the NUM for almost a decade, during which time hundreds of thousands of mineworkers had come to view him as their natural spokesman. The interim ANC provincial leaderships that had been put in place across the country were therefore unexpectedly well disposed towards the nomination and election of the young union leader.

One further factor in Ramaphosa's favour was that most of the senior positions in the movement were monopolised by an older generation of exile politicians hailing from the Eastern Cape. From the point of view of representivity – always a key consideration in the ANC – it was desirable to have a younger African from the domestic struggle, who was not a Xhosa, elected to a senior position. In such a role, Cyril might also have been preferred by many exiles to a potential rival such as Popo Molefe. He was not fully a part of the wider UDF structures that the repatriated Lusaka ANC was now keen to dismantle, and so he was less likely to protect them. In addition, his rivals may have recognised that tying Cyril to the demanding role of secretary-general would leave him with less time for personal campaigning in pursuit of the higher state offices that would soon become available.[5]

The decisive factor in overcoming Ramaphosa's reluctance to stand was that leaders of the SACP had asked him to do so.[6] If Cyril always 'wanted to be on the winning side',[7] SACP support came close to the guarantee of success he required. While Ramaphosa was never a Marxist, nor indeed was he ever a systematic theorist about politics, he was broadly sympathetic to the ideology's critical analysis of capitalism. The SACP was also a familiar presence in the union movement, which it viewed as an advanced force in the struggle for working-class mobilisation.[8]

The ANC cadres with whom he had the most contact in the late 1980s – Mac Maharaj, Govan Mbeki and Kgalema Motlanthe – were leading SACP members. Cyril was also influenced by members of the wider international communist movement. He met his English friend Vic Allen, who was to remain a communist and defender of the Soviet party after its 1990s implosion, in a boat off the coast of Cuba where they had both travelled to meet Fidel Castro.[9] Arthur Scargill, eccentric communist leader of the British NUM, also regularly attended South African NUM central committee meetings, and served as a conduit for funds and advice.[10] James Motlatsi, Cyril and Vic Allen visited the Soviet Union together clandestinely.

When Joe Slovo returned from exile, he and Cyril were to become very close friends and confidants. Slovo was in reality a pedestrian socialist theorist, but he adroitly used Marxist categories to justify his acute pragmatic judgements. His SACP, in truth, was an organisational rather than an ideological force, an institution that brought together the most capable cadres to neutralise the ethnic squabbling and patronage politics that were routine elsewhere in the ANC.

Was Ramaphosa an SACP member? William Gumede comments that Cyril 'allowed his membership to lapse', but characteristically offers no sources to support his contention that Ramaphosa was ever a member.[11] Cyril's friend Vic Allen 'once suspected he was a secret member of the party for a year or two in the late 1980s',[12] but no longer feels this was the case. Frederik van Zyl Slabbert speculates that Cyril 'joined the SACP as a matter of expediency just as Thabo Mbeki resigned'. Slabbert's contention is that both Mbeki and Ramaphosa recognised the great significance of the decline of the USSR. For Mbeki, there was no longer a relationship with Soviet power and resources to justify a continuing affiliation, and he resigned from the SACP Politburo at the end of the 1980s. For Ramaphosa, by contrast, SACP members seemed the liberation movement's most penetrating strategists.

If Ramaphosa found the SACP appealing, the party needed him even more. As a disproportionately white and Indian organisation, the SACP always desperately courted African leaders like Ramaphosa.[13] The party also required an insurance policy against the defection or debilitation of its long-term African figurehead, Chris Hani.

Evidence for a strong and multi-faceted relationship between Cyril and the SACP is certainly strong. His colleagues at the NUM, James Motlatsi and Marcel Golding, both counselled him against joining the party.[14] For Golding, this was an affiliation he simply did not need – he was already a major leader in his own right. For those who had created the black union movement, the aggressive entryism of the SACP was a constant threat. Its secretive membership recruitment and caucusing, and the dedication of its activists, allowed it to exercise vastly disproportionate influence in union bureaucracies. A pattern was already emerging in which the SACP depended on trade union 'donations' to secure its financial independence from the ANC. In consequence, the party felt the need to manipulate trade union elections to ensure that sympathetic union leaders would continue to divert resources to it.

In the NUM, there had been a steady rise of SACP penetration during the 1980s, and they were now found at senior level among the area and regional organisers. When Cyril was elected ANC secretary-general in 1991, and resigned in consequence from the union, the SACP moved to establish control. It would appear that it did so with the collusion, or at least passive acquiescence, of Ramaphosa.

Marcel Golding had been elected assistant general secretary after defeating communist rival Gwede Mantashe at a previous national congress. When Ramaphosa resigned, Golding immediately took over as acting general secretary – in accordance with the constitution of the union. He was soon subjected to a smear campaign, in which he was alleged to be linked to the CIA and to American mining interests. In reality, such accusations were absurd: Golding was simply hostile to the growing influence of the SACP within the union.

The next meeting of the central committee of the union was a torrid affair. Though this committee was a higher body of the union, it did not have the authority to appoint senior officers, a function reserved for the national congress. Nevertheless, the issue of the position of general secretary was raised, and strong criticisms were levelled at Golding. At the ringside, international communist party sympathisers Vic Allen and Arthur Scargill looked on. A communist putsch was evidently in the offing.

Golding vehemently opposed claims by members of the committee that they had the right and the obligation to replace him, but he was relentlessly brow-beaten and ultimately reduced to tears.[15] In contravention of the union's constitution, he was forced to arrange, and then to compete in, a ballot for acting general secretary that he considered totally illegitimate. During this vicious and unconstitutional manoeuvre, Ramaphosa was present, and he was asked to intervene. But he signally failed to back Golding's interpretation of the rules. In this way, an impression was created that Ramaphosa had enjoyed SACP support for his election as ANC secretary-general, and in return he had allowed the NUM to become the only major Cosatu union in which a majority of office-holders were SACP members.[16]

Despite this close and apparently symbiotic relationship with the SACP, it transpires that Ramaphosa never in fact became a member of the party.[17] Mac Maharaj did write to SACP general secretary Joe Slovo towards the end of the 1980s, asking that Cyril be recruited to what was known as 'Category D' membership.[18] This type of membership had emerged in the 1950s to permit high-profile individuals to join the party in complete secrecy. Category D members were allocated to cells or units that did not have highly active communists in them, in this way protecting them against inadvertent exposure through association with known activists.

The advantage of Category D membership to the party was that these hidden cadres could be mobilised suddenly at crucial moments. While Ramaphosa's application was in process, Maharaj insisted that he should meanwhile be treated as if he was already a member of the party. In Maharaj's view, Cyril was 'comfortable with the positions of the party', and the Vula commander had interacted with him repeatedly without a single breach of security occurring.[19]

The application was, however, never to result in membership. Fate intervened, in the unlikely form of Jacob Zuma, who had just been appointed to the Politburo. Zuma was a counter-intelligence specialist, and he was tasked with performing a 'background check' on Ramaphosa to ensure that he was not an infiltrator. This was the proper course of action. All the same, Zuma was already sympathetic to the theory – a precursor to today's culture of mediocrity in the ANC – that any accomplished young member of the liberation movement was quite likely a spy. If such a youngster was not in the employ of foreign powers or the state, how else could he have acquired his exceptional skills?[20]

Zuma took a very long while to report back. When he did so, he claimed that there were security question marks around Ramaphosa's past. Maharaj was outraged, given his complete confidence in Cyril and the indisputable fact that Maharaj himself had not been arrested despite associating with him. The regime, he observed, would have been thrilled to have secured his scalp. Eventually the Vula boss met with Zuma to hear his 'evidence' for himself. It transpired that Zuma's doubts rested on the already well-known fact that Cyril – like so many others – had once been imprisoned and released without being charged. Maharaj told Zuma he was not satisfied with the report, and sent him away to investigate further.[21] Events were soon to overtake these lumbering inquiries, and the opportunity to join the party was lost.

The fact that Cyril did not join the SACP was soon rendered

irrelevant. Mac Maharaj and Joe Slovo were key SACP power-brokers and their trust in him was absolute. Slovo quickly became Cyril's close friend on his return from exile. Maharaj was soon to storm out of the SACP himself, never to look back, once again in fury over Harry Gwala – this time over the volatile Natal firebrand's elevation to the SACP's central committee.[22]

An axis was emerging that cut across the boundaries between party and ANC and transcended divisions between exile and domestic cadres. Members of this new left axis included some SACP stalwarts from exile, certain former-SACP activists who had torn up their cards, and others who had never been, and would never become, members of SACP structures. Some of this last group were leftist but anti-communist intellectuals, such as Pallo Jordan. Others were 'inziles', often communist Cosatu or UDF activists such as Trevor Manuel, Cheryl Carolus and Valli Moosa, who were flexible and adroit enough to build bridges with their exile comrades. This wider left axis proved decisive in the nomination and election of Cyril to the position of ANC secretary-general. Its ambitions, however, did not stop there.

After the bombshell of Cyril's elevation to one of the great offices, the ANC's 48th conference moved on to the election of the NEC. The 50 members of this key decision-making body were elected from a list of 130 nominations. Much of the conference-floor discussion turned on the contest between Thabo Mbeki and Chris Hani, rivals for the future leadership of the ANC. Branch delegates were aware that the two men had been asked to relinquish competition for more senior office, and this made the outcome of their NEC contest all the more exciting. [23]

The election was by secret ballot, and involved each delegate casting multiple votes, almost equal to the number of positions that were to be filled. After a tension-racked count, the most successful of the candidates – Chris Hani and Thabo Mbeki – received 94.7 and 93 per cent of the vote respectively, indicating that almost every delegate had recognised these two candidates' claims to a place on the NEC. Despite the marginal nature of the 'victory', Thabo Mbeki had been defeated by the left's candidate, Chris Hani. Other SACP cadres who received more than 80 per cent support in the ballot included Joe Slovo, Ronnie Kasrils and

Harry Gwala, and the NEC's top 20 also included senior UDF activists 'Terror' Lekota, Steve Tshwete, Popo Molefe and Trevor Manuel.[24]

The conference then turned to policy issues. Among the resolutions adopted by the conference was a commitment to a negotiated settlement that would have been inconceivable just two years previously. It affirmed that 'the possibility exists of achieving the transfer of power to the people and the creation of a united, non-racial, non-sexist and democratic South Africa by peaceful means'. Care was taken to celebrate the role of all elements in the liberation movement, with the observation that 'This possibility has come about as a result of the heroic struggles of our people which have included mass action, armed struggle and underground work, supported by anti-apartheid actions of the international community'. Moreover, looking to the future, a resolution observed that 'To achieve the strategic objective of our struggle, it is vital that we continue to combine all forms of struggle, drawing in the widest spectrum of the people ... Gains made in the mass struggle will be reflected at the negotiations table' and the MK must 'maintain its combat readiness and vigilance to enable it to intervene decisively should the anti-democratic forces block the path to a peaceful settlement'.[25]

In reality, it was widely recognised that armed struggle had failed, and that negotiations now had a real chance of success. The focus of attention was correspondingly on practical steps to get negotiations moving. Conference called for rapid moves to an all-party congress and 'the adoption of a democratic constitution and the election of a parliament representative of all the people of South Africa'. The priority was for the newly elected NEC 'to take immediate steps to ensure that a comprehensive and representative team comprising all chief negotiators, working groups and researchers, which shall function under the supervision and direction of the NEC, is established. In the meantime, and subject to this resolution, Conference mandates the NEC to continue with the process of all-out talks and invests it with discretionary powers, within the policies of the ANC.'[26] A seismic shift was occurring. The ANC's current negotiators were about to be stripped of their powers.

At its first post-conference meeting in Soweto on 17 and 18 July 1991, the new NEC elected the 20-strong National Working Committee

(NWC) which would be responsible for the everyday management of the ANC. There was much excitement when Thabo Mbeki turned the tables on Chris Hani, securing 66 votes to Hani's 65, but the real story of the meeting was the rise of the UDF. Terror Lekota, Popo Molefe and Steve Tshwete each secured more than 60 votes. As a result of concerted and strategic voting by SACP and UDF members of the NEC, moreover, the NWC acquired a distinctively leftist imprint. Members included Joe Slovo, Cheryl Carolus, Joel Netshitenzhe, Sydney Mufamadi, Ronnie Kasrils and Trevor Manuel. Mac Maharaj was only narrowly defeated for the 20th position in the NWC.

In the first major realignment of forces in the liberation movement for decades, the left had secured its ascendancy. Pressing home its advantage at the first full meeting of the NEC on 31 July 1991, while Nelson Mandela was on an overseas trip, the left unleashed a putsch to displace the exile leadership from key policy-making and negotiating positions.[27] The ANC constitution stipulated that the NEC could allocate policy responsibilities to NWC members. In a shock decision, Western Cape UDF activists Trevor Manuel and Cheryl Carolus secured the plum portfolios of economic planning and health and human resources. This was the beginning of Manuel's rapid rise to the finance ministry. Meanwhile, the exiles were confined to now less-than-exciting portfolios such as the army (Joe Modise), international affairs (Thabo Mbeki) and intelligence (Joe Nhlanhla).

The key decision concerned the conference's mandate for a new negotiating department. The NEC chose Ramaphosa to take on this great responsibility. He was thrilled, and later explained his role in this way: 'Our conference in July decided that we should set up a negotiating team which will have the necessary back-ups, task forces and experts ... Our National Executive Committee has agreed that we should open up a department, what you could call a negotiations strategizing department, in the ANC. We call it the Negotiations Commission ... I have been charged with the responsibility for heading that Negotiations Commission.'[28] While the body also included Thabo Mbeki as one of its four members in a nod to exile sensitivities, the other two members were Joe Slovo and Valli Moosa, who were to play the central role, alongside Cyril and Mac Maharaj, in the ANC negotiating team.

The left's coup[29] or putsch[30] against the exile leadership had been a brilliant success. The negotiation commission's membership of

Ramaphosa (Cosatu), Valli Moosa (UDF–SACP) and Joe Slovo (SACP) – with the lonely exile figure of Mbeki – testifies to this new alignment of forces. The putsch was devastating. Exile leaders, and in particular the two old friends Jacob Zuma and Thabo Mbeki, had expected to dominate policy-making and to shepherd the negotiations to a conclusion. Zuma was now instructed to focus on the practicalities of rebuilding the ANC from the ground up. Mbeki's demotion in negotiations was close to a humiliation. He had been the man brave enough to enter into talks in 1989, when he and Jacob Zuma met with delegations from the National Intelligence Service in Switzerland. His principled case for negotiations had earned him the contempt of the left. Now, a few short years later, the same leftists had ousted him from the negotiations he had initiated. This was a turning point in Mbeki's political character, on one account marking the moment at which he became 'twisted' and the vindictive streak in his character gained an upper hand.[31]

The motivations behind the putsch were several and complex, and one was certainly pure political ambition. Although Mac Maharaj denies having any influence over the process – 'I did not even make it onto the NWC at the time'[32] – it is difficult to believe that the Vula network played no role in the strategic voting at conference and in the NEC. Domestic leaders like Ramaphosa, Carolus and Manuel reflected a wider desire for a more open politics than the exile leadership was able to countenance or understand.

The putsch was also motivated by growing frustration at the limited achievements of the existing ANC negotiating team. The Groote Schuur Minute, signed on 5 May 1990, had launched the negotiations on to a promising path. Working groups had been created to remove obstacles to negotiation such as inappropriate legislation, to smooth the repatriation of exiles and the release of political prisoners, and to address contentious matters such as the control of the armed forces, the granting of amnesty, and the curtailing of political violence. Very talented politicians such as Mathews Phosa, Pallo Jordan and Penuell Maduna had been put to work on these issues.

On the other hand, the ANC's team was hampered by the presence of dinosaurs such as Alfred Nzo and Joe Modise. Moreover, Nelson Mandela and Thabo Mbeki were themselves both obstacles to progress. Mandela's personality was not suited to the compromise and detailed work that negotiations required. He was a big gun best held in reserve.

While Mbeki was capable of managing the logistical and technical side of negotiations, he lacked the negotiating experience and human skills the task demanded. His approach was to dominate his team intellectually rather than to encourage and energise autonomous working groups.[33]

The time-frames for negotiation were already slipping out of control. What was to become known as Codesa I, the first stage of serious multi-party negotiations, was due to have begun in January 1991, but this deadline had passed with little progress being made. The wider implication of the NEC's appointment of a new negotiating body was that it believed and expected that Ramaphosa and his team would be able to give the whole process fresh impetus. Valli Moosa, indeed, immediately went on to the offensive, explaining that 'the leadership of the ANC has lost confidence in De Klerk' and accusing the President of 'being part of this double agenda which the regime is pursuing'. It was still possible to negotiate with the NP, he observed, even if its leader could not be trusted. 'We need to mobilize the strength we have to bring them to the point where they would have no choice but to adhere to agreements arrived at. That is the point at which we think negotiations can make sense.'[34]

The twin burdens of chief negotiator and secretary-general immediately fell upon Ramaphosa's shoulders. His task as secretary-general was not merely to rebuild the ANC, but to create it from scratch in areas where it had never been a mass movement. He had to keep in mind the likelihood that a negotiated settlement might soon produce an election, but that a collapse of talks would require quite different tactics to be adopted. A few weeks after his election he was exhausted. 'I have found that you do so many things at the same time that you hardly even have time to take a moment's breath. You don't even get time to sit down, to reflect on the many things that you are doing and [that are] happening around you.'[35]

Nelson Mandela expressed concern about Ramaphosa's duplicate roles, in charge of the organisation and also of the negotiations. He tried on a number of occasions to have the National Working Committee remove Cyril from Codesa so that he could focus his energies on building ANC structures across the country, a logistical task for which deputy secretary-general Jacob Zuma was evidently not well equipped. However, fellow negotiators Mac Maharaj and Joe Slovo insisted on Ramaphosa's indispensability, and Mandela ultimately relented.[36]

Cyril was unable to exercise much political power in his new office, his ANC role being 'more administrative than political'.[37] He needed to take painful decisions about staffing and costs, and he now lacked the time and freedom for personal promotion. However, he soon established reliable head-office systems under the redoubtable Marion Sparg, and he seconded able administrators such as the NUM's Simphiwe Nanise, and Donne Cooney from the ANC's Border region. The ANC fort was secure. Together with his team of Joe Slovo, Mac Maharaj and Valli Moosa it was time for Ramaphosa to return to the negotiating table.

PART FOUR
NEGOTIATING TRANSITION

CHAPTER 16

BC: NEGOTIATIONS, 1984 TO 1991

*It is legend now that the negotiations can be divided into two
distinct epochs, BC and AC – Before Cyril and After Cyril.*

– Tim Cohen[1]

*I can't see negotiations being successful. You know, I think that
people are a little bit utopian about this. I'm working to have them
perceive the realities.*

– Raymond Suttner[2]

The road to talks had been long and winding. Throughout the
1980s, powerful forces pushed the leaders of the ANC and the
NP towards negotiation.[3] By the time FW de Klerk seized the state
presidency in late 1989, there had been a wide variety of contacts between
liberation movement leaders and representatives of the regime's civilian
intelligence services. Equally importantly, South African business
had created channels of communication that would allow the second
'hidden transition' – in the economy – to take place without ideological
conflict.

While those driving these initiatives did not have the authority to
negotiate a post-apartheid settlement, they were able to create a deeper
understanding between leaders in politics and business about the
perspectives and demands of their antagonists. Most of the small coterie
of politicians who were to play major roles in the negotiations in the
early 1990s had valuable experience interacting with their enemy in the
long and violent years of the 1980s.

Of all the regime's participants in the negotiations process, Niel Barnard, head of the National Intelligence Service (NIS), had the most extensive interactions with the ANC. As a result of his domestic intelligence-gathering, he also had a clear sense of the foibles of the hardliners in the NP and the military. In December 1991, he would bring this wealth of experience to bear when he became director-general in the constitutional development department, later acting as one of government's three key negotiators alongside Roelf Meyer and constitutional adviser and state official SS 'Fanie' van der Merwe.

Barnard's NIS was descended from the notorious Bureau of State Security (BOSS) but it had started the 1980s as a junior to police intelligence and the military intelligence department (MID), which had both grown in power in a militarising state. The rise of NIS under Barnard was made possible by the failures of military intelligence and the police. According to historian James Sanders, 'the failure of MID and the police quickly to stem the insurrection of the mid-1980s and the disaster of Cuito Cuanavale in Angola destroyed the supremacy of the MID and reopened the door to Niel Barnard and the NIS.'[4]

Barnard was a very young and highly educated man with a quite distinctive perspective from that of the Afrikaner career bureaucrats dominating the security establishment. He had decided as early as 1984 that it was essential to reach an agreement with the ANC 'before our backs were against the wall'.[5] His number two at NIS, Mike Louw, and his number three, Maritz Spaarwater, were of like mind. Louw, who was to succeed Barnard as head of NIS in 1992, told *Financial Times* journalist Patti Waldmeir that 'We could see no light at the end of the tunnel ... We realised there had to be a total change of direction, otherwise we were simply going to fight to the last man, and whoever inherited this country would inherit a wilderness. And we knew that the longer we waited, the more difficult it was going to be to climb out of this hole – that it would be better to start negotiating while the government of the day still had some power, while South Africa was still a going concern.'[6] Barnard's insistence that negotiating now was better than negotiating later was to dominate the government's strategy right up until the 1996 signing of the final constitution. According to Tertius Delport, this presumption was a curse that also infected Roelf Meyer, who was to become the government's chief negotiator.[7]

It would be quite wrong to see the NIS as a bright light in the darkness of the apartheid state. On the contrary, a wider consensus had already emerged in much of the public service that negotiations should begin, and that multi-party democracy, a unitary state, the reincorporation of the Bantustans, the release of political prisoners and free political activity were all necessary and urgent concessions. NIS, by contrast, was engaged in a strategy of at best partial reform, seeking to divide the liberation forces in order to control them. This approach had various facets. NIS encouraged and supported Bantustan leaders like Mangosuthu Buthelezi and Lucas Mangope, believing them to be counterweights to the ANC and potential allies of the NP in a future dispensation. It sought to exclude the SACP from negotiations and drive a wedge between the party and the 'moderates' of the ANC. It also attempted to divide the internal ANC, and particularly the purportedly moderate Nelson Mandela, from the exile movement in Lusaka. Later, NIS tried to separate more moderate exiles, such as Thabo Mbeki, from their allegedly militaristic comrades such as Chris Hani.

Barnard's initial focus was on Mandela, who had initiated contact in 1985 by requesting a meeting with government. Mandela was alert to the danger of being lured into a reformist scheme without the consent of the leadership in Lusaka. Through the limited communication with Tambo that was made possible by George Bizos in 1986, he made it clear that he was not overstepping his authority.[8] An extraordinary sequence of 47 meetings between Mandela and representatives of the government took place, initially involving justice minister Kobie Coetzee. As we have seen, such meetings – and especially the later decision to request a meeting with President PW Botha – were a cause of great controversy in the ANC and the UDF. They were rendered legitimate according to ANC protocol largely retrospectively, once Operation Vula had established more direct communications between Pollsmoor and Lusaka.

While Kobie Coetzee initially convened meetings, Niel Barnard quickly became the key interlocutor in more formal meetings with Nelson Mandela, which began in May 1988. A team of four was assembled to meet regularly with Mandela, headed by Barnard, and including his deputy Mike Louw and the quiet official and career public servant Fanie van der Merwe, who was to become central to the later negotiations process. Barnard was to describe the meetings as 'an effort on the part of knowledgeable persons to establish "how Mandela's head worked".'[9] including trying to assess his positions on key questions such as economic management and nationalisation. The meetings also addressed thorny issues of great importance to the security establishments of the two antagonists: the amnesty process for combatants, the freeing of political and military prisoners, the definitions that would be adopted for war criminals, and the nature of guarantees of non-persecution of offenders in the event of a settlement. The meetings were also intended to readjust Mandela to the world he would find outside prison, one dramatically changed from the 1960s South Africa of his experience.

Bernard soon decided to initiate a wider range of meetings with the exile ANC. NIS was a facilitator of the 1987 meeting, organised by Frederik van Zyl Slabbert, in Dakar, Senegal, at which 50 Afrikaner intellectuals met representatives of the ANC. NIS also brokered contacts initiated by Tambo. The exile leader had requested Rudolph Agnew, chairman of British mining company Consolidated Goldfields, to fund and facilitate meetings between the ANC and Afrikaner intellectuals. Goldfields' communications director Michael Young identified Stellenbosch academic Willie Esterhuyse as a likely interlocutor. When Barnard became aware of the impending meetings, he asked Esterhuyse to report back on his contacts with the ANC. Esterhuyse agreed, but on condition that the ANC leaders were aware he was playing this role.

In this way, when Esterhuyse took around 20 Afrikaner academics to meet with the ANC in England in November 1987, in the first of a series of meetings that were to continue every few months until the middle of 1990, a *de facto* arm's length dialogue between the NIS and ANC was instituted. Thabo Mbeki headed the ANC delegations, and he was accompanied by senior figures such as Aziz Pahad and intelligence chief Jacob Zuma.[10] Despite the initial intention to divide and rule the ANC, Barnard did not keep Mandela entirely in the dark, on one occasion remarking, 'We hear Thabo Mbeki is somebody who wants negotiations. Have you any objection if we talk with him?'[11]

In June 1989, Barnard asked his now established channel, Willie Esterhuyse, to meet with Thabo Mbeki in a London pub and to organise a direct meeting between ANC and NIS intelligence heads. In the meantime, FW de Klerk had become Acting State President after pushing out the ailing Botha. At the first meeting of the State Security Council (SSC) under his chairmanship, on 16 August, he approved a carefully worded resolution that was designed to deceive him just as Botha had been deceived before. 'It is necessary that more information should be obtained on processes concerning the ANC, and the aims, alliances and potential approachability of its different leaders and groupings. To enable this to be done, special additional direct action will be necessary particularly with the help of the National Intelligence Agency functionaries.'[12]

In this way, the SSC unknowingly authorised clandestine meetings between NIS and ANC heads in Lucerne and then Berne, Switzerland, in September. Switzerland was the favoured venue because it was politically neutral, still did not demand travel visas for South Africans, and possessed confidential banking services. These meetings brought together Barnard, Louw, Maritz Spaarwater and Fanie van der Merwe with Thabo Mbeki, Jacob Zuma and the soon-to-be intelligence minister Joe Nhlanhla.[13] In these negotiations, contentious issues such as the repatriation of liberation movement fighters, how to define and deal with political prisoners, and the release of Mandela were discussed. All of those present were aware that the talks were not held with the knowledge or approval of either the State President or of Nelson Mandela – although Mbeki and Zuma would have been reporting their actions to Tambo and the NEC. Only later did Barnard brief De Klerk on his initiative – leading the President to respond with anger and then enthusiasm. As historian James Sanders observes, 'FW de Klerk did not have a security history as a politician and, far from adopting the NIS, [he] was, in effect, adopted by Niel Barnard.'[14]

For his part, Mbeki was severely criticised by some members of the NEC for talking to the NIS. He was vulnerable already as a 'black Englishman',[15] whose 1974 wedding contrasted starkly with the simultaneous upsurge in the detention and torture of domestic black consciousness activists. For later Mandela biographer Anthony Sampson, 'His Englishness is superficially apparent in his quiet style, his sports jackets, his curved pipe, precise speech and English friendships. He extended them through his marriage: he married Zanele Dlamini at Farnham Castle, where her sister, Edith, who had once been a cover-girl for the magazine *Drum*, then lived with her husband Wilfred Grenville-Grey, the son-in-law of the Earl of March – who as the Duke of Richmond later became Chancellor of Sussex University.'[16] The attacks on Mbeki were primarily positional, attempts by the left to establish the ascendancy of their favoured candidate, Chris Hani, as Tambo's heir-apparent.

While Barnard was reaching out to Mandela and Mbeki, NIS was also part of a wider state security system. At the zenith of this system was the SSC, the body charged with coordinating and directing state intelligence and military initiatives and reporting directly to the President. The SSC contained the heads of the armed forces, security police, NIS and MID, as well as the police commissioner. It had a strategic communications wing known as Stratcom, which engaged in propaganda work, disinformation, the infiltration of political organisations, and illegal activities such as assassination and sabotage.[17] The SSC also directed a National Security Management System (NSMS),[18] a network of 500 regional and local management centres. Their purpose was to harmonise intelligence-gathering and to coordinate the actions of the security police, national and municipal police forces, civilian commando units and other paramilitary units such as mine security. It was here, of course, that Barnard got to know Roelf Meyer, minister responsible for the NSMS between 1986 and 1988.

Through the SSC, Barnard was fully informed about government's funding of offensive paramilitary units which were later to destabilise negotiations. According to one confidential report, Barnard 'made major objections to the creation of such a force and indicated that the political risks associated with it were so great that he could not support it'. Ultimately SSC decided to go ahead, and members of Inkatha were indeed given paramilitary training.[19] As the third force moved from being a formal state-sponsored strategy to a more amorphous network of elements hostile to negotiation, especially after De Klerk began to unravel the state security system, Barnard continued to gather valuable intelligence about Inkatha, the white right and the military, as well as about his ANC opposite numbers.

The government team developed later into a triumvirate of key negotiators – Barnard, the official Fanie van der Merwe, and the politician Roelf Meyer – who were able to back up the judgement calls of their very active principal, De Klerk. Constitutional development minister Gerrit Viljoen was for a time an important intellectual presence (although not himself a negotiator) until he resigned as a result of illness later in 1992. One other figure, Tertius Delport, was to play a high-profile role in the 1992 collapse of Codesa. While the politicians were to come and go – with the exception of De Klerk and Meyer – Barnard and Van der Merwe would remain at the heart of the government negotiating team until the very end.

Unlike the surprisingly indiscreet spooks and spies, business people have mostly been quiet about the role they played in bringing the ANC and government together. Among scholars, only Merle Lipton has tried to register the importance of business interventions.[20] She emphasises that business is not homogeneous, and the interests and intentions of companies change over time. Apartheid initially benefited many businesses, as a result of access to a cheap and controlled workforce. But as the economy developed, some sectors began to demand a skilled and permanent workforce and so the removal of Bantu education and influx control. Other companies found that apartheid shrivelled the domestic consumer market, or undermined export performance. Over time, therefore, there was a growing convergence of the interests in favour of reform, and growing concerted pressure by business organisations to have apartheid brought to an end.[21]

The Federated Chamber of Industries (FCI) and the Associated Chambers of Commerce did sometimes come out openly against business-damaging aspects of apartheid, such as racial job reservation, the pass laws, segregated education, and restrictions on home ownership. Anglo American was of course prominent in 'modernising' initiatives such as the Urban Foundation.[22] White business people were, however, products of their time, and they were rarely motivated to abolish apartheid on moral grounds. One analyst who went to work for the Urban Foundation in 1981, and was put to work arguing for the abolition of influx controls, was told that moral arguments were specifically prohibited and the case needed to be made on pragmatic grounds only.[23] There was correspondingly almost no effort by business to recognise the human rights of Africans or to secure a universal franchise. One analyst who played a role in bringing business and ANC together, Christo Nel, describes the early 1980s commercial world as 'passive' and 'singularly ineffective in doing anything'. For Nel, business people were motivated primarily by their desire 'not to antagonise government'.[24]

A new wave of business activity was spurred in 1984 by a devastating piece of research conducted under the auspices of the Unisa Business School's rather Orwellian-sounding Project Free Enterprise. This research demonstrated that most South Africans (perhaps unsurprisingly) had a jaundiced and ill-informed view of business, understanding it as a rapacious exploiter of ordinary black people.[25] At the instigation of the chief executive of Barclays South Africa, Project Free Enterprise went on to explore what needed to be done to 'educate' the black workforce about the wholesome character and prudential advantages of free enterprise. Barclays SA was a wholly-owned subsidiary of Anglo American, and its involvement was almost certainly part of a wider strategy by newly installed Anglo chairman Gavin Relly to initiate contacts with the UDF using the giant company's network of subsidiaries.

By 1985, Christo Nel, the analyst recruited to conduct the research, had quickly concluded that it was impossible to educate people about the benefits of the capitalist system if they were in fact not deriving any. Business organisations began to see the need to argue openly and successfully against the evils of the apartheid system if popular views of the character of a market economy were to change. The president of the FCI, John Wilson, decided to take a clear stand against apartheid practices. In 1985 he launched a Business Charter of Human Rights. When Wilson intervened to oppose a specific instance of forced removals in the Brits area, however, and then argued publicly for the release of Nelson Mandela, the response by FCI's member companies was devastating. Dozens of them simply resigned their memberships and withdrew their funding, leading the federation to collapse.[26]

Christo Nel was then approached by a small group of businessmen who asked him to arrange a meeting with what they termed the 'legitimate black leadership'. This group significantly included Anglo's political strategist Zach de Beer and Chris Ball from Barclays SA, as well as Southern Life's Neal Chapman, prominent financier Mervyn King and well-known judge Anton Mostert. They provided Nel with a 'slush fund' to finance the logistics of the meetings they proposed.

Nel managed to link up with acting UDF head Murphy Morobe, who was in hiding, as well as treasurer Azhar Cachalia and president Albertina Sisulu. Other key UDF leaders, including Popo Molefe and Terror Lekota, were at that time being tried for treason. Through the services of their lawyer, George Bizos, Nel was later able to meet with them in their cells – the same dungeons in which the Rivonia trialists had been held – and to secure their assent to a series of meetings. Nel also approached heavyweight Cosatu leaders, including Cyril Ramaphosa, Sydney Mufamadi and Jay Naidoo, but they refused to participate – possibly because of the potential of such meetings to compromise them in the eyes of their members.

Across 1986, a small group of businessmen held late-night meetings with Azhar Cachalia and Murphy Morobe. By late 1986, a willingness had emerged to arrange for a more substantial meeting, and other UDF leaders, including Valli Moosa and Cas Coovadia, were becoming involved. However, the reticence of business leaders continued to be a stumbling block to meaningful talks. Christo Nel on one occasion brought more than a dozen business leaders to the Indaba Hotel north of Johannesburg for a meeting with Albertina Sisulu. Before leaving to collect Sisulu, he explained that they would be talking to a black leader subject to a banning order. They would therefore be breaking the law. When he returned with Sisulu, all but a handful of the businessmen had fled.[27]

Despite these difficulties, hundreds of small meetings, often one-on-one, continued between business, UDF and, increasingly, trade unions. A major step forward came in 1987, when Christo Nel and others went on Frederik van Zyl Slabbert's mission to Dakar. The exile ANC leadership had been in contact with the UDF about the negotiations with business, and they were able at Dakar to give their stamp of approval to a continuation of this internal dialogue.[28] Progress was interrupted by the arrest of Moosa and Morobe in late 1987, and a major intensification of the state of emergency in February 1988. Nevertheless, in August 1988, a meeting at last took place at the Broederstroom conference facility between around 25 business leaders, 15 sympathetic academics and a substantial part of the internal black leadership, most of whom were subject to restrictions. Azhar Cachalia, who with Nel was joint facilitator, began the meeting by joking that, as a result of his restriction order, 'I will be talking just to Christo Nel. If the rest of you want to listen in, that's up to you.'

The meeting divided immediately into two hostile camps: the black leaders were all clear in their demands for majority rule in a unitary state, to be brought about with immediate effect. Despite the fact that the business people were a self-selected fraction of the business class – those willing to break the law in order to talk to UDF leaders – they were simply unable to conceive of a South Africa governed by black people. Nel managed to overcome this 'sense of impossibility' by encouraging the white participants to work through a scenario in which, by 2050, there would be a black President.

Nel also developed an intellectual framework to take the racial emotion out of the opposition between groups at the meeting. In his schema, there were two main kinds of actors in South Africa (and at the conference). On the one hand, there were 'revolutionaries', who were seeking the overthrow of the existing order. On the other hand, there were 'reformers', seeking to change apartheid capitalism gradually. What was needed, Nel argued, was a small group of 'transformers', who would be able to form a bridge between the revolutionaries and the reformers.[29]

On the last day of the conference, the black leaders demanded that the business people form themselves into a body, with the threat that otherwise there would be no further talks. Very few executives walked away, but their caution was evident in their disagreement over the choice of a name. When Business Movement for Democracy was suggested, there was the threat of a walkout. In the end the name Consultative Business Movement (CBM) emerged.[30] Although it started with only a dozen paid-up members, the CBM quickly snowballed and within months more than a hundred businesses were signed up.

The CBM instituted a national consultative process that ran for almost two years, in 1989 and 1990. UDF and Cosatu organisers came together with business people, usually over a weekend, with the inclusion of time for informal socialising that was to prove so effective at breaking down barriers across the transition process. UDF and, later, MDM activists were almost always strongly anti-capitalist in orientation and many considered themselves to be Marxists. However, the business people at least had in their favour that they were not the NP, and behind the radical rhetoric of the UDF and Cosatu there was a good deal of pragmatism and willingness to engage with the concerns of business.[31]

This consultative process was significant in that issues fundamental to the future of the society were raised and discussed. One of these – the racial inequalities of ownership in the South African economy – allowed participants to develop the beginnings of what was later to become Black Economic Empowerment policy. Moreover, in the relationships that were built up between activists and business people, networks began to emerge that in later years were to turn into business relationships. The process also allowed the biggest force in the economy, Anglo American, to enter into indirect interaction with the liberation forces.

Anglo was initially very careful not to play a direct and obvious role in CBM. At the same time, important CBM leaders were executives in Anglo subsidiaries. Anglo was happy to play a conservative game with the South Africa Foundation, a developmental role with the Urban Foundation, and now a more reformist part with the CBM. When, in the course of 1990, it became clear that CBM was gaining ground, Anglo's Michael Spicer took up a position as deputy chair of the national consultative group of the CBM. Spicer was inevitably a decisive figure in shaping the deliberations and actions of the body thereafter, and he served as the eyes and ears of his hero and mentor Gavin Relly.[32] Nel describes him as a 'watchdog'. Other members of the committee joked that he was Cardinal Richelieu to Gavin Relly's King Louis XIII.[33]

On 2 February 1990, when President FW de Klerk announced the unbanning of the ANC and the impending release of Nelson Mandela, there were therefore already elaborate but fragmented relationships between various exile, intelligence, business and struggle leaders. Once the state of emergency was lifted, and exiles started to return in large numbers, lines of authority and communication inevitably became very confused. In March 1990, an agreement was reached to begin formal discussions on 11 April. Senior repatriated exiles Jacob Zuma, Mathews Phosa and Penuell Maduna were initially put in charge, and a steering committee was assembled to identify remaining obstacles to negotiation. Further arrivals of exiles, however, kept changing the composition of the negotiating team. On 27 April, major figures returned: Thabo Mbeki, head of the ANC's department of international affairs; Ruth Mompati; Joe Slovo, the general secretary of the SACP; Joe Modise, the commander of MK; and Alfred Nzo, ANC secretary-general.

The removal of obstacles to multi-party negotiations moved along extremely slowly, one narrative on the transition describing this period as 'talking about talking about talks'.[34] The Groote Schuur Minute, signed on 4 May 1990, committed the ANC and NP only in very general terms to a negotiated settlement and to the reduction of the climate of violence and intimidation. Matters were further complicated in July 1990, when Operation Vula operatives, including Mac Maharaj, were detained under the Internal Security Act. Maharaj had left the country secretly in May and re-entered legally in June, with the intention of joining the ANC negotiators 'above ground'. The arrest of Maharaj panicked the regime's intelligence services. Maharaj observes that it was only with his detention that 'they picked up evidence that Nelson was in communication with Oliver Tambo from Victor Verster Prison ... The strategy of dividing him from the ANC or dividing the ANC into two wings could not work and it could not work because they woke up with the shock that he was at one with OR.'[35]

While the regime adjusted its preconceptions, the ANC's primarily exile negotiators continued to be preoccupied with amnesty and armaments, issues that were central to them but ultimately marginal to an overall settlement. The Pretoria Minute, signed on 6 August 1990, addressed itself to the definition and release of political prisoners, and the suspension of armed actions. On 12 February 1991, the so-called DF Malan Accord was signed, clarifying the Pretoria Minute's agreement about arms control, committing the MK to register and control its weapons, and securing automatic indemnity for repatriated MK cadres.

By April 1991, the slow pace of movement was beginning to create frustration. Violence was escalating across the country, and ANC negotiators lamented the government's inability or unwillingness to address this problem directly. While De Klerk portrayed violence as a justification for delay, the ANC leadership argued that government itself was responsible, by commission or by omission, for the death and devastation. On 5 April 1991, the ANC demanded the removal of defence minister Magnus Malan and law and order minister Adriaan Vlok, and insisted that informal and paramilitary networks engaging in destabilisation across the country must be curtailed.

It was in the context of this frustration and violence that Ramaphosa's July 1991 election as secretary-general and, soon after, his appointment as head of the 'negotiations commission' must be understood. The new front-line negotiating team, including Joe Slovo, Valli Moosa and soon the omnipresent Mac Maharaj, were determined to step up the pace of negotiations and place the National Party under redoubled pressure.

Over time two key relationships emerged as the backbone of the negotiations. The first was between Fanie van der Merwe and Mac Maharaj. Like Maharaj, Van der Merwe was a details man and the *de facto* operational head of the government team. As a career civil servant, he had worked in the departments of justice and home affairs. As director-general with responsibility for prisons, he was one of the four officials, along with Niel Barnard, who attended formal meetings with Nelson Mandela. He discovered in Maharaj a shared admiration for Mandela and his idiosyncrasies. In 1989, he became what is known as the 'constitutional adviser' on constitutional development – the equivalent of the director-general in what was not then a full government department. From this position he was able to steer the thought and actions of his political principals, Chris Heunis, Gerrit Viljoen and finally Roelf Meyer.

The relationship between 'Mac and Fanie', as the conjoined pair became known, was probably more important to the negotiations than the more celebrated collaboration between Roelf Meyer and Cyril Ramaphosa. They met for the first time at the end of November 1990, in preparatory meetings to predetermine the stages through which a settlement would have to proceed. Already they were working in parallel, Mac effectively in charge of the ANC's detailed operations and Fanie in command of the government's. Their immediate mutual respect, dry sense of humour, and reticence about publicity marked them out as a perfect backroom team. They later composed the two-man secretariat of Codesa, and steered the agenda and deliberations of its management committee. In the later Multi-Party Negotiating Process (MPNP), they worked together on the ten-person planning committee, and formed (along with the IFP's token Ben Ngubane) the subcommittee that dealt with intractable issues.

Maharaj was a powerful personality and intellect within the ANC team, and through his Robben Island, SACP, Lusaka and Vula networks he had comprehensive knowledge of his own constituency. He was sometimes temperamental, as is indicated by his repeated resignations and conflicts with comrades. This made him less well-suited to the negotiating process itself than his colleagues Ramaphosa and Valli Moosa. Many years later when he was minister of transport, Maharaj was confronted in his office by a group of gun-packing Cape Flats taxi bosses, who shouldered their way past his security guards. His instinct was to respond with aggression, a testimony to the ascendancy that his anger could sometimes secure over his prudence.[36]

If Mac and Fanie had primary responsibility for ensuring that disputes were avoided through advance planning, Cyril Ramaphosa and Roelf Meyer were famously the resolving agents of those intractable disputes that did arise. Meyer is often portrayed by critics as a man of limited intelligence who was unable to comprehend the complexity of the negotiations.[37] It is true that, like Cyril, he was never destined to leave politics for a career in rocket science. However, to a far greater extent than FW de Klerk, who was more than his equal partner in decision-making, he has become a scapegoat for conservative Afrikaners who believe that too much was given away in the negotiations. His rival Tertius Delport always believed Meyer would stab the President (whom Delport adored) in the back, and forewarned De Klerk not to trust him.[38] 'He's skellum [*skelm*]. Do you know the Afrikaans word skellum? He's shifty, he's sly, he's not above a little bit of underhand dealings to get things his own way. I don't trust him, I don't believe everything he says.'[39]

Meyer's actions loyally followed De Klerk's instructions, however, and his thinking was in line with that of his senior, Gerrit Viljoen. Viljoen was a pragmatist who had softened the NP's negotiating position dramatically. In a confidential July 1991 interview, he conceded that 'I don't think it is likely that we will find it possible to negotiate a new constitution with ethnic definitions as a basis for political representation ... Once groups are defined in a constitution, there's a certain rigidity and a certain inflexibility which militates against the concept of voluntary association.' For this reason, he already accepted that 'you could not do more than provide guidelines and procedures in the constitution for groups who want to constitute themselves and have themselves recognized for the purpose of political protection in the constitutional set-up'. Indeed, Viljoen believed that NP thinking needed a 'third phase', in which 'the instrument to be considered is no longer so much groups as such but groups as articulating themselves through political parties ... the kind of protection that we should seek is not so much minority protection for ethnically-defined groups but minority protection for political parties.' In this way, Viljoen, as much as Meyer, was already close to embracing a conventional constitutional settlement.[40]

Meyer was also a vastly experienced politician. Between 1986 and 1988, he had been deputy minister of police, with special responsibility for overseeing the National Security Management System (where, it may be recalled, he helped Bobby Godsell to 'protect the civil rights' of non-striking mineworkers).[41] The job was one of the most politically sensitive in government and demonstrated the high regard in which he was held by Botha. It also exposed him to township and hostel violence, and left him in no doubt about the scale and depth of social unrest. Meyer was chosen by De Klerk to succeed an ailing Viljoen, in May 1992, in part because there was a serious dearth of talent in the cabinet.[42] However, he was also elevated because of his good relations with the ANC, his familiarity with Niel Barnard and the intelligence establishment, and perhaps especially for his perceived good relations with Cyril.[43] He had gone out of his way to cultivate these good relations. They had first met at Heathrow Airport in 1988, entirely by chance, while one was leaving and the other arriving. They agreed that they must soon meet and talk. When Cyril became head of the ANC negotiations commission in the middle of 1991, Meyer – who had been appointed minister of defence for a brief period but was still part of the NP's negotiating team – wanted urgently to get close to him. This resulted in a very famous, and very fishy, meeting.

Of all the events during the negotiations, one meeting in August 1991 has been the most widely reported. Allister Sparks, in the prologue to his sparkling 1994 book *Tomorrow Is Another Country*, tells the 'tale of the trout hook'.[44] On his account, Roelf Meyer and his family travelled by helicopter to Havelock Trout Farm in the Transvaal Lowveld at the behest of Sidney Frankel – a 'mutual friend' of Cyril and Roelf – who thought it would be a good idea for them to get to know one another better. Ramaphosa and his family were already at the farm. Just before the Meyers arrived, Frankel's daughter fell and broke her arm. Her parents were forced to leave on the helicopter that had conveyed Roelf. Cyril and Roelf, and their families, were left alone.

The Meyer children, observing that this was a trout farm, asked if they could try out fly fishing. Roelf had no knowledge of the sport, but Cyril volunteered to teach them at the dam below their chalets. When Roelf tried his hand, a hook became deeply embedded in a finger on his left hand. Despite the efforts of Cyril's second wife, Nomazizi – a trained nurse – they could not remove it. According to Sparks's account, Cyril uttered the famous words: 'Roelf, there's only one way to do this.' Cyril pulled out a bottle of whisky (from his pockets?) and encouraged Meyer to drink. Then he fetched some pliers. 'If you've never trusted an ANC person before,' Sparks obliged Cyril implausibly to remark, 'you'd better get ready to do so now!' Cyril wrenched the hook from Roelf's finger with a single pull. Meyer then purportedly remarked (imagine this), 'Well, Cyril, don't ever say I didn't trust you.'

The implausibility of the dialogue has led some critics to doubt the veracity of this story. Nevertheless, Sparks sourced the story from the fishing party's host, Sidney Frankel, and he then checked with both Meyer and Ramaphosa to ensure the versions were accurate and consistent.[45] It is curious, however, that Ramaphosa makes the following remarks to the writer Padraig O'Malley, in response to a question about the importance of trust in the negotiations, only a few days after he returned from the fishing trip: 'In a year's time when you come back … I will be able to tell you a very interesting story – I don't want to tell you now – but a very, very interesting story that has to deal with trust, how you build up trust because you build that up in the process.'[46]

While Ramaphosa might have had some quite different story in mind, cynics will speculate that Cyril had already elaborated the parable of the fish hook, but perhaps it was not yet in polished form. He had clearly tired of the parable by 1995, when he replied to Patti Waldmeir's question if he and Roelf had become friends. 'No, we haven't become friends.' Waldmeir countered that they were known to share in-jokes in the management committee, passing notes to each other and chuckling. Cyril responded, 'I think friendship goes beyond that. You want to meet your friend, have meals with him, spend time in their homes and they do the same with you, go fishing together.' They never fished together? 'No.' Waldmeir promised not to ask about the hook.[47]

The clearest evidence for the truth of the story is that it is almost too corny to have been made up. It captured the imagination of South Africans and well-wishers overseas, emphasising as it did the human dimension of negotiations. For Cyril, 'when you contest for state power you always find that negotiations are between enemies. Enemies don't usually trust each other and they don't really respect each other, but you see that grows out of a process. As you go on you build relationships, you cut deals on small little issues that may be insignificant, and, as you both deliver, as your stature grows in the eyes of the other, then you become more trustful of the other.'[48] This detached, even forensic, account of the nature of trust is of course silent about Ramaphosa's scarring experience at NUM, where those whom he trusted were unable to deliver on their promises.

The fish hook story unsettles some readers, sometimes because it is the white man, and not the black, who has to be helped out of his predicament. Roger Fisher and Daniel Fisher at the Harvard Negotiation Project, at least as reported in the *Harvard Gazette*, reverse the protagonists and so restore the narrative of the trusting native. Ramaphosa and Meyer 'forged a bond through their common interest in fly-fishing', they unpromisingly begin. 'Ramaphosa got a fishhook stuck in his thumb – and Meyer was able to extract it, relatively painlessly. Some weeks later ... the negotiations came to a particularly tricky point. Meyer turned to Ramaphosa and said "Trust me." With the memory of the fishhook fresh in his mind, Ramaphosa was able to trust, and the negotiation proceeded.'[49]

For Frankel himself, the story also has racial overtones. He recalls that the thought that struck him most forcibly on that fateful day was that 'While Mrs Meyer was anxiously watching over her shoulder, *this black woman had been touching the minister!*'[50] Most South African whites would by now have erased such a frank recollection from their memory of events.

The true significance of Sparks's story is that the host, Sidney Frankel, was chairman of Frankel Pollak, the largest stockbroker on the Johannesburg Stock Exchange. It was in the nature of Frankel's position that he acted as a facilitator of relationships between foreign and domestic business investors and government. By 1987 Frankel was well connected with the 'left' in government – with people such as Gerrit Viljoen, Barend du Plessis and Roelf Meyer – and he began to reach out to the UDF.[51] On one occasion, he recalls, PW Botha discovered that

Barend du Plessis was attending a Frankel Pollak conference, where he was talking to a senior UDF member. Botha had Du Plessis summoned to a telephone and instructed him to leave forthwith.

Frankel met Cyril at one of his own investment conferences. The two men, in his recollection, made 'an immediate connection' and soon became 'best pals'. Frankel was not a liberal on the Anglo model. Indeed, cutting remarks were made at the time, and still are today, about his late and rapid conversion to the cause of non-racial government.[52] He is a practical man rather than a liberal moralist, something that probably appealed to Cyril.

Once Mandela was released, and with Cyril in control of his diary, Frankel was able to bring the old man to the Johannesburg Stock Exchange. Designating himself 'Comrade Frankel', he telephoned Mandela towards the end of 1990 and invited him to visit the exchange for lunch. When Mandela and Frankel stepped on to the floor of the exchange together, trading stopped. At this time, Mandela was associated with the ANC's commitment to nationalisation. Out of sight of Mandela, one of the brokers spat on the floor next to Frankel and called him a 'Kaffir boetie'. After Mandela departed, Frankel received numerous abusive telephone calls, with one colleague telling him he was an 'arsehole' to bring the ANC leader to the exchange.[53]

Soon afterwards at Frankel's request, Ramaphosa arranged for a breakfast every six weeks at the opulent Transvaal Automobile Club, at which ANC leaders could informally chat with senior business people. Frankel remains uncertain as to what Cyril believed then – or believes now – about economic policy. Nevertheless, he is convinced that the constant interaction with the investment community was an important factor in changing Cyril's mindset, and in setting him against what Frankel believes was a genuine commitment to communism.

Cyril was, however, at a more advanced stage in thinking about the relationship between economics and politics than this account suggests. On one occasion, while Cyril was still NUM general secretary, Frederik van Zyl Slabbert organised a meeting between the mineworkers' leader and his arch opponent, the ageing Anglo magnate Harry Oppenheimer. Cyril remarked to the old man on how difficult life was for people in Soweto. Oppenheimer replied: 'That is fascinating, Mr Ramaphosa.' Cyril complained that he had to pay more for each unit of electricity he consumed in Soweto than Oppenheimer had to pay at Brenthurst. 'That is very fascinating, Mr Ramaphosa.' Finally Ramaphosa exploded, and launched one of his trademark tirades against big business, culminating in a threat: 'We're going to nationalise all of your mines!'

'That is very fascinating, Mr Ramaphosa, and that may be true,' the old man responded coolly. 'But a gold mine is only a hole in the ground.' Oppenheimer's point was that a working mine requires a complex system of skills and organisation, without which it is nothing. In the rather patronising opinion of Van Zyl Slabbert, this was a 'defining moment' in Ramaphosa's economic education.[54]

Business sponsors like Frankel made it possible for negotiators like Ramaphosa and Meyer to meet in comfortable and informal circumstances out of the public eye. One opportunity was Frankel Pollak's regular biannual investment conference, held in February and July each year. They also met at an investors' jamboree, organised by Frankel, on the opulent overnight Blue Train between Johannesburg and Cape Town. Meyer and Ramaphosa spent time together as well on a business-sponsored visit to Sabi Sabi game reserve, where Meyer remembers that night-time game drives provided an opportunity to talk in confidence for hours. When Meyer went to meet Ramaphosa at the trout farm, Frankel arranged the necessary transport for his family by calling up Sasol chairman Paul Kruger and requesting the use of one of the parastatal's fleet of helicopters.[55]

Frankel became sufficiently trusted to perform other services for the ANC. At one stage, he was asked to help repatriate offshore ANC funds, an immensely sensitive matter that required him to liaise with Reserve Bank governor Chris Stals. In the very last days of the old order, he received a call from Cyril at 2 a.m. to say that the IFP had re-entered the race, and glue was needed to stick IFP flyers to the bottom of ballot papers. Could Frankel, as chairman of ink manufacturer Sicpa, find some supplies? Three hours later, Frankel called Cyril back to say he had been successful. 'Sidney, I never thought you could do that so fast. I've already made another plan.'[56]

Ramaphosa convened a number of other meetings between business people and the ANC, recognising the importance of engagement between the entrenched economic elite and the emerging political leadership. One of the most fascinating meetings was Nelson Mandela's first encounter with a business person after his release from prison. Predictably, the first man in the queue was the most powerful chairman in South Africa, Anglo American's Gavin Relly. Relly and his assistant Michael Spicer went to see Mandela at his Soweto home, at a meeting Ramaphosa chaired. Outside the house, a large contingent of journalists gathered excitedly, speculating, in the aftermath of Mandela's declaration in favour of nationalisation, that this must be the subject under discussion. In fact, the four men did not even mention this topic, but instead ranged over other issues including industrial relations. As Relly and Spicer left, one of the throng of reporters asked, 'Are you anxious about nationalisation?' The calm and collected Relly commented, 'Nationalisation will be subject to the test of time and circumstance.'[57]

His confidence was based on Anglo's careful intelligence-gathering and bridge-building with the liberation movement. Relly's September 1985 journey to Lusaka, in defiance of the instructions of PW Botha and Harry Oppenheimer, had already shown him that OR Tambo, Thabo Mbeki, Mac Maharaj and Pallo Jordan were patriotic moderates.[58] Relly also understood that nationalisation was an immense practical task, requiring carefully planned administrative and legislative programmes. He returned confident that the ANC's leading economic thinkers, such as Thabo Mbeki, had no practical strategy for turning the idea of state ownership into a credible programme of nationalisation.[59]

The collapse of the USSR went on to discourage even die-hard proponents of nationalisation. Joe Slovo told a 19 July 1990 radio audience that 'We do not believe that the transfer of ownership from a board of directors to a board of bureaucrats will solve our economic problem.'[60] Essop Pahad told an interviewer in the same year that the SACP 'doesn't have concrete economic policies as yet ... The extent of the intervention must be determined by a whole lot of factors of which we are not even in control and on which we do not have information.'[61] Jeremy Cronin similarly observed that 'if you take away from Anglo American a whole lot of the economy, and then give it over to a bunch of bureaucrats ... workers have not been empowered, bureaucrats have.'[62] Trevor Manuel, shortly to become NEC economic policy head, concurred that 'the South African Communist Party would accept the existence of a "mixed economy".'[63]

Mandela sealed this implicit bargain between ANC and business. The liberation movement would protect private property and business freedom. In return, business would not obstruct transition, and would later move to redress the racial injustice that characterised the economy. Mandela even agreed to participate in meetings with the so-called Brenthurst Group, an informal panel of the half-dozen most powerful businessmen in South Africa, named after its meeting place – Harry and, later, Nicky Oppenheimer's home.

In October 1991, a meeting of liberation movement activists under the patriotic front umbrella proposed the creation of an interim government and a constituent assembly. To this, the NP responded with its vision of an interim constitution followed by a ten-year government of national unity. The distance between the moderates on both sides was closing. Ramaphosa observed that 'It is not inconceivable that we might have some of the people who have been in charge of certain departments in government in the new government ... You could have a Finance Minister who is still in office today being in office in, say, an ANC government. My own view, and this is a personal one, is that you could actually have the period of transition through an interim government.'[64]

He also observed that 'there isn't any difference between us and De Klerk with regard to a question of minorities'. De Klerk, he believed, had come round to the idea of a bill of rights to protect individuals rather than a constitution that explicitly defended unpalatable group rights. 'In many countries of the world,' Ramaphosa observed, 'it is the individual who enjoys maximum protection – much more than the group – and through that you are able to have checks and balances that will make sure that the group that the individual belongs to is not marginalized.'[65]

Roelf Meyer had reached broadly this view too, abandoning the idea of pre-defined group identities in 1990 and reiterating that majoritarianism had 'not been ruled out', although 'we wouldn't like to see a situation where any form of domination by the majority takes place at the expense of minorities'. Meyer proposed 'five mechanisms' to protect against this outcome: a bill of rights; the 'evolution of power to regional and local governmental levels'; 'autonomy of authority' at lower levels of devolved power; 'checks and balances' such as a bicameral parliament, and president and prime minister coming from different houses; and, finally, proportional representation. Reflecting on this moderate menu of constitutional instruments, he commented, 'One should most likely look at the combination of all these to find the right answer, constitutionally speaking.'[66]

A sense that the time was right for formal negotiations was in the air. The way the initiative was taken reflected the emerging significance of the channel between Ramaphosa and Meyer, notwithstanding the fact that Gerrit Viljoen was still in charge of the state's negotiating team. Meyer was invited by the journalist Rodney Pinder to attend a meeting of foreign correspondents one Friday evening in the middle of October 1991. Pinder saw to it that Meyer was seated at the same table as SACP general secretary Joe Slovo. As the evening progressed, and the wine flowed, the two conversed about how, under Ramaphosa's firmer hand, obstacles to negotiation had now been essentially removed or neutralised.[67]

The two parted amicably. On Sunday morning, Meyer received a phone call from Ramaphosa, who had a short message to convey. 'Madiba says it's time to start talking.'[68] Within days, the ANC and NP began to prepare for Codesa. For Meyer, the phone call signalled his growing status, and marked the beginning of his special relationship with Ramaphosa. At last the time had arrived for multi-party talks to begin.

CHAPTER 17

RETURN OF THE GREAT NEGOTIATOR

*Any, but any compromise or offer we can get today is better than
the one we can get tomorrow.*
— *Fanie van der Merwe*[1]

Making peace is like making love: no one can do it on your behalf.
— *Niel Barnard*[2]

Political scientist Jon Elster observes that there is a paradox at the heart
of the making of a constitution. On the one hand, any constitution
is designed to endure in an unforeseeable future, and so it must embody
the highest possible degree of foresight and detachment. Its creators
must abstract from the present, and design binding rules for a future
they can never know. On the other hand, constitutional settlements are
forged in times of political upheaval, in which negotiators are buffeted
by intense and immediate political and emotional pressure. In Elster's
evocative phrase, their task is to rebuild a boat while it is sailing on the
open seas.[3] To surmount such a challenge requires constitution-builders
who are able to combine powerful intellectual detachment with cunning
and the application of brute political force.

Nelson Mandela and FW de Klerk were unique and talented political
leaders, but they did not possess the right combination of skills to take
constitutional negotiations forward. Mandela was 'at the height of his
powers' by 1991,[4] in command of his own party and celebrated in the
international arena. While he had not chosen his negotiating team, there
was no reason to believe he was not happy with it. Yet his temperament

was not suited to the relentless grind of negotiation. His relationship with De Klerk deteriorated rapidly over the government's inability or unwillingness to tackle security force collaboration in violence.

For his part, De Klerk was the steady captain of a leaky and fractious NP ship. He played an active role throughout negotiations, and was more influential in his party's strategy than Mandela was in the ANC's. When an ailing Gerrit Viljoen resigned due to ill health – brought on in part by the stress of the negotiations – he quickly and perceptively promoted the youthful Roelf Meyer in his place.

Two small groups of negotiators were beginning to emerge, bringing stability to a process destabilised by violence. On the ANC side, Ramaphosa, Mac Maharaj, Valli Moosa and Joe Slovo held down the key positions on pivotal working groups and in management and planning committees. In issues of exceptional difficulty, such as the release of political prisoners, conflict in Natal, and the threat posed by the white right, they could call upon the additional talents of Jacob Zuma, Thabo Mbeki, Mathews Phosa and Penuell Maduna.

Part of the success of the ANC effort was that negotiators' skills were well matched to the challenges to which they were assigned. Zuma proved to be a genius at cooling passions in Natal, where he was deployed to work. Mbeki sold negotiating compromises to a variety of constituencies, including the youth, with his usual combination of dexterity and charm. He was a perfect intermediary for the white right. Moosa and Pravin Gordhan were masters of detail and composition – some would later complain of equivocation and ambiguity[5] – and their drafting skills were fully exploited. The outwardly quiet Slovo was at heart a tactician and showman. He had the leftist credibility to pull the ANC's mass constituency behind concessions such as 'sunset clauses' (which Slovo came erroneously to believe were his own idea).[6] Later in the negotiations, the planning committee finalised the election date on Slovo's birthday, and he was happy to accept acclaim for having brought about this milestone.[7]

The most complex and contested parts of the formal process were inevitably led by Ramaphosa. His negotiating skills were of a higher order than those of his colleagues, and he retained the ability to manage the mood and agenda of a discussion at will. Bantu Holomisa, head of the Transkei delegation that was allied to the ANC, observed that Ramaphosa had the experience to push aside NP equivocation and stalling. 'When De Klerk supported some faction in black-on-black violence, Cyril was the one who talked strong to him ... He said "we are not begging to negotiate with you – we are carrying a mandate from the people of South Africa".'[8]

Those on whom his negotiating skills were brought to bear naturally saw them differently. De Klerk later portrayed Ramaphosa's negotiating style in a very negative light, observing that his 'relaxed manner and congenial expression were contradicted by coldly calculating eyes, which seemed to be searching continuously for the softest spot in the defences of his opponents. His silver tongue and honeyed phrases lulled potential victims while his arguments relentlessly tightened around them.'[9] The NP's most obdurate Codesa negotiator, Tertius Delport, concurred, responding to the question whether Ramaphosa had impressed him with the words: 'Oh, he has impressed me for sure. Angered me ... I respect him for his ability, oh yes I respect him for his ability. I think Ramaphosa – let's forget about his policies – I think he is the outstanding personality in the ANC. He is superior by far to Mbeki, for instance, in terms of the sheer force of personality, the sheer presence. It's Ramaphosa all the way.'[10]

The first meeting of Codesa I – the Convention for a Democratic South Africa – took place on 13 November 1991, at a Holiday Inn near Johannesburg airport. The purpose of the Codesa meetings was to decide the rules according to which a multi-party negotiating process might unfold. Unfortunately, as Spitz observes, 'Codesa was responsible for exposing, rather than reconciling, basic differences between the parties.'[11] After preliminaries were completed, the first plenary meeting was held on 20 December at the World Trade Centre in Kempton Park, a venue chosen for its facilities and for its proximity to the then Jan Smuts international airport. The 20 delegations – 19 political parties and government – meant a total of around 400 delegates, and few venues could comfortably accommodate such a gathering.

The key product of Codesa I was a Declaration of Intent. It had been carefully prepared, largely in advance, by the operational heads of the core negotiating teams, Fanie van der Merwe and Mac Maharaj. It committed its 18 signatories – the IFP and the Bophuthatswana government did not sign – to strive for noble goals: a united, democratic, non-racist, non-sexist South Africa; a sovereign constitution; multi-party democracy; a separation of powers between three branches of government; the accommodation of the country's diverse cultures; and the protection of fundamental human rights.

Codesa I was organised around a management committee and used five working groups to make progress on key issues. The first group (WG1) was concerned with free political participation and the international community. WG2 was tasked with exploring constitutional principles and the constitution-making process. WG3 explored potential forms of interim government. WG4 dealt with the Bantustans. And WG5 looked at time frames. Each party was allowed two delegates and two advisers in each working group, and the groups were accountable to the management committee. Working groups started work on 20 January 1992, with the hope that a follow-up plenary, Codesa II, would be able to build upon whatever advances they were able to achieve.

Largely unnoticed at the time, Codesa I adopted a procedural convention that was to prove invaluable in difficult times ahead. The principle of 'sufficient consensus' became a standing rule of the negotiations despite a lack of clarity about what it might mean. This strange notion was introduced by Ramaphosa himself, prior to his appointment as chief negotiator. In workshops at Shell House, the ANC headquarters, he explained to activists that the negotiations must not get bogged down in numbers.

Albie Sachs recollects Cyril explaining that 'the minute you have numbers, the pressure is on to collect votes, not to find consensus, and we should be looking for consensus wherever possible. If it's just a matter of finding the votes, you elevate the tiny parties well beyond the status that they ought to have, and that allows them to bargain and auction themselves.' On Ramaphosa's view, the architecture of the negotiations was quite simple. Government was in power and controlled the state. Meanwhile, the ANC represented the overwhelming majority of the population. It was these two 'major forces' that needed to be bound together. Sufficient consensus was not some impossible unanimity, he explained, but rather the 'coming to an agreement' of just these key actors.[12]

Fanie van der Merwe had his own, slightly different, interpretation of sufficient consensus, seeing it as a method through which 'you place a document on the table and systematically work on that document. At every stage, you put a new draft or clause on the table, as soon as there is sufficient consensus to move forward, you go on to the next draft ... If enough of the parties supported the decision, and you could go forward without the process being disrupted, then the chairperson could declare that sufficient consensus had occurred.'[13]

Although Ramaphosa claimed that sufficient consensus was an idea borrowed from the NUM's negotiations, it seems just as likely that he simply invented it. It was sometimes joked by others that sufficient consensus was 'when Roelf and Cyril agree',[14] but Ramaphosa was always careful to stress that the agreement to which it referred was that between the two political parties.

When the Codesa II plenary convened, it became clear that WG2 was not moving towards a settlement. The issue at stake – the conditions in which a new constitution would be agreed in a Constitutional Assembly – went right to the heart of the process. The NP wanted important decisions about the future constitution to be taken immediately, in advance of any assembly, while its power was at its greatest. It demanded that a 70 per cent majority should be required for decisions in a constituent assembly that would write the final constitution. Where the bill of rights or regional powers were at stake, they claimed, this should rise to 75 per cent. The NP also wanted agreement then that the principle of power-sharing must be included.

For its part, the ANC proposed that a two-thirds majority was sufficient to decide what should go into the constitution. In itself, this was a bold concession, which Ramaphosa might have found hard to justify to his constituency. As he later observed, 'we would have had enormous problems in selling it – and in a way it was as well they did reject it ... Taking everything into account, the totality of everything, it would have looked like the ANC had actually sold out completely.'[15] The offer, however, was made by Cyril in the almost certain knowledge that the NP would reject it.

The problem for the ANC was that the NP might be able to

construct an alliance in the Constitutional Assembly large enough to exercise a veto. The country might then be trapped with an interim constitution based on power-sharing. As Gerrit Viljoen and Tertius Delport recognised, government might even be obliged to revert back to the old constitution.[16] On these grounds, Ramaphosa insisted that the ANC demand a deadlock-breaking mechanism: in the event that the constitution was not finalised within a period of six months, a popular referendum would be held as a deadlock-breaker.

This seemed to be a tempting offer, but the NP quickly realised it was one of Ramaphosa's tricks. The ANC would simply be able to stall for six months, and then trounce the NP in a referendum. It could then write the new constitution on its own. Codesa II deadlocked irreconcilably in the middle of this procedural morass. De Klerk and Mandela, who were going through one of the more positive phases of their relationship, met for evening coffee and salvaged something from the working group. They lowered the temperature, and referred the problems raised in WG2 back to the management committee.

The collapse of Working Group 2 created great confusion. There were many ANC negotiators present to whom the strategy had not been explained,[17] and Cyril certainly did not have any mandate from the ANC's National Executive Committee (NEC) for his approach. He had engineered a crisis, it appeared, and placed the blame for it on the NP.

One explanation for the breakdown was that Ramaphosa had decided to isolate Tertius Delport, who was the government's negotiator in that group. Delport took a good deal of flak from his own constituency for the deadlock, *Die Burger* and *Beeld* condemning his inflexibility and obstructionism. Today Delport argues that this was the point in negotiations at which the NP's strong hand was thrown away by anxious appeasers of ANC bullying. He was telling his party that 'the ANC had no physical or military presence. We could have held out.' He presented a memorandum to cabinet explaining that Codesa was not about percentages: 'We've just got to tell them – the ANC – to stop. We've got to crush them.'[18]

Delport's somewhat self-serving account forgets that positions adopted by Meyer, like those advanced by Viljoen and Delport, were the outcome of a collective process. Negotiators deferred to De Klerk and cabinet, and beyond Delport's empty words about crushing the ANC it was difficult to see what genuinely different approach was on offer. Nevertheless, the decline of Delport and the rise of Meyer probably did work to the advantage of Ramaphosa. De Klerk observes that Delport was a robust negotiator, 'and the ANC never forgave him for his dogged refusal to bow to their bullying tactics'.[19] The WG2 crisis 'undermined his position in the government negotiating team [because] he was seen as needlessly upsetting the ANC'.[20] Delport claims that Nelson Mandela later confessed to him, 'I had to ask Mr De Klerk to remove you as chief negotiator.'[21]

Once Roelf Meyer was in place, Delport believes, the ANC had 'an easy ride'.[22] 'Roelf was a waste of time. He would go in and ramble a bit. He takes decisions in advance.'[23] Another senior government official concurs: 'Ramaphosa played Meyer like the proverbial trout – he could play him at his will ... The great relationship that Roelf imagined he had was not really reciprocated. Roelf is a nice guy but not a very clever politician.'[24]

A second explanation for the deliberate deadlocking of Codesa II is that Ramaphosa was launching a 'Leipzig option' to remove the government through popular protest. The term refers to the mass protest that had soon before brought about the collapse of the East German regime through sheer force of numbers. In De Klerk's view, 'the fact is that by May 1992 the constitutional negotiations ... no longer suited the ANC and its allies'.[25] The SACP and Cosatu were looking to exercise greater power and had conceived the notion of a revolutionary seizure.[26] The idea behind the Leipzig option, according to Dave Steward, was that the ANC would 'bring the masses out, government would fall, and it would not be necessary to go through the tiresome negotiating process ... This is undoubtedly what they were trying to do.'[27]

In June 1992, a four-phase programme of 'rolling mass action' was launched. In the middle of this programme, on 17 June, a tragedy occurred at Boipatong, near Vanderbijlpark, when 46 residents of the township were massacred by local hostel dwellers. Mandela decisively withdrew the ANC from all Codesa contacts, and laid out a new set of demands for the resumption of negotiations. For De Klerk's camp, the conflict 'was starting to get dangerously out of hand'.[28] Worse still, the ANC had decided to topple the Bantustan governments, starting with Ciskei's government in Bisho, and some ANC cadres were shouting the slogan 'Bisho today then Ulundi tomorrow'.[29]

In the event, the mass action ended in Bisho, the capital of the tiny Ciskei homeland, and Cyril almost lost his life there. 'Independent' Bisho had a farcical history of coups and countercoups by members of its small military forces. The incumbent in 1992 was Colonel Oupa Gqozo, whom Ronnie Kasrils famously described as 'a pint-sized individual with an outsized military hat'.[30] Gqozo had successfully launched a 1990 coup, while the then military leader Lennox Sebe, himself a coup beneficiary, was in Hong Kong (allegedly shopping). Although Gqozo survived three coup attempts in the next two years, he was exceptionally unpopular and faced rebellion among his predominantly ANC-supporting subjects.

The ANC decided to mobilise the population against this illegitimate government. On 7 September, around 80,000 anti-Gqozo marchers, primarily from the locality, marched on Bisho demanding the military leader's removal. At their head were important representatives of the SACP, including Chris Hani and Ronnie Kasrils, together with John Gomomo from Cosatu, and prominent ANC leaders Steve Tshwete and Cyril Ramaphosa. Tshwete set the tone of the march in a speech in which he said they would 'drive the pig from the barn'.[31]

In the event, when Kasrils led a group of the marchers through a break in barbed wire, Ciskei soldiers opened fire on them. Kasrils describes how the firing 'spread to all sectors. People inside the stadium had been shot. Ramaphosa, and those with him at the razor-wire, had come under fire. Two marshals had thrown themselves over Ramaphosa to protect him. The crowd along the road, back into South Africa, had been mercilessly raked.'[32] In all, 29 people were killed and more than 200 were injured.

There were rumours of SADF involvement, and claims that Gqozo would not have acted without Pretoria's assent. Ramaphosa immediately accused the government: 'We blame De Klerk for this. The Ciskei is the creation of the apartheid system and it is responsible for the atrocities committed in its name.'[33] Behind the scenes, however, there were recriminations about the poor planning of the break-away group, and the hidden agendas of some of its SACP participants.[34] Raymond Suttner explains that, 'Based on [an] earlier march, when they had not opened fire, we miscalculated. Also, some groupings that broke away from the main march may have provoked the shooting. At any rate any idea of removing the "regime" evaporated under gunfire.'[35]

The massacre gave ANC participants pause for reflection. Ramaphosa, whose mother was desperate with shock and fear,[36] observed later that 'Bisho brought some measure of realism to bear on our mass action campaigns. After Bisho we felt that we did not need to take risks that could lead to the loss of life ... We tried [to do] everything we could to make sure that there was no loss of life, and I think to a large extent we did succeed.'[37]

De Klerk's chief of staff, Dave Steward, speculates that Bisho was a turning point in that the ANC leadership recognised 'the folly ... of pursuing the Leipzig option'.[38] However, even if there were some in the SACP who believed in it, the Leipzig option was always a red herring for Ramaphosa.[39] As he later observed, 'There was much talk about going to Ulundi [capital of Buthelezi's base of KwaZulu]. That was never really seriously on the cards.'[40] Instead, the breakdown of Codesa served primarily tactical purposes. Many ordinary ANC activists had been shaped by the insurrectionary climate of the 1980s or the militarism of exile, and they were fed up with unchecked 'third force' violence. Throughout the early negotiations popular support for the ANC was ebbing away. External sanctions had been lifted, the armed struggle was suspended, and the positions of external powers had shifted.[41] The break from talks allowed the leadership to 'rally the troops' by taking demonstrable action against what was widely perceived to be a violent and unprincipled enemy.

For Govan Mbeki, mass action gave the leadership an opportunity to rebuild links with their constituency. 'After so many years, the ANC has not yet succeeded to build the structures, effective structures right from the bottom up to the top ... You still get a situation where, and especially during the negotiations, where the top leadership arrives at certain positions with those with whom it is negotiating and that message doesn't go quickly to the grassroots because the structures have not yet been successfully established.'[42]

The breaking off of talks, as Ramaphosa later explained, 'marked an important return for the ANC to the politics of mass mobilization. It served to remind the regime that they were negotiating with a political movement which had the support of the majority of South Africans.'[43]

Indeed, De Klerk's insufficiently determined response to political violence allowed the ANC leadership to use it as a rallying point. 'Madiba is a man of integrity and accorded FW respect right at the beginning,' Cyril observed, but soon Mandela came 'face to face with the real FW'. Ramaphosa's account was inconsistent, however. On the one hand, he claimed that 'Madiba could never understand how a head of state who had all the apparatus of governance at his hand could not do something openly and meaningfully to stop the violence ... FW was still essentially playing politics at a great price, at a great cost to the lives of our people.'[44] Indeed, at one point, Ramaphosa remembered Mandela in effect accusing De Klerk of racism. Mandela would imply to De Klerk 'that you are involved in the violence ... If you were not involved you would stop it, it is because it is black people dying. Essentially at heart you are still a racist, you cannot accept that a black man can stand up to you and argue with you. [He said] stuff like that which would be very hurtful to a person who thought he had done a lot to bring the country to where it was.'[45]

On the other hand, Ramaphosa eventually accepted De Klerk's word that he was not sanctioning violence and that rogue elements were responsible. However, 'it's difficult not to blame the government because the rogue elements are never arrested and brought to book by a government that has strong surveillance capabilities. So I would say right now, indirectly at some level in government, there is liability.' Ramaphosa notes that, 'They have worked very hard to apprehend the perpetrators of massacre situations that involve white people ... but when it comes to black people ... no real follow up takes place ... That leads one to believe that at a particular level the security forces, or elements in the security forces, would be behind this.'[46]

In retrospect De Klerk is at pains to defend his record, and rebuts suggestions that he was pursuing a strategy of plausible deniability. 'As I understand the concept of plausible deniability it relates to situations where those in authority express vague – and often illegitimate – wishes to their subordinates, in the hope and expectation that the subordinates will use their own discretion to carry out what they perceive to be their superior's instructions. The supposed advantage is that those in authority can then deny any knowledge of their subordinates' actions, and if pressed can insist that their subordinates misinterpreted their wishes. The classic example is Henry II's *cri de coeur* referring to Archbishop Thomas à Becket, "Who will rid me of this troublesome priest!" When his knights carried out what they perceived (probably, quite correctly) to be the king's instructions by murdering Thomas, the King lamented that this had never been his intention!'[47]

De Klerk is happy to agree that 'culpability in such a case still lies with the instruction-giver'. Moreover, he has no doubt that 'the concept of plausible deniability was quite widespread in our security forces during the unrest of the eighties and that it was at the root of much of the malaise that was subsequently uncovered by [the commission of inquiry under Judge] Goldstone and the TRC. The trouble with plausible deniability is that it corrupts channels of communication and lines of authority. Decision-making devolves to relatively junior levels at times staffed by morally flawed people (often the only people prepared to carry out such "instructions"). They seek to "protect" their superiors by not informing them of the detail of their actions – but merely that "the job has been done".' Quite soon, he observes, 'those in command no longer know – or control – what is happening in their organizations. Emboldened by the absence of accountability those carrying out operations begin to act as they please – often for their own enrichment.'[48]

De Klerk vehemently denies having any two-track strategy in which violence and negotiations were running in parallel. 'I did not think that anything at all could be gained from ongoing violence on the one hand, while proceeding with negotiations on the other.' He concedes that 'it is possible that Ramaphosa, Mandela and other ANC leaders might at a certain stage genuinely have thought that this was indeed the case. Such suspicions would have explained in part the deterioration in relations between me and the ANC leadership. At the same time it is also possible that the ANC leadership was quite aware that I was not involved in any way in violence, but nevertheless used such allegations for propaganda purposes.'

He goes on to observe: 'Violence seriously undermined the negotiations on which I had staked my presidency. Accordingly, I consistently and repeatedly ordered the security forces to confine themselves to their statutory duties and did everything I could to try to get to the root of allegations concerning "third force" violence ... Thus, regardless of whatever convoluted suspicions Ramaphosa might or might not have had in this regard, there was absolutely no basis in fact for the idea that I was following a policy of plausible deniability with regard to the violence that continued to afflict South Africa during my presidency.'[49]

Whatever the truth behind the government's inability to grapple with violence, De Klerk's own triumphalism also set him on a collision course with Mandela. De Klerk had badly misread the implications of his victory in a whites-only referendum. It had been held after a shock defeat of the NP by the Conservative Party in February 1992 in the hitherto rock-solid NP constituency of Potchefstroom. De Klerk demonstrated his tactical brilliance by calling a snap referendum on the negotiations for 17 March, and he secured an almost 70 per cent mandate to continue with negotiations.

'After the referendum,' Cyril observed, 'De Klerk was too confident, became very arrogant, became very reckless and I think squandered his good fortune ... He thought he was riding on the crest of a wave and his vision for the future became too narrow and too short sighted. After that referendum he could have moved decisively to reach a settlement with the ANC, at the Multi-Party [Negotiating Process] of course, on a multi-party basis. We could have reached an agreement at Codesa II and we could have settled the apartheid question last year [1992] even.'[50] Kader Asmal concurs that De Klerk 'miscued the whole nature of that mandate' and drew the wrong conclusion from the ANC's seeming weakness. By personalising matters, he created a need for Madiba too to develop a mandate of his own. '[Mandela] needed to be able to stand up and say, "We also speak from a degree of strength and social power."'[51]

If Ramaphosa and Mandela's condemnation of De Klerk served primarily tactical purposes, the period of stalemate also allowed them to shake up the NP's negotiating strategy. Roelf Meyer described how the majority within the NP had not yet come to terms with the reality that 'the actual basis for agreement had to be found between the NP and the ANC because the one had the power and the other had the numbers'.[52] The NP foolishly continued to negotiate with the erratic IFP and with other even more eccentric Bantustan conservatives, and it was still arguing for a three-way rotating presidency in which Mandela would alternate with Buthelezi and De Klerk. 'There was the stated intention on our side, by some of our people, that it should be a tripartite sort of agreement,' Meyer recalls. 'Looking back at the situation I don't think that was ever part of the reality of how things could develop.'[53] The following August, Ramaphosa reflected: 'Their need to have alliances actually ... made the negotiation process flounder ... That is an important lesson that they had to learn. They are now able to make an input in the negotiation process in a much more constructive way.'[54]

The majority of Meyer's team still harked back to a group rights or ethnic power-sharing solution. In retrospect, for Roelf Meyer, the period between Mandela's post-Boipatong withdrawal from Codesa structures and from ANC–NP bilaterals and the Record of Understanding signed in September was 'the most productive part of the entire process'.[55] The Codesa crisis forced the NP to 'go back to the drawing board' and 'rethink our whole position on group rights'.[56] Further advances were made through what came to be known as the 'channel bilateral' – a formal line of communication between the two parties that firmly established the privileged character of the NP–ANC relationship.

In fact, communication between Meyer and Ramaphosa had never been broken off. When Nelson Mandela announced that the ANC was terminating all bilateral meetings with the NP after the Boipatong massacre, Roelf Meyer was sitting at home watching Mandela speak on the television. Ten minutes later Cyril called: 'When can we talk?' Ramaphosa had been authorised by Mandela to continue discussions, and Meyer immediately called De Klerk to get clearance from his principal. It was only on 31 August, however, that the ANC's National Working Committee gave its formal mandate for such a channel to be established.

The channel bilateral did not involve just Cyril and Roelf. It involved the core negotiating teams from both sides: Maharaj, Ramaphosa, Zuma, Slovo and Moosa dealing primarily with constitutional issues; Mathews Phosa and Penuell Maduna handling political prisoners; and others, such as Billy Cobbett and Hassan Ebrahim, dealing with violence in the hostels. Niel Barnard, Roelf Meyer and Fanie van der Merwe were the key members of an equally substantial government team.

The government and ANC negotiators were already of a mind on the overall shape of a realistic constitutional settlement. They were now mandated to proceed quickly and unencumbered by the need to report back to their own sides. On the key constitutional issue, the idea of an interim government with a Constitutional Assembly had been more or less agreed. ANC determination to see Inkatha hostels fenced and traditional weapons banned finally drove a permanent wedge between the NP and the IFP. After the Record of Understanding was signed in September 1992, Buthelezi withdrew from contact with the NP. His unpromising reserve strategy was to build an alliance – called the Concerned South Africans Group (Cosag) – with the Conservative Party, Oupa Gqozo of Ciskei, Lucas Mangope of Bophuthatswana, and other assorted far right and Bantustan elements. He also began ominously to set out proposals for unilateral secession and the creation of a Zulu state.

On the morally murky issue of the release of political prisoners, Mandela seemingly 'threw down the gauntlet',[57] by grandstanding for the unconditional release of political prisoners such as Robert McBride whom the regime had claimed it wanted to keep in prison. In reality, of course, both sides were happy for a resolution that protected their security forces from prosecution when they had blood on their hands.[58] Unfortunately for De Klerk, he had carelessly and publicly stated his opposition to the releases, and Mandela was determined to humiliate him. In a closed meeting, Mandela attacked De Klerk, saying to him that 'you must never put forward a position of intransigence, like saying "never", when you know in the end you are going to have to give in … When you do give in, you will be humiliated, and I am trying to save you from humiliation.'[59]

The NP agreed to a constituent assembly bound only by general constitutional principles, and accepted the ANC's deadlock-breaking mechanisms.[60] Progress was so fast that De Klerk and Mandela agreed to hold a Kempton Park bilateral on 26 September 1992, to confirm their position on the interim government and Constitutional Assembly, to address the issue of 'cultural weapons', and to set out their deal on the unconditional release of political prisoners. The milestone Record of Understanding was signed at the end of this meeting.

Both De Klerk and Mandela were able to claim successes. The ANC accepted a role for binding principles in the Constitutional Assembly, and agreed to reconsider its strategy of mass action.[61] The NP had decisively broken its relationship with the IFP and abandoned group rights solutions. Mandela spoke for everyone when he observed, 'There is no reason why a political settlement should not be achieved within a relatively short period. This will pave the path to peace. This will pave the path to the economic recovery we all yearn for. But we will only achieve this if all parties and all our people, black and white, put South Africa first.'[62]

Roelf Meyer explains the importance of the deal thus: 'They got confirmed from us that we are looking at a two-phase process providing for an elected constitution-making body at the end of the process ... From our side we got what was important, and that is confirmation that there will be constitutional continuity, that there will be in the transitional phase a constitution drafted now which will be a complete constitution preventing a constitutional hiatus. So those two elements were both addressed in the end result in the Record of Understanding. That was their fundamental aspiration as far as the constitution-making process is concerned and the other one was our fundamental one as far as the substance is concerned.'[63]

The Record of Understanding, in Kader Asmal's view, 'established an ineluctable route towards a final settlement'.[64] The core negotiators had succeeded in bringing their own constituencies behind the process. There was still much to do: a formal multi-party negotiations process now had to begin to agree the detail of the interim constitution, and the manner in which transitional authority would be exercised. The leaders also now needed to bring on board the parties that had remained outside the process, most importantly the IFP and the white right.

Joe Slovo was now a close friend and confidant of Ramaphosa, and he was proving to be a 'sheep in wolf's clothing'.[65] On 23 November, the ANC's NEC adopted his paper 'Strategic Perspectives', which set out steps towards majority rule. It included concessions to current public sector employees, and defended the employment rights and pensions of existing state officials. It was important that this proposal came from a person with impeccable leftist credentials. In fact, key ideas in the document, such as sunset clauses, probably originated with Thabo Mbeki.[66]

Meanwhile, the bilateral meetings between the ANC and NP that followed the Record of Understanding cemented agreement on how the process should move forward. On 4 and 5 March 1993, a planning conference was held at the World Trade Centre to lay the groundwork for a Multi-Party Negotiating Process (MPNP) scheduled to begin on 1 April. The MPNP was aided by the fact that there was now common purpose between the two key parties. It was also a more efficient institution. Codesa's unwieldy working groups contained upwards of 80 people, and their deliberations were too open. In effect, large groups of politicians were making public their negotiating positions, and therefore finding it impossible to compromise without incurring the wrath of their followers. MPNP also had an open plenary to which each party could send 10 delegates, and a negotiating council to which they could send 4, and this served as a focal point for public attention.

Meanwhile, the real action was behind the scenes, in closed 'technical committees' partly composed of 'apolitical' technical experts. These committees deliberated on constitutional issues, human rights, the media and the transitional executive. Because they took written submissions from all parties, they were able to draft and redraft documents, emerging with comprehensive positions that took account of the concerns of all the different contributors.

At the centre of the MPNP was a ten-member planning committee, and at the heart of the planning committee was a subcommittee of Mac Maharaj and Fanie van der Merwe, together with Ben Ngubane of the IFP. The familiar talents of Ramaphosa and Joe Slovo were supplemented by Zam Titus, representing ANC ally Transkei where he was state legal adviser, and Maharaj's Vula contact Pravin Gordhan, who was chair of many of the key sessions. Ramaphosa managed the personalities and the processes of the committee; on one account 'he even controlled everyone's diaries'.[67]

This combination of small and closed technical committees, and a tightly organised management committee, resulted in very rapid progress. When the gender committee's Baleka Kgotsile[68] demanded that each negotiating team must have a woman on it, aggressive male posturing also declined. An effective secretariat, run by the Consultative Business Movement's (CBM's) Theuns Eloff, ensured effective administration.

Eloff was a compromise choice to run the secretariat, acceptable to both key parties. His assistant, Gillian Hutchings, who was the exceptional minute-taker during the committees' meetings, has said: 'For the first few meetings, the minutes I had taken were very carefully scrutinized. Everyone was aware that minutes can be skewed and that wording is always on a knife-edge. After a time this scrutiny became cursory – they knew I had mastered the business and that I understood that neutrality was of fundamental importance.'[69]

Hutchings paints a picture of relentless effort and energy. The committee would sometimes work for 48 hours at a stretch. Despite occasional outbursts of anger, trust and camaraderie grew.[70] The only bitter row pitted Ramaphosa against the Democratic Party's representative, Colin Eglin, with whom the argument became racialised. Eloff remembers that Ramaphosa 'made racial remarks' towards Eglin. 'It was the one time I thought Cyril might have a chip on his shoulder with regard to racism.'[71]

Eloff also had clashes with his fellow workaholic Ramaphosa. He insisted on working as 'custodian of the process', as the rules demanded, rather than acting as a servant of one of the major parties. Eloff complains, 'Cyril sometimes tried to treat me as a party political apparatchik. He thought I should understand that I was now working for him ... But eventually Cyril trusted me.'[72] When the negotiators were celebrating the completion of the constitution at a dance in 1993, it transpired that neither side had really trusted Eloff. Roelf Meyer told him: 'We thought you were ANC.' Cyril laughed: 'We thought you were National Intelligence.'

There was also some humour in the talks. Roelf and Cyril would often pass notes to each other and chortle. When Mac and Fanie, very much the mature pairing in the room, found somebody's behaviour amusing, they would look at each other with poker faces. A serious-looking Joe Slovo on one occasion lambasted the administrative team for the piles of document packs and papers piled up around the room. With sadness, he concluded that it was time to fire them all. The other members of the committee played along, until Slovo gestured at the papers and remarked, 'I am, of course, speaking as the representative of the Green Party.'[73]

Ramaphosa's endurance and negotiating skills helped ensure rapid progress. 'Cyril had the ability to get people to do whatever he wanted,' observes Hutchings. Eloff recalls in particular his facility for changing the question under discussion without other participants noticing. 'He would look confused and ask for clarification on some matter, and when the other person answered him they would suddenly realise they had fallen into a trap.'[74] Eloff reflects that 'It is not a good idea to underestimate Cyril, especially if you are his enemy. He knows about things and he knows things.'

The negotiations were moving ahead well when, on 10 April 1993, Chris Hani was assassinated outside his home in Boksburg by a Polish anti-communist immigrant. Hani was not at the centre of the negotiations. His importance, alongside figures such as Peter Mokaba and Winnie Mandela, was in popular mobilisation, and in selling a negotiated settlement to an angry constituency. His death threatened to crystallise lingering discontent with the negotiations process. It also exposed De Klerk's impotence, Mandela having to call in a televised speech for 'all South Africans to stand together against those who, from any quarter, wish to destroy what Chris Hani gave his life for – the freedom of all of us'.

Mandela's own name was found on a hit-list at the assassin's residence. Exploiting the redoubled pressure and tension, Ramaphosa arranged for new technical committees to be established to address violence, the creation of an Independent Electoral Commission, control of the media, and the functioning of the transitional executive. Meanwhile, the CBM wheeled out business leaders to lobby the Cosag alliance to fight political instability, and Cosatu called for clear and demonstrable progress in talks. The ANC, as Ramaphosa later stated, took advantage of the crisis to pressure De Klerk for the immediate setting of an election date.[75] De Klerk conceded, and the date of 27 April 1994 was agreed. As an editorial in the *Sunday Times* observed, 'The act of setting a date for national elections, however hedged about with qualifications, has carried South Africa into the final stretch of its journey from racial oligarchy to mass democracy.'[76]

At the MPNP, the technical committee on the interim constitution was now in a race against time. Like the other technical committees, its members lacked high political profiles, and had been chosen for their acceptability to all parties. Bernard Ngoepe, today judge president of the Transvaal Division, remembers the committee's extended debates over drafts of key sections, and the process of consultation that accompanied it.[77] The lawyers sat surrounded by international constitutions, and drew clauses from countries as diverse as India, Canada and the US. The Namibian constitution was especially influential, given that members of the technical committee had been involved in drafting it.

Ngoepe credits Ramaphosa with imbuing the negotiating process with the appropriate spirit. 'A constitution is merely pieces of paper,' considers Ngoepe. 'And the spirit of a constitution has to be built – people have to work to generate that spirit that gives life to a constitution … Cyril helped build bridges, and bridged divides, to create the unity and consensus that gave a spirit to this constitution'.[78]

By the end of October, a draft constitution was almost complete. All that remained were assorted residual points of difference. But the task was harder than it sounded, because differences that had endured to the end of negotiations were inevitably the least tractable. Moreover, Ramaphosa's deliberate strategy was to leave the thorniest issues until last, when accumulated trust and the momentum of negotiations would hopefully carry them over their final hurdles.

Late in the evening of 16 November, the two lead negotiators, Cyril and Roelf, and their principals, Mandela and De Klerk, met in a crucial bilateral meeting, and struck what was later known as the 'six-pack' deal.[79] The issues were well known, and the possibilities for compromise had already been explored again and again. The meeting was to last just four hours, indicating that the negotiators had clarified the broad outlines of a deal in advance. The ANC conceded security of tenure for public servants (without whom they could not anyway conceivably hope to govern) and agreed to a compromise on official languages that would in effect protect Afrikaans by proliferating the number of 'special' languages to 11. There was broad agreement on the role of a Judicial Services Commission in appointing judges. Mandela conceded that provinces would have the power to write their own constitutions, but only in a manner consistent with the national constitution. In a further time-limited concession, the ANC agreed to protect whites' 30 per cent representation on councils to be elected in 1996 local government elections. This 'concession' would succeed in painting the NP as hold-outs for racial codification.

On the key issues, compromises favoured the ANC. Cabinet decision-making had been a matter of long-standing contention, with the NP pressing for minority vetoes. For Tertius Delport, indeed, the whole issue of power-sharing had now been reduced to this one issue. 'What majority in Cabinet for a decision? We said 75 per cent all along. It was referred for a long time, nearly a year, to the channel, Roelf [and] Ramaphosa.'[80] Cyril later explained how his discussions with Meyer unfolded. 'I just told him, you have known me long enough to know I can't give you a bargaining position that is false on this issue ... And you know too that it will not be accepted by the ANC ... The best thing for you and me is to reach an agreement that cabinet will work on the basis of majority ... As soon as I prefaced everything like that, he knew it was pointless even to argue. We had developed that type of rapport, we didn't need to take false positions on certain crucial matters.'[81]

On the advice of Meyer, De Klerk conceded that 'Cabinet shall function in a manner which gives consideration to the consensus-seeking spirit underlying the concept of a government of national unity as well as the need for effective government'. Decisions would be taken by consensus, but with the understanding that the majority could prevail.[82]

The final key NP concession concerned deadlock-breaking mechanisms for the Constitutional Assembly. It was agreed that if the assembly was unable to reach agreement, only 60 per cent support in a referendum would be required for the adoption of a contested draft constitution. The 60 per cent threshold was so low that a threat thereafter hung over the heads of NP negotiators.

Meyer and Ramaphosa had steered their principals to an historic agreement. Ramaphosa ascribed the success to their sense of detachment. 'There were a number of issues which were left hanging ... I knew that we would get a better deal if things were handled that way, because we would discuss things without being emotional.'[83] He believes that 'in a way that had to do with the chemistry that we had developed ... One of the key things in negotiations is to find a whole lot of mechanisms to resolve problems ... and maybe identifying two people on both sides who get on well together ... They usually come up with a solution, that's what happened with Roelf and me.'[84]

Ramaphosa's fullest statement about his relationship with Meyer came in August 1993: 'As we went on, it became logical that we would relate at a personal level. The need to relate at a personal level was mainly directed at having a firm basis on which we can solve problems, because we knew that problems were inevitable ... We knew that it was only through some understanding between us that we could make a real attempt to resolve the problems. I wouldn't say we have become friends. I think we have a relationship that lends itself to enabling us to resolve problems. At the same time we know that we are adversaries. We know that when we go for elections we are going to be fighting the elections on different sides, and we are people who come from different backgrounds. We have different interests, we have different history, we have different aspirations for the future, but at a broad level I think we are bound by a common vision of making sure that we move our country from an apartheid society to a democratic one and that is what binds us together.'[85]

Behind Ramaphosa's mostly generous words, there still lurked a fear of betrayal, traceable perhaps to the collapse of the bonds built in the NUM's negotiations with Anglo American. 'I never wanted to come back home knowing that we had been hoodwinked, we had not achieved our objectives and we had been defeated at the hands of people like Roelf.'[86]

The deal had been struck by four remarkably self-confident politicians. Mandela's aristocratic self-possession has been much analysed. De Klerk, likewise, was 'a supremely confident politician', who 'comes from a very old and well-established political family'.[87] Meyer enjoyed an equally distinguished lineage, his prodigious political success at a young age coming easily to a scion of one of the Afrikaner community's most powerful families. Ramaphosa, in this respect, was the outsider. Though one journalist has described his 'almost awe-inspiring sense of self-confidence',[88] his self-possession was not secured by the authority and history of his family, or by any special social status in his community.

At seven the following morning, FW de Klerk presented the details of the six-pack agreement to a special meeting of his cabinet. Meyer explained that this was a 'package deal', before De Klerk broke the news about cabinet decision-making. Then minister of local government Tertius Delport's recollection of his words was as follows: 'We decided it would not be wise to have a set majority in Cabinet because then you start off with a voting process.' Instead, he continued, 'What must be developed is a process of consultation ... I see eye to eye with Mr Mandela. Between the two of us we will make this work ... I need him, he needs me, and he realises it ... and we will run the country.'[89]

There was a stunned silence. Delport viewed the six-pack deal as a 'total surrender'. When De Klerk called for a short break, Delport rushed over to Dawie de Villiers, Cape leader of the party, saying that he would have to resign. He then followed De Klerk to his office. Taking hold of him, and full of emotion, he cried out, 'You have given it all away!' His eyes welling with tears, he spoke for an hour to De Klerk, pleading with him to reconsider. De Klerk insisted that he would sign the agreement that morning. Turning back now, he claimed, would lead to a revolution.[90] 'I was prepared, thank God it never happened, thank God I didn't get it my own way, I was prepared to face a revolution. I was prepared for a short period of grief instead of a very long, drawn-out period of grief. But then maybe it's correct to call me a hawk, or reckless, or whatever. So maybe, thank God, FW didn't listen to me.'[91]

On 22 December the interim constitution was adopted by parliament. Immense attention to detail was displayed in its drafting, with powers and rules precisely specified, and the transitional executive (the ultimate executive authority in the run-up to the election) regulated by detailed statutes. The process had not been the one envisaged by De Klerk when he announced the release of Nelson Mandela in 1990. To Ramaphosa's mind, 'They thought they could manage it, [but] they didn't have a long-term vision ... I guess in the end they knew that there would be a president from the ANC, that Mandela would be president ... They could have held out a lot longer but they had no option.'[92] As De Klerk's

chief of staff, Dave Steward, perceptively observed, 'The final package was determined not so much by the relative skill of the negotiators as by the "objective circumstances" – as the ANC would put it.'[93]

Time was now short to bring the recalcitrant right and the IFP into the fold. In De Klerk's view, 'The ANC was far more concerned about the threat from the Afrikaner right than they were about the IFP. They felt the IFP could, if necessary, be crushed – but they were worried about the military threat posed by rightwing Afrikaners.'[94] The best efforts of Thabo Mbeki had partly enticed the stubborn conservative constituency. De Klerk also helped persuade the right to participate in the elections, lobbying for the inclusion of a possibility of Afrikaner self-determination in the interim constitution.

The IFP maintained its brinkmanship almost up to the wire. Buthelezi became increasingly isolated as his local allies – first the NP, then the white right, and finally the Bantustan leaders – fell by the wayside or rejoined the process. Even his international friends, such as British prime minister Margaret Thatcher, advised him to participate in the elections.[95] Just a week before the date of the ballot, Buthelezi capitulated. His decision was brought about in part by the firmness with which Ramaphosa's negotiating team dispatched international mediators Henry Kissinger and Lord Carrington. Kissinger later observed, 'If we had stayed we would have become part of the problem. In a way, our failure achieved success.'[96] In reality, Ramaphosa had insisted they not meddle, and that the only meaningful concession they could make – a postponement of the election – was absolutely not on the cards.

An old Nigerian law professor called Washington Okumu had been brought in to facilitate Buthelezi's climb-down. Okumu flew down to Mandela – accompanied by two executives of Anglo American – to explain Buthelezi's terms. The IFP leader wanted protection for the status of the Zulu monarchy and the re-introduction of an international mediation process after the elections.[97] With the ballot a week away, there were some logistical problems preparing the ballot papers. However, the move was not unanticipated. The IFP, for its part, unrolled a very carefully planned and punchy election campaign, suggesting that it had prepared long and hard for just this eventuality.

When South Africa's first democratic election began on the morning of 27 April 1994, Ramaphosa decided not to cast his ballot in a suburb or in Soweto. He drove out to Kloof Gold Mine in Westonaria, Gauteng, the first mine the NUM had organised in 1982. He recalls that 'There were about ten thousand miners waiting to vote. They had queued up, and it was the longest queue I had ever seen ... They glowed, and the glow in their faces is what I kept remembering ... I was stopped by one [old] miner ... who said, "We are very pleased that you are here ... I can now go and retire because what we fought for all these years, and what you also came and fought for, has now been attained, and I can go and retire and die. Your coming here shows that you have come home, you belong to us miners."'98

CHAPTER 18

TRIUMPH AND DESPAIR

Behind the extraordinary historical drama of the election, there was logistical and administrative chaos. When the smoke cleared, it became evident that political accommodation had been preferred to a mechanical counting of votes. The result was almost too good to be true. The NP secured a win in the Western Cape, and the IFP snatched 51 per cent in KwaZulu-Natal, results that bound both parties into the outcome. When Natal firebrand Harry Gwala called for voting abuses to be investigated, the ANC silenced him. In the national result, the NP squeaked past the 20 per cent threshold for De Klerk to secure the second deputy presidency. When the ANC vote began creeping up towards two-thirds, 'they just stopped counting'.[1]

This was not the right occasion for moralising about electoral manipulation, nor was it sensible for the ANC to press home its advantage fully. Ramaphosa reflected the combination of cynicism and relief common among professional politicians. He commented, 'Everyone emerged a winner. There was no outright loser who would have wanted to take up arms to destabilise everything ... The "miracle" was in the end properly packaged, and that in itself gave legitimacy to the processes that we have gone through. In the end one can say that the end, in a way, justified the means ...'[2]

Ramaphosa, Slovo, Moosa and Maharaj did not have long to enjoy the fruits of their labours. The leftist putsch, through which they had been propelled to control of the negotiations, had been followed by a powerful counter-reaction. The ANC's NEC remained a more conservative and exile-dominated body than the left's 1991 tactical triumph had suggested.

While the leaders of the left axis had been embroiled in negotiations over the country's future, the right was preparing to reassert what it believed was its natural right to lead the liberation movement. An immediate focus was the first deputy presidency of the country. Whoever secured this position would be well placed to succeed the ageing Nelson Mandela, who was already known to favour only one term of office.

Many former UDF and Cosatu activists believed the deputy presidency should go to one of their number. Cyril's triumph in the negotiations made him their inevitable choice. According to Bantu Holomisa, who was then a favoured son of Nelson Mandela, 'There was a legitimate expectation on Ramaphosa's part – and on the part of many members of the ANC – that he might be deputy president to Mandela.'[3] Saki Macozoma, who had experienced the ANC on Robben Island and in exile, but who had nevertheless been formed in the same domestic struggle as Cyril, concurs: 'It was a surprise when he was not made deputy president. Most people thought Ramaphosa would be made deputy president. Cyril certainly thought so.'[4]

In retrospect, Mandela's choice of Mbeki was not so surprising, even for Cyril himself. In the draft of his authorised biography of Mandela, Anthony Sampson observed that 'Mandela appeared often to favour Ramaphosa, and saw the advantage in having a non-Xhosa as his deputy'. However, Mandela's notes in the margin of the manuscript explain that he consulted widely among top ANC, SACP and union leaders 'without indicating his own feelings'.[5] It was likely that Ramaphosa's relationship with Mandela had cooled. Mandela did not fully trust Cyril,[6] and he may have become 'disillusioned with Cyril's naked ambition'.[7]

In the event, Mandela consulted many comrades he already knew would support Mbeki. One was Jacob Zuma, Mbeki's ally and the man who had obstructed Cyril's entry to the SACP, and who in turn was displaced by him from a leading role in the negotiations. Another was Thomas Nkobi, whose close friend, Alfred Nzo, Ramaphosa had humiliated in the election for secretary-general in 1991.[8] Mandela also approached Walter Sisulu, who would have respected Tambo's wishes, Kenneth Kaunda and Julius Nyerere, who could not have known Ramaphosa at all, and two or three union leaders unsympathetic to him.[9] Of all those consulted, only Joe Slovo is known to have supported Cyril.

The most likely interpretation is that Mbeki was the better-prepared man for the job, and that Mandela in fact favoured him. James Myburgh's partly persuasive revisionist account suggests that 'between 1994 and 1996, not only did Mandela make various decisions which almost guaranteed Mbeki's ascent, but he was seen, both inside and outside the party, as favouring Mbeki as his successor. He could have always chosen someone else, or at least kept the contest open. He did neither ... By 1999 Mandela may have regretted not choosing Ramaphosa over Mbeki in 1994 ... but the contemporaneous evidence simply does not support the assertion that he preferred Ramaphosa at the time.'[10]

Mbeki certainly appeared a more prudent choice. As one observer remarked at the time, 'Mbeki is close to Jacob Zuma and together they are seen as the moderate wing of the national executive. Ramaphosa usually has Joe Slovo at his side.'[11] Moreover, while Cyril had been embroiled in the negotiations, Thabo Mbeki had moved closer to Mandela, serving humbly as his speechwriter, and building on their mutual affection for Tambo.[12] Mbeki continued to bask in the respect accorded to Tambo, and acquired seniority from the relationship. Mbeki was also a hard worker, an organisational fixer and a details man, who, like Mandela, had bravely advanced the case for negotiation while others were trapped in an irrelevant militaristic paradigm.

If Mandela broadly favoured Mbeki at the time, why was there such an elaborate show of consultation? One reason is that Mandela did not want to be seen to be engineering the rise of a fellow Xhosa, because this might raise dangerous perceptions of ethnic favouritism. Certainly, ethnicity must have played some role in Ramaphosa's fate, in the indirect sense that he was not part of longstanding Xhosa political and familial networks in the Eastern Cape.

Ramaphosa, like many others, also had difficulty engaging with the ethnic chauvinists of the Zulu royal court. The problem was not the IFP leader, Mangosuthu Buthelezi, who may have been a 'complex and frustrating interlocutor',[13] but was not a crude ethnic nationalist. According to Penuell Maduna, there was never any effort on Buthelezi's part to exclude ANC negotiators on ethnic grounds.[14] Rather, it was King Goodwill, who had a curious conception of the place of the tribe in political life. During his negotiations with the NP, he demanded a kingdom that embraced not just Natal, but also the southern Transvaal, some of the Eastern Cape and parts of the Free State. He was not impressed by FW de Klerk's pertinent observation that the people living in those places might not want to be his subjects. The king pronounced himself willing to tolerate rule by whites, because they had defeated the Zulu in battle, but was unwilling to be ruled by the Xhosa. Moreover – and Steward emphasised that 'the Venda dimension was very important in these discussions' – one of the Zulu princes proclaimed that 'We are not prepared to be ruled by the Venda dog Ramaphosa'.[15]

It was inevitably Afrikaners who offered the most uncomplicated interpretations of the implications of tribalism for Cyril's leadership ambitions. Roelf Meyer, reflecting on the matter in 1996, conceded that it was difficult for an outsider to speculate successfully. However, he observed that 'Thabo is coming from the tribe that forms the basis and still plays a dominant role in the organisation'.[16] Tertius Delport's less nuanced 1996 judgement was that 'It's ethnic politics again. I think he's a Venda, you can't have a Venda ... He's from a minority and not well liked, not even minority but seen as an inferior little tribe, whatever. So, Ramaphosa: never, never, never.'[17]

As we shall see later, such outsider judgements underestimated the capacity and determination of the ANC to strive for the equitable treatment of ethnic groups. From the perspective of the organisation and its leader, it would certainly have been desirable for Mandela's successor precisely not to be a Xhosa. Indeed, this may be one of the reasons why Mandela considered Ramaphosa seriously enough to have sounded him out about his ambitions.

On Bantu Holomisa's view, Ramaphosa's expectation that he would become Mandela's deputy was probably built up by the old man himself. If Mandela was considering Cyril, he would certainly have 'sounded out Cyril about this in advance', perhaps giving him the impression that the job was already his.[18] Only this course of events, according to Holomisa, can account for Ramaphosa's 'overreaction' when Mandela chose Thabo Mbeki instead. Cyril was offered a consolation prize – the post of foreign minister – but he declined it.[19] Indeed he stormed off that same day, in what was widely believed to be a sulk, to fish with his old friend Rick Menell. ('He arrived late, and caught a very big fish.')[20] Nthato Motlana derided this behaviour as 'running off to stay with some white boy in the suburbs'.[21]

Cyril then boycotted Mandela's 10 May inauguration, which, in Holomisa's view, 'was a little childish, but one must think what made him behave in this manner ... His overreaction was perhaps understand-able.'[22] Ramaphosa's now largely estranged wife, Nomazizi Mtshotshisa, attended the event with veteran journalist Allister Sparks.[23]

So disappointed was Cyril that some close acquaintances believed he had decided to quit politics altogether. Roelf Meyer recalled that 'Cyril's disappointment first originated when he was not appointed deputy president, and he wanted then already to leave … Cyril asked [Mandela] in 1994 to leave and he denied him the opportunity to go … I don't think Cyril would have been able or been prepared to serve under Thabo.'[24]

Ramaphosa's decision not to accept a cabinet post, however, may not have been motivated by a desire to step aside from active politics. A more plausible explanation is that Ramaphosa wanted to concentrate his attention on internal ANC machinations. He was rumoured to have refused Mandela's offer of a cabinet post on the grounds that he had not had the opportunity to do justice to the office of ANC secretary-general.[25] Now that his commitment to the negotiations was behind him – or so he thought – he wanted the chance to do the job properly. Mandela was willing to concede on these grounds – and it must be remembered that the old man could have compelled him to serve in the cabinet had he wished.

Inevitably, a whispering campaign was immediately launched, suggesting that Ramaphosa was preparing to 'go back to the branches' to prepare a grassroots campaign for the leadership. He was shortly to be placed number two in the ANC's complex list process, in effect ranking him behind only Nelson Mandela in the party's informal hierarchy. It was still conceivable that he might secure the post of ANC deputy president at the December 1994 ANC conference, and then rise to the position of ANC president – and so successor-designate to Mandela – at the movement's 1997 conference.[26]

It quickly became clear that such a scenario could never unfold. The first reason was that Ramaphosa had become alienated from certain key constituencies in the ANC. While he had never been popular himself, Thabo Mbeki had built alliances with popular activists such as Winnie Mandela and Peter Mokaba.[27] Ramaphosa's late 1980s membership of the Mandela Crisis Committee, assembled to rein in the increasingly violent behaviour of Winnie Mandela's bodyguards, earned him Madikizela-Mandela's enmity thereafter. When she returned to prominence as president of the ANC Women's League in 1994, she was relatively easy for Thabo Mbeki to court.

While the exile ANC had dithered over the practice of 'necklacing' championed by Winnie Mandela in 1986, Ramaphosa was an unequivocal critic. Just when Winnie was beginning her rehabilitation, in April 1992, and her supporters were drawing a veil over the necklacing issue, Ramaphosa drew attention to it once again: 'We cannot condone threats to resort to necklacing. It is a barbaric and unacceptable method of execution which the ANC has never condoned. ANC Secretary General, Cyril Ramaphosa, has requested [a recent proponent of necklacing] Mr Mathusa to come to the ANC Headquarters and account for his statements as reported in the press.'[28]

Ramaphosa also earned the ire of the ANC Youth League's mercurial leader, Peter Mokaba. Mokaba was a powerful organiser and orator, who had built the ANC's youth wing into a 1.5-million-strong league. He was almost as popular as Ramaphosa, but with a quite different base of support, and he shared with Winnie Madikizela-Mandela the ability to sway opinion. Mokaba was famous for his use of the slogans 'Roar, young lions, roar!' and 'Kill the Boer, kill the farmer', the second of which the ANC decided to ban. But Mokaba continued to relish its use, and in a major public humiliation Ramaphosa one day cut him dead at a mass meeting and scolded him for using the phrase. As Chris Barron observes, 'Ramaphosa's silencing of Mokaba might have been the final nail in the coffin of his presidential hopes.'[29]

Mbeki's courting of Mokaba demonstrated the exile's keen tactical sense, and the young firebrand became a long-term collaborator during his rule. As well as being his sometime electoral strategist, Mokaba helped Mbeki develop some of his less conventional policy positions. In particular, he helped justify the government's controversial HIV/AIDS policy, penning a notorious condemnation of an 'omnipotent apparatus' trying to force Mbeki to embrace anti-retroviral treatments.[30] Moreover, he was author of the ANC discussion document 'Through the Eye of a Needle', designed to promote centralisation and leadership control over internal ANC elections.[31] While Ramaphosa remained vastly more popular than Mbeki, the new deputy president leveraged his own support through alliances with the two most important populists in South African politics.

A second reason why Ramaphosa's ambitions were unrealisable was that the leftist realignment of 1991 had been reversed. Even in that year, only one-quarter of the NEC were former UDF activists, and the implications of the collapse of actually-existing socialism had not yet been fully absorbed. By 1994, the personnel, practices and conventions of the Lusaka ANC had gained the ascendancy in the centre, and Mbeki's rise was a natural concomitant of this reconstitution of exile power.

Away from the centre, former UDF activists inevitably dominated regional institutions. The ex-UDF contingent had organisational capacity and the ability to turn out the vote. However, tensions grew in national institutions around organisational and ideological questions. The UDF had built real, if unevenly applied, conventions of internal debate and argumentation (themselves inherited from an earlier ANC tradition). On the other hand, exile conditions placed a premium on discipline and secrecy, and had reduced the new leadership's toleration of robust debate and argument.

After the 1994 election, Mandela entrenched this pattern by appointing key UDF leaders to provincial premierships that were themselves quickly subordinated to the centre: Lekota to the Free State, Molefe to the North West, and Stofile to the Eastern Cape. Other 'inziles' were assigned roles in a parliament that was soon to become the servant of the executive. Trevor Manuel, the devious organisational genius of the UDF in the Western Cape, was, as always, the exception to the rule, securing a powerful office as minister of trade and industry and later becoming finance minister and the most powerful member of Mbeki's cabinet.

The waning influence of the left axis was evident in the cabinet positions to which they were appointed.[32] Mandela's one-time favourite, and hero of the negotiations process, Mac Maharaj, was assigned the miserable post of transport minister. Joe Slovo was allocated the grave-yard portfolio of housing. A whole generation of talented domestic activists, it seemed, were also being simply bypassed. Meanwhile, mediocre exile place-men secured plum portfolios such as foreign affairs, defence and intelligence.

A third explanation for Ramaphosa's inability to compete for the leadership was an increasingly dirty campaign of smears and character assassination. This was a harbinger of the vicious disinformation campaigns that were to scar the decade of Mbeki's rule. As the historian of the NUM recalls, 'The stories that were peddled to discredit Ramaphosa began soon after he became the secretary-general and was seen as the heir apparent. Some were disturbingly malicious. All, to my knowledge, were false.'[33]

Drawing on half-truths and naked fabrications, the whispering campaign was often so crude as to be laughable. For Ramaphosa, it was presumably no laughing matter. Reference was made to his recently deceased policeman father being a servant of apartheid, and Zuma's old concern, that Cyril was arrested but not prosecuted, was recycled. It was alleged that he had worked for Anglo American, and ordered the great strike of 1987 to be abandoned just as the workers were about to topple the apartheid state.

Such tales served to create division and mistrust between former allies. Frans Baleni, a former underground mineworker, long-term member of the SACP, and today general secretary of the NUM, remembers, 'These people were telling dirty smear stories. They were telling us that the NUM constitution was written at the Anglo American headquarters in Main Street. But they were telling this to mineworkers who were at the very congress where it was written.'[34]

The most comical accusations were that Cyril was a CIA agent, and that he also enjoyed a homosexual relationship with Roelf Meyer – or sometimes Bobby Godsell, it did not seem to matter. In one possibly apocryphal account, which is nevertheless widely believed in NUM circles, a former official of the union was present at a meeting at which Sydney Mufamadi claimed that Ramaphosa was gay. Given Ramaphosa's well-deserved reputation, at that time, for womanising, it was almost impossible for the official to keep a straight face. As Baleni observes, 'We were all inclined to believe that Cyril veered the other way.'[35]

The association with Meyer was nevertheless astute psychological warfare. Just as Meyer had been spurned by much of the Afrikaner community, Ramaphosa was vulnerable to the accusation that he had been too close to the enemy, and allowed whites to keep their ill-gotten apartheid gains. The old complaint that Ramaphosa was 'not really ANC' also resurfaced, and he was portrayed as a black consciousness leader with no track record in the liberation movement. This claim was accompanied by a new and disturbing swagger among some returned exiles.

James Motlatsi was present at an incident that crystallised this concern in his mind. He had been asked by the ANC in 1993 to handle the logistical arrangements and security for Chris Hani's funeral. The atmosphere was highly charged, and there was the scent of violence in the air. Motlatsi organised teams of mineworkers to search funeral-goers at the entrances to the stadium where the funeral was being held. One man, a flashy-looking exile with expensive sunglasses and a foreign suit, tried to shoulder aside the mineworkers who wanted to search him, while shouting, 'Get off me, you can't fucking search me.' The man seemed to have a firearm under his jacket, and the mineworkers persisted. The man stepped back and stared at them furiously: 'Don't you ever forget this: we liberated you!' Motlatsi believes this attitude has done untold damage. 'We all liberated South Africa together. It was a result of our collective actions, and not just the doing of Robben Island prisoners or exiles.'[36]

Bantu Holomisa makes a similar point in ridiculing the pretensions of those who claim that Ramaphosa 'is not ANC'. 'People are tired of the exiles ... They must be reminded that the ANC did not organise the '76 events. These exiles are strong on public relations, and they find any opportunity to brief that "we are in charge".' In truth, he claims, 'the exiles climbed onto the bandwagon. Does one have to have gone to prison on Robben Island, or into exile in Lusaka, to understand and become part of the ANC? Those who say Cyril is not ANC must think twice. Ramaphosa found a home in the ANC and he worked for it.'[37]

Ramaphosa was relatively sanguine about such personal attacks on his political history. Beneath his smooth performance as a union leader and negotiator, however, Cyril had undergone a series of personal reversals since the late 1980s. The 1987 strike had been perhaps the most significant event in the lives of those who participated in it. For many years after the strike ended, its leaders felt a profound sense of despair, guilt, and responsibility for failure.

Whenever the pressure of NUM activity relented, Ramaphosa would take upon himself other responsibilities, particularly in Cosatu and the local politics of Soweto. Much of the extra-union work was heartbreaking and stressful. Ramaphosa, for example, was asked by a pastors' peace committee to intervene in an unrelenting conflict in the township of Bekkersdal, 7 km east of Westonaria. The township was a bare and inhospitable place of misery, built in the 1950s to house Africans working on nearby gold mines. Now, conflict had broken out between Azapo supporters in the township and local IFP-affiliated hostel dwellers. By the start of 1991, there were bodies on the streets almost every morning. Many of those involved were mineworkers, who smuggled sticks of dynamite to throw at adversaries in night-time battles. Ramaphosa, together with other leaders such as Steve Tshwete and Lybon Mabasa, were instrumental in bringing opposing forces together in a process that culminated, after a year, in a peace rally.³⁸

Cyril's family life was also in some disarray. Ramaphosa's father, Samuel, died in 1987 after a long illness, removing an important source of practical counsel. Cyril would continue, in the African way, to talk to his late father in periods of stress and difficulty.³⁹ As the eldest son, he had to shoulder responsibility for his siblings, and for the care of his mother Erdmuthe, who was still living in Tshiawelo.

The excitement of building the NUM had rescued Cyril from his post-detention depression and the failure of his first marriage to Hope Mudau. As one of his union colleagues had flippantly remarked, Ramaphosa was now married to the union.⁴⁰ In the middle of the 1980s he remarried, to Nomazizi Mtshotshisa, a woman with strength of character and ambition to match his own. She had been a nurse at Baragwanath Hospital in Soweto, before becoming a legal officer and then a lawyer. However, external pressures never relented, a family friend observing that Cyril had 'no space for a private life'.⁴¹ His second marriage was also to end in divorce.

Once Thabo Mbeki had been chosen deputy president, it was up to the senior members of the movement to ensure that a disappointed Ramaphosa's capacities were put to use. Mandela would also have been keen to dispel rumours that Ramaphosa might be using the office of secretary-general to campaign in the branches for a personal resurgence. In any event, when the time came for the head of the Constitutional

Assembly to be chosen, Mandela summoned Cyril to his office in the Union Buildings. There was a pressing task to be completed: the negotiation of a final constitution that would guide South Africa towards political stability and prosperity. Most senior Codesa and MPNP negotiators had agreed to take up jobs in the executive, unlike Cyril, and he was now the only candidate to chair the constitution-making process.

Ramaphosa protested that he wanted to remain full-time secretary-general in order to devote himself to the organisation-building task for which he had been elected. But Mandela believed it was unthinkable that the key negotiator of the settlement should remain outside the Constitutional Assembly.[42] Cyril had already turned Mandela down once; there was no way he could turn him down again. Ramaphosa would have to put his nose back to the grindstone and lead negotiations for the final constitution.[43]

Cyril put behind him the conflict of the previous years, and focused on the task ahead. The liberation election of 1994 marked the end of the peace-making era. Now, 400 members of the National Assembly and 90 members of the Senate – already preoccupied with overhauling apartheid laws – had to sit together as the Constitutional Assembly and determine the character of the new South Africa's final basic law.[44] They had two years, after which dangerous deadlock-breaking mechanisms would kick in.

Between 1992 and 1994, the ANC had sought as free a hand as possible to make a constitution after the elections. The NP had tried to entrench binding rules that would limit the freedom of action of the new Constitutional Assembly. The compromise had been a constitution-making process bound by 34 'constitutional principles'. The Constitutional Court would determine the constitutionality of the final constitution in terms of its consistency with these principles.

There were more practical considerations if the constitution was to be embraced as the collective product of the society. All the major negotiating parties wanted a unifying constitution that could be adopted by the Assembly as a whole. Most believed that the constitution should be understood by and 'owned by' ordinary citizens, for which reason there was also a public consultation process that was strenuous, if studiously ignored by negotiators.

Ramaphosa's deputy was the NP's Leon Wessels, a steady facilitator with no major political constituency or ideological position of his own. There were continuities of personnel from the earlier negotiations, including Roelf Meyer and Valli Moosa, whose new governmental responsibilities overlapped with their constitution-building ones. The experience of Codesa and MPNP also proved invaluable in setting up efficient institutions. A management committee of 12 met weekly to drive forward the negotiations, and a 44-member constitutional committee was the main negotiating and coordinating body. The management committee had a smaller subcommittee with 20 members, whose composition was tailored to the problem at hand.

The 34 constitutional principles set out in Schedule 4 of the interim constitution were the basis for a division of the work of negotiators into 6 'themes' – dealing with the character of the state, the structure of government, relations between levels of government, rights, the legal system and judiciary, and 'specialized structures of government' such as the security services and financial institutions. Each 'theme committee' (TC), which ran between September 1994 and June 1995, had 30 members, three rotating chairs and a steering committee. The composition of these committees was more or less a cross-party 'who's who' of the emerging political establishment. The negotiations were an opportunity for intensive networking between rising and declining elites. Learning from MPNP, each theme had its 'apolitical' technical committee, to take the edge out of partisan opposition.

Ramaphosa shone. Hassan Ebrahim observes that 'Cyril Ramaphosa's masterful chairing of meetings ensured that negotiators never lost their good humour. His personality, charm, and wit enabled him to deal with difficult and unhappy people from all parties. He was able to command the respect of all and able to steer the process through very difficult waters.'[45] The smooth process also testified to the MPNP's success. 'Fundamentally it's not different from the 1993 constitution,' Kader Asmal observed. 'The fundamental assumptions are not different. The distribution of power is not different. [And] that's what a constitution is about.'[46]

As Ramaphosa saw it in early 1995, they should 'take care not to reinvent the wheel, but at the same time we cannot just take everything that is in the interim constitution as it stands and put it in the new constitution … We are using the interim constitution as a reference document … We will always have it at the back of our minds as we write the new constitution [and] we are bound by the constitutional principles that are enshrined in it.'[47] Meyer adopted this same language, confirming 'We don't have to reinvent the wheel. That is the approach that is developing more and more.'[48]

Ramaphosa's reconciliatory approach was underpinned by a cool-headed analysis of the interests of white South Africans. 'There aren't many white people, in the end, who will want to sacrifice everything they have, the good life they have had, to fight a struggle and a cause which does not look winnable, where the strongest political organisation or movement in the country has set a palatable menu on the table for many white people: reconciliation, forgetting the past, and so forth. Their immediate interests as individuals are not under threat [and] they know that. Their rights in terms of culture, language and religion ... are not under threat. And the idea of a *volkstaat* is an emotional one, but many Afrikaners know it is not feasible because they haven't got a territory to fight for and defend.'[49]

A draft constitution was ready as early as September 1995, once again with contentious issues set aside for resolution at the end. When the multi-party stage of negotiations moved towards finalisation in early 1996, there were almost 70 issues outstanding, but rapidly these were reduced to a small number of deadlock issues: the constitutionality of the death penalty; the promotion of the rights of cultural and linguistic groups; the acceptability of a 'lock-out clause' in industrial relations disputes; and the nature of the 'property clause' and how it would constrain options for land reform; the process for appointing judges and the auditor-general; and the rights and prerogatives of traditional leaders. In a carefully prepared multilateral meeting at the sleepy fishing village of Arniston, away from the prying eyes of the media, substantial advances were made. Ramaphosa was able to remark that 'It defies logic. All parties are happy with their scores. It's a win-win situation for everybody.'[50]

When deadlock on some issues nevertheless persisted into May, and the deadline for completing the constitution loomed, Ramaphosa raised the temperature a little: 'We are now in a danger zone. If we take a wrong turn in the next 24 hours, we could do something we could regret.'[51] The 'channel bilateral' had already been formally re-established to break residual deadlocks on 16 April 1996. By now, Ramaphosa and Meyer were using 'the channel' routinely to resolve outstanding problems between the parties.

Kader Asmal, who was an ANC representative on TC4, which dealt with 'fundamental rights', remembers Ramaphosa's unflappable style. 'We were reporting back to Cyril after a morning session. We briefed him on our problem. We told him there had been an intractable deadlock, a serious problem, and we could not see a way to move forward. We explained it all to him.'

Cyril did not say a word. He turned his back, and seemed to be contemplating the wallpaper. 'What do we do?' Asmal pleaded anxiously. 'We don't have much time.' After another minute of silence, his back still turned to them, Ramaphosa broke his silence: 'I'll talk to Roelf.' At five minutes before two, just as the afternoon session was about to start, Cyril wandered over casually: 'It's agreed.' Asmal observes that it was easy to underestimate Ramaphosa's achievement in the negotiations because of his systematic but quiet effectiveness. 'He ran the negotiations; but not in an obtrusive way.'[52]

Ramaphosa's secret weapon was the deadlock-breaking mechanism that he had pushed through as part of the six-pack agreement. If no agreement was reached within two years, the draft would go to a referendum where only 60 per cent support would carry the day – a figure that the ANC could muster with ease. This threat hovered like a dark cloud over the recalcitrant NP negotiators. 'We didn't have to spell it out but it helped to remind them towards the end ... I kept on saying to them that if they remained intransigent on a few issues ... they were actually just giving the ANC a blank cheque to write the new constitution.' Cyril added the hint that the ANC might withdraw previous concessions before such a referendum, which 'must have terrified them'.[53]

While Ramaphosa had the NP over a barrel, he was careful not to push its negotiators into a settlement that would further divide their constituency. For FW de Klerk, the key disappointment was the 'ANC's flat refusal to include any aspect of power-sharing at the executive level in the final constitution', an aspiration that most commentators had already written off as unrealistic.[54] However, the NP did secure property and language rights concessions that would allow middle-class Afrikaners to perpetuate their affluence across generations.

After mostly technical amendments, the final text of the constitution was adopted on 8 May 1996. Constitutional Court scrutiny of the text in September identified eight respects in which the text was not consistent with the required constitutional principles. After a flurry of last-minute amendments, the constitution was resubmitted and certified. Like the interim constitution, it was a substantial accomplishment. It would have been difficult to have improved on the final outcome.

The achievement marked perhaps the high point in public affection for Ramaphosa. He was widely hailed as the man who had steered South Africa into a new era of stability. Kader Asmal, describing the process as historically unique, commented that its success 'was largely due to the role that the chairperson had played'.[55]

While Ramaphosa was steering the constitutional process towards a successful conclusion, his political hopes were undergoing dramatic reversal. The first the public knew of this was an announcement by Nelson Mandela in Cape Town, on 13 April 1996, when he told a surprised nation – and a surprised NEC – that 'Comrade Cyril Ramaphosa, secretary-general of the ANC, will be taking up a senior position in the private sector ... once the constitution-writing process is completed'.[56] His destination soon became clear. He was going to become deputy chairman of an investment holding company called New Africa Investments Limited, or Nail, whose chairman was the legendary Soweto businessman and Committee of Ten founder, Nthato Motlana.

Why was Ramaphosa making this extraordinary move? And why was there no time for the NEC or NWC to consider the matter before the decision was taken? One prominent newspaper commented that 'Cyril Ramaphosa did not jump, he was pushed'. The paper speculated that 'Ramaphosa had his eye on becoming finance minister once he discharged his duty of steering through the new constitution, and he was given indications this would become a reality. However, these then evaporated – and the job went to former trade and industry minister

Trevor Manuel. Mandela's statement that there would be no further reshuffle is said to have been the last straw.'[57]

It is highly unlikely that Ramaphosa had ambitions in this direction, however, because the position had long been earmarked for Manuel, who had been head of the ANC's department of economic planning, and was being groomed for the finance post in the department of trade and industry. In any case, the finance ministry had been reserved for NP and 'neutral' white ministers, to soothe the nerves of the financial markets.

Ramaphosa's departure was most likely the result of a combination of factors: the resurgence of the exile right, hostile and personal campaigning, and the growing pattern of intolerance among Mbeki's circle for political challengers. Pallo Jordan, a leftist whose intellectual sophistication arguably exposed the hollowness of Mbeki's pretensions, had been fired. In some eyes, he had also been a supporter of the putsch that removed Mbeki and Zuma from the negotiations.[58] The RDP office run by former Cosatu head Jay Naidoo had been closed down, and its key functions incorporated into Mbeki's own deputy presidency. In August 1996, deputy minister Bantu Holomisa was sacked and then hounded from the party, after he accused cabinet minister Stella Sigcau of taking a cut from a bribe from Sol Kerzner,[59] and Thabo Mbeki and Steve Tshwete of accepting favours from the casino magnate.[60] Other purported aspirants to leadership roles, such as Mathews Phosa and Tokyo Sexwale, were later to be swept aside and obliged to make new careers for themselves in business.

At the same time, Mandela's friends and allies fell away, and he proved unable to prevent an unhealthy consolidation of power around Mbeki and Zuma's conservative exile faction. In November 1996, Mandela began to backtrack on his support for Mbeki as his successor, observing that 'we have a number of gifted and experienced leaders. Any one of them could qualify.'[61] He expanded on his position in a leaked NEC briefing, noting, 'There has been a perception that I have already chosen my successor. There is talk that comrade Mbeki is the heir apparent but all this is not true. I have not chosen anyone to take over. The whole matter is in the hands of Congress.'[62] However, Mandela was neither decisive enough, nor any longer powerful enough, to inhibit Mbeki's rise to the ANC presidency in December 1997. He could not even prevent Mbeki hand-picking his deputy president, Jacob Zuma, although convention dictated that the position should go to a different wing of the party.[63]

On the choice of his future career, the ANC magazine *Mayibuye* reported as fact Cyril's presumably tongue-in-cheek claim that he had stumbled upon the idea of going into business while he was shopping for furniture. 'What I'm doing is born out of the belief that the economy of this country is run by black people. If you go to any company – be it a furniture manufacturer, a car manufacturer, a mine or a food manufacturer – you will find that everything is made by black people. Black workers do everything in this country ... Yet it is a few white people who control the economy.'[64] Ramaphosa's interest in business was in fact longstanding and genuine. 'I had always said that one of the important areas where transformation had to take place was the economy ... Political stability and social harmony is really dependent on the transformation that needs to take place in the economic sphere.'[65]

At the age of 43, Ramaphosa could afford to wait out a Mbeki presidency and return to fight again as a relatively young man. Just such an argument was put to Nelson Mandela by Dr Nthato Motlana, his old physician from Soweto, and the doyen of black business people in South Africa. The 70-year-old Motlana had been an ANC activist at Fort Hare University in the 1940s, qualified as a medical doctor in 1952, and went on to be secretary of the ANC's Youth League in the 1950s. He lived in the same multi-ethnic township as the Ramaphosas, Western Native Township, and he had been prominent in campaigns to prevent forced removals. Motlana was an entrepreneur whose successful businesses included a substantial clothes manufacturer and a large private medical clinic. He had been a major figure in the Committee of Ten, in which role he had known a younger and more reticent Cyril. 'He was young and quiet, very much on the side. He was not much involved in the committee in the 1970s.'[66]

By 1993, Motlana was ready to enter the big business league. He joined forces with other aspirant black magnates, such as Dikgang Moseneke, Franklin Sonn, Paul Gama and Sam Motsuenyane, and together they launched Nail. Motlana was very much not a patronage businessman. 'Don't talk to me about black economic empowerment, because I don't come from that bloody genre. I come from a time when [black enrichment] was impossible, and yet I did it. That's where I come from, not from some bloody political patronage.'[67] At the core of his executive team was an ambitious young businessman called Jonty Sandler, who recognised the importance of political connections. Confident of his own business acumen, he wanted partners who could exert influence at the highest levels in South Africa and across the continent. He began lobbying Motlana in earnest to court Ramaphosa as early as 1994. Cyril was also an attractive target because he was well connected in the mining industry, and Nail had its eye on a deal in that sector. [68]

When Cyril's options in government and the ANC were closed down, Motlana approached Mandela for a meeting. He suggested Sandler and Cyril should come along. Motlana and Sandler pointed out to Mandela the advantages for Ramaphosa of a ten-year break from politics. Cyril was ten years younger than Mbeki. He would emerge after a decade in business with a long future in politics still ahead of him. Motlana remarked to Ramaphosa that, as a wealthy man, 'You will have enough money to be incorruptible.' Ramaphosa did not find this comment remotely amusing, and asked him not to talk in that way again.[69]

Ramaphosa was not immediately fully persuaded that this was where his future lay. However, when faced with a choice between a desperate battle and a prudent withdrawal to fight another day, he had a place to go. There was one piece of Motlana's advice that Ramaphosa rejected when he joined Nail: he turned down the suggestion that he should resign from the National Executive Committee of the ANC.[70] Ramaphosa stayed on, and consolidated his position as one of the two or three most popular candidates in NEC elections to come. He was determined to keep his finger on the pulse of the ANC, and to remain immersed in its policy debates and personality clashes. But, for the foreseeable future, business was to be at the centre of his life.

PART FOUR
TREADING WATER

CHAPTER 19

CHAIRMAN CYRIL

You don't have to be a rocket scientist to be a businessman.
– Cyril Ramaphosa[1]

No one can serve two masters. He will either hate one and love the other, or be devoted to one and despise the other. You cannot serve God and mammon.
– Matthew 6. 24

As Nthato Motlana predicted, Ramaphosa has gone on to become a very rich man indeed over the past ten years. The investment company that Cyril joined, New Africa Investments Limited (Nail), was one of a number of major black business groups looking to exploit new opportunities to participate in the mainstream economy. They circled, in the early days, around Anglo American, waiting for the giant mining house to fulfil the quiet promise it had made to the ANC to participate in the new era of black economic empowerment (BEE).

Anglo's strategy was to take a large subsidiary company, Johnnies, and break it up into three constituent units, two of which would be made available for bold empowerment deals. The first was Johnnic, a holding company for industrial assets; and the second was JCI, a mining house. The two companies could not have been more different. Johnnic held substantial, but never controlling, stakes in giant South African companies such as South African Breweries (SAB) and Toyota South Africa. JCI, by contrast, was an operating company, essentially a self-contained business, and a gold-mining house to boot. By the middle of

1995, the unbundling was complete and Anglo was ready for its first sale. It decided to complete its disposal of its stake in Johnnic first.

Ramaphosa had long expressed an ambition to run a mining house. He felt confident that he had learnt enough in his years at NUM to run mines as profitably as – and he believed more humanely than – Anglo ever could. Cyril's NUM background was also one of his main attractions in the eyes of Nail chairman Nthato Motlana and chief executive Jonty Sandler. For all of them, JCI was an attractive prize. However, Anglo's determination to sell Johnnic first created a dilemma: Nail could not afford to miss out on the second prize of Johnnic, not knowing for sure that it would then win the first prize of JCI. Nail's directors decided to buy into Johnnic first – and then look to buy into JCI too.

The great Johnnic deal with which Ramaphosa's business career was launched was the first significant empowerment venture of the new era. Motlana, Sandler and Ramaphosa used all their efforts to win the contest against other empowerment groups. First, Nail muscled its way into a 'broad-based' investment vehicle called the National Empowerment Consortium (NEC), which was already in negotiations with Anglo over Johnnic. The NEC had brought together a plethora – perhaps 50 – of smaller established black businesses, trade union funds, and trusts made up of small black investors.

When Nail joined the NEC, it had four times as much capital available for investment as the rest of the consortium, and it took effective control of the Johnnic bid. Relationships between different investors continued to be fractious. NEC members had been keen to develop Johnnic's industrial interests, especially SAB and Premier Foods, whereas Motlana and Sandler were more interested in its holdings in media and communications. Ramaphosa's first task was to use his negotiating skills to keep the consortium together.

Johnnic looked like a wonderful prize. It had a total market capitalisation of R8.5 billion, making it a very substantial company.[2] Anglo American was avowedly keen to cement its place in the new order, and the Johnnic deal was its first opportunity to demonstrate its commitment to 'voluntary empowerment'. All these factors promised that Anglo would try its hardest to make the deal a rewarding one for investors. It was widely celebrated that Anglo was selling Johnnic at just R50 per share, which represented a 6 per cent discount on the market price. The NEC, with Nail as dominant party, was ultimately victorious, buying 20 per cent of Johnnic initially. It rapidly increased its stake to more than 34 per cent. Ramaphosa – who it should be remembered had no real money of his own to invest in the company – became Johnnic's non-executive chairman, a capacity that left him responsible for broad strategic direction, the management of the board, and the selection and succession planning of senior executives. At a Carlton Centre dinner staged to celebrate the sale, Anglo American executive director Michael Spicer toasted Ramaphosa's success: 'I think we can call you Chairman Cyril now, rather than Comrade Cyril.'[3]

A first disappointment for Ramaphosa quickly followed. Now that it had sold a substantial stake in Johnnic, Anglo moved ahead with the sale of its shareholding in the mining house JCI. Suddenly it became clear that Nail's path to a second major deal was obstructed by another politically well-connected empowerment group, Capital Alliance Holdings (CAH), chaired by former Robben Islander Mzi Khumalo. NUM's own Mineworkers Investment Company was ironically a major investor in this holding company. Khumalo had assembled a powerful consortium around CAH, which he called Africa Mining Group (AMG).

The Anglo executive committee indicated that it would decide between competing bids on the basis of price. Khumalo's consortium was less encumbered with debt than Nail, and willing to pay 50 cents more per share for JCI. Anglo's own stated preference was to empower a broad section of the black community, rather than just a single consortium, so it was happy to decline Nail's offer on grounds of price. It sold its 35 per cent of the gold-mining house to Khumalo in February 1997. It also promised AMG first refusal on its remaining 13 per cent stake.

Ramaphosa was devastated. 'We at Nail have decided to pursue an industrial strategy,' he commented. 'I am disappointed, but we were beaten fair and square on price. That's business.' The reality was that Mzi Khumalo had walked away with a controlling stake in a mining house, realising precisely the ambition that Ramaphosa had long harboured. Cyril, by contrast, was left at the helm of a holding company with a very uncertain trajectory.[4]

Johnnic was a product of Anglo American's response to the business conditions of late apartheid. In the era of financial sanctions it had been rational for successful companies to expand by means of domestic acquisition. In consequence, Johnnic was not a focused business, but rather a holding investment trust conglomerate containing a wide array of asset types and classes. It operated in a broad range of unrelated sectors. It owned 14 per cent of the massive national monopoly brewer, South African Breweries (SAB); 27 per cent of Premier Foods; 26 per cent of Toyota South Africa; and 43 per cent of Omni Media, which in its turn owned between a quarter and a half of assets such as retailer CNA Gallo, publisher Caxton, broadcaster M-Net, and M-Cell. Omni also held 91 per cent of Times Media Limited, of which Ramaphosa was also soon to become chairman.

Confronted with this spread of largely unrelated assets, Ramaphosa's executive team set about building some business logic to the company's holdings. Nail's own communications holdings, in particular, were major complicating factors queering Johnnic's strategic pitch. At the same time, the very large number of diverse investors who made up the NEC possessed diverse and irreconcilable objectives. The deal was debt-financed using hopelessly inappropriate funding structures. Putative black shareholders were in fact merely 'borrowing' the shares of institutional investors, and sharing with them only the growth in their value.[5] At the end of the funding period, black investors would be able to buy shares with their portion of any 'upside', which was usually 20 or 30 per cent of share price growth. For most investors, a strategy of 'unbundling' the company, eliminating assets not central to the business and so unlocking value for the shareholders, was always their priority.

Within this tight set of constraints, Ramaphosa's team followed a coherent and quite orthodox strategy. There was no hope of Johnnic ever exercising control over companies such as SAB, Premier and Toyota South Africa, and these stakes were rapidly sold off. The plan was to remake the company around its faster-growing sectors and those in which it might be possible to build controlling stakes. Funds released by asset sales – where these were not returned to thirsty investors – were concentrated in the media, telecommunications and entertainment sectors in which Johnnic's new bosses believed it had its greatest potential. There was an element of fashion in this decision: the idea of a convergence between telecommunications and media businesses was at that time the flavour of the month in European and American investment circles.

By the turn of the new century, Johnnic had become somehow less grand, comprising a telecoms company, a set of media assets, and a holding company for assorted gambling and hotel interests. By 2003, the company had even unbundled its MTN shares, in most investors' eyes the most potentially exciting of the company's assets. The telecommunications strategy fashioned by Johnnic had conferred a shine upon MTN. However, institutional shareholders were determined to remove the inherent discount that resulted from the pyramid holding structure of the company.

Critics complained that while Johnnic's management professed to recognise the cell-phone company's promise, they never took decisive action to buy a controlling stake. When the unbundling came, moreover, it left a sour taste in many mouths because it created wealth for only some of the company's shareholders.

The problem, one commentator has observed with the benefit of hindsight, was that 'each successive theoretical business strategy seemed to depend on selling or distributing yet another limb, until there were no legs to carry the company forward … Johnnic never managed to convince the market it could win without dismembering itself.'[6] Far from being strengthened by these consecutive waves of asset disposals, the company seemed to veer from one near-crisis to another.

In 2005, it quite inadvertently lost control over the media group Johncom, which, as the part-owner of the *Sunday Times* and *Business Day*, was the political jewel in the Johnnic crown. The company was perhaps unprepared for this turn of events. The Johannesburg Stock Exchange pressured Johnnic to collapse the pyramid structure between the two companies, and so to unlock the discount at which Johnnic shares traded. It had to unbundle its whole 62.5 per cent stake in one go. The consequent loss of black ownership of the *Sunday Times*, in particular, was a major symbolic blow to enthusiasts for empowerment.[7] Johncom, now also the owner of the *Sowetan*, still has no substantial black shareholder today.

Johnnic, in which such high hopes had been invested, was now reduced to a casino and hotels group – and things were about to get spectacularly worse. The company became embroiled in a struggle over its single most promising asset, its stake in Tsogo Investment Holdings (TIH) which was the majority shareholder of the money-spinning casino operation Tsogo Sun. Johnnic was pursuing a majority stake in TIH so that it could secure control of Johannesburg's Montecasino, Durban's Suncoast, East London's Hemingway's, Witbank's The Ridge and Nelspruit's Emnotweni – all expressions of the vulgar, if energetic, materialism of early 21st-century South Africa.

Unfortunately for Johnnic, another company, Hosken Consolidated Investments (HCI), also had a significant stake in TIH through three of its subsidiaries, and it too was determined to wrest control. The contest became front-page news because HCI was run by two former trade unionists: one-time textile union head Johnny Copelyn and Cyril's former NUM comrade Marcel Golding. These two men had abandoned careers as members of parliament in 1999, in order to run the investment companies of trade unions Saccawu and the NUM, which later became HCI.

HCI was well known as the owner of South Africa's only free-to-air commercial television station, e.tv, which Golding and Copelyn had rather spectacularly turned around. In the process, the two men developed formidable reputations as analytic and tough businessmen. Copelyn, in particular, was picked out by established business leaders as an exceptional and hard-nosed rising star. He was to create great hilarity when he accused Christine Ramon, Johnnic's chief executive officer, of having an 'aggressive style'.[8]

As the battle for Tsogo unfolded between HCI and Johnnic, HCI proved to have a decisive advantage. It was itself a major shareholder in Johnnic, holding more than 30 per cent of its competitor. As a union investment vehicle, HCI was a 'black' investor and a key element in Johnnic's black empowerment profile. Copelyn and Golding realised they could avoid a frontal battle for TIH. Instead they could acquire a controlling stake in Johnnic itself, and in that way indirectly secure control of Tsogo, their real quarry.

In pursuit of this strategy, Copelyn sought election to the Johnnic board in 2005, on the basis of HCI's substantial shareholding in the company. Ramaphosa's reaction was stony. In a letter to Johnnic shareholders in August 2005 advising them to rebut Copelyn's advances, he complained that 'HCI has embarked on an unsolicited and hostile offer to the shareholders of Johnnic in order to acquire Johnnic's assets'.

Ramaphosa's position had a good deal of merit: for Copelyn and other HCI directors to sit on the Johnnic board might be construed as creating a conflict of interest. After all, both of the companies were pursuing the same quarry in Tsogo, and joint HCI–Johnnic directors might be perceived to be selling out Johnnic to the benefit of HCI. Ramaphosa's position was that the interests of Johnnic's investors could not simply be ignored.

Johnnic's shareholders mostly fell into line behind chairman Cyril, and they rebutted Copelyn's overtures. Television cameras at the Johnnic shareholders' meeting captured Marcel Golding and Johnny Copelyn jumping out of their seats, and then holding their heads in their hands when the rebuff by shareholders was announced. So much interest had been stirred up by this battle that the tussle was a top news story on all television channels – including Golding's own e.tv.

Behind the scenes, however, questions were being asked whether this battle was necessary or desirable, given that HCI was not really interested in acquiring control of Johnnic at all. Many disinterested observers believed that it was highly predictable that HCI would prevail in the end in its pursuit of control of Tsogo. It had a very clear battle plan and the backing of Investec, a major investment bank. It was also believed to be offering Johnnic a very attractive deal – in the words of one businessman who was involved, it was almost a 'no-brainer'. HCI was keen to secure 51 per cent of Tsogo Sun for purposes of accounting and voting control. However, in order to avoid a hostile encounter with Johnnic, Copelyn was even believed to be happy for Cyril to become chairman of Tsogo Sun.

Speculation about the reasons for Ramaphosa's alleged intransigence turned to personal issues. 'He was not willing', one insider believes, 'to make a pitch to Marcel … Cyril couldn't cut a deal with someone he saw as his junior or his subordinate … He didn't even want to chat – he wouldn't even pick up the phone. I tell you, if Marcel was to become head of the PIC [Public Investment Commissioners] Cyril wouldn't be able to pitch to him for the same reason.'[9] Others speculated that the real problem lay with Copelyn, whose aggressive approach conflicted with Ramaphosa's determination to protect the interests of Johnnic's shareholders.

Whatever Ramaphosa's motivations, once it was clear that he would not do a deal on Tsogo, Copelyn and Golding moved very rapidly to secure control of Johnnic. They employed a range of robust and admirable tactics to overcome Johnnic, the most elegant if underhand of which was engineering a technical deal that robbed Johnnic of its empowerment status. The 'black' company HCI technically sold its shares in Johnnic to its own white directors, in this way destroying Johnnic's black empowerment status with the Mpumalanga Gaming Board.

By January 2006, the battle was over. HCI had control of Johnnic, and Copelyn had installed himself as chairman. Eight months later Golding took his place and Copelyn took up executive control as CEO. Ramaphosa and three of his non-executive directors, together with company CEO Christine Ramon, resigned. Commentators remarked that Copelyn and Golding had qualities that marked them out as true business animals: the ability to cut a favourable deal, and the cut-throat instinct to dispatch a rival.

The demise of Johnnic has come to represent the disappointed hopes of the first era of black economic empowerment. The company once promised to be at the vanguard of a new age of black business expansion, in which the commanding heights of the economy would come under the influence of black capital. In the end, its demise occurred during a scramble for the control of money-spinning casinos.

Over the years that Cyril was at the helm, many of Johnnic's long-term investors made a reasonable return. Nevertheless, the story of the company was mostly one of disappointed hopes. Ramaphosa tried to make light of his eviction from Johnnic after a decade at the helm. 'Frankly speaking, I didn't have skin in the game,' he shrugged, alluding to the fact that his own money was not invested in Johnnic. 'I just happened to be there when the skirmishes took place.'[10]

The fact that Ramaphosa did not 'have skin in the game' also represented a wasted personal opportunity. Johnnic could have been the instrument of Ramaphosa's own rise, its assets making possible deals to benefit both Johnnic shareholders and Cyril personally. Ramaphosa's former CEO at Shanduka, Ndoda Madalane, believes Cyril has a blind spot when it comes to seizing the opportunity to create personal wealth. 'Things were pitched to him from my own bank AMB [African Merchant Bank], but Cyril would have had to sell them to his board. He was very sensitive about pushing something on to the agenda that might benefit him personally. This made it impossible for him to use Johnnic as his own vehicle.'[11]

During the better days of the company, Ramaphosa's involvement in Johnnic allowed him, as chairman of Times Media Limited (TML), a Johnnic-controlled company, to become one of South Africa's new generation of press barons.[12] The print media had been dominated under apartheid by Afrikaans-medium apologists for the National Party, Nasionale Pers and Perskor, and by Anglo American's English-language groups, TML and Argus. The NP was able to subsidise its media supporters through the award of state printing contracts. The liberal press, meanwhile, was protected by Harry Oppenheimer from NP-aligned predators.

As part of its overall strategy of ostentatious de-politicisation, Anglo began to seek buyers for Argus and TML in the early 1990s. In March 1993, immediately before the transitional election, it sold the Argus Group to Tony O'Reilly, Irish owner of the Independent newspaper group, and today a close confidant of President Thabo Mbeki (on whose International Investment Council he sits). O'Reilly rapidly sold off the group's *Sowetan* newspaper to Nthato Motlana at Nail, Mandela's doctor, who therefore became the first black media baron of the new era.

Anglo's talks with Pearsons – UK-based owner of the *Financial Times* and *The Economist* – dragged on into the new dispensation without reaching a clear conclusion. Since TML was part of the Johnnic stable, Anglo decided to dispose of these politically sensitive assets as part of the overall Johnnic transaction. When it acquired its stake in Johnnic, the National Empowerment Consortium took control of almost 20 per cent of the country's newspaper market. Ramaphosa became chairman not just of Johnnic but also of TML.

In part because of their specialised character, two of TML's smaller but most important publications, *Business Day* and *Financial Mail*, trading as BDFM, were 50 per cent acquired by Pearsons, with 50 per cent owned by the National Empowerment Consortium and Johnnic. Pearsons expressed its unwillingness to allow politically unpopular editors to be 'executed' by TML. One part of the uneasy relationship that emerged revolved around concerns about editorial independence. Perhaps as a result of racial stereotyping, the threat posed by O'Reilly was largely ignored while black investors were carefully scrutinised for signs of political interference in editorial decisions.

Ramaphosa was initially known as a very hands-off chairman by BDFM editors, never involving himself in the editorial policy of the papers and magazines in the Johnnic stable. Indeed, his prominence as a black chairman conferred upon him responsibility without much power. He was held responsible for the editorial positions of TML publications despite his careful efforts not to meddle with them. In the most remarkable example of this problem, Zimbabwean president Robert Mugabe took Ramaphosa to task with his usual gusto after taking exception to analyses in *Business Day* and *Financial Mail* of the deteriorating economic situation north of the Limpopo.

'There are some blacks who have acquired these media conglomerates. It appears they have joined these whites in attacking Zimbabwe. Well, they are black white men and they are really putting on the master's cap.' Precisely mirroring a smear campaign against Ramaphosa within the ANC itself, Mugabe continued: 'In some cases, you will discover that the wealth they say they have, they have acquired through some bosses or through some conditional lending from some multi-national benefiting them.' In a remark that demonstrated how vicious and unstable he had already become, he described Ramaphosa as 'a white man in a black man's skin'.[13]

On the same day that Mugabe launched his attack, Ramaphosa was also on the front pages of Johnnic's own newspapers as a result of his seemingly acrimonious departure from Nail. Ramaphosa had joined Nail, in the first instance, to help close the deal with Johnnic, a transaction that was already well advanced. It had always been difficult 'batting' for the two closely interrelated companies at the same time, given the divergent interests of their distinct shareholder bases. Nail's other directors may have been pushing for a merger between the two groups, a move Ramaphosa would probably have resisted at the behest of the union-based component of the National Empowerment Consortium, Johnnic's key shareholder.[14]

However, his departure was surrounded by darker rumours. Some commentators argued that Ramaphosa had been stretched too thin by his multiple directorships, which at that time included Anglo American, South African Breweries, Times Media Limited and First National Bank. The Sunday newspapers were also full of speculation that he had been evicted forcibly by board members purportedly aligned with Thabo Mbeki, in particular Dikgang Moseneke and Zwelakhe Sisulu.[15] Indeed, the deputy president's office felt obliged to issue a denial, commenting that 'The Deputy President has no personal or financial interest in the affairs of any private company, including Nail, to determine the future of its directors – nor does the Deputy President have any interest in the personal fortunes of Mr Cyril Ramaphosa ... The decision by Mr Ramaphosa to quit his post is an internal matter between Nail directors and Mr Ramaphosa and they have nothing to do with the Deputy President.'[16] Such denials, of course, coming from Mbeki's spokesman, only served to heighten speculation.

It was later also observed that Ramaphosa left Nail just before controversy exploded around R130 million in African Merchant Bank options, with which Nail chairman Nthato Motlana and executive director Jonty Sandler proposed to reward themselves for their sterling efforts at the company – a scandal that soon brought about their own departures. Whatever the precise combination of factors that precipitated Ramaphosa's resignation, many observers of Nail's stubborn and strong-headed executive directorship were not surprised by the eventual outcome: Motlana, Sandler, Moseneke and Ramaphosa simply represented 'too many bulls in the kraal'.[17]

It was not long after these controversies were splashed across the front pages that Ramaphosa infringed the principle of editorial independence. Immediately before the 1999 national elections, the *Financial Mail* surprisingly trumpeted on its front page its endorsement of the electoral ambitions of the United Democratic Movement (UDM), a curious party jointly led by Bantu Holomisa and Roelf Meyer. Peter Bruce, then editor of the *Financial Mail*, did not intend the endorsement of the party to be taken entirely seriously. The UDM fancifully brought together Roelf Meyer's leftist refugees from the NP with Bantu Holomisa's personal following in the Eastern Cape. 'It was a kind of jolly jape,' explains Bruce, 'designed to shake things up a little.'[18]

Somewhere, however, this endorsement touched a nerve. Holomisa had been evicted from the ANC for making what were widely believed to be well-grounded accusations of corruption and improper conduct against government ministers and officials. He had a powerful constituency in the Eastern Cape heartland of the party. Meyer, for his part, had over-reached himself in trying to topple FW de Klerk from the NP leadership, and he was more or less out in the cold. For those who wrongly suspected that Ramaphosa wielded influence over his editors, it might have appeared that he was deliberately supporting Mbeki's antagonist and his old negotiating partner by giving them the *Financial Mail*'s endorsement.

Whatever his reasoning, Ramaphosa's reaction was fierce and immediate. 'Cyril called me up,' remembers Bruce. 'His voice was chilling. I have never, ever, been spoken to in that way before – and never [have been] since. He made, I would say, a strong demand for a right to reply.' Bruce capitulated to Ramaphosa's demand, and allowed him to write a response – something of a tirade – in the next issue of the magazine. Bruce, he claimed, had given his own views primacy, and had 'commandeered' the magazine for his own ends. 'The call for a vote for any specific political party seriously compromises the editorial independence and credibility of the *Financial Mail* [and] tarnishes its record of independence, fairness and unbiased coverage.'

Ramaphosa was then very roundly and sanctimoniously condemned, in his turn, in particular in the news media that Johnnic did not own. The *Mail & Guardian* observed that 'in many parts of the world rich men who are anxious to enjoy the fruits of their money buy newspapers in the belief that this makes their voice more powerful than when exercised over the dinner table or in the boardroom … The effect of Ramaphosa's intervention at the *Financial Mail* is to place his fine stable of publications – including *Business Day* and the *Sunday Times* – in an extremely invidious position.'[19]

Bruce recently recalled that 'The ensuing uproar was both colourful, if you were out there reading it, and terrifying for me. I aged (or perhaps matured) ten years in a month.'[20] Looking back, however, he doubts that Ramaphosa's heart was in the 'chilling' call to his office on that day, or in the sentiments he expressed in his published reply. 'I think he was under pressure from his investors.'[21] Bruce, moreover, was firmly backed by BDFM's co-owner, Pearsons, and the general consensus in the industry against editorial meddling was bolstered. When Johnnic's media interests were ultimately unbundled, they adopted Pearsons' own protocols, which explicitly entrenched editorial independence from the board.[22]

Almost immediately after Ramaphosa's departure from Nail, he was obliged to become operationally involved in Molope Group, a company of which he had been non-executive chairman since 1996. Molope was a food and beverage provider with which Cyril had long been familiar because it was a major player in the mine catering industry. It was a relatively small business, its market capitalisation around R1.2 billion in 1999. In May 1999, Ramaphosa was appointed executive chairman and chief executive of the company.

Behind the fanfare about Ramaphosa's enthusiasm for an operational role, the truth was that the company was in trouble. Indeed, Molope almost foundered under Ramaphosa's non-executive chairmanship, although the causes of its troubles remain shrouded in legal and accounting confusion. What is clear is that chief executive Anthony Bock and non-executive director Richard Grantham soon left the company under a cloud, after it became clear that Molope had expensively acquired Grantham's own food company. The crisis was sufficiently serious for Cyril to step in as chief executive primarily to secure a rescue plan.

Some market analysts once again whispered that Ramaphosa had been overstretched, and this had left him incapable of properly overseeing the management board. Less forgiving critics claimed that the Molope débâcle was indicative of Cyril's inattention to detail. According to someone who has worked for him, it also exemplified his tendency to delay. 'He does not want to deal directly with issues that arise, he drags things out.'[23] Financial journalist Jabulani Sikhakhane more charitably observes that 'Cyril was out to do the right things, but he was also trying to do too many things. He was just too spread out. It must be remembered that he was inexperienced, and perhaps he placed too much trust in his CEO. Or perhaps the directors of the company simply moved in different circles and networks to him.'[24]

Despite his heavy business commitments, Ramaphosa's attention never drifted very far from the political world he had claimed to put behind him. At the ANC's 1997 conference, he effortlessly came in first in the NEC election, which is viewed as a 'beauty contest' – at least by those ANC leaders who do well in it. Despite the authority this gave him, he maintained a studious silence about the new Mbeki government's various travails. At the end of August 2000, however, the Sunday newspapers were deliberately leaked rumours of a supposed plot, instigated by 'unnamed British and American business persons' dissatisfied with South African policy over AIDS and Zimbabwe, to oust Thabo Mbeki and replace him with Ramaphosa. It was alleged that intelligence minister Joe Nhlanhla had taken it upon himself, after informing Mbeki's office, to investigate the matter further. Penuell Maduna, who was at that time acting intelligence minister – Nhlanhla was seriously ill – denied that any such investigation was taking place.[25]

Ramaphosa immediately described the allegations as 'ludicrous' and 'insane'. He trotted out the correct line, commenting that such stories about plots 'are aimed at destabilizing the ANC and undermining the unity of its membership and leadership ... I am fully in support of the government, and our president, who is my leader.'[26] Suspicions were soon confirmed that the alleged plot was nothing more than a crude disinformation campaign ahead of the 2002 ANC conference, aimed to undermine leaders perceived to be Mbeki's rivals. In April 2001, safety and security minister Steve Tshwete announced to an astonished nation that Ramaphosa, former Gauteng premier Tokyo Sexwale, and former Mpumalanga premier Mathews Phosa were being investigated for spreading 'disinformation' that might endanger the life of the President. This second implausible plot was related to already widespread rumours that Mbeki had been involved in the assassination of his then rival, Chris Hani, in 1993.

In a bizarre television interview, Mbeki himself linked the supposed conspiracy to the forthcoming December 2002 ANC conference. 'Some people want to be President of South Africa,' he commented. 'That's fine. The matter that is arising is the manner in which people pursue their ambitions. If there is any talk of plotting, those who have information must come out openly and say this is what they know about the plotting, who is involved, and so on.' He went on: 'It's a conspiratorial thing. I know you have business people who say we will set up a fund to promote our particular candidate and we will then try to influence particular journalists.'[27]

Mbeki's manner of conducting politics through media leaks and innuendo inevitably took its toll in a coarsening of national political debate and a widespread lack of trust. Today, political attacks and accusations, such as those that have been levelled against former deputy president Jacob Zuma, are greeted by political activists with immediate and profound suspicion, in part because of a long history of deliberate deceit.

Since 2000 Ramaphosa has conducted his personal business dealings through his investment vehicle, Millennium Consolidated Investments (MCI), later renamed Shanduka (Venda for 'change'). Thirty per cent of Shanduka is owned by the Ramaphosa family, 25 per cent by management and staff, 15 per cent by associates such as James Motlatsi and a series of community trusts, and the remaining 30 per cent by Investec and Standard Bank.

Shanduka has divisions dealing in resources, property, energy and financial services. The company does very little government business, Ramaphosa always aware that there was little likelihood of success in pursuing public sector contracts. In terms of value, the company is overwhelmingly a financial services investor. Shanduka acquired 16 per cent of Alexander Forbes in 2003, 1.2 per cent of Standard Bank in 2004, and 1.5 per cent of Liberty Life in 2005. It also holds 2.25 per cent of the giant Bidvest distribution group. Such small holdings in very large companies do not allow control, or even much influence, over the business concerned. The primary purpose of such investments is to take advantage of the empowerment discounts with which they are bought.

BEE deals of this kind have led to accusations that beneficiaries are 'fat cats', securing benefits without adding value to the company concerned. Ramaphosa was criticised for the Standard Bank deal, in particular, because he was perceived to be making overtures to two banking groups – Standard Bank and the First Rand group – at the same time. Ramaphosa had joined First Rand at the start of 2001 (Mac Maharaj was then also on the board) and resigned in July 2004 while the banking group was preparing a major BEE transaction. It would appear that Ramaphosa had been in negotiations about BEE with First Rand and Standard Bank at the same time. Although there was no question of improper behaviour, some commentators snidely, but conceivably accurately, remarked that Ramaphosa seemed ready to go wherever the returns were fatter.

Ultimately he joined Saki Macozoma's giant Standard Bank empowerment deal. Ramaphosa argued that the deal should be a 50:50

split between the two men, and Macozoma had to write to Cyril explaining that he was now a veteran on the Standard Bank board and that the deal was primarily his.[28] Ramaphosa took this in reasonably good grace, and accepted 40 per cent to Macozoma's 60.[29] The sums of money involved were substantial, and Shanduka's 1.2 per cent stake in the bank was for many years its biggest asset, only recently surpassed by the group's resources businesses. While such calculations are almost meaningless in the absence of information about the debt-financing behind them, the value of the Standard Bank shares is certainly in excess of a billion rands.

In its investments, in resources, paper and packaging, property and now energy, Ramaphosa views Shanduka as a 'hands-on' investor. One analyst observes of Shanduka that 'Close one eye and you could see it as cautious and value-accretive: first it dips a toe in with a minority investment, then explores how it can help the business grow ... Close the other eye and it looks mercenary: Shanduka gets in cheap, gets a look at the books and the talent, finds managers loyal to itself, then takes over the company... Ramaphosa seems to genuinely have a foot on either side of the line.'[30]

It is difficult to assess the wealth Ramaphosa holds through Shanduka. The company does not disclose financial information, although it acknowledges that its investments have totalled more than R5 billion. Only half a dozen of the more than 20 companies in which Shanduka invests are listed entities. Moreover, the complex financing structuring behind deals makes it impossible to guess how much wealth Ramaphosa will ultimately be able to realise from his holdings. Some would estimate his fortune at R500 million and others might guess double that.

Despite his substantial wealth, many people who have closely observed Ramaphosa's business dealings believe that he is not a natural or enthusiastic businessman. Nthato Motlana, the man who brought him into Nail in 1996, is critical of his decision to remain a member of the ANC's NEC. Motlana contrasts Ramaphosa's performance with Patrice Motsepe, the brother of Cyril's current wife Tshepo, who is perhaps the most successful of the current generation of empowerment pioneers.

'He has no connections with the ANC. His life is business. He went to the mining houses and told them he wanted to work their redundant mines. Then he went out and talked to the engineers and the workers, face to face, and he explained to them that they could all make money together ... That is a real businessman.'[31]

Ramaphosa's experiences at Johnnic and Molope, in particular, ensure that for him the jury is still out when it comes to his achievements in business. His consensus-building style sometimes seems to prevent him from taking the unequivocal decisions that business success demands. He lacks an appetite for the fine detail that can make or break a deal or a company. His reticence about selling deals that benefit him personally, and his inability to pitch to subordinates, limit his range and dynamism as an entrepreneur.

Ramaphosa's depressing days at Johnnic and Molope are, however, only part of a wider story. Responsibility for Johnnic's sad decline was shared with the boards of directors that oversaw it and the chief executives who ran it. Many of the problems confronting Johnnic, moreover, were generic. Nail, for example, followed a similar depressing trajectory, and for many of the same reasons. Preoccupied with a lack of investor confidence, Motlana and Sandler first disposed of 'non-core' assets such as Nail's media businesses, and later cut the company's asset base in half by unbundling African Bank Investments and African Merchant Bank Holdings. Their rationale was to focus on insurance company Metropolitan Life, in which they held a controlling stake. In the end, their successors disposed of Metropolitan Life too.

Shanduka has been a very successful company, making Cyril and many of those associated with him rich beyond imagining. Ndoda Madalane, Ramaphosa's CEO at Shanduka for seven years, remembers that 'Cyril was excited and enthusiastic in the early stages ... He had wider ambitions, particularly to see a pan-African business grow ... He built a stronger team at Shanduka than comparable companies, he had very wide-ranging relationships, and he was in many respects a good person to work for. Most of us trusted him, and he supported members of the team in building the business.'[32]

Ramaphosa has also enjoyed successes as a non-executive chairman, most notably with MTN, the cellphone company that has become a black empowerment champion and a pioneer of South African business in Africa. It was under Ramaphosa's chairmanship that MTN boldly and brilliantly expanded into Nigeria, and then spread out across much of Africa and the Middle East.

Yet, even here, analysts are inclined to give little credit to Ramaphosa, perhaps because of his reticence about celebrating his own achievements publicly. The grand vision and boldness of MTN are mostly attributed to its former CEO. Its current successes are ascribed to the dynamic current CEO. 'Phuthuma Nhleko', one businessman observes, 'uses Cyril well. Ramaphosa knows how to talk to an Obasanjo, or to meet with the other politicians, so Nhleko needs a heavy hitter like Cyril. But Cyril is not involved in the detail of the business.'[33]

Ramaphosa combines a superficially consensual approach to decision-making with a determination to get his own way. His former CEO Ndoda Madalane describes the problem in this way: 'I came from an investment banking background. I was used to clearly articulated positions from my head of division. The person running the division must make the call – it has to be clear who has taken a decision, and why it has been taken … But Cyril prefers discussion to decision. He likes to shape the evolution of a collective decision, and he just refuses to take a clear decision himself. There are many people who do not like the feeling of being coaxed by Cyril into saying they agree with him.'[34]

Ramaphosa has had stormy relationships with some of the strong-willed CEOs who have worked with him. Nthato Motlana observes that Jonty Sandler was initially keen for Cyril to be on board at Nail, but the two were quickly at loggerheads when they had to take decisions together. Echoing Motlatsi's recollection of Ramaphosa at NUM, Madalane observes that 'Cyril really is stubborn. At some point logic stops, and he becomes stubborn. This is ok in Shanduka, but it is a problem when working with others … No, it is a problem even in his own company.'

For Madalane, Ramaphosa is not a businessman but a politician. 'He is a lot like Saki [Macozoma]. When he was at Transnet, Saki said to Coleman Andrews, "You fix the business side of things and I will deal with the politics."'[35] Michael Spicer, former Anglo American executive director and political strategist, concurs: 'Cyril's first love is politics. He is not terribly interested in business … For him it is just a convenient way-station. It is just a vehicle for the necessary accumulation of wealth.'[36]

CHAPTER 20

PHILOSOPHER AND STATESMAN

The man to lead South Africa in the long run.
– Margaret Thatcher[1]

Rather than focusing on amassing a great fortune, Ramaphosa has devoted much of his time over the past decade to reflection on the character of post-apartheid business. His former CEO at Shanduka despaired at his unwillingness to focus on making money. 'If you went through Cyril's diary, treating him as a real businessman, you could cancel 70 per cent of his meetings.'[2] Much of his more philosophical activity has nevertheless been at the intersection between business and politics, where he has been able to apply his experience to the resolution of intractable policy problems.

He has spent close to a decade embroiled in debates over 'black economic empowerment' (BEE), the controversial attempt to increase ownership, management and control of South African businesses by black citizens.[3] Today's BEE policy is 'broad-based' in response to widespread criticism of the elite enrichment that purportedly marked its first phases. It seeks to support skills and small business development, to make finance more readily accessible to black entrepreneurs, and to use 'preferential procurement' by the state and its agencies to spread empowerment across the private economy.

Ramaphosa has been an unrelenting champion of BEE. In an analogy with the political deal-making of transition, he has described it as 'another revolution ... it is not grab and run – it is taking place in as orderly a way as our political transformation ... The ethos and culture of the negotiated deals that have a transformative component are remarkable'.[4] Post-1994 BEE, however, has been very controversial, even for those who strongly support its underlying objectives. The President's brother, Moeletsi Mbeki, famously described BEE as 'buying' black members into the 'consumer-exploitative' club of established white South African business.[5] A former head of the South African Chamber of Business similarly summarised BEE as 'characterized in the main by crony capitalism, fronting, enrichment and debt-burdened deals'.[6]

The acrimonious economic transition of BEE, like the political transition before it, can be divided into two periods: before Cyril and after Cyril. Before Ramaphosa became involved in BEE policy, it went through fits and starts. It had evolved after 1994 more or less as a direct continuation of post-1976 National Party initiatives to build a black middle class, until Thabo Mbeki superimposed his own project of creating a patriotic bourgeoisie upon it. This convoluted history of empowerment cannot be understood in isolation from the systematic and legalised black disempowerment that preceded it.

After the NP's 1948 election victory, the exploitation of black South Africans began to depart dramatically from conventional imperial suppression of native advance. While other colonies moved towards independence, the NP introduced new laws to deepen blacks' disempowerment. The Native Laws Amendment Act of 1952 intensified black exclusion from urban areas,[7] the 1953 Bantu Education Act limited black education to a level deemed fit for menial work and manual labour,[8] and the 1959 Extension of University Education Act excluded black students from white campuses and confined them to the 'bush colleges'.[9]

Alongside this pattern of legislated exclusion from economic opportunity, government channelled ambitious blacks into the professional, business and artisan classes of the homelands. Black people could train as artisans in the building trade, for example, so long as they were employed in skilled work only in a black-designated area. The Bantu Investment Corporation Act[10] facilitated African financial, commercial and industrial projects – again in areas designated black.[11]

In the aftermath of 1976, government and business alike threw themselves more energetically into the project of creating a black middle class. Government recapitalised the Bantu Investment Corporation and increased homeland development subsidies in a new and more explicit empowerment policy. While anti-capitalist sentiment remained strong across the country in this period, these programmes – together with business initiatives such as the Urban Foundation – laid the ground for a later reconciliation of political freedom with a market economy.[12]

The exile liberation movement was meanwhile torn between different perspectives and priorities for the post-liberation economy. Ultimately it was unable to resolve upon a coherent policy for black economic re-empowerment. Exile leaders such as SACP general secretary Joe Slovo had passed enough time in the Eastern bloc to be sceptical about the sustainability of actually existing socialism.[13] Senior exiles had experienced the triumph of social democracy and the mixed economy in their travels across Western Europe and Scandinavia.

There remained a formal commitment to nationalisation of the commanding heights of the economy, which were understood to comprise the mines, heavy industries, and financial institutions. This aspiration to public ownership was almost entirely undeveloped in policy terms, however, and there were almost no attempts to map out the practical and legislative requirements for such a programme to become a reality. As Gavin Relly was to discover on his trip to Lusaka in 1985, even before the collapse of the Soviet model, ANC nationalisation was more or less entirely a matter of rhetoric.

In a more robust strand of thinking, communists were presciently preoccupied with the danger of parasitic nationalist elites. SACP concerns stemmed from the experiences of post-colonial liberation movements elsewhere, which had fallen victim to a syndrome of parasitic dependency on state resources.[14] The ANC's 1969 *Strategy and Tactics* document insisted that 'our nationalism must not be confused with the classical drive by an elitist group among the oppressed people to gain ascendancy so that they can replace the oppressor in the exploitation of the masses'.[15] Nelson Mandela echoed this hope three decades later when he promised South Africa would never see 'the formation of predatory elites that thrive on the basis of looting of national wealth and the entrenchment of corruption'.[16]

Before the political transition really got under way, ANC economic policy debate was thrown further into turmoil by changed international conditions. The collapse of the Soviet Union, and the decisive discrediting of its economic model, created a crisis of intellectual confidence across the socialist world. Meanwhile, the 'new right' policy revolutions of

Reagan's America and Thatcher's Britain were accompanied by a rediscovery of classical and 'Austrian school' economic thought. A so-called 'Washington consensus' favouring economic liberalisation, privatisation, reduced barriers to trade, a 'rolling back of the state' and fiscal conservatism achieved ascendancy just as the endgame of apartheid was decisively under way.

Established business prepared the ground for compromise through its assiduous cultivation of domestic and exile struggle constituencies. Business was convinced that sustainable growth in the 1990s would depend on rapid re-entry to international capital markets, enhanced competitiveness, and the removal of tariff walls and sanctions. It was happy in principle to trade the racial monopoly of ownership for liberal economic conditions. Economist Stephen Gelb has described the result as an 'implicit bargain' between the ANC and big business, which immediately preceded the political transition.[17] According to this bargain, the liberation movement committed itself to orthodox fiscal policy, macroeconomic stability and the dismantling of barriers to the movement of goods and money across South Africa's borders. At the same time, business pledged itself to 'capital reform' that would open ownership to black citizens. Given that the transition was a negotiated process rather than a seizure of state power, capital reform and deracialisation were conceived by both the ANC and business as gradual.

Ramaphosa did not possess any formal economics education, but he had been exposed from the mid-1970s to the voices of business: through his relationship with the Menells, at the board meetings of the Urban Foundation, and in his negotiations at NUM. Moreover, he came from an immediate family of fairly successful entrepreneurs. Although he listened in admiration to the theories of Marxist die-hards such as Govan Mbeki, he was immune to the temptations of theoretical fundamentalism in economics just as in politics.

Mandela's post-1994 government was obliged to ostentatiously adopt conservative macroeconomic policies. It needed to build confidence in nervous international financial institutions and markets. Continuity of personnel in the finance ministry and the Reserve Bank went hand in hand with a conciliatory approach to black economic redress. A rudimentary employment equity policy was introduced, the National Empowerment Fund was created to channel privatisation proceeds, public sector procurement policy ostensibly favoured emerging companies, and new government agencies provided managerial advice and finance to small enterprises. All in all, however, the approach was a very tentative one, behind which lay not just prudence but also fundamental philosophical division. As Mandela has observed, the ANC is a coalition in which some members 'support free enterprise, others socialism. Some are conservatives, others are liberals. We are united solely by our determination to oppose racial oppression.'[18]

In the early years of the new democracy, increased black ownership was left to voluntary business initiatives. Many ANC members saw the economy as a hostile realm of 'investment strikes' and 'malicious acts of capital flight'.[19] Yet, by its 1997 Mafikeng conference, the ANC's *Strategy and Tactics* document for the first time characterised the black middle class and the black bourgeoisie as significant 'motive forces' in the 'national democratic revolution'.

Government had by then controversially adopted the Growth, Employment and Redistribution (Gear) economic stabilisation programme. Perceived by activists as a 'neo-liberal' policy foisted upon the liberation movement by international capital, Gear was responsible for a political backlash against the market economy. In the ANC-aligned labour movement, in particular, the austere fiscal policy to which the cabinet committed itself was lambasted. The removal of import controls and the exposure of unionised sectors such as textiles to international competition had already caused severe job losses in Cosatu member unions, and this in the midst of a wider and growing unemployment crisis.

In such circumstances, it was imperative that the voluntary process of black empowerment deliver results. Unfortunately, it was cruelly but predictably undermined by an international crisis in financial markets that erupted in 1997 and 1998. Ramaphosa later observed that BEE deals were mostly financed through 'special purpose vehicles' (SPVs) established solely to facilitate the purchase of equity in white businesses.[20] SPVs used shares as collateral against the loans used to buy them, and tougher economic conditions led the banks to wind most of them up rapidly. When all unsustainable financial structures had collapsed, black ownership on the JSE had been drastically reduced from around 7 per cent of total JSE market capitalisation at the start of 1997 to little more than 2 per cent.[21]

Voluntary empowerment had decisively failed to produce a sustainable and substantial increase in black ownership, unemployment was biting deep, and Gear was stoking up ideological antagonisms.[22] Black business people began to press for a strategy less dependent on the questionable good faith of white business. While Thabo Mbeki's economic thinking was instinctively conservative, he had always insisted, as one exile essay confirms, that 'non-racialism in politics has to be accompanied by non-racialism in the economy'.[23] When he became State President, in 1999, he announced boldly that 'we must strive to create and strengthen a black capitalist class'.[24]

His first model was Afrikaner economic nationalism. Afrikaners' long march towards equality with English speakers began in the 1920s, when organised farmers secured tariff protection and agricultural subsidies.[25] After the NP's 1948 election win, Afrikaner nationalists lobbied successfully for affirmative procurement, targeted state contracts, and employment creation in the parastatals. They also built ethnic insurance companies and banks, and transformed their language and their educational institutions into economic assets. Govan Mbeki wrote that their giant business enterprises were 'the main pillars around which ... large concentrations of Afrikaner enterprise were to take shape'.[26]

Thabo Mbeki also admired the Malaysian empowerment model.[27] In 1970, the United Malays' National Organisation launched a programme to transfer equity from the minority ethnic Chinese, who dominated the economy, to the Malays and Indians who between them made up more than 60 per cent of the population.[28] Twenty-year targets were set for the transfer of a third of all commercial and industrial equity. Mahathir bin Mohamad, Malaysian prime minister from 1981 to 2003, insisted that privatised state assets should not be given as 'hand-outs' to the poor, but rather be directed towards the wealthy Bumiputera (sons of the soil) who could build on them.

Malaysian empowerment has been tarnished by the Malays' dependency on government favours, and Mahathir himself has lamented the creation of empowerment speculators or 'Ali Babas' trading in state contracts and licences.[29] Nevertheless, it provided a template for Mbeki's project to build a patriotic bourgeoisie, an initiative that bought the ANC time to rethink the very purpose of black economic empowerment.

Ramaphosa's involvement in all this came through the watershed Black Economic Empowerment Commission (BEECom), which he chaired in 2000. The need for a commission was first mooted by the Black Management Forum's 1997 conference, and political pressure redoubled during the financial crisis of 1998, which slashed black JSE capitalisation. The issue was taken up by the Black Business Council, an umbrella body representing 11 black business organisations, which in tandem with the ANC initiated BEECom's creation.

Ramaphosa was elected chairperson at the first meeting of the commission, where it was clear the body enjoyed the tacit blessing of the ANC. The key issue they had to address, as he saw it, was how to combine the transfer of equity to black hands with broader empowerment to spread prosperity across the economy. BEECom's quasi-official status allowed it to 'think the unthinkable', and its radical proposals included the creation of a national procurement agency and the appropriation of public sector pension funds to finance empowerment. BEE, for Ramaphosa's commission, was an historical project to 'redress the imbalances of the past', but it was also a practical plan to shift the apartheid economy on to a higher and more sustainable growth path.[30]

BEECom's final report had the backing of the ANC. As a member of the NEC's economic transformation subcommittee, Ramaphosa could test the commission's proposals against the views of party heavyweights. Moreover, he collaborated with finance minister Trevor Manuel to ensure Treasury's concerns were reflected in the commission's conclusions.[31]

The Broad-Based BEE Act of 2003 which ultimately emerged out of parliament was a complex and multi-faceted piece of legislation. It assembled hitherto discrete initiatives in capital deracialisation, employment equity, business development, preferential procurement and skills enhancement – and it did so in a framework of voluntary compliance flexible enough to accommodate the full diversity of businesses. At the start of 2007 the legislation came into effect. Its key instrument is a 'balanced scorecard' that measures every enterprise against wide-ranging criteria for 'broad-based' empowerment. These criteria are spelt out in 'codes of good practice' that are applied by state agencies in procurement, licensing, concessions, public–private partnerships and the sale of state-owned assets.[32]

BEE has created a good deal of concern, relating in particular to overall feasibility, economic costs, distorting effects on the state, and implications for ANC unity.

The most devastating criticism is that it just won't work. On the one hand, there is a danger that business will evade the requirements of the Act through the exploitation of legal loopholes – such as the creation of trusts – or through a technique called 'fronting'. This practice involves black managers being employed but discouraged from participating in the operations of the business. One sceptic observes that fronting is likely to migrate down the supply chain to small and medium-sized companies where it will be harder to detect, because 'fat and underperforming' big business will try to hide its own poor ownership, skills and employment equity performance by boosting empowerment procurement ratings.[33]

Ownership change may largely be financial smoke and mirrors that does little to increase overall black ownership. One empowerment professional observes that 'it is quite easy for any white company to abide by the legislation and still not comply with the spirit of BEE ... Legislation won't work on a problem of this scale.'[34]

BEE may also fail simply because resources are not available to address the scale of the challenge. It is proposed that a quarter of the private economy will be owned by black South Africans within a decade. Around R200 billion has so far been committed. Yet private sector assets total around R5 trillion (five thousand billion rands) and it remains unclear how such a massive scaling-up can be financed. One further concern is that resources that are used will be diverted from productive uses. A low savings rate in South Africa already makes government's 6 per cent growth target tough. Tying up perhaps R450 billion in transfers of shares to black South Africans may make the target still harder.[35]

Black business people already face an uphill struggle to access capital.[36] As Ramaphosa discovered at Johnnic, black entrepreneurs must borrow from third parties at high cost, leaving their deals vulnerable to economic downturn. The current generation of BEE transactions may not prove more sustainable than the last.[37] Financiers always promise to square the circle, reducing the direct debt obligations carried by the BEE investors, and using option schemes or deferred shares.[38] The only certainty to such financial structuring is that it will bring the investment bankers fat fees.

The 'net equity' that black entrepreneurs purportedly possess is merely paper wealth. 'Lock-in' provisions have been widely used to prevent the early sale of the shares, because such sales would dilute black equity and so lead to a loss of empowerment credentials.[39] This need for lock-in exposes the fundamental tension between vendors' desire to maintain high black shareholding levels and empowerment shareholders' yearning to sell shares to repay debt and realise value from their investments.

Company earnings will almost invariably be insufficient to cover interest and capital repayments, obliging BEE players to sell down shares at the end of the term.[40] Some claim that such considerations point to the need for a massive downscaling of expectations around BEE. Even if economic conditions continue to be favourable to empowerment transactions, only a modest fraction of the hoped-for ownership transformation of the private economy will occur over the next decade. But for Ramaphosa, such problems merely indicate that efforts must be stepped up a gear, to ensure that meaningful change is brought about within an acceptable period of time.

Ramaphosa rebuts allegations that BEE entrepreneurs have benefited from patronage. 'None of us have been able to make headway in business riding on the coattails of government. I've been an entrepreneur from the age of 16. What could have been a business career for me was interrupted by apartheid. I started as a hawker buying and selling things. But that had to stop because there was a struggle to be prosecuted.'[41] As BEE activity grows, however, patronage-based empowerment partnerships are likely to grow. It is becoming increasingly difficult for established businesses to build meaningful operational partnerships with black managers in their industry.[42] 'Broad-based' development trusts, union funds or employee share schemes can be put together, but they usually lack any economic rationale, and bring benefits only over an inordinately long period. For this reason, partnerships are increasingly struck for reasons of influence-buying, where political and procurement power is sometimes the bait.

Such deals are sometimes castigated for not creating value, a criticism Ramaphosa disputes. 'First you become a financial investor to accumulate capital, because capital does not fall from the sky. Once you're accumulating capital, you begin to acquire skills and skilled people whom you can deploy in various businesses. The third stage is acquiring control of companies and beginning to be an operator, running a proper business.' Being an entrepreneur, Ramaphosa observes, is not simply running a business. 'A guy like Warren Buffett has never run a business in his life. He's the greatest and richest entrepreneur in the world. He manages money. He invests money. That's what he does.'[43]

Many established businesses remain sceptical about the merits of today's BEE model. The most 'empowered enterprises' in the country are probably Eskom and Telkom, rightly celebrated for employment equity, preferential procurement and business development achievements. Nevertheless, these scorecard darlings are associated with escalating prices, abused monopoly powers and cowed regulators.

Political sensitivities around BEE make it difficult to learn lessons from experience. Moreover, many investors are concerned that empowerment lacks clear time-frames. In ten years, they query, will empowerment obligations simply be renewed, or will they even be intensified?

A third cause for concern about BEE is the questionable character of the emerging empowerment state. SACP deputy general secretary Jeremy Cronin laments that 'established and emerging capital have succeeded in exerting considerable dominance over the state'.[44] If the state becomes a slave of narrow interests, it can never become the 'developmental state' that the government needs to rescue millions from poverty. If BEE disguises growing patronage relations between officials and entrepreneurs, ultimately every business may believe it needs state patrons to land government contracts or to secure licences.

Industrial policy might become a life-support system for politically well-connected companies, and public sector and parastatal pension funds might be drained in support of risky investments. Government departments might increasingly act at the behest of individuals rather than in the national interest. Intelligence services and the diplomatic corps might be put at the disposal of companies with high-risk foreign investments simply because of their close relationships with ministers or officials.[45] Major infrastructure investments – in power generation and transmission, nuclear energy or new-generation rail systems – might be still more often secured by golf-course hand-shakes rather than by social and economic cost-benefit calculations.[46] The key financial beneficiaries will remain established businesses, but with politically connected empowerment partners brought into the established white business oligarchies.

When influential BEE groups battle for licences or contracts they may damage regulatory institutions, destroy the careers of rigorous regulators, and abuse the power of the public broadcaster. Recent big oil and armaments transactions, always a first choice for entrepreneurs seeking to secure nest eggs or build war chests, have seen BEE vehicles allegedly used as instruments of personal enrichment, and media houses used to tarnish rivals.

'Revolving doors' problems, and conflicts of interest, have increasingly been raised as a result of the deal-making of former and current public servants. The circulation of talented individuals between state and business is desirable, of course, bringing mutual understanding and aiding the internal transformation and corporate culture of both sectors. Nevertheless, confidentiality requirements and new regulations ensuring appropriate time delays are urgently needed, and new conflict of interest regulations need to be formulated and applied.

A fourth set of concerns surrounds the integrity and stability of the ANC itself. Highlighting deals involving Manne Dipico, Popo Molefe and Valli Moosa – but with Ramaphosa very much in its sights – *City Press* has even asked rhetorically if the ANC is 'mortgaged to private capital'.[47] Empowerment vehicles have also been implicated in the alleged abuse of preferential procurement to bring 'retro-kickbacks' to ANC funds, and in the purported interference of business in the presidential succession processes. SACP deputy general secretary Jeremy Cronin observes that 'political tensions within the state and ANC leadership are "resolved" by allowing some to be "deployed" into the private sector. However, the converse of this is that the leading financial and mining conglomerates are increasingly reaching into the state and the upper echelons of the ANC and its Leagues – actively backing (betting on) different factions and personalities, and seeking to influence electoral outcomes and presidential succession.'[48]

Any legal and regulatory framework for BEE may be exploited for private gain unless there are more successful ANC initiatives to police the activity of its own cadres. It remains an open question whether a liberation movement already changed by its interaction with economic power will continue to be able to steer empowerment in a benign direction.

Ramaphosa and his fellow BEE magnates are more aware than anyone of the potential damage that the abuse of empowerment deals can bring. For him, however, empowerment remains a political and moral imperative. Black economic advance will be driven primarily by the actions of individuals, and entrepreneurs will look to exercise their new-found freedom to make deals. Established businesses will meanwhile seek out the skills and connections that black partners can bring, and many of them will hunger for access to government contracts and the ear of powerful decision-makers.

The central case for creating a black bourgeoisie remains the need to build effective communications between business and politics. It is reasonable to believe that a black elite can open up more honest and direct lines of communication between politicians and business people, and nurture the confidence upon which long-term investment is based. A successful BEE policy will therefore be one that not only encourages more intense interaction between black business, established capital and the state, but also establishes clearer rules to manage such relationships. The return of ANC business tycoons to political work will be necessary if conduct in the fast-moving BEE landscape is to be successfully regulated.

Ramaphosa's sense of urgency about BEE is probably driven by a final and largely unarticulated worry. The first voluntary phase of empowerment failed to produce a sustainable increase in black ownership and control when the 1998 emerging market crisis led banks to wind up BEE financing vehicles. Black entrepreneurs have again borrowed at high cost, and deals remain vulnerable to higher interest rates or a slowing economy. If the current generation of transactions proves no more sustainable than the last, we will see another dramatic reversal of the project to bring a degree of racial equity to ownership patterns.

Today, however, a far wider range of broad-based beneficiaries, an over-borrowed new middle class, and more numerous politically connected empowerment partners will suffer the consequences. Any resulting political turbulence might generate a counter-reaction against a market-friendly and voluntary BEE programme. It might therefore bring disturbing consequences for South African businesses, and for the wider social progress that is ultimately dependent upon a flourishing private economy. Uncertainty about the future of the BEE project is already damaging to the development of the longer time-horizons and business confidence that are prerequisites for the achievement of the government's pressing economic and developmental goals.

Ramaphosa's instincts are clear. There are costs and risks to a rapid process of scaling up empowerment. All the same, the risks and costs of delay are immeasurably greater. Michael Spicer, one-time Anglo American executive director, believes this is the one aspect of Cyril's approach to economic policy that is quite distinctively his own. 'His real passion is for BEE – it is his only genuine business passion. He believes we need to do this quickly. He is not interested in an incremental approach.'[49]

Beyond BEE, Ramaphosa has sought out other opportunities to shape the views of established businesses. His quiet influence is exercised primarily through the wide range of directorships he maintains. He is currently non-executive chairman of MTN Group, Alexander Forbes Africa Holdings, Bidvest Group and re-insurance entity Sasria. He is a board member of Standard Bank and of the global brewing giant SABMiller, and he also sits on the board of a number of smaller companies, including MacSteel and Medscheme.

Cyril's multiple board memberships have been a matter of some debate. A politician like Ramaphosa is still sometimes treated by company chairmen as a weapon of last resort, able to open doors to political leaders or officials at critical moments. Yet this notion is sorely misplaced. 'When there has been a screw-up,' Cyril's former CEO, Ndoda Madalane, observes, 'the chairman's head will inevitably turn to the black non-executive directors. But when a company has messed up, say, a service to a municipality, the worst thing they can do is to bring in someone like Cyril.'[50]

Non-executive directors like Ramaphosa rarely possess unique or specialised knowledge of a particular business. Rather, their value lies precisely in their wide range of other directorships, which allows them to 'read' changes in the overall business environment. Ramaphosa would certainly claim to be able to offer such a service to the companies he serves.

He also sits on the executive committee of the major lobbying group for big business, Business Leadership South Africa (BLSA), formerly the South Africa Foundation. BLSA's membership includes the largest companies on the JSE and the biggest multinational names with a presence in the country. Its chair observes that some international business people are 'maddened by Cyril's hands-off approach ... There is a perception that Cyril does not attend boards, that he is too exposed and only does what he is interested in ... If the meeting is a grind, he will not go.'[51]

Ramaphosa certainly seems less dedicated to routine board attendance than to becoming a prominent voice for Africa in global business forums. America's *Time* magazine earlier in 2007 declared Ramaphosa one of the world's 'one hundred most influential people'.[52] In a laudatory profile, former United States ambassador to the UN Richard Holbrooke described Ramaphosa as 'a beacon of hope for Africans – and the rest of us'. Referring to Ramaphosa's move to business, he observed that Cyril 'saw an opportunity to show the way to a generation of black South Africans who would gradually control the South African economy. He reached out to white business leaders, but he made black economic empowerment his new issue, tirelessly promoting it and warning that it had to happen.' Holbrooke effusively continues: 'There are many who hope that Ramaphosa, just 54, will emerge as South Africa's next president.'[53]

Holbrooke became acquainted with Ramaphosa through a curious institution, the Coca-Cola Advisory Board. This board is a repository of many of the great and good of our times, charged to provide 'strategic insight for the chairman and senior management team', and to 'enlarge our strategic networks of key leaders around the world in government, business and non-profit sectors'. Alongside Holbrooke, Cyril rubs shoulders on this board with the chairman of the supervisory board of Deutsche Bank and several former US cabinet ministers. Representatives from the South include a former Brazilian foreign minister, an economic research specialist from Beijing, the director-general of the Confederation of Indian Industry, and Ernesto Zedillo, the former Mexican finance minister. To round things off, the council boasts the chairman of Goldman Sachs International, Italy's Renato Ruggiero and 'Ben' Makihara, the legendary chairman of Japan's Mitsubishi Corporation. This is indeed a curiously high-powered body, dedicated ultimately to increasing the global intake of fizzy drinks.

Ramaphosa's other international board memberships give him access to equally high-powered, but distinctive, networks. His position on the Unilever Africa Advisory Council gives him a voice in a company that operates across the African continent. Although chaired by Lynda Chalker,[54] a former British minister for overseas aid and development, it is composed primarily of Africans with wide business experience – for example the chairman of the Nigerian Investment Promotion Agency, the managing director of Barclays Bank Ghana, and the chief executive officer of Kenya Airlines.

Ramaphosa has also been deputy chairman of the Commonwealth Business Council (CBC). The CBC was inspired by a Nigerian head of the Commonwealth who believed that business leaders needed to work with politicians to address the developmental and governance challenges faced by poorer Commonwealth countries. With the agreement of British prime minister Tony Blair and his South African counterpart Thabo Mbeki, Ramaphosa was brought together with Simon Cairns,[55] a British financier with a profound interest in development, to set the CBC in motion in the late 1990s.

CBC quickly expanded beyond its initial remit, to address a whole range of developmental challenges across the Commonwealth.

Its formal mission is 'to provide a bridge between the private sector and governments, between emerging markets and developed markets and between small businesses and [the] international private sector'. It pursues these goals by changing negative international perceptions of countries' investment climates, sharing experiences about global trade and environmental negotiations, and attempting to 'bridge the digital divide' between the North and South. In one of its most recent conferences in October 2006, for example, the CBC and the Nepad secretariat[56] together lobbied the German government to keep African development on EU and G8 radars during its presidencies. Ramaphosa observed that 'whether the G8 wish it or not, they share a mutuality of interest with Africa which demands their attention'.[57]

Like all such international institutions, it is the informal networks they create that are of most importance. CBC's board includes James Bolger, the prime minister of New Zealand between 1990 and 1997, who oversaw a remarkable turnaround in the country's economy; Bryan Sanderson, chairman of Standard Chartered; Tan Sri Dato' Mohd Hassan Marican, the chief executive officer of Petronas, the Malaysian petrochemicals giant; and Lakshmi Mittal, chairman and chief executive of Mittal Steel, by some margin the world's largest steel producer.

Ramaphosa has also become quietly involved in the international battle against HIV/AIDS. He has been very careful not to make any open intervention in the domestic controversy over anti-retroviral drug treatment, an issue which unfortunately remains surrounded by exceptional political sensitivity within the ANC.[58] His commitment to a practical approach was signalled when he became vice-chair of the Global Business Coalition on HIV/AIDS, Tuberculosis and Malaria. This coalition has more than 200 member companies, committed to 'harness the power of the global business community to end the HIV/ AIDS, tuberculosis and malaria epidemics', in particular by improving the quality and reach of country prevention and treatment programmes, fostering private–public–voluntary partnerships to fight HIV/AIDS, and using the lobbying power of business to push AIDS, TB and malaria up national political agendas.[59] The board includes eccentric entrepreneur Richard Branson, with whom Cyril launched a new anti-AIDS initiative at the Cida campus in Braamfontein in November 2004.[60]

Ramaphosa's foreign policy initiatives have included his participation, together with a former president of the Philippines and the deputy speaker of the Russian Duma, in the International Commission on Intervention and State Sovereignty. This body was established by the Canadian government in response to UN Secretary-General Kofi Annan's post-Rwanda challenge to the international community to prevent future genocides. While the commission was a time-consuming distraction from the travails of Johnnic, Ramaphosa's then personal assistant remarks that 'You just don't say no to the UN Secretary-General'.[61]

The commission argued that 'sovereign states have a responsibility to protect their own citizens from avoidable catastrophe – from mass murder and rape, from starvation – but when they are unwilling or unable to do so, that responsibility must be borne by the broader community of states'.[62] The commission's findings were sadly overshadowed by the events of 11 September 2001.[63]

A second major foreign policy involvement was the Northern Ireland peace process. Much to the surprise of the populations of Ireland, north and south of the border, Ramaphosa and a former president of Finland, Martti Ahtisaari, were jointly appointed in 2000 to oversee the decommissioning of the weapons of the Irish Liberation Army (IRA), and to ensure that they were kept securely and 'beyond use'. Ahtisaari had a formidable reputation as a peace-broker in southern Africa and the Balkans. As special envoy of the European Union, he had famously tamed Slobodan Milošević. Ramaphosa, for his part, was familiar with the 'Irish problem', and on close terms with many leaders of the IRA's political wing, Sinn Fein.

The seemingly natural affinity between the ANC and Sinn Fein is a comparatively recent creation. The ANC's conventional anti-colonialist analysis of Ireland did predispose its members to support the IRA. Irish nationalists, for their part, traditionally identified with the Afrikaner project of defiance against British colonial rule. In the early 1980s, however, Sinn Fein exploited the ANC's international prestige by likening Northern Ireland to an Afrikaner homeland. Margaret Thatcher and Ronald Reagan, by refusing to negotiate with the 'terrorists' of the ANC and IRA alike, helped to reinforce this parallel.

Having hitched the legitimacy of its struggle to the ANC, the IRA was caught off balance by rapid progress in South Africa. Nelson Mandela even undiplomatically suggested that the time had come for the IRA and the British government to commence peace talks of their own. He invited Gerry Adams to visit in June 1995, a trip the wily republican leader used to remind sceptics at home that the problems they faced, such as prisoner amnesty and arms decommissioning, were not insuperable. Adams also learnt from Roelf Meyer that violent ANC tactics in the 1980s had simply entrenched regime intransigence, by deepening the security establishment's stranglehold over policy. The securocrats always viewed deep-seated political problems through the lenses of security, and their control had to be broken before political compromise could begin.

In 1997, when Tony Blair's Labour Party won its historic general election victory, long-term ANC and Sinn Fein sympathisers were propelled into positions of power. Many of this generation of politicians subscribed to an anti-colonialist analysis of the Irish troubles. In April 1998, the British government invited Ramaphosa, Valli Moosa, Mac Maharaj and Mathews Phosa to the UK to advise their Irish counterparts on potential initiatives to advance talks. They seized upon the notion of 'sufficient consensus' to justify the marginalisation of smaller parties, and they came to understand the importance of personal relationships in creating the conditions for negotiation.

The South African government also hosted the Northern Ireland protagonists in a retreat in the small fishing village of Arniston in the Western Cape. The loyalist delegates carefully refused, however, to interact socially with their republican opposite numbers, although Ramaphosa, as the host of the engagement, did his best to bring the two sides together. While Ramaphosa enjoyed his closest relationship with Gerry Adams of Sinn Fein, even the Unionists recognised his impartiality and skill as a facilitator.[64] After the encounter, Roelf Meyer stayed in touch with members of Ian Paisley's party, and even spent a period in Northern Ireland attempting to guide them towards negotiations. Both Ramaphosa and Meyer were willing to devote time and energy to helping in this conflict situation, which many others had abandoned in despair.[65]

When Tony Blair called Ramaphosa on 6 May 2000 from Downing Street, to ask him to take up this new role, it was therefore not a complete surprise. It was all the same flattering that Gerry Adams of Sinn Fein had put forward his name as the international mediator in whom Sinn Fein had trust.[66] When Sinn Fein and the Democratic Unionist Party finally reached their historic agreement, on 26 March 2007, to restore power-sharing institutions in the province, Gerry Adams wrote to the ANC that 'a new and unprecedented opportunity for progress now exists in Ireland. People are more hopeful now than at any time since the Good Friday Agreement ... To all of you who played a role, however large or small, I want to say a very sincere thank you.'[67]

In Sinn Fein's own newspaper, *An Phoblacht*, he not only thanked the usual presidents and prime ministers, but also picked out a number of special individuals: British politicians Ken Livingstone, Tony Benn and Jeremy Corbyn; American senators Mitchell and Kennedy; and Fidel Castro, Cyril Ramaphosa and Martti Ahtisaari. 'I want to say a very public and heartfelt *go raibh maith agaibh* – thank you – to all of them. We are where we are because of their trust and confidence in us. They never gave up – even when things looked bad.'[68]

Some South Africans fear that President Thabo Mbeki is almost irreplaceable because of his experience in foreign policy. He has propelled both the idea of African Renaissance and the institution of Nepad to international prominence. He has sponsored significant partnerships with India, China and Brazil, the new giants of the South. While recent paralysis over Zimbabwe has tarnished his record, and the HIV/AIDS controversy has weakened his influence over fellow world leaders, ANC activists believe that 'the chief' still punches above his weight in international forums.

It is therefore understandable that many ANC members believe that Mbeki, his African project at best half complete and recently suffering many reversals, should be given more time to bring his breathtaking agenda to fruition. At the very least, some claim, his skills and experience must not be lost to the movement and to the country. It is vital that he remain available, in one capacity or another, as a guiding hand behind the foreign policy of the nation.

While potential successors such as Tokyo Sexwale and Kgalema Motlanthe are indeed short of foreign policy experience, Ramaphosa has quietly built a major international reputation. His relationships with fellow leftists date back to his 1980s career in the National Union of Mineworkers, of course. As NUM general secretary, he worked with Southern African Mineworkers' Union leader Morgan Tsvangirai, Cuban president Fidel Castro, and British mineworkers' leader Arthur Scargill. International socialist and labour leaders still find it easy to communicate with Ramaphosa. It was no surprise when newly elected Bolivian president Evo Morales made a special point of visiting and publicly greeting Ramaphosa during his visit to South Africa in 2006.

After a decade of international network-building, Ramaphosa now also has significant experience of international business and political leadership. He has unobtrusively become the best equipped of the current generation of ANC leaders to take forward Thabo Mbeki's ambitious and path-breaking international agenda. It is intriguing to speculate what might have been, had he accepted Nelson Mandela's 1994 offer to serve his country in the capacity of foreign minister.

PART SIX
HORIZONS

CHAPTER 21

A DEEPENING NATIONAL CRISIS

The biggest threat to the future is the inability of an ANC
government to meet the legitimate needs of the people ... They
want clean water, they want shelter, they want education for their
kids, they want the possibility of work. And unless the government
meets the very legitimate aspirations, and unless white society
understands that they must be met, that's the biggest threat, that's
what will destabilise the emerging democratic order.
*   – Kader Asmal, February 1994*[1]

We're seeing parents burying their children. We need to be doing
much more. We need to get to grips with this [HIV/AIDS]
pandemic, arrest it and reverse it.
*   – Cyril Ramaphosa, November 2004*[2]

The ANC is likely to be the party of government for the foreseeable
future. Its internal political processes must forge the society's sense
of collective purpose and select its leaders.

Since coming to power in 1994, the ANC has recorded many substantial
political and economic achievements.[3] It has secured political stability,
almost eliminating the territorial conflict that characterised the 1994
elections in Natal. It has maintained public participation in democratic
elections, albeit at decreasing levels,[4] and it has put together integrated
programmes that have helped citizens to understand what they can
reasonably expect of their government. In this way, it has retained a degree
of trust among poor citizens for whom the first decade of democracy
often brought a deepening of poverty rather than relief from it.[5]

Finally, the ANC has performed the crucial role of discouraging racial and ethnic conflict. Racial antagonisms are an inevitable product of a history of racially exploitative rule, in which Africans were mostly confined to Bantustans and segregated townships, restricted to unskilled or semi-skilled work, prohibited from property accumulation, and denied the basic social infrastructure required to lead a dignified and productive life.[6]

Because it is so central to South Africa's future, there is widespread concern that the moral fabric of the liberation movement seems to be disintegrating. The extended succession struggles over the presidencies of the ANC and state have exposed underlying grievances and ideological divides, as well as demonstrated a blind determination among many of the movement's leaders to secure power, or to retain it, at almost any cost.

A movement embracing as wide a diversity of interests as the ANC is always susceptible to division, and inevitably depends both on central discipline and on consensus-building to maintain internal unity. The ANC's ability to maintain unity and to consolidate alliances with partners such as Cosatu and the SACP is sometimes explained in terms of African social conservatism and a preference for consensus over contestation. Nelson Mandela has celebrated the idealised democracy of tribal meetings he observed in his childhood, in which the fundamental equality of men was purportedly expressed through a right and freedom to speak regardless of rank and social position. 'All men', Mandela claims, 'were free to voice their opinions and were equal in their value as citizens ... majority rule was a foreign notion. A minority was not to be crushed by a majority.'[7] In addition, many former exiles and communists idealise a participatory democracy. All the same, the ANC's ability to secure consensus in a complex and class-divided society must be explained by reference to wider intellectual systems and organisational practices.

The ANC explains its own project in terms of a struggle to achieve a more just society through a 'national democratic revolution' (NDR). This revolutionary understanding of democracy was introduced in the 1960s by communist intellectuals trying to conceptualise the relationship between the overarching goal of international socialism and the immediate anti-colonial project of national liberation.[8] The SACP sought political alliances that might bring national liberation without jeopardising a socialist future. NDR has been characterised as 'a process of struggle that seeks the transfer of power to the people', whose 'strategic objectives' in this 'current phase' include the creation of 'a non-racial, non-sexist, democratic and united South Africa'.[9] Since 1994, however, its content and interpretation have become controversial.

NDR is unspecific about time-frames and about the strategic relationships between avowed immediate (national) and ultimate (international socialist) objectives. This fundamental ambiguity has allowed the discourse to survive in post-apartheid and post-communist conditions, and to maintain a commitment to an overarching project – however vaguely defined – that holds the ANC together despite a growing divergence of interests.[10] The NDR framework has mostly been used pragmatically to justify necessary compromises between ANC constituencies and goals, and to support a hitherto benign form of social democracy.[11]

Despite its considerable achievements in power, the ANC now faces an almost bewildering range of internal and external challenges. Internally, the seeming policy consensus of the past decade has in fact papered over deeper ideological conflicts. There are profound disagreements about the abuse of office and how it can be contained; the significance of ethnicity and race; the degree to which liberal constitutionalism should be respected; and the relevance of socialism in a 'neo-liberal' world order.

Because the ANC dominates government across the country, leadership positions are fast becoming seen as an essential step towards public office and potential private gain. ANC secretary-general Kgalema Motlanthe used the ANC's National General Council to lament that 'the central challenge facing the ANC is to address the problems that arise from our cadres' susceptibility to moral decay occasioned by the struggle for the control of and access to resources. All the paralysis in our programmes, all the divisions in our structures, are in one way or another, a consequence of this cancer in our midst.'[12]

Younger activists have no direct experience of the struggle for liberation, and no intrinsic respect for conventions of authority in the movement. Many older ANC supporters are uncertain whether their tradition of reconciling diverse interests in the pursuit of 'national democratic revolution' will survive generational change. Meanwhile, senior office-holders' threats to impose disciplinary action or redeployment lack moral authority. Local and provincial politics involve routine accommodations with questionable power-brokers. The leadership is compromised by its own open pursuit of wealth and its own ethically dubious behaviour.

Ethnic politics has also made disturbing headway within the ANC. The collapse of the IFP in KwaZulu-Natal handed control of the province to the ANC and left a cohort of ethnic activists looking for a new political home. Soon afterwards, the perceived guarantor of conservative Zulu interests, Jacob Zuma, was undermined. Zuma's supporters have advanced conspiracy theories about a plot to prevent the rightful succession to the presidency of a Zulu. Mbeki's second-term cabinet reshuffle meanwhile resulted in 13 cabinet ministers and 6 deputy ministers being Xhosa speakers, an insensitive tilt away from ethnic balance.

Race remains another potential flashpoint. Many whites and Indians have capitalised on their skills and asset advantage to benefit from higher wages in the 'knowledge economy' and from capital gains in the property market. Although there is no longer an apartheid state to enforce segregation, there has been a 'privatisation of apartheid' as a result of new security estates, guarded shopping complexes, private health services, and fortress business parks and leisure centres. Whites' denialism about their culpability for apartheid meanwhile reinforces a submerged racial antagonism that might yet be exploited by political entrepreneurs.

Liberal institutions are also vulnerable a decade after Ramaphosa's Constitutional Assembly seemingly entrenched them. Some ANC activists view bourgeois democracy as a Western imposition that entrenched the privileges of a property-owning white elite. Among the wider citizenry, only a third of South Africans consider the procedural components of the political system – majority rule, regular elections, freedom to criticise government, and multi-party competition – as 'essential' to its democratic character. Citizens more often consider 'delivery' to be the key aspect of democracy.[13]

The ANC leadership has not defended the legislature against executive arrogance,[14] and the ANC caucus code of conduct privileges party over parliamentary policy authority.[15] While the ANC has shown more respect for the courts, ANC leaders sometimes mobilise behind critics of the bench, and controversial legislation was recently mooted – although then withdrawn – to place the administration of the courts in the hands of the executive, and strip the Judicial Services Commission of some of its key powers.

A dominant party like the ANC can in principle sustain the 'founding pact' of a democracy, using its strength to prevent old hostilities re-emerging and to promote reconciliation.[16] But dominant parties can also become undemocratic monsters, intimidating minorities and participating only in elections they are sure they will win. When a genuine electoral challenge finally emerges, the dominant party may simply make it impossible for the majority to express its will through the ballot box.

One final concern, though not the least, is that many activists view a market economy as, at best, an unappealing necessity. The ANC has recognised the importance of international capital markets and trade, and it has determinedly stuck to an orthodox fiscal and monetary policy. However, government's economic programme was packaged in the ideologically unpalatable form of Gear, and imposed upon ANC and alliance structures without the case for stabilisation being made and accepted. Conflict continues within the tripartite alliance about the fundamental orientation of the economy. For business, the resulting uncertainty inhibits long-term investment. For activists, the illusion persists that there is some assured alternative to 'neo-liberal' Gear that will bring quick gains in jobs and wealth.

While the ANC has been embroiled in internal ideological power struggles, the external environment has decisively worsened in three key respects. First, South Africa is facing a maturing HIV/AIDS epidemic which is beginning to have major economic and political repercussions. Soon a million South Africans who need anti-retroviral drugs (ARVs) will be denied them, and obstacles to sustainable and universal ARV provision are likely to remain entrenched. There are too few health professionals and dramatically insufficient capacities for counselling, testing, monitoring and management of supply chains. The AIDS crisis will continue to deepen, and the number of citizens needing medication is going to grow dramatically over the next decade.

Second, the politics of local service delivery is becoming increasingly torrid. Many municipalities exhibit dramatic human resource deficiencies, and most labour under growing debt burdens. It is likely that the intractable nature of the service delivery challenge will result in increasing recourse to protest and violence in local-level politics.

Third, despite the ANC's orthodox economic policy, the economy presents growing political challenges. Inequality and poverty remain entrenched, most importantly because of an intractable unemployment crisis. A more open economy and fiscal prudence have done nothing to reduce South Africa's vulnerability to capital outflows and foreign exchange crises. If the buoyant global economy slows, reduced growth would necessitate trade-offs between welfare and investment and threaten multiple compromises between business, the new middle class, organised labour and the rural poor. The black middle class so essential to political stability is heavily indebted as it seeks to make up for its assets deficit. Meanwhile, today's black economic empowerment deals are vulnerable to economic downturn. Worsening economic conditions would therefore bring rising unemployment, a debt crunch for the new middle class, and the collapse of empowerment deals that implicate both the black business elite and 'broad-based' beneficiaries.

Given vicious internal conflict and this potentially torrid external environment, the significance of the succession process cannot be over-emphasised. Does the ANC have the collective ability to identify and support the new leadership that it so evidently needs? And will Ramaphosa play any role in the struggle to rescue the liberation movement, and the country, from a deepening crisis?

Ramaphosa's political history, constituency and personality make him one of a very small number of credible candidates to step in and heal the divisions that have been opened up by the battle between Thabo Mbeki and Jacob Zuma.

He is uniquely able to build on the moral authority of the 1996 constitutional settlement and restore life to the practice of democracy. Power has already been pulled from society to state, from the provinces to Pretoria, and from legislature to executive. Within national government, the presidency has grown inexorably. A successor will probably seek ways to mobilise the efforts and capacities of the wider society. Ramaphosa's trade union background has left him open to a democratic approach to decision-making; he once observed that dissent helps negotiators to develop informed positions.[17] Roelf Meyer commented that Cyril would in his heart like a 'normal democracy where parties oppose each other [and] where anyone could win the next election'.[18]

Ramaphosa believes that democracy and development will rise or fall together. 'Democracy requires development,' he insists, because 'the value of electing public representatives … is severely undermined if people have few resources and even less opportunity to make of their lives what they want'. Yet development also requires democracy. 'Any despot can build a million houses. But to truly meet the needs of the people demands the involvement of the people in the development process.'[19]

Ramaphosa is also well placed to drive forward the black empowerment that he both understands and champions. At the same time, he could serve as a bridge between the left and economic orthodoxy. Socialists see him as a man of the left.[20] Indeed, as late as 1987 he was calling for a country 'where socialist principles are adhered to', in which 'the wealth of the country is shared equally by everyone'.[21] Business people by contrast consider him an 'artful pragmatist' who 'spoke the socialist rhetoric required of the time, and periodically raised the flag of nationalisation'.[22] As business leader Michael Spicer observes, 'Cyril is a pragmatist, although I would not expect a Ramaphosa government to be in any way an "easy wicket" for business.'[23]

Ramaphosa accepts that capitalism limits government power, but he also believes such limits must be explained to activists rather than imposed on them. The case for the Gear programme of economic stabilisation was never made, and activists persist with the illusion that 'neo-liberal' policy can simply be abandoned. Ramaphosa might win over leftist critics to an accommodation with business that would encourage the increased savings and investment upon which any anti-poverty strategy will ultimately depend.

A Ramaphosa presidency would also ensure a visible ethnic rotation of power. Some ANC activists in KwaZulu-Natal have seen Zuma as victim of a plot to secure continued Xhosa domination. Such ethnic confrontations work in favour of a potential successor not strongly associated with the major Nguni groups. Most leaders, in particular, consider it unwise to choose a third Xhosa president in a row. Bantu Holomisa observes that 'Ramaphosa's strength, if he were to go for that office [of President], is that he is from a minority group, call it tribe ... it is a good idea to get away from the Nguni groups'.[24]

Ramaphosa might also be able to defuse some of the society's racial tensions. Whites benefit from skills and assets accumulated under apartheid. Yet they noisily trumpet their comfortable incomes in the knowledge economy and their capital gains in the property market as well-deserved rewards for merit and 'hard work'.

Ramaphosa's appeal cuts across racial lines to an unusual degree for a South African politician, and he may be uniquely able to engage with whites and to encourage them to understand their moral obligation to make redress for the past. The fact that he is a figure whites feel comfortable with is, however, very much to his disadvantage in the internal politics of a southern African liberation movement.

Ramaphosa remains unwilling to engage in racial gesture politics in public. (As we have seen, he has always enjoyed trying to scare white captains of industry in private.) It should always be recalled that as a child he was pushed into a ditch by white soldiers. As a youth he was detained and interrogated by white security police. His mineworkers' union was famous for its all-black leadership, and his executive management teams in business – unlike those of many other so-called 'black empowerment tycoons' – have been overwhelmingly black.

His reading of his white countrymen can be quite cutting. In 1996, he observed that 'bigotry manifests itself in many, many ways ... [including] this well-practised and well-finessed way of white people just hiding their heads in the sand like an ostrich, completely oblivious to what's happening in this country. They were [supposedly] not aware [of apartheid abuses] and some of them did not even want to know ... I think the same is happening again with the Truth and Reconciliation Commission. They don't want to know ... But it is sad, it is very, very sad that white people are indifferent and this is something that is going to catch up with us as a nation ... What type of a political life do we have if we have not come to terms with what happened in the past, all of us collectively, and have [not] dealt with it and have [not] truly forgiven?'[25]

Ramaphosa is also the pragmatist that South Africa's HIV/AIDS crisis has been waiting for. HIV/AIDS requires not only wider collaboration but also the open discussion of complex moral and emotional issues – exactly the kind of task at which Ramaphosa is especially adept.

Finally, Ramaphosa is probably the best foreign-policy President South Africa could now muster, equally respected and influential on the international left, in the capitals of the West, and in Africa and the South.

His objective suitability for the highest office is evident. However, key questions remain. Is Ramaphosa up to the job? And does he want it?

CHAPTER 22

VISIONARY PRAGMATIST

E ven as a young child Ramaphosa's self-possession and charisma impressed his peers and his elders. He was a natural leader who enjoyed an easy mastery of others. Strong familial and religious frameworks helped him rise above the role models of Tshiawelo street culture and the ethnic slurs aimed at Venda children. He became a relentless worker, a scrupulous student, and an attentive son. With his impeccably groomed hair, immaculate clothes and a Bible always in his hands, he was indeed, as a friend remarked, 'the personification of perfection'.[1]

Through evangelism and preaching, he learnt the humility to engage the emotion and intellect of poorer and uneducated people. He also developed the ability to disengage his public persona – the sincere and later urbane face he presented to the world – from the more conflicted emotions with which he wrestled. Ramaphosa's conservative religious upbringing entrenched in him confident intuitions about social justice, and helped to build the sense of invulnerability that eventually surrounded him. Religion was also a cage, demanding deferential responses to a government that abused its power.

When Ramaphosa and his contemporaries were swept into black consciousness politics, Cyril was fortified by an increasingly radical interpretation of his religion. When confronted by racial oppression, he simply could not believe that God loved whites better than blacks: black and white alike were made in God's image.

His rise at university was rapid, the first of the three great waves of political activity in his life. When the banning of more radical organisations brought his Student Christian Movement to prominence, Ramaphosa's organisational skills and relentless energy helped him to exploit his opportunities to the full. His unique ability was to bridge the divide between religious rural students from the north and highly politicised Soweto activists.

This first wave of Ramaphosa's political rise broke when he was detained, first in 1974 and then again in 1976. As with many other released detainees, particularly those kept in solitary confinement, a carefully managed façade concealed psychological and emotional wounds that could never be fully healed. Detention left in its wake bitterness and pain, the destruction of old friendships, and extended periods of deep depression.

Incapable of anything less than relentless work, Ramaphosa applied himself tirelessly to his law studies, legal clerking, and youth organisation, and he finally married Hope Mudau. Knocked back by the loss of Douglas Ramaphosa to exile, his family prospered to the limited degree that apartheid conditions allowed. The hand of fate that brought Cyril into contact with the Menell family gave him an early introduction to the limitations of white paternalism. It also allowed him to secure work with a prestigious law firm, and held out the possibility of comfortable suburban prosperity as a member of the new black elite.

Underlying his hard work and study, a second wave of anger and political ambition was building. Surveying the terrain ahead, Ramaphosa had already identified the trade union movement as blacks' key vehicle for political mobilisation. Fate rather than calculation led him to the Cusa federation, to the organisation of mineworkers, and to his indispensable friend and partner, James Motlatsi. His personal demons were swept aside as Ramaphosa committed himself to the struggle of mineworkers and their families. As a strategist and negotiator he thrived on relentless pressure and conflict. He was also developing a growing awareness of the systematic forces that lay behind the brutal facts of exploitation. His reputation and authority spread within South Africa, across the subcontinental labour empire of the mines, and among ANC exiles in Lusaka.

Across the 1980s, Ramaphosa worked like a driven man. One of the NUM's external lawyers recalls the singular quality of Cyril as being 'not so much his charm or his intellect [as] his tenacity. He showed extraordinary stamina in what were always taxing times, day in and day out, month after month. Unlike other people I have come across who show staying power, he was not so much energetic – in fact he often (for good reason) displayed weariness – as unstoppable.'[2]

This second great wave of Ramaphosa's political ascendancy also had to break. With the inevitable defeat of the great 1987 mineworkers' strike, Ramaphosa's hopes for the union were crushed too. Though the NUM's leadership had no option other than to battle on, Ramaphosa and his fellow officials came close to despair.

Engaged by now in the wider battle to make the country 'ungovernable', Ramaphosa began to interpret the impending denouement of apartheid in increasingly cataclysmic terms. Yet, like the minister of religion who preaches that the end of the world is nigh while planting young fruit trees, Ramaphosa could not commit his imagination to Marxist revolutionary fantasies. He worked hard to create institutions of self-government in Soweto while also battling to destabilise the state, demonstrating an ingrained pragmatism and a determination to keep open multiple potential doors to the future.

The third wave of Ramaphosa's political rise was more deliberately crafted than its predecessors. He positioned himself to become a prominent spokesman for the ANC, and actively sought out a network of alliances in the UDF and the SACP. Many of his trade union friends were sceptical of his avowed conversion to leftist class doctrines. However, without SACP support, he could not have been propelled into the office of ANC secretary-general or risen to the leadership of its negotiation commission.

Another period of breathtaking personal achievement followed. Ramaphosa's mastery of negotiation was showcased to great effect by the Kempton Park process. His seemingly irresistible rise appeared for a time to be propelling him towards the state deputy presidency. His hopes and expectations were, however, dashed by Mandela's decision to choose the older and better-prepared Thabo Mbeki for this role. The internal politics of this struggle for office were rough and added bitter cynicism to Ramaphosa's views of some members of the exile elite.

Despite his initial devastation at being bypassed, Ramaphosa rode over the reversal and produced a stunning performance as chairman of the Constitutional Assembly. For many observers, his achievements highlighted the short-sightedness of Mandela's – and the ANC leadership's – choice of Mbeki as deputy president. When Ramaphosa left for business in 1996, his departure was accomplished with some dignity, his resilience fortified by his marriage of the heart to his third wife.

Ramaphosa probably always found the exposure of public life problematic. Former University of Cape Town Vice-Chancellor Mamphela Ramphele once described him as 'a very private person'. She speculated that 'this deep privacy is common amongst the people from his area of origin, Venda. I remember some of the children I grew up with in that area would deny any knowledge of the whereabouts of their parents … *Thidebe* (I don't know) was their first response to any question.'[3]

Whether or not such stereotypes are genuinely illuminating, Ramaphosa certainly hated the regimented life he was forced to lead as ANC secretary-general. He was forever surrounded by bodyguards, and with no time to call his own. The burden of public life on his young children was also never far from his mind.[4] Now he had time to spend on himself. Would his ingrained and powerful ambitiousness relent?

Ramaphosa has gradually accommodated himself to wealth and comfort, and to his status as an elder statesman of the ANC renowned for his role in the trade union movement and the constitutional negotiations. He has known his wife, Tshepo Motsepe, for more than 20 years. They were married on 17 November 1996 at the Sandhurst home of Cyril's lawyer acquaintance Billy Gundelfinger.[5] They have three children.

Ramaphosa's first son, Andile, lived with his mother, Hope Ramaphosa, until the age of 12. He then decided that he wanted to live with his father. Andile was quickly brought into the family. Although such blessings always come with complex problems, Cyril's delight was evident when he and the family went to watch Andile, a prop forward, playing rugby for the Golden Lions: 'We were non-rugby people before, but his playing the game has made the whole family get into it. He has taught us rugby.'[6]

Ramaphosa lives with his family in an exclusive Johannesburg suburb. Although his work schedule is still more than full, he has a more rounded domestic life than a professional politician can enjoy. He spends most Sundays and Mondays at the family's substantial farm at the foot of Mpumalanga's Hlumuhlumu Mountains, 300 km east of Johannesburg, where he indulges his favourite pastime of trout fishing on his own lake and with his own boathouse. He loves to invite friends to stay on the farm, and to explain to them the finer points of fly-fishing: the art of seduction, the need for patience, and the futility of using force when fishing.

The farm boasts a herd of Kenyan Boran cows which are spectacular animals – for those who adore cows, at least. (They are 'God's gift to cattlemen' in the admittedly partial opinion of the journal *Boran South Africa.*) In addition there is a herd of Ugandan Ankole cattle, bought from Ugandan President Yoweri Museveni, which is Ramaphosa's pride and joy. On a business trip to Uganda he saw the cows and fell deeply in love.[7] Cyril even brought back photographs of the Ankole and showed them to everyone who wanted to see them – and to many who didn't.

Ramaphosa, who is also a breeder of Bonsmara cattle, recently earned the admiration of the farming community for his response to a rude white youngster at a stud auction in the North West. A young man at the auction's registration table asked Ramaphosa for his name, to which he replied 'Cyril'. The editor of *Farmer's Weekly* takes up the story:

'The kid, obviously no great current affairs enthusiast, squints uncomprehendingly at arguably the best-known black businessman in South Africa, before shaking his head disappointedly. "Ag nee wat," he starts. "Dis mos nie 'n naam vir 'n swart man nie. Ons noem jou sommer Piet." [No man, that's not a name for a black man, we'll just call you Piet.] To say that there was a rather awkward silence around the table is maybe somewhat of an understatement.'[8]

With a wry smile, Cyril picked up his name tag, with 'Piet' scrawled upon it, and made his way to his seat without a word. When Ramaphosa began buying expensive bulls, the youngster must have discovered the error he had made, and he fled in his bakkie. 'Besides the obvious and uniquely South African humour of the story of the hapless auctioneer's assistant,' the editor of *Farmer's Weekly* observed, 'the maturity with which Ramaphosa dealt with the situation speaks volumes. Recognising the situation for what it was – ridiculous human folly – he thought better of it than to make a huge fuss, and in the process won the respect of all the farmers who witnessed the jarring faux pas.'

The mouthpiece of the country's farmers concluded that it is 'through strength of character, and not by indulging insecurities, that such idiots are put squarely in their place ... In the process, a constructive lesson is imparted to all. It is no understatement to say that this country, and agriculture specifically, needs more men and women of Ramaphosa's stature.'[9]

When pressed by journalists, Cyril's office lists his hobbies as reading biographies, trout fishing, playing golf, listening to jazz, watching motor racing, and playing tennis. These are more or less the same interests as Cyril and his then wife Hope Mudau professed in *Black Who's Who* almost 30 years ago.[10] The difference lies in the degree of indulgence that great wealth can bring: a tennis court of one's own, a fishing lake on the farm, a personal library, expensive musical and electronic equipment, and a garage full of high-performance cars.

Some ANC veterans – and even more white liberal observers – have struggled to come to terms with the affluence of the new black elite. Journalists love to dwell on 'ostentatious displays of wealth'. One 1998 polemic ridiculed 'the readiness of a liberation movement to be liberated into the bourgeois lifestyle of its opponents'. It commented that 'Daring ties, silk and quasi-military style suits predominate among the male liberators; fancy hats and ostentatious dresses among the newly elevated female elite.' Ramaphosa was singled out in this attack for his 'weakness for fly-fishing and single-malt whiskies'.[11]

For Ramaphosa such reporting has subtle racist undertones. 'It's almost like, "Here they are, the Johnny-come-latelies ... Look at the type of cars they drive; look at the clothes they wear." I find it despicable. Because quite often black people who are succeeding in business are not recognized for what they are achieving, but for how different they have now become.'[12]

Ramaphosa sees no contradiction between the struggle for justice and the enjoyment of luxury. At times, and by necessity, Ramaphosa has lived a very modest life. Working at NUM in the middle of the 1980s, he was often at his desk for days at a time, with almost no sleep, earning R600 per month. But even as a student, he revelled in 'bourgeois pleasures' and there was nothing he liked better than to entertain. When he and his school friends took the train from Soweto to Doornfontein for their holiday work in the early 1970s, Cyril loved to dress up smartly in a suit and tie – and, above all, to buy a first-class ticket.[13] At the NUM he would fly first-class on union business.[14]

The scholar Padraig O'Malley once asked Ramaphosa about the contrast between Nelson Mandela's lavish inauguration and the wider poverty of the society. The ANC, after all, had indulged in a three-day post-election celebration at the Carlton Hotel in which 'even the drapes were done in satin in ANC colours'. Ramaphosa's comment was that 'In the end, I think life has to be good for all our people'.[15]

Such a statement is consistent with Ramaphosa's earlier behaviour as NUM general secretary. He would insist – despite the union's financial deficit – that union delegates must stay at the Johannesburg Sun Hotel. 'I want the best for mineworkers,' he would explain, arguing that they deserved to enjoy the same comforts as their mining-house counterparts.[16]

Ramaphosa's version of socialism seemingly demands that equality must be achieved by raising up and not by levelling down. Education, culture and the arts – but also good food, vintage wine, beautiful clothes, and fast cars – should not be reserved to the rich. Why should rich whites monopolise access to material and aesthetic goods?

The late Peter Mokaba wrote a discussion paper entitled 'Through the Eye of a Needle' that today guides ANC branch members in the choice of their leaders. The biblical reference seems to imply that it is easier for a camel to pass through the eye of a needle than for a rich man to enter the kingdom of the presidency. However, the eye of the needle is in fact an apocryphal gate in biblical Jerusalem providing access to the city after dark. The gate was built low so that a wealthy merchant's camel would have to be unloaded of its treasures in order that the animal might crawl humbly and unburdened of wealth, on its knees, into the city.

It remains unclear if Ramaphosa would be willing to sacrifice his wealth for political office. Matthew 6. 24 is sometimes cited against him: 'No one can serve two masters. He will either hate one and love the other, or be devoted to one and despise the other. You cannot serve God and mammon.'[17]

In Ramaphosa's youth, this passage would have been interpreted as concerning God's insistence that human beings should not be preoccupied with money or with the necessities of life: 'Look at the birds in the sky; they do not sow or reap, they gather nothing into barns, yet your heavenly Father feeds them. Are not you more important than they?'[18] Anxiety about material consumption is a sign that one is not yet fully committed to being a child of God. The desire to protect and provide for ourselves demonstrates that we have not yet understood that it is God, and not we, who is in control of the circumstances of our lives.

Today's post-religious Ramaphosa exhibited some real sensitivity to allegations of crass materialism when a spokesman for DaimlerChrysler claimed in 2005 that Cyril had purchased a Maybach 62. The Maybach was priced at R3 million and it was widely reported to boast a television, a DVD player, and a 21-speaker surround sound system. Other advertised features included a refrigerator, a heated steering wheel, a golf-bag holder, and a set of fitted sterling silver champagne flutes.

For Ramaphosa a Maybach would have been 'far too much of a conspicuous display of wealth in a sea of enormous poverty'.[19] He complained that 'I have spoken to DaimlerChrysler several times and asked them to apologise, but they have refused ... I drive a BMW and I felt embarrassed to be associated with a car that is worth millions ... They must correct the impression they have created.'[20]

The company backed down and in settlement paid an undisclosed amount into one of Ramaphosa's educational charities. Ramaphosa then had to respond to media speculation that the legal action was designed to protect his image because he wanted one day to return to politics. 'That is absolute, absolute rubbish. That is really stretching it. I am acting to protect my personal interests.'[21]

Ramaphosa's charitable ventures are too haphazard and poorly advertised to be motivated by political calculation. As early as 1996, he began collecting money for a student support fund using collections during speeches and sending out annual requests for donations. His experiences in helping to equip his own childhood primary school, Tshilidzi Primary in Tshiawelo, with basic facilities persuaded him to exchange *ad hoc* interventions for more systematic action. After giving the school a fax machine and photocopier, he realised Tshilidzi also needed major investment in new classrooms. Through the Adopt-a-School Foundation he started in 1999, such help is now made available to a wide range of schools.[22]

Only the most cynical observers greeted the recent creation of the

Shanduka Foundation, a charitable arm of the investment company, as harbinger of a return to politics.[23] A relatively modest initial commitment is spread between the Adopt-a-School initiative, a business development vehicle, and an educational scholarships trust. The Foundation is run by ANC loyalist and Ramaphosa's trusted PA of 11 years standing, Donne Cooney, an indication that the vehicle could rapidly expand should it become necessary to shed personal wealth in preparation for a return to high office.[24] This, of course, would be the act of a wealthy merchant, whose camel had to be unloaded of its treasures in order for it, and him, to crawl unburdened through the eye of the needle.

Ramaphosa has also adopted a number of unlikely local causes in recent years. The youth who was a dreadful footballer[25] has become chairman of Wits United soccer club, known as the 'Clever Boys' because of their affiliation with the Witwatersrand University. In September 2006, he became patron of the Johannesburg Philharmonic Orchestra, using his influence to secure the orchestra sponsorships and publicity.

The profile Ramaphosa presents to the world is that of a politician turned businessman. Despite his continued membership of the ANC's National Executive Committee, and his participation in its subcommittee work, his actions send out the message that he has no personal ambition to return to the fray. His official curriculum vitae, posted on Internet sites wherever his name is cited, likewise emphasises that politics is firmly a thing of the past. He is happy to reflect back on his achievements: on the 1987 Olaf Palme prize, a string of honorary doctorates from prestigious universities, and the respect and acclaim of his peers for the role he played in South Africa's negotiated settlement. His attention in the present and for the foreseeable future is purportedly focused on the business world and his ambitions for Shanduka, his investment holding company, as a pan-African business.

Ramaphosa is described as both arrogant and humble. His self-confidence is no doubt so well developed that it is sometimes hard to distinguish from arrogance. His apparent humility, meanwhile, is sometimes slightly smug, as when he begins his contribution to a meeting by remarking 'I am just a humble businessman'.

His pride in rubbing shoulders with presidents and prime ministers was palpable in the early 1990s.[26] And he has an evident weakness for high-profile advisory boards, loving nothing more than being the centre of attention and having his brains picked by the leading international diplomats and politicians of his generation.[27]

A genuine yearning for approval and acceptance is also sometimes revealed in sensitivity to criticism. Cyril recently attended a weekend business strategy workshop at which the participants, sitting around small tables, had to identify and write down good and bad characteristics of other members of their team. The purpose of such excruciating exercises is to encourage participants to be more open about feelings they hide in the office. When the anonymous contributions were read out, most participants took criticism of themselves in good grace. Cyril, however, looked very cross about what were only mildly critical remarks, and went on to sulk for the entire weekend.[28]

Ramaphosa can muster the aggression to strike fear into the hearts of his victims even over the telephone.[29] Yet he is also careful to treat ordinary employees and acquaintances sensitively, and he softens any honest criticism he may have with a balancing compliment. He will make space to attend and speak at the weddings of friends, and to visit them when they have suffered bereavements. His friend Simon Cairns, an exceptionally charming and gracious hereditary British Earl, observes of Cyril: 'At the end of a meeting, Cyril will always be very careful to thank everybody present – including the caterers. There is an inverse relationship between the social status of an individual and the amount of time he devotes to them.'[30]

In the middle of the negotiated transition, Ramaphosa's one-time employer from Jeppe Street legal chambers, Henry Dolowitz, came across Cyril walking down the street in downtown Johannesburg. Ramaphosa was accompanied by Joe Slovo and surrounded by a phalanx of bodyguards. Dolowitz was hesitant to approach him, but Cyril rushed over to introduce him to Slovo. When Dolowitz mentioned that he was due to get married the following Sunday, Ramaphosa insisted he must come. Flicking through engagements in his diary, however, he ruefully remarked, 'That morning I have breakfast with Nelson Mandela and FW de Klerk.' Come Sunday morning, Ramaphosa arrived at the wedding – a little late – and told Dolowitz he had cut short his breakfast. 'What did you tell them?' asked Dolowitz. 'I told them I had something more important to do.'[31]

Ramaphosa invites old friends to his farm to share with them the good fortune he has enjoyed. Even quite distant acquaintances feel that he cares about them and listens to what they have to say.

It is characteristic of Ramaphosa to retain old friends and networks rather than to abandon them. The Lutheran Church belongs primarily to his youth and to his family, and he will respect both that world and the people who are part of it. Few of Ramaphosa's acquaintances would any longer describe him as a Christian, although all would recognise the importance of religion in the formation of his character. A bishop in the Lutheran Church who has been a family friend for decades observes that Cyril is no stranger to the church.[32] Indeed, any visitor to the Tshiawelo Lutheran congregation can observe the pews recently donated by Cyril, and his church subscription is almost certainly fully up to date.

Ramaphosa likewise meets with his old friends from high school and university every year, usually on 16 December. And he has recently assembled together his entire extended family, the Ramaphosa clan, and persuaded them to communicate through a closed website and to contribute to an annual 'family report'.

Others who call themselves his friends – people he has met through business or politics – are kept at arm's length in their own quite distinct social spaces. Among his old trade union friends, Cyril is taken as a union man who still has the interests of ordinary workers close to his heart. His communist friends believe he is deep down a sympathiser, and social democrats and African humanists likewise claim him as one of their own. Business people meanwhile feel that Cyril has absorbed the fundamental lessons of the post-socialist age and pragmatically accepts the ascendancy of capitalism. Despite this tendency to claim Ramaphosa as one of their own, most friends from his diverse social and political constituencies regard him as fundamentally a 'pragmatist'.

Ramaphosa's conciliatory nature, pragmatism and immaculate presentation have never fully concealed a wild streak in his personality. As a young man, he was a socialite and an entertainer who could quickly cast off the staid Christian demeanour required for preaching and evangelism. His seeming unconcern about the threat of violence and detention was later accompanied by a sanguine approach to his union's alarming financial deficits.[33]

He has always been a dare-devil driver. In the long drives that were part of union life, Cyril would push his increasingly decrepit BMW at full throttle, routinely breaking traffic laws and spectacularly exceeding speed limits.[34] In the early 1990s, Cyril was driving two visitors from England at his usual breakneck speed along a rural road. They flashed past a speed trap, and traffic police raced after them. As he pulled over to the side of the road, Cyril observed to his passengers that the policemen were all black brothers. He placed his ANC card on top of his driving licence as he handed it to one of the policemen.[35]

Despite the conservatism of his upbringing, such experiences show that Ramaphosa cannot be accused of making a fetish out of obeying the law. In his younger days, likewise, his many relationships with women demonstrated a disregard for the exaggerated propriety and moralising aspect of the churches. As one acquaintance explains it, Cyril is a man of true integrity. However, 'he has a pragmatic sense of the limited depth and range of God's interest in man's misdemeanours'.[36] For Ramaphosa, as for his boyhood friend Lybon Mabasa, God is not petty.

Ramaphosa's capacities as a conciliator and an ameliorator also run partly counter to one further trait that has struck all those who have worked closely with him: he is stubborn. This trait has formed part of his armoury as a negotiator, bringing an added element of indeterminacy to the calculations of his adversaries.

As a negotiator or a businessman, stubbornness means Ramaphosa must always be brought on board early. Once he has taken up an entrenched position, it is virtually impossible to get him to abandon it. He would rather endure days or even weeks of not talking to those closest to him than back down in the face of pressure.

Ramaphosa does not acknowledge this quality in himself. Indeed, perhaps like most people, he sees himself as an exceedingly reasonable man. When he has taken major decisions in his life, for example when he decided to leave politics for the world of business, he consulted widely with friends. Nevertheless, whether knowingly or not, he talked only to those who would not condemn a decision he had already taken.[37]

This pragmatic consensus-seeker also harbours a controlling streak. In the early days of the NUM, Ramaphosa was the hands-on manager of a shoestring operation, micro-managing the office 'down to the paper clips'.[38] His endless designing and redesigning of strategic plans and constitutions demonstrate a perfectionist tendency.[39] Unable to control this tendency, he conceals it beneath consultative procedures. On joining the Student Christian Movement in Turfloop and the Youth Alive ministry in Soweto, he immediately insisted on writing a new constitution. He then forced everyone else to deliberate upon, and agree to, its beneficent character in a democratic process that none of the participants wanted or enjoyed.[40]

One business colleague observes of Cyril's 'control obsession' that 'he tries so hard to camouflage [it]. He wants to have the final say on everything – even the colour of everybody's jackets. He hides his control aspect but it comes out at awkward times and in awkward ways.'[41]

On his farm Ramaphosa insists that his household staff must choose the colour of their own uniforms – a choice he oversees and inevitably shapes.[42] This is, of course, a benign control: Cyril wants to know the name of every employee and he questions their working conditions, pay and food. Are they getting enough healthy vegetables to eat?

Ramaphosa is accustomed to securing control simply by exercising an easy influence over those he knows. Since his childhood, he has been a person in whom others place trust. Cyril's Turfloop contemporary Reuel Khoza, an accomplished scholar of theories of leadership, observes that the 'mystery of leadership' lies in the fact that 'power comes from those who are led': leaders are powerful only because they can build 'willing coalitions of supporters'.[43] Ramaphosa, in Khoza's view, has an uncanny ability to resolve the paradoxes of leadership because he has both 'the common touch' to engage with ordinary people and the uncommon capacity to act as a heroic visionary.[44]

Ramaphosa's ability to build trust rests on perceptions that he demonstrates a deeper integrity that sets strict boundaries to his actions. He plays the games of politics and business but he does so according to his own code of personal ethics.

Pragmatism and trust were central factors in the success of constitutional negotiations. Ramaphosa's pragmatic streak did not allow him to become fixated on the pristine character of the final document. For him it was a complex solution to political and practical problems. Kader Asmal observes that the first section of the constitution, entitled 'Founding Provisions', includes a section on language policy inserted, most unusually, before the bill of rights. Most constitutional lawyers saw this as an anomaly to be rectified. For Ramaphosa, this placing of language policy was part of a hard-nosed compromise struck with recalcitrant National Party negotiators. When asked to consider repositioning the section, he responded, 'What does it matter?' The benefits of the compromise were greater than the costs, in Ramaphosa's view, and this was sufficient for him to give it the go-ahead.[45] While he is a lawyer, he was not acting as a lawyer, or in a legalistic way, during the negotiations.[46]

The document was also infused by the trust that Ramaphosa built between the participants. The judge president of the Transvaal, Bernard Ngoepe, who was a member of the committee that drafted the interim constitution, observes that what were merely pieces of paper somehow developed a compelling moral character. Ramaphosa nurtured trust and commitment in the process and its outcome among diverse negotiators, and in this way he gave the document itself the spirit that it continues to possess.[47]

As an ameliorator[48] and a processor[49] Ramaphosa transforms the antagonisms of others into an unexpected consensus. His own deeper beliefs and opinions remain hidden. People who have known him for many years have no idea what his position might be on central aspects of economic or foreign policy.[50]

Ramaphosa's thinking has deep and complex ideological roots and he returns repeatedly to a preoccupation with the origins and persistence of the fundamental disadvantage of black people.[51] Beneath his bonhomie and charm, moreover, there is a coldness and dispassionate quality. According to one of his oldest friends, he is not a 'prisoner of friendship' who would feel obliged to pay back his friends for their loyalty. 'If he was president, he would be a president.'[52]

For a successful politician of the modern era, he has been almost uniquely immune to the political blackmail of populists like Peter Mokaba and Winnie Madikizela-Mandela. He has been the 'tough guy' who 'tells people to get off when they are out of order... He draws a line and says "no further."'[53]

Ramaphosa's primary achievement as a political leader has been more mundane and yet far more important. The key disappointment since 1994 has been the government's inability to create new institutions to solve intractable problems. This is exactly the capacity that has marked Ramaphosa's entire political career. The National Union of Mineworkers remains a powerful testimony to Ramaphosa's ability to build an institution that can endure. The nation's constitution, an achievement hard to imagine without Ramaphosa, seems set to shape national politics for decades to come. Even the Bold Evangelical Christian Organisation is still performing the evangelical work for which Ramaphosa created it.

Many South Africans see the problem-solving and institution-building Ramaphosa as an obvious choice as a future State President of South Africa. At first he rose without effort. When as a teenager he astonished journalist Denis Beckett with his claim that he would be President, he was ascending naturally to the leadership of almost every organisation he joined.

Excluded from Turfloop after his detention in 1974, Cyril lamented his separation from his constituency. Despite all that he had been through, he still wanted to be Student Representative Council president.[54] He switched from the languishing Young Ambassadors youth club to the more successful Youth Alive in the mid-1970s.[55] His took the NUM out of Cusa and into the growing and glamorous Cosatu he had helped to create.[56]

As his political career matured, however, Ramaphosa's ambition was tempered by a fear of losing. His decision to stand for the position of secretary-general of the ANC in 1991 was not one he found easy to take, but not for want of ambition. He hoped to be on the winning side, and he wanted to be wanted.[57] A former trade union colleague observes that 'Cyril will not stand unless he wins. He is not a chancer and not a number two.'[58]

Ramaphosa is a natural politician who gravitates towards and embraces power. It would not be a surprise to find that his time, at last, has come.

NOTES

Preface

1 Mark Gevisser, 'Rhodes, Rupert, Ramaphosa', *Mail & Guardian*, 11 October 1996.

2 Ibid.

3 These remarks are not in quotation marks because I was sufficiently intimidated not to write them down as they were spoken. They may not be arranged exactly as uttered.

4 Unnamed journalist, quoted in Gevisser, 'Rhodes, Rupert, Ramaphosa'.

5 William Mervyn Gumede, *Thabo Mbeki and the Battle for the Soul of the ANC*. Cape Town, Zebra Press, 2005.

6 Dirk Klopper, 'In pursuit of the subject: Towards a biography of Arthur Nortje', *Journal of Southern African Studies*, 30: 4, 2004, p. 871.

7 Cited in ibid., p.869.

8 Frank Chikane, *No Life of My Own: An Autobiography*. London, Catholic Institute for International Relations, 1988.

9 Klopper, 'In pursuit', pp. 881–2.

10 Vic Allen, *History of Black Mineworkers in South Africa: Volume 3*. Keighley, The Moor Press, 2003.

11 His involvement in the project began in 1989. Confined with Ramaphosa on a boat off the coast of Cuba, while waiting to meet Fidel Castro, Allen was persuaded to take on the task of writing this comprehensive history, and to do so explicitly from the perspective of black mineworkers themselves.

12 Per Strand, *Decisions on Democracy: The Politics of Constitution-Making in South Africa, 1990–1996*. Doctoral dissertation in political science, Department of Government, University of Uppsala, 2000.

Chapter 1

1 Oswald Mtshali, 'Just a passerby', *Sounds of a Cowhide Drum*. London, Oxford University Press, 1972, p. 56.

2 Godfried Dederen, personal communications with author, 27 and 28 February 2007; Samu Zulu, 'A tribute to Cyril Ramaphosa's late mother, Munyadziwa', *The Enquirer*, 8 November 2001.

3 This account is adapted from Anthony Butler, *Contemporary South Africa*. New York, Palgrave Macmillan, 2004, Chapter 1.

4 Twentieth-century South Africa was notorious for institutionalised racial and ethnic segregation. Apartheid required the enforced classification of a fluid and diverse population as white/European, native/Bantu, Indian or coloured. Such categories have been contested politically by many of those to whom they have been applied. Their use in this book should not be taken as an endorsement of assumptions about racial or ethnic difference that have no scientific validity.

5 Leonard Thompson, *History of South Africa*. New Haven, Yale University Press, 1995, pp. 207-9.

6 Philip Bonner et al. (eds.), *Apartheid's Genesis 1935–1962*. Johannesburg, Witwatersrand University Press, 1993, pp. 15–21.

7 The war economies of the north provided a ready market for almost any manufactured export from the south. At the same time, a shortage of formerly imported manufactured goods resulted in an explosion of import-substituting domestic industries, creating finished products from local raw materials. This boom was also fuelled by expanding markets across the African continent. Anthony Butler, *Democracy and Apartheid*. London, Macmillan, 1998, pp. 20–3.

8 Monica Cole, 'The Witwatersrand conurbation', *Transactions and Papers of the Institute of British Geographers*, 23, 1957, p. 258.

9 Elinor Sisulu, *Walter and Albertina Sisulu: In Our Lifetime*. Cape Town, David Philip, 2003, p. 89.

10 Douglas Ramaphosa, author's interview, Parktown, Johannesburg, 22 November 2006.

11 Cole, 'Witwatersrand conurbation', p. 258.

12 Ibid.

13 Philip Bonner and Lauren Segal, *Soweto: A History*. Cape Town, Maskew Miller Longman, 1998.

14 Diamond Atong, author's interview, Tshwane University of Technology, Pretoria, 29 August 2006.

15 With improbable accuracy, Lybon Mabasa ventures 4,271 units. Author's interview, Rosebank Johannesburg, 17 August 2006.

16 Ishmael Mkhabela, author's interview, Braamfontein, Johannesburg, 15 August 2006.

17 Ibid.

18 Author's interviews with Tom Manthatha, Parktown, Johannesburg, 16 August 2006; Ishmael Mkhabela; Lybon Mabasa; Peter Phaswani, Jabavu, Soweto, 31 August 2006.

19 Douglas Ramaphosa, author's interview. Cyril remains a paid-up member of this burial society to this day.

20 Rams Ramashia, author's interview, Waterfront, Cape Town, 31 October 2006.

21 Cyril Ramaphosa interview with Patti Waldmeir, 19 January 1995, Historical Papers, University of the Witwatersrand, A2508.

22 Douglas Ramaphosa, author's interview.

23 Peter Phaswani, author's interview.

24 Rams Ramashia, author's interview.

25 Tshitasini literally means 'place near the mission station'.

26 Griffith Zabala, author's interview, Kyalami Estate, Johannesburg, 15 August 2006.

27 Ibid.

28 Ibid.

29 Caesar Molebatsi, author's interview, Johannesburg, 5 October 2006.

30 Peter Phaswani, author's interview. For details of the plot, see *The Star* or *The Sowetan*, 4 March 1994.

31 Zulu, 'Tribute to Cyril Ramaphosa's late mother'.

32 Peter Phaswani, author's interview.

33 Douglas Ramaphosa, author's interview.

34 Ibid.

35 Ibid.

36 Ibid.

37 BBC News online, 'Ramaphosa hopeful on weapons', 9 May 2000, available at <www.bbc.co.uk/1/hi/northern_ireland/741129.stm> accessed on 3 October 2006.

38 Leroy Vail (ed.), *The Creation of Tribalism in Southern Africa*. London, James Currey, 1989.
39 I am very grateful to Godfried Dederen from University of Venda for his explanation of this history. Personal communications with author, 27 and 28 February 2007.
40 Tshenuwani Farisani, *In Transit*. Grand Rapids, Michigan, Eerdmans Publishing, 1990, p. 86.
41 Today around two million people speak Venda in their homes, while ten times as many speak Zulu or Xhosa. Butler, *Contemporary South Africa*, p. 29.
42 Urban Foundation, *Profile of Greater Soweto*, 1976. National Archive, Cape Town, A2562 V/2. In contemporary usage, Tsonga and Venda tend to be described as distinct languages – indeed they are both 'official languages' in the new South Africa – and the word Shangaan is mostly applied to people living over the border in Mozambique.
43 Ishmael Mkhabela, author's interview.
44 Tom Manthatha, author's interview. Cyril did not attend such a camp.
45 Ishmael Mkhabela, author's interview.
46 Erdmuthe also became a staunch supporter of the ANC.
47 I have drawn in this discussion on Sheldon Wolin, *Politics and Vision*. Boston, Little, Brown, 1960, especially Chapter 5; and J Atkinson, *Martin Luther and the Birth of Protestantism*. London, Morgan and Scott, 1982. I am also grateful to Peter Phaswani and Tshenuwani Farisani for discussion.
48 I am grateful to Peter Phaswani for drawing my attention to the significance of this passage for Cyril's parents.

Chapter 2

1 Tshenuwani Farisani, 'South Africa: Unasked questions and unquestioned answers', in *Journal of Law and Religion*, 5: 2, 1987, p. 263. Farisani is sometimes known as 'Simon' Farisani.
2 Today he heads the Interfaith Community Development Association in Johannesburg.
3 Ishmael Mkhabela, author's interview, Braamfontein, Johannesburg, 15 August 2006.
4 Ishmael Mkhabela, author's interview.
5 Ishmael Mkhabela, author's interview.
6 Duma Ndlovu, author's interview, Northcliff, Johannesburg, 5 October 2006.
7 Ibid.
8 Griffith Zabala, author's interview, Kyalami Estate, 15 August 2006.
9 Ibid.
10 Tshenuwani Farisani, author's interview, Sandton, Johannesburg, 24 November 2006.
11 Griffith Zabala, author's interview.
12 Ibid.
13 Tom Manthatha, author's interview, Parktown, Johannesburg, 16 August 2006.
14 Peter Phaswani, author's interview, Soweto, Johannesburg, 31 August 2006.
15 Author's interviews with Griffith Zabala, Ishmael Mkhabela and Lybon Mabasa.
16 Jeremy Seekings, *The UDF: A History of the United Democratic Front in South Africa 1983–1991*. Cape Town, David Philip, 2000, p. 5.
17 Raymond Suttner, 'The UDF period and its meaning for contemporary South Africa', *Journal of Southern African Studies*, 30: 3, 2004, p. 694.
18 The importance of taking pride in one's blackness had been an important strand in black nationalism in the United States as far back as Civil War thinker Martin Delany.
19 Duma Ndlovu, author's interview.
20 Ishmael Mkhabela, author's interview.

21 Ibid.
22 Lybon Mabasa, author's interview, Rosebank, Johannesburg, 17 August 2006.
23 The acting head of SCM in Ramaphosa's absence was later killed in detention.
24 Peter Phaswani, author's interview.
25 Cyril Ramaphosa, interview with Julie Frederikse, 13 August 1985. Julie Frederikse Collection, Historical Papers, University of Witwatersrand, AL2460.
26 TS Ntsandeni, author's interview, Sibasa, Limpopo, 27 October 2006.
27 Ibid.
28 Ibid.
29 I am grateful to the current principal of Mphaphuli for unearthing the matriculation records of Ramaphosa's cohort.
30 Peter Phaswani, author's interview.
31 Ibid.
32 Griffith Zabala, author's interview. On one account he was 'a sociologist', *Black Review*, 1974/75, Chapter 1.
33 The Mphephu were a prominent part of the Singo clan.
34 *Black Review*, 1975/75, Chapter 1.
35 Douglas Reed, *The Siege of Southern Africa*. Johannesburg, Macmillan, 1974, available at <www.douglasreed.co.uk/siege.html> accessed on 12 August 2006.
36 Peter Phaswani, author's interview.
37 Reuel Khoza, author's interview, Sandton, Johannesburg, 26 October 2006; Hope Mudau, telephone conversation with author, 15 September 2006.
38 Today Farisani is Speaker in the Limpopo legislature.
39 Tshenuwani Farisani, author's interview.
40 Farisani, 'South Africa: Unasked questions', p. 265.
41 Tshenuwani Farisani, *In Transit*. Grand Rapids, Michigan, Eerdmans Publishing, 1990, pp. 103–4.
42 Tshenuwani Farisani, author's interview.
43 Farisani, *In Transit*, p. 92.
44 Ibid., p. 91.
45 Tshenuwani Farisani, author's interview.
46 Ibid.
47 Ibid.
48 Luke 4. 16–20.
49 Exodus 3. 4–9 and 16–22.
50 Farisani, *In Transit*, p. 84.
51 Peter Phaswani, author's interview.
52 Denis Beckett, telephone conversation with author, 6 November 2006.
53 Genesis 1. 26–8.
54 See, in particular, the first two chapters of Farisani, *In Transit*.
55 Tshenuwani Farisani, author's interview.
56 Douglas Ramaphosa, author's interview.
57 Simon Robinson, 'Welcome to the club', *Time Europe*, 29 May 2005.
58 Ishmael Mkhabela, author's interview.
59 Griffith Zabala, author's interview.
60 Ibid.
61 'A' grades were virtually unknown in the Venda school system at this time. TS Ntsandeni, author's interview.
62 Ishmael Mkhabela lost a leg as a child and was unable to make the walk. He joined them later in Cape Town by train.
63 Griffith Zabala, author's interview.
64 Observed by numerous respondents, including Kate Carey and Henry Dolowitz.

65 Griffith Zabala, author's interview; Duma Ndlovu, author's interview.

66 Wally Serote, *Selected Poems*. Johannesburg, Ad Donker, 1982, pp. 69–70.

Chapter 3

1 Tshenuwani Farisani, *In Transit*. Grand Rapids, Michigan, Eerdmans Publishing, 1990, p. 87.

2 The Extension of University Education Act, No. 45 of 1959, legislated the ethnic provision of higher education for black people.

3 *Black Review*, 1972, Chapter 12.

4 For example, The University of the North Act, No 49 of 1969.

5 *Black Review*, 1972, Chapter 12.

6 Ibid.

7 The bursary was from Syfrets Trust.

8 *Black Review*, 1972, Chapter 12.

9 Nkosinathi Gwala, 'State control, student politics and the crisis in black universities', in Robin Cohen and Billy Cobbett (eds.), *Popular Struggles in South Africa*. London, James Currey, 1988, pp. 163–82.

10 Radical black students' rejection of Nusas may have been a major factor in the rise of black consciousness.

11 Griffith Zabala, author's interview, Kyalami Estate, 15 August 2006.

12 Frank Chikane, *No Life of My Own: An Autobiography*. London, Catholic Institute for International Relations, 1988.

13 This account of Tiro's speech and its immediate aftermath is drawn from *Black Review*, 1972, Chapter 12; and from Thomas Karis and Gail Gerhart (eds.), *From Protest to Challenge, Volume 5: Nadir and Resistance, 1964–1979*. Bloomington, Indiana University Press, 1997, Chapter 5. The full text of Tiro's speech is also reprinted in this volume.

14 Karis and Carter, *From Protest to Challenge*, p. 498.

15 *Black Review*, 1972, Chapter 12.

16 Author's interview with Reuel Khoza, Sandton, 26 October 2006.

17 Website of the Azanian People's Organisation (Azapo), www.azapo.org.za accessed on 20 September 2006.

18 I am grateful for this recollection to my colleague Lungisile Ntsebeza who was at that time studying at Fort Hare.

19 Website of the Azanian People's Organisation (Azapo), www.azapo.org.za accessed on 20 September 2006.

20 Karis and Gerhart, *From Protest to Challenge*, Chapter 5.

21 Barney Pityana, author's interview, Unisa, Pretoria, 5 October 2006.

22 Griffith Zabala, author's interview.

23 Reuel Khoza, author's interview, Sandton, Johannesburg, 26 October 2006.

24 Today the director-general in the office of the President.

25 Chikane, *No Life of My Own*, p. 37.

26 Ibid., pp. 36–8.

27 Ibid., p. 37.

28 Frank Chikane, author's interview, Tuynhuys, Cape Town, 2 November 2006.

29 Barney Pityana, author's interview.

30 Chikane, *No Life of My Own*, p. 38.

31 Frank Chikane, author's interview.

32 Barney Pityana, author's interview.

33 Ibid.

34 Ibid.

35 Reuel Khoza, author's interview.

36 Frank Chikane, author's interview.
37 Reuel Khoza, author's interview.
38 Griffith Zabala, author's interview.
39 Chikane, *No Life of My Own*, p. 39.
40 Griffith Zabala, author's interview.
41 Frank Chikane, author's interview.
42 Reuel Khoza, author's interview.
43 Lybon Mabasa, author's interview, Rosebank, Johannesburg, 17 August 2006; Caesar Molebatsi, author's interview, Johannesburg, 5 October 2006.
44 Nigel Worden, *The Making of Modern South Africa*, 2nd edition. Oxford, Blackwell, 1995, p. 118.
45 Kgomotso Moroka, daughter of Dr Nthato Motlana, was secretary of the Saso branch.
46 Makhudu Sefara, 'Does Cyril have what it takes?', *City Press*, 30 July 2006, p. 21.
47 Such as himself, presumably. Barney Pityana, author's interview.
48 Reuel Khoza, author's interview; Frank Chikane, author's interview.
49 Chikane, *No Life of My Own*; Karis and Carter, *From Protest to Challenge*.
50 Ibid.
51 Pandelani Nefolovhodwe, telephone conversation with author, 22 August 2006.
52 Griffith Zabala, author's interview; Frank Chikane, author's interview; anonymous informant.

Chapter 4

1 Tshenuwani Farisani, *In Transit*. Grand Rapids, Michigan, Eerdmans Publishing, 1990, p. 84.
2 The General Laws Amendment Act of that year provided for detention without trial for 12 days. The Internal Security Act and Suppression of Communism Act of 1950 provided for 'preventive detention' and for the detention of state witnesses. Legislation introduced in response to the early 1950s Defiance Campaign allowed detention only after the declaration of a state of emergency. I am grateful to Colin Bundy for his advice on this legislation.
3 Don Foster, *Detention and Torture in South Africa: Psychological, Legal and Historical Studies*. Cape Town, David Philip, 1987, p. 25.
4 Ibid., p. 25.
5 Ibid., p. 5.
6 Raymond Suttner, *Inside Apartheid's Prison*. Melbourne, Ocean Press, 2001, p.29.
7 Ellen Kuzwayo, *Call Me Woman*. Randburg, Ravan Press, 1996 [1985], p. 205.
8 Tshenuwani Farisani, *Diary from a South African Prison*. Philadelphia, Fortress Press, 1987, p. 37.
9 Ibid., p. 39.
10 Griffith Zabala, author's interview, Kyalami Estate, 15 August 2006.
11 Ibid.
12 Chetty was posthumously reinstated on the roll of attorneys only in 2006.
13 Website of the Azanian People's Organisation (Azapo), www.azapo.org.za accessed on 20 September 2006.
14 Saths Cooper, author's interview, Killarney, Johannesburg, 17 August 2006.
15 Saths Cooper, author's interview. In a strange twist of history, Singh was the former public relations officer of Cyril's mentor Tshenuwani Farisani.
16 Pandelani Nefolovhodwe, telephone conversation with author, 22 August 2006.
17 Saths Cooper, author's interview; Tshenuwani Farisani, author's interview, Sandton, Johannesburg, 24 November 2006.
18 Saths Cooper, author's interview.

19 Tshenuwani Farisani, author's interview.
20 Tom Manthatha, author's interview, Parktown, Johannesburg, 16 August 2006.
21 Lybon Mabasa, author's interview, Rosebank, Johannesburg, 17 August 2006; Ishmael Mkhabela, author's interview, Braamfontein, Johannesburg, 15 August 2006; Griffith Zabala, author's interview.
22 Tom Manthatha, author's interview.
23 Saths Cooper, author's interview.
24 Frank Chikane, author's interview, Tuynhuys, Cape Town, 2 November 2006; Griffith Zabala and Tom Manthatha, author's interviews.
25 Cyril Ramaphosa interview with Patti Waldmeir, 19 January 1995. Historical Papers, University of the Witwatersrand, A2508.
26 Anonymous source.
27 Suttner, *Inside Apartheid's Prison*, p. 29.
28 Saths Cooper, author's interview.
29 Ibid.
30 Tom Manthatha, author's interview.
31 Testimony of a former detainee, in Foster, *Detention and Torture*, p. 152.
32 Cyril Ramaphosa interview with Julie Frederikse, 13 August 1985. Historical Papers, University of the Witwatersrand, AL2460.
33 Cyril Ramaphosa interview with Waldmeir, 19 January 1995.
34 Ibid.
35 Tshenuwani Farisani, author's interview.
36 Farisani, *Diary*, p. 36.
37 Rams Ramashia, author's interview, Waterfront, Cape Town, 31 October 2006.
38 Ishmael Mkhabela, Lybon Mabasa and Griffith Zabala, author's interviews.
39 Foster, *Detention and Torture*.
40 Ishmael Mkhabela, author's interview.
41 Rams Ramashia, author's interview.
42 Cyril Ramaphosa interview with Waldmeir, 19 January 1995.

Chapter 5

1 From Dennis Brutus, 'Remembering June 16, 1976', in *Remembering Soweto 1976*. Elmwood, Canada, Whirlwind Books, 1992.
2 Jeremy Seekings, *The UDF: A History of the United Democratic Front 1983-1991*. Cape Town, David Philip, 2000, p. 11; William Beinart, *20th Century South Africa*. Oxford, Oxford University Press, 1994, p. 219.
3 Alistair Boddy-Evans, 'The Afrikaans Medium Decree', *About African History*, available at <http://africanhistory.about.com/library/bl/blsaJune16decree.htm> accessed on 27 February 2007.
4 Frank Chikane, author's interview, Tuynhuys, Cape Town, 2 November 2006.
5 Ellen Kuzwayo, *Call Me Woman*. Randburg, Ravan Press, 1996 [1985], p. 41.
6 Thompson puts the numbers at 3,000–10,000 and Worden at 15,000. Leonard Thompson, *A History of South Africa*. New Haven, Yale University Press, 1990, p. 212. Nigel Worden, *The Making of Modern South Africa*. Oxford, Blackwell, 1995, p. 119. Some estimates are even higher.
7 Thompson, *History of South Africa*, p. 212.
8 Ishmael Mkhabela, author's interview, Braamfontein, Johannesburg, 15 August 2006.
9 Cyril Ramaphosa interview with Mark Gevisser, quoted in Gevisser, 'Rhodes, Rupert, Ramaphosa', *Mail & Guardian*, 11 October 1996.
10 Rams Ramashia, author's interview, Waterfront, Cape Town, 31 October 2006.
11 Douglas Ramaphosa, author's interview, Parktown, Johannesburg, 22 November 2006.

12 Ibid.

13 Cyril Ramaphosa interview with Julie Frederikse, 13 August 1985. Historical Papers, University of the Witwatersrand, AL2460.

14 Douglas Ramaphosa, author's interview.

15 Ramaphosa interview with Patti Waldmeir, 19 January 1995. Historical Papers, University of the Witwatersrand, A2508.

16 Ellen Kuzwayo, *Call Me Woman*. Randburg, Ravan Press, 1996 [1985], p. 41.

17 Muofhe is survived by his wife, Professor Lillian Muofhe, and by a daughter, both of whom live in the United States.

18 *Truth and Reconciliation Commission*, vol. 3, p. 542.

19 Imtiaz Cajee, 'A journey to reclaim an uncle, comrade and martyr', *Umrabulo*, 23, June 2005.

20 Imtiaz Cajee, *Timol: A Quest for Justice*. Cape Town, STE Publishers, 2005. Student activist Matthews Mabelane was to fall in February 1977 from the same tenth-floor window.

21 Douglas Ramaphosa, author's interview.

22 Ibid.

23 Ramaphosa interview with Waldmeir, 19 January 1995.

24 Diamond Atong, author's interview, Tshwane University of Technology, Pretoria, 29 August 2006.

25 Diamond Atong, author's interview.

26 Henry Dolowitz, author's interview, Orange Grove Johannesburg, 30 August 2006.

27 Ibid.

28 Ibid.

29 Ibid.

30 Ibid.

31 Ibid.

32 Don Foster, *Detention and Torture in South Africa: Psychological, Legal and Historical Studies*. Cape Town, David Philip, 1987.

33 Ishmael Mkhabela, author's interview.

34 Tshenuwani Farisani, 'South Africa: Unasked questions and unquestioned answers', *Journal of Law and Religion*, 5: 2, 1987, p. 263.

35 Ramaphosa interview with Waldmeir, 19 January 1995.

36 Caesar Molebatsi, author's interview, Johannesburg, 5 October 2006.

37 Tom Manthatha, author's interview, Parktown, Johannesburg, 16 August 2006; Rams Ramashia, author's interview.

38 Peter Phaswani, author's interview, Soweto, Johannesburg, 31 August 2006.

39 Rams Ramashia, author's interview.

40 Strike Thokoane, author's interview, Pretoria, 24 November 2006.

41 Douglas Ramaphosa, author's interview.

42 Duma Ndlovu, author's interview, Northcliff, Johannesburg, 5 October 2006.

43 Tshenuwani Farisani, author's interview, Sandton, Johannesburg, 24 November 2006.

44 Rick Menell, author's interview, Main Street Johannesburg, 25 October 2006.

45 Ramaphosa interview with Waldmeir, 19 January 1995.

46 Rams Ramashia, author's interview; Caesar Molebatsi, author's interview.

47 Caesar Molebatsi, author's interview.

48 Ibid.

49 Ramaphosa also sat on the board of an umbrella organisation, the South African Christian Leadership Assembly (SACL). See Sheila Keeble (ed.), *Black Who's Who of Southern Africa Today*. Johannesburg, African Business Publications, 1979, p. 242.

50 Peter Phaswani, author's interview.

51 Rams Ramashia, author's interview.

52 Griffith Zabala, author's interview.
53 Rams Ramashia, author's interview.
54 Griffith Zabala, author's interview.
55 Martin Nicol, author's interview, Cape Town, 24 August 2006.
56 Kate Carey, personal conversation, Keighley, West Yorkshire, 14 July 2006.
57 Diamond Atong, author's interview.
58 National Archive, Cape Town. A2562 A/28.
59 Griffith Zabala, author's interview, Kyalami Estate, 15 August 2006.

Chapter 6
1 Chris van Wyk, *It Is Time to Go Home*. Johannesburg, Ad Donker, 1979, p. 28.
2 Duma Ndlovu, author's interview, Northcliff, Johannesburg, 5 October 2006. Ndlovu remembers that he was another of those contacted by Beckett.
3 Ellen Kuzwayo, *Call Me Woman*. Randburg, Ravan Press, 1996 [1985].
4 Helbron Vilakazi, telephone conversation with author, 1 September 2006.
5 Cyril Ramaphosa interview with Patti Waldmeir, 19 January 1995. Historical Papers, University of the Witwatersrand, A2508.
6 Kuzwayo, *Call Me Woman*.
7 Ibid., Chapters 1–3.
8 Barney Pityana, author's interview, Unisa, Pretoria, 5 October 2006; Duma Ndlovu, author's interview, Northcliff, Johannesburg, 5 October 2006.
9 Nthato Motlana, author's interview, Johannesburg, 24 November 2006.
10 The events are detailed by Kuzwayo, *Call Me Woman*.
11 Memorandum from the Transvaal Chamber of Industries to the Prime Minister of the Republic of South Africa, 29 July 1976.
12 In reality the game originated in the Roman Empire with the game Harpastum, which involved two teams trying to carry a stuffed leather ball over each other's goal line. Harpastum itself was probably derived from ancient Chinese and Japanese sports or perhaps from the ancient Greek pastime Episkyros. See Richard Bath (ed.), *The Ultimate Encyclopedia of Rugby*. London, Hodder & Stoughton, 1997.
13 The language is that of their son Rick Menell, author's interview, Main Street, Johannesburg, 25 October 2006.
14 Irene Menell, author's interview, Parktown, Johannesburg, 26 October 2006.
15 Rick Menell, author's interview.
16 Ibid.
17 Irene Menell, author's interview.
18 *Mail & Guardian*, 'Arms deal: Who got R1bn in pay-offs?', 12 January 2007; *Mail & Guardian*, 'How arms dealer got its hooks into the ANC', 19 January 2007.
19 Irene Menell, author's interview.
20 Frederik van Zyl Slabbert, author's interview, Craighall, Johannesburg, 21 November 2006.
21 It is not known whether there were countervailing influences that can explain Mufamadi's subsequent moral trajectory.
22 Irene Menell, author's interview.
23 Ibid. Tutu, of course, might have turned his question back on himself.
24 Frederik van Zyl Slabbert, author's interview.
25 Irene Menell, author's interview.
26 André du Toit, personal communication with author, 23 January 2007.
27 Ibid.
28 Irene Menell, author's interview.
29 Ibid.
30 David Pallister, Sarah Stewart and Ian Lepper, *South Africa Inc.: The Oppenheimer*

Empire, 2nd edition. London, Corgi, 1988, Chapter 5.

31 Tshenuwani Farisani, author's interview, Sandton, Johannesburg, 24 November 2006.

32 Quotation from unattributed participant, conference publicity materials, untitled and undated, National Archive, Cape Town, A2562 J/5.

33 Ebbe Dommisse, *Anton Rupert: A Biography.* Cape Town, Tafelberg, 2005, p. 238.

34 Ibid., pp. 238–41.

35 Businessmen's Conference on the Quality of Life of Urban Communities, 'Resolutions', 29 November 1976. National Archive, Cape Town, A2562, V/2.

36 Jan Steyn, letter to Harry Oppenheimer, 8 December 1976. National Archive, Cape Town, A2562 B/7.

37 Dommisse, *Anton Rupert*, p. 239.

38 Submission by the Urban Foundation: Transvaal Region to the Urban Foundation National Review and Planning Meeting, 7 March 1980, p. 2. National Archive, Cape Town, A2562 J/5.

39 Irene Menell, author's interview.

40 Fred Phaswana, author's interview, Constantia, Cape Town, 10 October 2006.

41 Dan Smit, 'The Urban Foundation: Transformation possibilities', *Transformation*, 18, 1992, p. 36.

42 Urban Foundation Transvaal Region, Minutes of a strategy and budget committee meeting, Monday 9 October 1978. National Archive, Cape Town, A2562 A/2.

43 Letter from Clive Menell to Jan Steyn, 8 August 1978. National Archive, Cape Town, A2562 P/7.

44 John Kane-Berman, 'The search for a black middle class', *Energos*, 1, 1980.

45 Nigel Unwin, author's interview, Diagonal Street, Johannesburg, 30 August 2006.

46 Jan Steyn, 1980 correspondence. National Archive, Cape Town, A2562 B/8.

47 By the middle of 1981 he was attending fewer than one in two meetings.

48 National Archive, Cape Town, A2562 I/7.

49 Ibid., A2562 I/7.

50 Ibid., A2562 D/10.

51 Ibid., A2562 D/7.

52 Irene Menell, author's interview.

53 National Archive, Cape Town, A2562 D/7.

54 Ibid., A2562 B/8. The owner of Oranjemund was Consolidated Diamond Mines, a wholly owned subsidiary of De Beers.

55 Today the Indaba Hotel.

56 Rick Menell, author's interview. Margaret Malikolo Motumi was a social worker with the UF.

57 Rick Menell, author's interview.

58 Bob Tucker, author's interview, Johannesburg CBD, 31 August 2006; anonymous informant. Ramaphosa did complete his BProc degree after leaving EFK Tucker.

59 Bob Tucker, author's interview.

60 Cyril Ramaphosa interview with Julie Frederikse, 13 August 1985. Historical Papers, University of the Witwatersrand, AL2460.

61 Smit, 'Urban Foundation', p. 35.

62 Barney Pityana, author's interview.

63 Margaret Motumi, 'Assessment of Soweto Tour'. National Archive, Cape Town, A2562 A/34. Later studies were more equivocal, for example 'Report on Perceptions of the UF amongst Community Leaders', November 1985. National Archive, Cape Town, A2562 V/6. Ellen Kuzwayo observed that there are 'many black people who criticize the Foundation as an arm of government which tries to make some blacks comfortable to protect the white community'. Kuzwayo, *Call Me Woman*, p. 205.

64 Frank Chikane, author's interview.

65 Michael Spicer, author's interview, Parktown, Johannesburg, 24 October 2006.
66 Saki Macozoma, 'Business seals success of new work drive in black and white', *Sunday Times*, 4 October 1998.
67 Frank Chikane, author's interview, Tuynhuys, Cape Town, 2 November 2006.
68 Fred Phaswana, author's interview.
69 Ibid.
70 Bob Tucker, author's interview.
71 Rick Menell, author's interview.
72 Rams Ramashia, author's interview, Waterfront, Cape Town, 31 October 2006.
73 Fred Phaswana, author's interview.
74 Henry Dolowitz, author's interview, Orange Grove, Johannesburg, 30 August 2006.

Chapter 7
1 Arrie Paulus speaking in 1979, quoted in David Pallister, Sarah Stewart and Ian Lepper, *South Africa Inc.: The Oppenheimer Empire*, 2nd edition. London, Corgi, 1988, p. 205.
2 This section draws heavily on Rob Lambert and Eddie Webster, 'The re-emergence of political unionism in contemporary South Africa', in William Cobbett and Robin Cohen (eds.), *Popular Struggles in South Africa*. Trenton, Africa World Press, 1988.
3 Lambert and Webster, 'Re-emergence', pp. 23–25.
4 Vic Allen, *The History of Black Mineworkers in South Africa: Volume 3*. Keighley, The Moor Press, 2003, pp. 79–81.
5 Ibid., p. 81.
6 The gold price had fallen from a high of $800 per ounce in 1980 to around $300 in 1982.
7 Pallister, *South Africa Inc.*, pp. 26–9.
8 Ibid., p. 26.
9 Ibid., pp. 9–15.
10 Ibid., p. 26.
11 Ibid., p. 26.
12 Ibid., pp. 29ff.
13 Ibid.
14 Ibid., pp. 30ff.
15 Ibid.
16 Michael Spicer, author's interview, Parktown, Johannesburg, 24 October 2006.
17 Michael Spicer, author's interview.
18 'The House' is a nickname for Christ Church.
19 Pallister, *South Africa Inc.* reports that six out of eight divisional heads at Anglo in 1984 had been Rhodes Scholars.
20 This judgement about the intellectually undemanding character of PPE has raised the hackles of some readers of the manuscript. It is based on the experiences of the author as a student in this honour school.
21 C Wright Mills, *The Power Elite*. Oxford, Oxford University Press, 1956.
22 Ralph Miliband, *Capitalist Democracy in Britain*. Oxford, Oxford University Press, 1982.
23 Michael Spicer, author's interview. Spicer was then working at SAIIA.
24 Nelson Mandela, in *Liberation*, June 1953; quoted in Pallister, *South Africa Inc.*, p. 9.
25 The famous 'Sullivan codes' were introduced in 1977.
26 RM (Bobby) Godsell, *Liberal Ethics in South Africa since 1948*. MA dissertation, University of Cape Town, 1972.
27 Bobby Godsell, author's interview, Diagonal Street, Johannesburg, 17 January 2007.
28 *Sunday Times*, 25 February 2007.

29 Nigel Unwin, author's interview, Diagonal Street, Johannesburg, 30 August 2006.
30 Bobby Godsell, author's interview.
31 Jay Naidoo, author's interview, Rosebank, Johannesburg, 13 September 2006.
32 Today the head of the South African Revenue Service (SARS).
33 Ishmael Mkhabela, author's interview, Braamfontein Johannesburg, 15 August 2006.
34 Cyril Ramaphosa interview with Patti Waldmeir, 19 January 1995. Historical Papers, University of the Witwatersrand, A2508.
35 Griffith Zabala, author's interview, Kyalami Estate, Johannesburg, 15 August 2006.
36 Ramaphosa interview with Waldmeir, 19 January 1995.
37 Phiroshaw Camay, author's interview, Rosebank, Johannesburg, 17 August 2006.

Chapter 8

1 Tshenuwani Farisani, 'South Africa: Unasked questions and unquestioned answers', *Journal of Law and Religion*, 5: 2, 1987, p. 265.
2 Phiroshaw Camay, author's interview, Rosebank, Johannesburg, 17 August 2006.
3 Vic Allen, *History of Black Mineworkers in South Africa: Volume 3.* Keighley, The Moor Press, 2003, pp. 3–77 and 238–77.
4 Anglo American Corporation, *Perceptions and Behaviour Patterns of Black Mineworkers on a Group Gold Mine.* Johannesburg, AAC Manpower Resources Division, 1976, p. 15.
5 Bobby Godsell, author's interview, Diagonal Street, Johannesburg, 17 January 2007.
6 Michael Spicer, author's interview, Parktown, Johannesburg, 24 October 2006.
7 Nigel Unwin, author's interview, Diagonal Street, Johannesburg, 30 August 2006.
8 Michael Spicer, author's interview.
9 T Dunbar Moodie, 'Getting the gold out of the ground: Social constraints and financial limitations on technical capacity in South African deep-level mining', Paper presented to the African Studies Association, 16–19 November 2006.
10 Quoted in ibid.
11 Chamber of Mines, quoted in Francis Wilson, *Labour on the South African Gold Mines, 1911–1969.* Cambridge, Cambridge University Press, 1972, fn, 16.
12 Other unions actively organising black mineworkers in September 1982 included the Tucsa-affiliated Federated Mining, Explosives and Chemical Workers' Union (FMECWU), the Black Mineworkers' Union, the Municipal and General Workers Union of South Africa, and the Black Allied Mine and Tunnel Workers' Union. Georgina Jaffee, 'Unionizing mine workers', *Work in Progress*, 24, 1983.
13 Clive Thompson, personal communication with author, 1 January 2007.
14 Allen, *History*, pp. 86–7.
15 Clive Thompson, personal communication.
16 Allen, *History*, pp. 81–6.
17 Ibid., p. 82.
18 T Dunbar Moodie, *Going for Gold: Men, Mines and Migration.* Johannesburg, Witwatersrand University Press, 1994, p. 250.
19 Allen, *History*, pp. 65–6.
20 Ibid.
21 Phiroshaw Camay, author's interview,
22 Vic Allen, personal communication with author, 20 January 2006.
23 Rick Menell, author's interview, Main Street, Johannesburg, 25 October 2006.
24 Author's interviews with Bobby Godsell and Phiroshaw Camay; personal communication from Clive Thompson.
25 Clive Thompson, personal communication.
26 Johann Liebenberg, author's interview, Cape Town, 28 September 2006.
27 In his retirement to the coast, purportedly to sail, this pathological negotiator has

become chairman of the Port Nolloth yacht-owners' association, through which his negotiating urges presumably find an outlet. Johann Liebenberg, author's interview.

28 Despite a number of approaches, only one black union (FMECWU) had been recognised by the Chamber – in September 1982.

29 Johann Liebenberg, author's interview.

30 Ibid.

31 Allen, *History*, p. 91.

32 Clive Thompson, personal communication.

33 Moodie, *Going for Gold*, p. 250. On Vic Allen's account, Salae had been in dispute over wages with his Teba supervisor. He consulted a Catholic priest who advised him to contact Cusa, where Camay put him in touch with Ramaphosa. Allen, *History*, p. 89.

34 Allen, *History*, p. 89.

35 James Motlatsi, author's interview, Selby, Johannesburg, 31 August 2006.

36 Ibid.

37 Ibid.

38 Allen, *History*, pp. 89–91.

39 Ibid., p. 92.

40 Ibid., p. 92.

41 Ramaphosa himself put the number of delegates at 1,800, whereas there should only have been 200 voting delegates present. Allen, *History*, pp. 98–9 and xxi.

42 James Motlatsi, author's interview.

43 William B Gould IV, 'The emergence of black trade unions in South Africa', *Journal of Law and Religion*, 5: 2, 1987, pp. 495–500.

44 Johann Liebenberg, author's interview.

45 Ibid.

46 Cyril Ramaphosa interview with Patti Waldmeir, 19 January 1995. Historical Papers, University of the Witwatersrand, A2508.

Chapter 9

1 A favourite dictum of Cyril Ramaphosa, as reported by Irene Charnley, author's interview, Roodepoort, Johannesburg, 24 October 2006.

2 Membership data from Vic Allen, *History of Black Mineworkers in South Africa: Volume 3*. Keighley, The Moor Press, 2003, pp. 99, 124, 236.

3 Ibid., p. 236.

4 Ibid., especially pp. 3–77 and 238–77.

5 Allen's *History* includes references.

6 Ernest Cole, *House of Bondage*. London, Allen Lane, 1967, pp. 23–4.

7 Anglo American Corporation, *Perceptions and Behaviour Patterns of Black Mineworkers on a Group Gold Mine*. Johannesburg, AAC Manpower Resources Division, 1976, pp. 15–33.

8 Ibid., p. 15.

9 Simphiwe Nanise, author's interview, Braamfontein, Johannesburg, 30 August 2006.

10 T Dunbar Moodie, *Going for Gold: Men, Mines and Migration*. Johannesburg, Witwatersrand University Press, 1994, p. 251.

11 Francis Wilson, *Labour on the South African Gold Mines, 1911–1969*. Cambridge, Cambridge University Press, 1972.

12 Allen, *History*, p. xxix.

13 Ian Macun, 'Dynamics of trade union growth in South Africa: 1970–1996', *Labour Studies Report Series*, No. 10. Johannesburg, University of Witwatersrand Sociology of Work Unit, 2002, p. 36.

14 The total workforce was 4.7 million.

15 Cyril Ramaphosa interview with T Dunbar Moodie in 1984, cited in Moodie, *Going for Gold*, p. 251.
16 Ibid., p. 251.
17 Ibid., pp. 250–6.
18 Vic Allen, author's interview, Keighley, Yorkshire, 15 July 2006.
19 Jonathan Crush, 'Mine migrancy in the contemporary era', in Jonathan Crush and Wilmot James (eds.), *Crossing Boundaries*. Cape Town, Idasa, 1995, pp. 14–34.
20 Martin Nicol, author's interview, Cape Town, 24 August 2006.
21 Cyril Ramaphosa interview with Julie Frederikse, 13 August 1985. Historical Papers, University of the Witwatersrand, AL2460.
22 Anonymous union representative.
23 Martin Nicol, author's interview.
24 James Motlatsi, author's interview, Selby, Johannesburg, 31 August 2006.
25 Christine Randall, author's interview, Sandton, Johannesburg, 12 September 2006.
26 Irene Charnley, author's interview, Roodepoort, Johannesburg, 31 August 2006.
27 Christine Randall, author's interview.
28 James Motlatsi, author's interview, Selby, Johannesburg, 6 October 2006.
29 Cyril Ramaphosa interview with Patti Waldmeir, 19 January 1995. Historical Papers, University of the Witwatersrand, A2508.
30 Johann Liebenberg, author's interview.
31 Christine Randall, author's interview
32 Martin Nicol and Christine Randall, author's interviews.
33 James Motlatsi, author's interview, 31 August.
34 Ibid.
35 Johann Liebenberg, author's interview; James Motlatsi, author's interview, 6 October.
36 Charles 'Chuck' Sabel, unpublished paper.
37 James Motlatsi, author's interview, 31 August.
38 Johann Liebenberg, author's interview.
39 Ibid.
40 James Motlatsi, author's interview, 6 October.
41 Cyril Ramaphosa interview with Patti Waldmeir, 19 January 1995.
42 Ibid.
43 James Motlatsi, author's interview, 31 August.
44 Cyril Ramaphosa, interview with Waldmeir.
45 James Motlatsi, author's interview, 31 August.
46 Ibid.
47 Cyril Ramaphosa, Address to the South African Institute of Race Relations, May 1985; published in shortened form as *Organizing on the Mines*. Johannesburg, SAIRR Publications, 1985.
48 Allen, *History,* p. 511.
49 Ibid., pp. 511–14.
50 Martin Nicol, author's interview.
51 Ibid.
52 Ibid.

Chapter 10

1 Frans Baleni, 'A silent crime in the mines', *Mail & Guardian*, 13 November 2006. Between 1984 and 2005, more than 11,000 miners died underground, and more than 200 miners have been killed in each year since 2000.
2 Paul Benjamin, author's interview, Cape Town, 23 August 2006.
3 Clive Thompson, personal communication with author, 1 January 2007.

4 Ibid.
5 Ibid.
6 Paul Benjamin, author's interview.
7 Ibid.
8 Kuben Pillay, author's interview, Sandton, Johannesburg, 12 September 2006.
9 Paul Benjamin and Kuben Pillay, author's interviews.
10 Clive Thompson, personal communication.
11 Vic Allen, *History of Black Mineworkers in South Africa: Volume 3*. Keighley, The Moor Press, 2003, p. 238. Benjamin himself is uncertain about this interpretation, believing that Cyril might have been referring to a policy of not employing professionals on the head office staff. Paul Benjamin, author's interview.
12 Kuben Pillay, author's interview. Pillay today works for media giant Primedia.
13 Ibid.
14 Ibid.
15 Ibid.
16 Ibid.
17 Ibid.
18 Ibid.
19 Ibid.
20 Mono Badela, 'Leader with a heart of gold', *South*, 1988, date unknown. Archived in the Julie Frederikse collection, Wits Historical Archives, AL2460.
21 Sheryl Raine, 'SA mining faces its "Cyril factor,"' *Sunday Star*, review section, 28 September 1986.
22 Cited in Roger Omond, *The Apartheid Handbook*. New York, Penguin, 1985, p. 194.
23 Marcel Golding, author's interview, Cape Town, 20 October 2006.
24 Ibid.
25 Ibid.
26 Ibid.
27 Allen, *History*, p. 202.
28 Ibid., p. 485.
29 Ibid., p. 485.
30 Ibid., p. 114.
31 Ibid., pp. 114–15.
32 Ibid., pp. 115–16.
33 Simphiwe Nanise, author's interview, Braamfontein, Johannesburg, 30 August 2006.
34 Ibid.
35 Allen, *History*, details the evolution of NUM's relationships with the international federations. His account, however, should be read with the caution that he was a partisan of the IMO.
36 Ibid., pp. 437–9.
37 Ibid., p. 439. It was only after Ramaphosa's departure from the NUM in the early 1990s that conflict broke out between supporters of the IMO, such as Kgalema Motlanthe, and those, such as James Motlatsi, who believed the end of the Cold War promised its long-overdue demise. By this stage, Ramaphosa and Motlatsi had freed the union from its external dependency by persuading the congress to adopt a policy of setting union dues at 1 per cent of members' salaries, an innovation that led to a massive swelling of resources.
38 Andeya Baleni, author's interview, Eastgate, Johannesburg, 16 August 2006.
39 Allen, *History*, p. 171.
40 Ramaphosa's prescience in this regard can be seen in current disputes over inequality in the NUM. Unlike members' subscriptions, the 'agency fee' collected from non-

members is retained at branch level.

41 Irene Charnley, author's interview, Roodepoort, Johannesburg, 24 October 2006. Charnley is an executive director of MTN.
42 Ibid.
43 Ibid.
44 Allen, *History*, pp. 175–6.
45 Andeya Baleni, author's interview.
46 James Motlatsi, author's interview, Selby Johannesburg, 31 August 2006.
47 Andeya Baleni, author's interview.
48 Ibid.
49 James Motlatsi, author's interview, 31 August.
50 Allen, *History*, pp. 173–7.
51 Ibid., p. 175.
52 Ibid., p. 175.
53 James Motlatsi, author's interview, 31 August.
54 Allen, *History*, p. 176.
55 James Motlatsi, author's interview, 31 August.
56 Ibid.
57 Cyril Ramaphosa interview with Julie Frederikse, 13 August 1985. Historical Papers, University of the Witwatersrand, AL2460.
58 Clive Thompson, personal communication.
59 Ibid.
60 Bobby Godsell, author's interview, Diagonal Street, Johannesburg, 17 January 2007.
61 Nigel Unwin and Bobby Godsell, author's interviews.

Chapter 11

1 Vic Allen, *History of Black Mineworkers in South Africa: Volume 3.* Keighley, The Moor Press, 2003, pp. 118–19.
2 Ibid., pp. 120–3.
3 Cyril Ramaphosa interview with Patti Waldmeir, 19 January 1995. Historical Papers, University of the Witwatersrand, A2508.
4 David Pallister, Sarah Stewart and Ian Lepper, *South Africa Inc.: The Oppenheimer Empire*, 2nd edition. London, Corgi, 1988, p. 215.
5 'Labour Action', *Work in Progress*, 37, 1985.
6 Quoted in Pallister, *South Africa Inc.,* p. 220.
7 Quoted in ibid., p. 218.
8 Quoted in ibid., p. 218.
9 Simphiwe Nanise, author's interview, Braamfontein, Johannesburg, 30 August 2006; Frans Baleni, author's interview, Boksburg, Johannesburg, 25 October 2006.
10 James Motlatsi, author's interview, Selby, Johannesburg, 30 August 2006.
11 Johann Liebenberg, author's interview, Cape Town, 28 September 2006. Conservatives saw communists and agitators behind workers' protests, reacting to worker protest with the same misconceptions the Chamber displayed when faced with the great 1946 African mineworkers' strike. Frans Baleni, author's interview.
12 SS Terreblanche, 'The manpower situation in South Africa and its effects on the gold-mining industry', Lecture prepared for Anglo American Corporation's Training Division. Pretoria, South African Institute for Manpower Research and the Human Sciences Research Council, 1980.
13 Bobby Godsell, author's interview, Diagonal Street, Johannesburg, 17 January 2007.
14 Terreblanche, 'Manpower situation', p. 21.
15 The gold price soon fell from $750 per ounce to $250.
16 Nicoli Nattrass, 'South African gold mining: The 1980s and beyond', in Jonathan

Crush and Wilmot James (eds.), *Crossing Boundaries: Mine Migrancy in a Democratic South Africa*. Cape Town, Idasa, 1995, p. 170.

17 Michael Spicer, author's interview, Parktown, Johannesburg, 24 October 2006.

18 Ibid.

19 Ibid.

20 Quotations from Allen, *History*, pp. 276–8.

21 Head of Anglo American's Gold and Uranium Division, Peter Gush, did respond in detail soon after the deadline, committing Anglo to further hostel upgrades and the dismantling of the induna system. Allen, *History*, pp. 280–1.

22 Truth and Reconciliation Commission, Amnesty Committee: Application for Amnesty in terms of Section 18 of the Promotion of National Unity and Reconciliation Act. AC/99/0349.

23 *Dispatch Online*, 30 July 1998. Available at ‹http://www.dispatch.co.za/1998/07/30/southafrica/TRC1.HTM› accessed on 8 November 2006.

24 Ibid.

25 Kuben Pillay, author's interview, Sandton, Johannesburg, 12 September 2006.

26 Johann Liebenberg, telephone conversation with author, 8 November 2006.

27 Bobby Godsell, author's interview.

28 James Motlatsi, author's interview, Selby, Johannesburg, 6 October 2006.

29 Bobby Godsell, author's interview.

30 Johann Liebenberg, author's interview.

31 Allen, *History*, p. 307.

32 Nigel Unwin, personal communication with author, 18 October 2006.

33 Pallister, *South Africa Inc.*, p. 227.

34 Nigel Unwin, personal communication with author.

35 Allen, *History*.

36 *New York Herald Tribune*, 10 August 1987, cited in ibid., p. 307.

37 Quoted in Allen, *History*, p. 359.

38 *The Star*, 14 August 1987, quoted in Allen, *History*, p. 359.

39 Bobby Godsell, author's interview.

40 Allen, *History*, pp. 303–4.

41 Ibid., p. 304.

42 NUM Strike Press Conference, 3 August 1987, quoted in Allen, *History*, p. 305.

43 *New York Herald Tribune*, 10 August 1987, cited in Allen, *History*, p. 307.

44 Michael Spicer, author's interview.

45 Frans Baleni, author's interview.

46 Marcel Golding, author's interview, Cape Town, 20 October 2006.

47 James Motlatsi, author's interview, 31 August 2006.

48 Allen, *History*, p. 313.

49 Johann Liebenberg, author's interview. In 1987 Liebenberg, as the Chamber's spokesman, insisted that a maximum of 240,000 workers were on strike. The 300,000 figure is closer to the 333,000 strikers estimated by the Labour Monitoring Group at the time. See Peter Alexander, 'South Africa's great miners' strike of 1987: Towards a re-examination', unpublished paper, p. 3.

50 Cyril Ramaphosa interview with Patti Waldmeir. The National Executive Committee of the NUM had delegated the decision about the precise date of the strike's commencement to Ramaphosa and Motlatsi.

51 Allen, *History*, p. 320.

52 Frans Baleni, author's interview.

53 Simphiwe Nanise, author's interview.

54 Kuben Pillay, author's interview.

55 Cyril and the other officials scarcely slept for days on end in the run-up to and during

the strike. After almost two weeks without leaving the office, lawyer Paul Benjamin and another colleague announced that they had had enough. They were going to go home. Ramaphosa remonstrated with them, demanding that they justify leaving the office when workers were on strike. 'I need to change my underwear,' Benjamin pleaded. Ramaphosa immediately responded that he himself had not changed his underwear for two weeks. Benjamin quickly left the building, but he returned a little later in the day bearing a bag of underwear for Cyril.

56 Allen, *History*.

57 Ibid.

58 Ibid.

59 *Wall Street Journal*, 13 August 1987, quoted in ibid., p. 329.

60 The report was leaked and extracts were later published in *South African Labour Bulletin*, 4: 5, 1978.

61 Pallister, *South Africa Inc.*, p. 199.

62 Godsell observes that security police intelligence was often of higher quality than that which the mines could provide for themselves. Bobby Godsell, author's interview.

63 Roelf Meyer, author's interview, Killarney, Johannesburg, 18 January 2007.

64 Speaking on the *Today* programme, BBC Radio 4, 10 August 1987.

65 Bobby Godsell, author's interview.

66 Ibid.

67 Nigel Unwin, author's interview, Diagonal Street, Johannesburg, 30 August 2006.

68 Bobby Godsell, author's interview.

69 Marcel Golding, author's interview.

70 Nigel Unwin and Bobby Godsell, author's interviews.

71 This information was provided on a non-attributable basis by a senior informant with no identifiable motivation to mislead the author.

72 The information was supplied to James Motlatsi, and reported in Allen, *History*, pp. 362–3.

73 Bobby Godsell, author's interview.

74 Ibid.

75 Unwin remembers he was unaware of the problem of collapsing stopes until the middle of the strike, a recollection Michael Spicer describes as 'Astonishing!'. Nigel Unwin and Michael Spicer, author's interviews.

76 Bobby Godsell, author's interview.

77 Johann Liebenberg, telephone conversation with author.

78 T Dunbar Moodie, 'Getting the gold out of the ground: Social constraints and financial limitations on technical capacity in South African deep-level mining', Paper presented to the African Studies Association, 16–19 November 2006, fn. 38.

79 Allen, *History*, p. 382.

80 James Motlatsi, author's interview, 6 October 2006.

81 Allen, *History*, p. 385.

82 Ibid., p. 385.

83 Moodie, 'Getting the gold out of the ground', p. 21; Jonathan Crush, 'Mine migrancy in the contemporary era', in Crush and James (eds.), *Crossing Boundaries*, p. 22.

84 Martin Nicol, author's interview, Cape Town, 24 August 2006.

85 National Union of Mineworkers, *Biennial Report*. Johannesburg, NUM, 1989.

86 Kuben Pillay, author's interview.

87 Frans Baleni, author's interview.

88 Ibid.

89 Ibid.

90 James Motlatsi, author's interview, 31 August.

91 James Motlatsi, author's interview, 6 October. The probable reason for the hard line

taken against Motlatsi is that he had instigated the act of resistance most terrifying to the mine owners. Correctly predicting that workers would be forced underground at gunpoint, he instructed them in public meetings that they should in such an eventuality remain underground and continue the strike from there. Some workers in this situation began to take out their anger at being forced underground by destroying equipment and machinery, leading to some of the most severe losses of the dispute.

92 Vic Allen, personal communication with author, 20 January 2006.

93 For one luminous example, see Peter Clarke, *A Question of Leadership*. London, Hamish Hamilton, 1991.

94 Vic Allen, personal communication.

95 Ibid.

96 Neva Makgetla, 'In praise of labour movement's overlooked virtues', *Business Day*, 25 August 2006.

97 The building was designed for Anglo American Property services by Chicago architect Helmut Jahn, a disciple of Mies van der Rohe. Those antagonised by its vulgarity will be pleased to hear that it offers a terrible work environment, baking in summer and freezing in winter. Nigel Unwin, author's interview.

98 Union officials like Charnley and Golding testify to the humanity of Godsell and Unwin, and Motlatsi emphasises that the character of hard-line negotiators like Gush should not be judged from their style of doing business. Irene Charnley, Marcel Golding and James Motlatsi, author's interviews.

99 Cyril Ramaphosa, 'Organizing on the mines', in *Topical Opinion*. Johannesburg, SAIRR Publications, 1985.

100 Vic Allen, personal communication.

101 Simphiwe Nanise, author's interview.

102 Ibid.

103 Frans Baleni, author's interview.

Chapter 12

1 Oliver Tambo, 'We are a force', *Sechaba*, October 1984, p. 13.

2 Anthony Butler, *Contemporary South Africa*. New York, Palgrave Macmillan, 2004, Chapter 1.

3 Howard Barrell, *Conscripts to Their Age: African National Congress Operational Strategy, 1976–1986*. D.Phil. thesis, Faculty of Social Studies, University of Oxford, 1993.

4 Dave Steward, author's interview, Plattekloof, Cape Town, 26 September 2006. Steward was perhaps the most successful career diplomat of his generation, and served as De Klerk's chief of staff from 1992.

5 All quotations from Barrell, *Conscripts to Their Age*.

6 FW de Klerk. *The Last Trek: A New Beginning*. London, Macmillan, 1999, pp. 92–3.

7 Raymond Suttner, 'The UDF period and its meaning for contemporary South Africa', *Journal of Southern African Studies*, 30: 2, 2004, pp. 692–3.

8 For analysis of the UDF, see Jeremy Seekings, *The UDF: A History of the United Democratic Front in South Africa, 1983–1991*. Cape Town, David Philip, 2000.

9 Dave Steward, author's interview.

10 Ivan Pillay interview with Howard Barrell, 20 July 1989, Mayibuye Centre Archives, University of the Western Cape; Ivan Pillay interview with Wolfie Kodesh, 24 April 1993, Mayibuye Centre Archives, University of the Western Cape.

11 Ivan Pillay interview with Wolfie Kodesh.

12 Seekings, *UDF*, p. 7; Suttner, 'UDF period', p. 697.

13 Quoted in *The Guardian*, London, 15 April 1986. The following analysis appeared in different form as 'The ambivalent flames of history', *Business Day*, 13 April 2006.

14 Quoted in *Time Magazine*, New York, 5 August 1985.

15 George Bizos, interviewed on *Carte Blanche*, M-Net Television, 29 April 2001.

16 United Democratic Front, Submission to the Truth and Reconciliation Commission, Cape Town, 6 May 1998.

17 Ronald Suresh Roberts, *No Cold Kitchen: A Biography of Nadine Gordimer.* Johannesburg, STE Publishers, 2006, pp. 447–9.

18 Ibid., p.452.

19 Nelson Mandela, *Long Walk to Freedom.* London, Abacus, 1995, p. 166.

20 Roberts, *No Cold Kitchen*, p. 453.

21 Joanna Ball, *Ritual of the Necklace.* Johannesburg, Centre for the Study of Violence and Reconciliation, 1994.

22 Quoted in *The Times*, London, 14 September 1986.

23 James Matthews. Untitled. *Poisoned Wells and Other Delights.* Cape Town, Blac, 1990.

24 African National Congress, *Green Book.* Report of the Politico-Military Strategy Commission to the ANC National Executive Committee, August 1979. Available at <www.anc.org.za/ancdocs/history/mk/green-book.html> accessed on 1 April 2007.

25 Ibid., Appendix B.

26 For fuller analysis see Rob Lambert and Eddie Webster, 'The re-emergence of political unionism in contemporary South Africa', in William Cobbett and Robin Cohen (eds.), *Popular Struggles in South Africa.* Trenton, Africa World Press, 1988.

27 Jay Naidoo, author's interview, Rosebank, Johannesburg, 13 September 2006.

28 My two sources on this aspect of inter-union conflict asked not to be quoted on this issue.

29 Jay Naidoo, author's interview.

30 Indeed, it was not to be until 19 March 1990 that an historic meeting between Sactu and Cosatu, in Kafue, Zambia, agreed that Sactu would wind itself up and integrate its members into Cosatu unions on their return to South Africa.

31 Vic Allen, personal communication with author, 20 January 2006.

32 Phiroshaw Camay, author's interview, Rosebank, Johannesburg, 17 August 2006.

33 Lybon Mabasa, author's interview, Rosebank, Johannesburg, 17 August 2006.

34 Cyril Ramaphosa interview with Julie Frederikse, 13 August 1985. Historical Papers, University of the Witwatersrand, AL2460, pp. 3–4. His contemporary Reuel Khoza concurs that Saso was 'sweeping across university campuses' and that Cyril simply 'articulated the ideas of the time'. Reuel Khoza, author's interview, Sandton, Johannesburg, 26 October 2006.

35 Cyril Ramaphosa interview with Frederikse, p. 4.

36 Ishmael Mkhabela, author's interview, Braamfontein, Johannesburg, 15 August 2006.

37 Martin Nicol was the first white appointee to a key position in the union in 1988.

38 The term was suggested by Saki Macozoma, author's interview, Melrose Arch, Johannesburg, 21 November 2006.

39 Vic Allen, *History of Black Mineworkers in South Africa: Volume 3.* Keighley, The Moor Press, 2003, pp. 166–7.

40 Jay Naidoo, author's interview.

41 Cited in Allen, *History*, pp. 165–6.

42 Vic Allen, personal communication.

43 My informants did not wish this judgement to be attributed to them.

44 Vic Allen, personal communication.

45 Ibid.

Chapter 13

1 Oyama Mabandla, author's interview, Sandton, Johannesburg, 12 September 2006.

2 Phiroshaw Camay, author's interview, Rosebank, Johannesburg, 17 August 2006.

3 Saki Macozoma, author's interview, Melrose Arch, Johannesburg, 21 November 2006.

4 Barney Pityana, author's interview, Unisa, Pretoria, 5 October 2006.

5 Ishmael Mkhabela, author's interview, Braamfontein, Johannesburg, 15 August 2006.

6 Vic Allen, *History of Black Mineworkers in South Africa: Volume 3.* Keighley, The Moor Press, 2003, pp. xxx and 443.

7 Jay Naidoo, author's interview, Rosebank, Johannesburg, 13 September 2006.

8 Ibid.

9 Ibid.; Oyama Mabandla, author's interview, Sandton, Johannesburg, 12 September 2006.

10 Phiroshaw Camay, author's interview.

11 Cyril Ramaphosa interview with Patti Waldmeir, 19 January 1995. Historical Papers, University of the Witwatersrand, A2508.

12 Oyama Mabandla, author's interview.

13 Cyril Ramaphosa interview with Waldmeir.

14 Ibid. Every January 8, in celebration of the founding of the ANC, the NEC issues a statement setting out the direction the movement should follow in the coming twelve months.

15 Waldmeir's account, in Cyril Ramaphosa interview with Waldmeir.

16 Jay Naidoo, author's interview.

17 Ibid.

18 Oyama Mabandla, author's interview.

19 Ibid.

20 Vic Allen, conversation with author, Keighley, Yorkshire, 15 July 2006.

21 *The Times*, London, 26 August 1987; cited in Allen, *History*, p. 442.

22 I am grateful to Padraig O'Malley for this account of events. Interview with author, Hout Bay, Cape Town, 15 December 2006.

23 ANC Department of Information and Publicity, 'ANC Statement on the Release of Govan Mbeki', Lusaka, 5 November 1987.

24 Allen, *History*, p. 496.

25 Wolfie Kodesh interview with Ivan Pillay, Durban, April 1993. Mayibuye Centre, MCA 6 – 348 b (2). Pillay is head of compliance at the South African Revenue Service (SARS).

26 Howard Barrell, *Conscripts to Their Age: African National Congress Operational Strategy, 1976–1986.* D.Phil. thesis, Faculty of Social Studies, University of Oxford, 1993.

27 James Sanders, *Apartheid's Friends: The Rise and Fall of South Africa's Secret Service.* London, John Murray, 2006, pp. 299–300.

28 Fanie van der Merwe, author's interview, Sunnyside, Pretoria, 26 October 2006.

29 Mac Maharaj, author's interview, Morningside, Johannesburg, 16 January 2007.

30 Ibid.

31 His tolerance did not extend to the antics of the international labour federations whose own pro- and anti-Western political agendas diverted the energies of union leaders. Mac Maharaj, author's interview.

32 Maharaj was due to have been accompanied by Chris Hani, but Hani was made chief of staff of MK and so could not participate.

33 Mac Maharaj, author's interview.

34 Ibid.

35 Ibid. I am grateful to O'Malley for discussing with me the Vula communications sources used in his recent biography of Maharaj, author's interview.

36 Vic Allen, personal communication with author, 20 January 2006.

37 Cyril Ramaphosa interview with Waldmeir.

417

38 Ibid.
39 Ibid.
40 Mac Maharaj, author's interview.
41 Nelson Mandela, Document presented to PW Botha, July 1989, available at <www.anc.org.za/ancdocs/history/mandela/doc890705.html> accessed on 11 April 2007.
42 Padraig O'Malley, author's interview. There was speculation at the time that unknown ANC cadres had taken out a contract for the assassination of Mandela.
43 Cyril Ramaphosa interview with Waldmeir.
44 Allen, *History*, pp. 512–13.
45 Ibid., p. 513, fn 75. Allen was the fourth passenger in the car.
46 Isaac Mogase, now the ANC's chief whip in parliament, was a member of the delegation.
47 Frederik van Zyl Slabbert, author's interview, Craighall, Johannesburg, 21 November 2006.
48 Lynda Schuster, 'The struggle to govern Johannesburg: The transition to nonracial rule is proceeding more slowly – and more viciously – than expected', *Atlantic Monthly*, 276: 3, 1995.
49 Ibid.
50 Ibid.
51 Ibid.
52 Quoted in ibid.
53 Frederik van Zyl Slabbert, author's interview.
54 Saki Macozoma, author's interview.

Chapter 14

1 Michael Spicer, author's interview, Parktown, Johannesburg, 24 October 2006. Spicer had just joined Anglo and attended the speech at Gavin Relly's request.
2 FW de Klerk. *The Last Trek: A New Beginning*. London, Macmillan, 1999, p. 121.
3 Nthato Motlana, author's interview, Fourways, Gauteng, 24 November 2006.
4 Frederik van Zyl Slabbert, Craighall, Johannesburg, 21 November 2006.
5 De Klerk, *Last Trek*, pp. 129–130.
6 My informant refused to be attributed as a source of this anecdote and I have not been able to confirm it.
7 He performs the same role as executive head of the De Klerk Foundation. Dave Steward, author's interview, Plattekloof, Cape Town, 26 September 2006.
8 Padraig O'Malley, author's interview, Hout Bay, Cape Town, 15 December 2006.
9 Frank Chikane, author's interview, Tuynhuys, Cape Town, 2 November 2006.
10 Saki Macozoma, author's interview, Melrose Arch, Johannesburg, 21 November 2006.
11 Van Zyl Slabbert, author's interview.
12 Frank Chikane, author's interview.
13 Saki Macozoma, author's interview.
14 Mac Maharaj, author's interview, Morningside, Johannesburg, 16 January 2007.
15 Ibid.
16 Ibid.
17 Cyril Ramaphosa interview with Patti Waldmeir, 19 January 1995. Historical Papers, University of the Witwatersrand, A2508.
18 Ibid.
19 Padraig O'Malley, author's interview.
20 Samu Zulu, 'A tribute to Cyril Ramaphosa's late mother, Munyadziwa', *The Enquirer*, 8 November 2001.
21 Kader Asmal, author's interview, Parliament, Cape Town, 13 December 2006.

22 Mac Maharaj, author's interview.
23 Kader Asmal, author's interview.
24 Nelson Mandela, Speech to the rally outside the Cape Town City Hall, 11 February 1990, available at <http://www.sahistory.org.za/pages/classroom/pages/projects/grade12/lesson11/mandela-speech.htm>, accessed on 1 April 2007.
25 Padraig O'Malley, author's interview.
26 Ibid.
27 James Sanders, *Apartheid's Friends: The Rise and Fall of South Africa's Secret Service.* London, John Murray, 2006, pp. 299–300.

Chapter 15

1 Oyama Mabandla, author's interview, Sandton, Johannesburg, 12 September 2006.
2 Saths Cooper, author's interview, Killarney, Johannesburg, 17 August 2006.
3 James Motlatsi, author's interview, Selby, Johannesburg, 31 August 2006; Kader Asmal, author's interview, Parliament, Cape Town, 13 December 2006.
4 Kader Asmal, author's interview.
5 Penuell Maduna, author's interview, Sandton, Johannesburg, 23 November 2006; Asmal, author's interview.
6 Ramaphosa reported to Frederik van Zyl Slabbert that 'They have asked me to stand for secretary-general of the ANC', where according to Slabbert 'they' referred to the SACP. Frederik van Zyl Slabbert, author's interview, Craighall, Johannesburg, 21 November 2006.
7 Also the opinion of Vic Allen, personal conversation, Keighley, 15 July 2006.
8 Jeremy Baskin, *Striking Back: A History of Cosatu.* Johannesburg, Ravan Books, 1991, pp. 60–6.
9 Vic Allen, *History of Black Mineworkers in South Africa: Volume 3.* Keighley, The Moor Press, 2003, p. xxiii.
10 Marcel Golding, author's interview, Cape Town, 20 October 2006.
11 William Gumede, *Thabo Mbeki and the Struggle for the Soul of the ANC.* Cape Town, Zebra Press, 2005, p. 42.
12 Vic Allen, personal communication with author, 20 January 2006.
13 Frederik van Zyl Slabbert, author's interview.
14 Marcel Golding, author's interview; James Motlatsi, author's interview.
15 Frans Baleni, author's interview, Boksburg, East Rand, 25 October 2006.
16 This account is from author's interviews with Marcel Golding, Vic Allen, James Motlatsi, Frans Baleni, and two anonymous interviewees.
17 In author's interviews, Penuell Maduna, Bantu Holomisa and Frans Baleni all strongly repudiate the claim that Ramaphosa was ever a member of the party.
18 Mac Maharaj, author's interview, Morningside, Johannesburg, 16 January 2007.
19 Ibid.
20 This position in expressed in Jacob Zuma's interview with Howard Barrell, Lusaka, 18 August 1989. UWC, Mayibuye Archive.
21 Mac Maharaj, author's interview.
22 Padraig O'Malley, author's interview, Hout Bay, Cape Town, 15 December 2006.
23 Penuell Maduna, author's interview, Sandton, Johannesburg, 23 November 2006.
24 The full list and results are available at <http://www.anc.org.za/ancdocs/history/conf/iecrep48.html> accessed on 20 January 2007.
25 ANC, 'Resolutions on negotiation adopted by the 48th National Conference of the ANC'.
26 ANC, 'Resolutions on negotiation'.
27 ANC Department of Information and Publicity, 'Restructuring of the Departments of the Organisation and the Allocation of Portfolios to Members of the National

Working Committee of the ANC', issued by the ANC, Marshalltown, 2 August 1991.
28 Cyril Ramaphosa interview with Padraig O'Malley, 16 August 1991. All O'Malley interviews are available online at <www.omalley.co.za>
29 This term is Mabandla's, author's interview.
30 I am grateful to Kader Asmal's for offering this more precise term, author's interview.
31 The source asked not to be identified.
32 Mac Maharaj, author's interview.
33 Kader Asmal, author's interview.
34 Valli Moosa interview with Padraig O'Malley, 25 July 1991.
35 Cyril Ramaphosa interview with Padraig O'Malley, 16 August 1991.
36 Anonymous informant.
37 Saki Macozoma, author's interview, Melrose Arch, Johannesburg, 21 November 2006.

Chapter 16
1 Tim Cohen, 'Cyril Ramaphosa and a cautionary tale for BEE', *Business Day*, 16 January 2006.
2 Raymond Suttner, interview with Padraig O'Malley, 27 August 1990.
3 Kader Asmal, 'The making of a constitution', *Southern African Review of Books*, 36, 1995.
4 James Sanders, *Apartheid's Friends: The Rise and Fall of South Africa's Secret Services*. London, John Murray, 2006, p. 227.
5 Quoted in ibid., p. 231.
6 Mike Louw, quoted in Patti Waldmeir, *Anatomy of a Miracle*. New Brunswick, Rutgers University Press, 1998, pp. 49, 51; cited in Sanders, *Apartheid's Friends*, p. 227.
7 Tertius Delport, author's interview, Parliament, Cape Town, 7 November 2006.
8 Allister Sparks, *Tomorrow Is Another Country: The Inside Story of South Africa's Negotiated Revolution*. Sandton, Struik Publishers, 1994, pp. 28–30.
9 Niel Barnard, interview in *Die Burger* in 1992; cited in Sanders, *Apartheid's Friends*, p. 244.
10 Sanders, *Apartheid's Friends*, pp. 240–1; there is also a broadly consistent account in Sparks, *Tomorrow*.
11 Anthony Sampson, *Nelson Mandela: The Authorised Biography*. New York, Vintage Books, 1999, p. 362.
12 Sanders, *Apartheid's Friends*, pp. 240–1, 246.
13 Sparks, *Tomorrow*, pp. 102–4; Sanders, *Apartheid's Friends*, pp. 247–8.
14 Sanders, *Apartheid's Friends*, p. 249.
15 The phrase is Frederik van Zyl Slabbert's. Mbeki contrasts with Ramaphosa, who is 'indigenous' and 'knows the locals'. Frederik van Zyl Slabbert, author's interview, Craighall, Johannesburg, 21 November 2006.
16 Anthony Sampson, 'President select', *The Observer*, London, 10 June 2001.
17 Sanders, *Apartheid's Friends*, p. 230.
18 Ibid., p. 228.
19 Ibid., pp. 267–8.
20 Merle Lipton, 'The role of business under apartheid', in Hans Erik Stolten (ed.), *History Making and Present Day Politics: The Meaning of Collective Memory in South Africa*. Uppsala, Nordiska Afrikainstitutet, 2007, pp. 292–305. For a short statement of her original position, see Merle Lipton, 'Capitalism and apartheid', in John Lonsdale (ed.), *South Africa in Question*. London, James Currey, 1988, pp. 52–63.
21 Lipton, 'Capitalism and apartheid', pp. 58–60; 'Role of business', pp. 294–7.

22 Lipton, 'Role of business', p. 293.
23 Ann Bernstein, author's interview, Cape Town, 5 April 2007.
24 Christo Nel, author's interview, Hout Bay, Cape Town, 2 April 2007.
25 Ibid.
26 Ibid.
27 Ibid.
28 Ibid.
29 Theuns Eloff, author's interview, Stellenbosch, 13 December 2006.
30 Christo Nel, author's interview; Theuns Eloff, 'The business community ten years after apartheid', Paper delivered at the After Apartheid conference, August 2006, Cape Town. See also Consultative Business Movement, *The Consultative Business Movement: 1998–1994. A Submission to the Truth and Reconciliation Commission.* CBM, Johannesburg, 1994.
31 Theuns Eloff, author's interview.
32 Michael Spicer, author's interview, Parktown, Johannesburg, 24 October 2006.
33 Christo Nel and Theuns Eloff, author's interviews.
34 Richard Spitz with Matthew Chaskalson, *The Politics of Transition.* Johannesburg, Witwatersrand University Press, 2000, p. 18.
35 Mac Maharaj interview with Padraig O'Malley, 18 August 1993.
36 I am grateful to Adrian Crewe for this anecdote.
37 Tertius Delport, author's interview. One other senior negotiator made the same anonymous assessment of Meyer's limitations.
38 Tertius Delport, author's interview.
39 Tertius Delport interview with Padraig O'Malley, 9 May 1996.
40 Gerrit Viljoen interview with Padraig O'Malley, 26 July 1991.
41 Bobby Godsell, author's interview, Diagonal Street, Johannesburg, 17 January 2007.
42 Dave Steward, author's interview, Plattekloof, Cape Town, 26 September 2006.
43 This last is Roelf Meyer's opinion, author's interview, Killarney, Johannesburg, 18 January 2007.
44 Sparks, *Tomorrow*, pp. 3–4.
45 Roelf Meyer, author's interview; Allister Sparks, telephone conversation, 19 April 2007.
46 Cyril Ramaphosa interview with Padraig O'Malley, 16 August 1991.
47 Cyril Ramaphosa interview with Patti Waldmeir, 19 January 1995. Historical Papers, University of the Witwatersrand, A2508.
48 Cyril Ramaphosa interview with O'Malley, 16 August 1991.
49 Ruth Walker, 'Feelings are key to negotiation', *Harvard Gazette*, 13 October 2005. Parables of this kind, when used in business school settings, are presumably not expected to be literally true.
50 Sidney Frankel, author's interview, Waterfront, Cape Town, 31 October 2006.
51 Ibid.
52 One senior banker who asked not to be quoted recalled Frankel using foul language to turn down a request to support bursaries for black South Africans to visit the United States in the late 1980s.
53 Sidney Frankel, author's interview.
54 Theuns Eloff, author's interview; Frederik van Zyl Slabbert, personal communication, 2 February 2007.
55 Sidney Frankel, author's interview.
56 Ibid.
57 Michael Spicer, author's interview.
58 Sidney Frankel, author's interview.
59 Michael Spicer, author's interview.

60 This interview is archived on the O'Malley website at <www.omalley.org.za> accessed on 29 January 2007.
61 Essop Pahad interview with Padraig O'Malley, 24 August 1990.
62 Jeremy Cronin interview with Padraig O'Malley, 26 August 1991.
63 Trevor Manuel interview with Padraig O'Malley, 6 August 1990.
64 Cyril Ramaphosa interview with Padraig O'Malley, 16 August 1991.
65 Ibid.
66 Roelf Meyer interview with Padraig O'Malley, 17 December 1990.
67 Ibid.
68 Ibid.

Chapter 17
1 Fanie van der Merwe, government negotiator, quoted by Tertius Delport, interview with Padraig O'Malley, 9 May 1996.
2 Niel Barnard, head of the NIS, quoted in James Sanders, *Apartheid's Friends: The Rise and Fall of South Africa's Secret Services*. London, John Murray, 2006, p. 249.
3 Jon Elster, *Rebuilding the Boat in the Open Sea: Constitution-Making in Eastern Europe*. Discussion Paper 24, Oxford, Centre for European Studies, 1993; see also Jon Elster, 'Constitution-making in Eastern Europe: Rebuilding the boat in the open sea', *Public Administration*, 71: 1, 1993, pp. 169-217.
4 Kader Asmal, author's interview, Parliament, Cape Town, 13 December 2006.
5 Tertius Delport, author's interview, Parliament, Cape Town, 7 November 2006.
6 Anonymous informant.
7 The senior negotiator who made this comment asked not to be attributed.
8 Bantu Holomisa, author's interview, Parliament, Cape Town, 5 September 2006.
9 FW de Klerk, *The Last Trek: A New Beginning*. Basingstoke, Pan Macmillan, 2000, p. 238. It is possible that this uncharacteristically florid passage was in fact penned by Dave Steward who assisted De Klerk in the preparation of the book.
10 Tertius Delport, interview with Padraig O'Malley, 9 May 1996.
11 Richard Spitz with Matthew Chaskalson, *The Politics of Transition*. Johannesburg, Witwatersrand University Press, 2000, p. 19.
12 Spitz interview with Albie Sachs, quoted in ibid., p. 57.
13 Spitz and Chaskalson, *Politics of Transition*, pp. 57-8.
14 Gillian Hutchings, author's interview, Parktown, Johannesburg, 6 October 2006.
15 Cyril Ramaphosa interview with O'Malley, 17 August 1993.
16 Tertius Delport, author's interview.
17 Mac Maharaj, author's interview, Morningside, Johannesburg, 16 January 2007.
18 Tertius Delport, author's interview.
19 De Klerk, *Last Trek*, p. 238.
20 Dave Steward, author's interview, Plattekloof, Cape Town, 26 September 2006.
21 Tertius Delport, author's interview.
22 Ibid. The meeting between Delport and Mandela occurred in 1994 in Eastern Cape when Delport was serving as provincial MEC for agricultural and environmental affairs. Delport also refers to a BBC documentary on the *Death of Apartheid* that he believes confirms his view. Tertius Delport, author's interview.
23 Ibid.
24 The interviewee, who was close to the centre of the negotiations, asked that these comments not be attributed to him.
25 De Klerk, *Last Trek*, p. 239.
26 Jeremy Cronin, 'The boat, the tap and the Leipzig way', *African Communist*, 130, 1992.
27 Dave Steward, author's interview.

28 Ibid.

29 Ibid. Bisho was the capital of the Ciskei homeland and Ulundi of KwaZulu.

30 Ronnie Kasrils, *Armed and Dangerous*, 2nd edn. Johannesburg, Jonathan Ball, 1998. Trevor Manuel likes to describe Kasrils as 'armless and harmless'.

31 Ibid., p. 360.

32 Ibid., p. 360.

33 Quoted in ibid., p. 360.

34 Mac Maharaj, author's interview.

35 Raymond Suttner, 'African National Congress as dominant organisation', Paper presented at Rhodes University, 25 August 2006.

36 Peter Phaswani, author's interview, Soweto, Johannesburg, 31 August 2006.

37 Cyril Ramaphosa interview with Padraig O'Malley, 17 August 1993.

38 Dave Steward, author's interview; De Klerk, *Last Trek*, p. 247.

39 Roelf Meyer, author's interview, Killarney, Johannesburg, 18 January 2007; Fanie van der Merwe, Mac Maharaj and Theuns Eloff, author's interviews.

40 Cyril Ramaphosa interview with Padraig O'Malley, 17 August 1993.

41 Kader Asmal interview with Padraig O'Malley, 4 August 1992.

42 Govan Mbeki interview with Padraig O'Malley, 27 July 1992.

43 Cyril Ramaphosa, 'Negotiating a new nation: Reflections on the development of South Africa's constitution', in Stephen Ellmann and Penelope Andrews (eds.), *Post-Apartheid Constitutions: Perspectives on South Africa's Basic Law*. Johannesburg, Witwatersrand University Press, 2001, pp. 71–84.

44 Cyril Ramaphosa interview with Patti Waldmeir, 19 January 1995. Historical Papers, University of the Witwatersrand, A2508.

45 Ibid. Did Mandela actually accuse De Klerk of being racist? Ramaphosa: 'Not the word racist but it was clear. It was a sad sight.'

46 Cyril Ramaphosa interview with Padraig O'Malley, 17 August 1993. Ibid.

47 FW de Klerk, personal communication with author, 6 December 2006.

48 Ibid.

49 Ibid.

50 Cyril Ramaphosa interview with O'Malley, 17 August 1993.

51 Kader Asmal interview with Padraig O'Malley, 4 August 1992.

52 Roelf Meyer interview with Padraig O'Malley, 25 November 1996.

53 Ibid.

54 Cyril Ramaphosa interview with O'Malley, 17 August 1993.

55 Roelf Meyer, author's interview.

56 Ibid.

57 Hassan Ebrahim, *Soul of a Nation: Constitution-Making in South Africa*. Cape Town, Oxford University Press, 1998, p. 140.

58 De Klerk, *Last Trek*, pp. 249–50.

59 Cyril Ramaphosa interview with Waldmeir, 19 January 1995.

60 Ebrahim, *Soul of a Nation*. I have drawn heavily on this invaluable volume in the section that follows.

61 De Klerk, *Last Trek*, pp. 249–53.

62 Nelson Mandela, press statement on the Record of Understanding between the ANC and NP, World Trade Centre, Kempton Park, 26 September 1992.

63 Roelf Meyer interview with Padraig O'Malley, 13 August 1992.

64 Kader Asmal, author's interview.

65 Allister Sparks, *Tomorrow Is Another Country: The Inside Story of South Africa's Negotiated Revolution*. Sandton, Struik Publishers, 1994, p. 181.

66 Kader Asmal, author's interview. Confirmed by an anonymous interviewee.

67 Bantu Holomisa, author's interview.
68 Today, parliamentary Speaker Baleka Mbete. Gillian Hutchings, author's interview, Parktown, Johannesburg, 6 October 2006.
69 Gillian Hutchings, author's interview.
70 Ibid.
71 Theuns Eloff, author's interview, Stellenbosch, 13 December 2007.
72 Ibid.
73 Gillian Hutchings, author's interview.
74 Theuns Eloff, author's interview.
75 Kader Asmal, author's interview.
76 *Sunday Times*, Johannesburg, 6 June 1993; quoted in Ebrahim, *Soul of a Nation*.
77 Bernard Ngoepe, author's interview, Pretoria, 24 November 2006.
78 Ibid.
79 This section draws heavily on Padraig O'Malley, 'Overview of 1993', archived at www.omalley.co.za; De Klerk, *Last Trek*; and Ebrahim, *Soul of a Nation*.
80 Tertius Delport interview with Padraig O'Malley, 9 November 1996.
81 Cyril Ramaphosa interview with Waldmeir, 19 January 1995.
82 Waldmeir reports Joe Slovo's astonishment: 'It was something I thought we should never win.' Patti Waldmeir, *Anatomy of a Miracle*. London, Viking, 1997, p. 232.
83 Cyril Ramaphosa interview with Waldmeir, 19 January 1995.
84 Ibid.
85 Cyril Ramaphosa interview with Padraig O'Malley, 17 August 1993.
86 Cyril Ramaphosa interview with Waldmeir, 19 January 1995.
87 André du Toit interview with Padraig O'Malley, 2 August 1990.
88 Quoted in Mark Gevisser, 'Rhodes, Rupert, Ramaphosa', *Mail & Guardian*, 11 October 1996.
89 Tertius Delport interview with Padraig O'Malley, 9 November 1996.
90 Tertius Delport, author's interview.
91 Tertius Delport interview with Padraig O'Malley, 9 May 1996.
92 Cyril Ramaphosa interview with Waldmeir, 19 January 1995.
93 Dave Steward, author's interview. As De Klerk puts the same insight in his autobiography, written with Steward's assistance, 'the skill and cunning of our respective negotiators probably did not play so decisive a role as the objective circumstances within which negotiations took place'. De Klerk, *Last Trek*, p. 388.
94 De Klerk, *Last Trek*, p. 310.
95 Anthony Sampson, *Nelson Mandela: The Authorised Biography*. New York, Vintage Books, 1999, p. 479.
96 Ibid., p. 481.
97 Ibid., p. 480.
98 Cyril Ramaphosa interview with Padraig O'Malley, 26 May 1994.

Chapter 18

1 Kader Asmal, author's interview, Parliament, Cape Town, 13 December 2006.
2 Cyril Ramaphosa interview with Padraig O'Malley, 28 February 1995.
3 Bantu Holomisa, author's interview, Parliament, Cape Town, 5 September 2006.
4 Saki Macozoma, author's interview, Melrose Arch, Johannesburg, 21 November 2006.
5 Anthony Sampson, *Nelson Mandela: The Authorised Biography*. New York, Vintage Books, 1999, p. 485.
6 Kader Asmal, author's interview.
7 As Clive Menell, on his deathbed, told Theuns Eloff. Author's interview, Stellenbosch, 13 December 2006.
8 Mandela, *Sampson*, p. 485; Oyama Mabandla, author's interview, Sandton, Johannes-

burg, 12 September 2006.

9 William Mervin Gumede, *Thabo Mbeki and the Battle for the Soul of the ANC*. Cape Town, Zebra Press, 2005, p. 47; Oyama Mabandla, author's interview; Gumede, *Thabo Mbeki*, p. 32; Mark Gevisser, 'The Chief', *Sunday Times*, Johannesburg, 20 June 1999; James Myburgh, 'Some notes on the idea that in 1994 Nelson Mandela preferred Ramaphosa as his successor', available at <www.ever-fasternews.com> accessed on 10 August 2006.

10 Myburgh, 'Some notes'.

11 Anton Harber, 'Round one in the deputy president bout', *Mail & Guardian*, 29 April 1994.

12 Kader Asmal, author's interview.

13 Dave Steward, author's interview, Plattekloof, Cape Town, 26 September 2006.

14 Penuell Maduna, author's interview, Sandton, Johannesburg, 23 November 2006.

15 Dave Steward, author's interview.

16 Roelf Meyer interview with Padraig O'Malley, 25 November 1996.

17 Tertius Delport interview with Padraig O'Malley, 9 May 1996.

18 Bantu Holomisa, author's interview.

19 Kader Asmal and Bantu Holomisa, author's interviews.

20 Rick Menell, author's interview, Main Street, Johannesburg, 25 October 2006.

21 Nthato Motlana, author's interview, Fourways, Johannesburg, 24 November 2006.

22 Bantu Holomisa, author's interview.

23 Allister Sparks, telephone conversation with author, 19 April 2007.

24 Roelf Meyer interview with Padraig O'Malley, 25 November 1996.

25 Anonymous informant close to Ramaphosa.

26 An anonymous informant close to Ramaphosa set out these versions of events.

27 Kader Asmal, author's interview.

28 ANC, 'Statement on necklacing', issued by ANC Department of Information and Publicity, 27 April 1992.

29 Chris Barron, 'Peter Mokaba: King of the young lions had a reputation for enjoying the good things in life', *Sunday Times*, Johannesburg, 16 June 2002.

30 Peter Mokaba and anonymous others, *Castro Hlongwane, Caravans, Cats, Geese, Foot and Mouth and Statistics: HIV/AIDS and the Struggle for the Humanisation of the African*. 2000. <www.chico.mweb.co.za/doc/aid.Castro.Hlongwane.doc> accessed on 8 September 2004. The document was created on Thabo Mbeki's computer for which reason he is often considered to be one of the probable authors.

31 ANC, 'Through the Eye of a Needle: Choosing the Best Cadres to Lead Transformation'. Discussion document of the National Working Committee of the ANC, 2001. A member of the NEC informed me that Mokaba was the author of this document.

32 Anton Harber, 'Feuds 'n debts shaped cabinet', *Mail & Guardian*, 20 May 1994.

33 Vic Allen, personal communication with author, 20 January 2006.

34 Frans Baleni, author's interview, Boksburg, East Rand, 25 October 2006.

35 Ibid. Such anecdotes may have contributed to Mufamadi's very uneven reputation in the union movement, which resulted in him being booed extensively at the 2006 Cosatu congress.

36 James Motlatsi, author's interview, Selby, Johannesburg, 31 August 2006.

37 Bantu Holomisa, author's interview.

38 Helbron Vilakazi, author's telephone interview, 1 September 2006.

39 Vic Allen, personal communication with author.

40 Widely known phrase; original source not identified.

41 Rams Ramashia, author's interview, Waterfront, Cape Town, 31 October 2006. Nomazizi Mtshotshisa was eventually to become chairperson of Telkom and a prominent business woman in the new South Africa.

42 Anonymous source.
43 Gaye Davis, 'How potential Mandela successor was edged out', *Mail & Guardian*, 19 April 1996.
44 Hassan Ebrahim, *Soul of a Nation: Constitution-Making in South Africa*. Cape Town, Oxford University Press, 1998.
45 Ibid.
46 Kader Asmal interview with Padraig O'Malley, 15 May 1996.
47 Cyril Ramaphosa interview with Padraig O'Malley, 28 February 1995.
48 Roelf Meyer interview with Padraig O'Malley, 24 March 1995.
49 Cyril Ramaphosa interview with Padraig O'Malley, 26 May 1994.
50 Hassan Ebrahim, *Soul of a Nation*, p. 196.
51 Ibid., p. 207.
52 Kader Asmal, author's interview.
53 Cyril Ramaphosa interview with Padraig O'Malley, 24 May 1996.
54 FW de Klerk, *The Last Trek: A New Beginning*. Basingstoke, Pan Macmillan, 2000, p. 358.
55 Hassan Ebrahim, *Soul of a Nation*, p. 220.
56 Nelson Mandela, Statement on the future of comrade Cyril Ramaphosa, Cape Town, 13 April 1996.
57 Gaye Davis, 'How Cyril was edged out by Thabo', *Mail & Guardian*, Johannesburg, 19 April 1996.
58 Oyama Mabandla, author's interview.
59 South African Press Association, 'Holomisa has signed his own death knell in the ANC: Tshwete'. Johannesburg, SAPA, 1 August 1996.
60 Ibid.
61 *Sowetan,* 11 November 1996.
62 Newton Kanhema, 'Mandela drops Mbeki bombshell', *The Star*, 11 November 1996.
63 Sampson, *Mandela*, p. 529.
64 ANC, 'Cyril wants to transform the economy', *Mayibuye*, 7: 6, July 1996.
65 Ibid.
66 Nthato Motlana, author's interview, Fourways, Johannesburg, 24 November 2006.
67 Quoted in the *Mail & Guardian*, Editorial, 19 April 1996.
68 Ndoda Madalane, author's interview, Morningside, Johannesburg, 22 November 2006.
69 Nthato Motlana, author's interview.
70 Ibid.

Chapter 19
1 Cyril Ramaphosa, interviewed in the *Sunday Independent*, 31 August 1997.
2 Tim Cohen, 'Cyril Ramaphosa and a cautionary tale for BEE', *Business Day*, 16 January 2006.
3 Michael Spicer, quoted in *The Nation*, 29 September 1997.
4 'Mzi snatches JCI's pot from under Cyril's nose', *Business Times*, 1 December 1996.
5 Black shareholders had the right to vote for the shares but the institutional investors that owned them would receive 70 or 80 per cent of any growth in the share price. The black investors were also paying a fee to the institutions for this service.
6 Cohen, 'Cyril Ramaphosa'.
7 One anonymous observer comments that this should never have been seen as a shock because the black shareholders were just a front for white institutional investors all along.
8 *Business Times*, 1 November 2005.
9 Private information from a source requesting anonymity.

10 Phillip de Wet, 'Man at the crossroads', *Maverick*, 1: 5, April 2006, p. 40.
11 Ndoda Madalane, author's interview, Morningside, Johannesburg, 22 November 2006.
12 David Kovarsky 'Fourth estate becomes the property of the new power elite', *Sunday Times*, 24 November 1996.
13 'Mugabe turns his wrath on Cyril', *Business Day*, 22 February 1999.
14 'Outside interests not the problem', *Business Day*, 22 February 1999.
15 *Sunday Times*, 21 February 1999.
16 Statement issued by Ronnie Mamoepa, Office of the Deputy President, 21 February 1999.
17 *Business Day*, 22 February 1999.
18 Peter Bruce, author's interview, Rosebank, Johannesburg, 11 September 2006.
19 '*Cyril's faux pas*', *Mail & Guardian*, 14 May 1999.
20 'Thick end of the wedge', *Business Day* 21 May 2007.
21 Peter Bruce, author's interview.
22 Ibid.
23 Anonymous informant.
24 Jabulani Sikhakhane, author's interview, Rosebank, Johannesburg, 6 October 2006.
25 Jaspreet Kindra, 'Government denies Ramaphosa investigation', *Mail & Guardian*, 1 September 2000; James Sanders, *Apartheid's Friends: The Rise and Fall of South Africa's Secret Services*. London, John Murray, 2006, p. 353.
26 *Business Day*, 28 August 2000.
27 Chris McGreal, 'ANC veterans accused of plot to harm Mbeki', *Guardian*, London, 26 April 2001.
28 Saki Macozoma, author's interview, Melrose Arch, Johannesburg, 24 November 2006.
29 Ndoda Madalane, author's interview; Saki Macozoma, author's interview.
30 De Wet, 'Man at the crossroads', pp. 42–3.
31 Nthato Motlana, author's interview, Fourways, Johannesburg, 24 November 2006.
32 Ndoda Madalane, author's interview.
33 Ibid.
34 Ibid.
35 Ibid.
36 Michael Spicer, author's interview, Parktown, Johannesburg, 24 October 2006.

Chapter 20

1 Former British prime minister Margaret Thatcher's judgment of Ramaphosa, quoted in Hugh Murray, 'The privatisation of Cyril Ramaphosa', *Leadership*, July 1997, p. 23.
2 Ndoda Madalane, author's interview, Morningside, Johannesburg, 22 November 2006.
3 For a general statement of his position, see Cyril Ramaphosa, 'Black empowerment: Myths and realities', in F Sicre (ed.), *South Africa at 10*. Cape Town, Human and Rousseau, 2004, pp. 72–84.
4 Quoted in John Reed, 'South Africa's "cappuccino effect": Will economic empowerment do more than create a sprinkling of black tycoons?', *Financial Times*, London, 5 November 2003, p. 11.
5 Ibid., p. 11.
6 Kevin Wakeford, 'Empowerment must be an investment, not a cost', *Business Day*, 9 September, 2004.
7 Section 10 notoriously limited this to those born in a specific town with 15 years' residence in it, those with 15 years' continuous employment, and those who had worked for 10 years for the same employer.
8 Act No 47 of 1953.

9 Act No 45 of 1959.
10 Act No 34 of 1959.
11 Brian Bunting, *Rise of the South African Reich*. London, International Defence and Aid Fund for South Africa, 1986 [1964]; N MacDermott, 'Self-determination in the "independent" Bantustans', in ES Reddy (ed.), *Apartheid, South Africa and International Law*. United Nations Centre Against Apartheid, Notes and Documents Series 13/85, 1985.
12 OC Iheduru, 'Black economic power and nation-building in post-apartheid South Africa', *Journal of Modern African Studies*, 42: 1, 2004, pp. 4–5.
13 Penuell Maduna, author's interview, Sandton, Johannesburg, 23 November 2006.
14 Joe Slovo, 'The South African working class and the National Democratic Revolution'. *Umsebenzi Discussion Pamphlet*, South African Communist Party, 1988.
15 African National Congress, *Strategy and Tactics of the African National Congress*. ANC, April–May, 1969.
16 Nelson Mandela, 'Report by the president of the ANC', ANC National Congress, Mafikeng, 16 December 1997.
17 Jo Beall, S Gelb and S Hassim, 'Fragile stability', *Journal of Southern African Studies*, 31: 4, 2005, p. 693.
18 Nelson Mandela, interview in the *Washington Post*, 26 June 1990.
19 African National Congress, 'Tasks of the National Democratic Revolution and the mobilization of the motive forces', *Umrabulo*, 8 May 2000, Section C.
20 Ramaphosa, 'Black empowerment'.
21 Beall, Gelb and Hassim, 'Fragile stability', p. 693.
22 Iheduru, 'Black economic power'.
23 Thabo Mbeki, 'This seed must grow into a tree', in Thami Mazwai (ed.), *Black Business Pioneers*. Houghton, Black Enterprise, 1994, p. 2.
24 Thabo Mbeki, 'Speech at the annual national conference of the Black Management Forum', Kempton Park, 20 November, 1999, available at http://www.anc.org.za/ancdocs/history/mbeki/1999/tm1120.html, accessed on 13 March 2006.
25 Dan O'Meara, *Volkskapitalism: Class, Capital and Control in the Development of Afrikaner Nationalism*. Cambridge, Cambridge University Press, 1983.
26 Govan Mbeki, *Learning from Robben Island: The Prison Writings of Govan Mbeki*. London, James Currey, 1991, p. 23; cited in Jeffrey Herbst, 'Mbeki's South Africa', *Foreign Affairs*, November/December 2005.
27 Thabo Mbeki, 'The eradication of poverty in South Africa', *ANC Today*, 1: 12, 13 April 2001, available at http://www.anc.org.za/ancdocs/anctoday/2001/at12.htm, accessed on 13 March 2006.
28 John Daniel, R Southall and J Lutchman, 'Introduction: President Mbeki's second term: Opening the golden door?', in Daniel, Southall and Lutchman (eds.), *State of the Nation: South Africa 2004–2005*. Cape Town, Human Sciences Research Council Press, 2005, p. xxx.
29 Jenny Cargill, 'Black corporate ownership: Complex codes can impede change', in Sue Brown (ed.), *Conflict and Governance: Economic Transformation Audit 2005*. Cape Town, Institute for Justice and Reconciliation, 2005, p. 25.
30 BEECom, Executive Summary of the *Report of the BEEC*, Black Economic Empowerment Commission, 2001, available at <www.bmfonline.co.za/bee_rep.htm> accessed on 7 January 2006.
31 BEECom participant Jabulani Sikhakhane, author's interview, Rosebank, Johannesburg, 6 October 2006.
32 The various sectoral 'transformation charters' already negotiated or under negotiation are now dead in the water because they are unlikely to pass the test of substantial compatibility with the new codes.

33 Wakeford, 'Empowerment must be an investment'.

34 Quoted in Reed, 'South Africa's "cappuccino effect,"' p. 11.

35 Cargill, 'Black corporate ownership', pp. 23–5.

36 Ibid., p. 22.

37 Ibid., p. 23.

38 'Rising danger', *Financial Mail*, 24 February 2006, p. 16.

39 Vuyo Jack, 'Empowerment partnerships', *New Agenda*, 20, 4th Quarter 2005, p. 30.

40 Cargill, 'Black corporate ownership', pp. 23–5.

41 Simon Robinson, 'Welcome to the club', *Time Europe*, 29 May 2005.

42 Jack, 'Empowerment partnerships', pp. 27–30.

43 Robinson, 'Welcome to the club'.

44 Cronin, 'The people shall govern'.

45 Eskom has served as an instrument of South African external policy since 1994, for example, and it has been understandable and largely desirable that the state has reciprocally acted as an instrument of Eskom Enterprise's foreign policy (which in many respects is more ambitious than government's). It would be quite undesirable, however, if South African intelligence systems and political capital were routinely put at the disposal of mining companies with high-risk investments in sub-Saharan African countries.

46 Muller observes that we are trying too hard 'to create internal opportunities for our new economic elite'. He speculates that the east coast transmission line that would have averted the Cape's current power crisis would not have been delayed if it did not threaten the profitability of a new BEE power generator in the Eastern Cape. Mike Muller, 'Switching on SA's energy regulators', *Business Day*, 7 March 2006.

47 T Msomi, 'ANC mortgaged to private capital', *City Press*, 27 November 2005.

48 Cronin, 'The people shall govern'.

49 Michael Spicer, author's interview, Parktown, Johannesburg, 24 October 2006.

50 Ndoda Madalane, author's interview.

51 Michael Spicer, author's interview.

52 'The Time 100: The most influential people in the world', *Time*, New York, 27 April 2007.

53 Richard C Holbrooke, 'Cyril Ramaphosa', *Time*, 27 April 2007.

54 She is known as 'Baroness Chalker' under the system of patronage-based quasi-traditional leadership prevalent in the UK.

55 Simon Cairns is a senior hereditary traditional leader formally known as The Rt. Hon. The Earl Cairns.

56 Ramaphosa was also a member of the United Nations Secretary-General's Panel on International Support to the New Partnership for Africa's Development (Nepad).

57 Commonwealth Business Council, 'CBC urges Germany not to let Africa slip from G-8 agenda', available at <http://allafrica.com/stories/2006/200610190266.html> accessed on 14 February 2007.

58 Anthony Butler, 'South Africa's HIV/AIDS policy 1994–2004. How can it be explained?', *African Affairs*, 104: 417, pp. 591–614; Anthony Butler, 'The negative and positive impacts of HIV/AIDS on democracy in South Africa', *Journal of Contemporary African Studies*, 23: 1, pp. 3–26.

59 The Global Business Coalition website is at <www.businessfightsaids.org> accessed on 14 January 2007.

60 'Branson, Ramaphosa launch Aids drive', 5 November 2004. <http://iafrica.com/news/sa/6637.htm> accessed on 14 January 2007.

61 Donne Cooney, author's interview, Sandton, Johannesburg, 19 March 2007.

62 International Commission on Intervention and State Sovereignty, *The Responsibility to Protect: Report of the ICISS*. Ottawa, International Development Research Centre,

2001.
63 Chair of the Commission Gareth Evans, Australian foreign minister between 1988 and 1996, remembers Cyril as 'always a fount of good humour and robust common sense'. Gareth Evans, personal communication with author, 1 January 2007.
64 Padraig O'Malley, author's interview, Hout Bay, Cape Town, 15 December 2006.
65 Ibid.
66 Ramaphosa then immediately wrote to Thabo Mbeki to inform him of the invitation. Donne Cooney, author's interview, Sandton, Johannesburg, 19 March 2007.
67 Gerry Adams, 'A defining moment in Irish history', *ANC Today*, 8: 13, 6 April 2007.
68 'Adams says thank you to international community', *An Phoblacht*, 29 March 2007.

Chapter 21

1 Kader Asmal interview with Padraig O'Malley, 15 February 1994.
2 'Branson, Ramaphosa launch Aids drive', 5 November 2004, available at <http://iafrica.com/news/sa/6637.htm> accessed on 14 January 2007.
3 This section draws in part on an earlier paper 'The state of the ANC', in Roger Southall et al. (eds.), *State of the Nation: South Africa 2006–2007*. Cape Town, HSRC Press, 2007.
4 86 per cent of eligible voters in 1994, 72 per cent in 1999, and 58 per cent in 2004. These are the calculations of Jessica Piombo, 'The result of the election '04: Looking back, stepping forward', *Centre for Social Science Research Working Paper, No. 86*. Cape Town, University of Cape Town Centre for Social Science Research, 2004.
5 Charles Simkins, 'Employment and unemployment in South Africa', *Journal of Contemporary African Studies*, 22: 2, 2004, pp. 253–78.
6 Cyril Ramaphosa, 'Black empowerment: Myths and realities', in F Sicre (ed.), *South Africa at 10*. Cape Town, Human & Rousseau, 2004, p. 74.
7 Quoted in Andrew Nash, 'Mandela's democracy', *Monthly Review*, 50: 11, 1999, available at http://www.monthlyreview.org/498nash.htm, accessed on 30 October 2004.
8 ANC, *Strategy and Tactics of the ANC*. African National Congress, April–May 1969, available at http://www.anc.org.za/ancdocs/history/stratact.html, accessed on 27 October 2004; Joe Slovo, 'The South African working class and the National Democratic Revolution', *Umsebenzi Discussion Pamphlet*. South African Communist Party.
9 Joel Netshitenzhe, 'The NDR and class struggle: An address to the executive committee of Cosatu', *The Shop Steward*, 9: 1, 2000; Jeremy Cronin, 'Thinking about the concept "national democratic revolution"', *Umrabulo*, 1, 4th quarter 1996.
10 Jeremy Cronin, 'Here comes the sun: Drawing lessons from Joe Slovo's "No Middle Road"', *African Communist*, 163, 1st quarter 2003.
11 ANC, 'Tasks of the NDR and the mobilisation of the motive forces', ANC discussion document, *Umrabulo*, 8, 2000, Section C, Sections A4 and A6.
12 Motlanthe Kgalema, 'ANC secretary-general's organisational report', ANC National General Council, June 2005.
13 Bob Mattes, 'South Africa: Democracy without the people', *Journal of Democracy*, 13: 1, 2002, pp. 22–36; Bob Mattes et al., 'Democratic governance in South Africa: The people's view'. *Afrobarometer Working Papers No. 24*, January 2003.
14 Firoz Cachalia, 'Good governance needs an effective parliament', *Umrabulo*, 11, 2nd quarter 2001.
15 Tom Lodge, 'The ANC and the development of party politics in modern South Africa', *Journal of Modern African Studies*, 42: 2, 2004, p. 209.
16 Vicky Randall and L. Svasland, 'Political parties and democratic consolidation in Africa', *Democratization*, 9: 3, 2002, pp. 30–52.

17 Cyril Ramaphosa, interview with Padraig O'Malley, 26 May 1994.

18 Roelf Meyer, interview with Padraig O'Malley, 15 May 1996.

19 Cyril Ramaphosa, 'Rising together', in Kader Asmal, David Chidester and Wilmot James (eds.), *Nelson Mandela: From Freedom to the Future*. Cape Town, Jonathan Ball, 2003, pp. 179–85.

20 Vic Allen, author's interview, Keighley, Yorkshire, 15 July 2006.

21 Quoted in Alan Fischer and Michel Albedas (eds.), *A Question of Survival*. Johannesburg, Jonathan Ball, 1987, p. 286.

22 Clive Thompson, personal communication with author, 1 January 2007.

23 Michael Spicer, author's interview, Parktown, Johannesburg, 24 October 2006.

24 Bantu Holomisa, author's interview, Parliament, Cape Town, 5 September 2006.

25 Cyril Ramaphosa, interview with Padraig O'Malley, 24 May 1996.

Chapter 22

1 Duma Ndlovu, author's interview, Northcliff, Johannesburg, 5 October 2006.

2 Clive Thompson, personal communication with author, 1 January 2007.

3 Mamphela Ramphele, *A Life*. Cape Town, David Philip, 1996, pp. 191–2. The correct Venda translation for 'I don't know' would be *A thi divhi*.

4 Donne Cooney, author's interview, Sandton, Johannesburg, 19 March 2007.

5 Gundelfinger is a celebrated divorce lawyer.

6 'Ramaphosa junior does dad Cyril proud with driving play', *City Metro*, 10 July 1999.

7 Donne Cooney, author's interview.

8 'When Piet is much more than just a name', *Farmer's Weekly*, Johannesburg, September 2007.

9 Ibid.

10 Sheila Keeble (ed.), *Black Who's Who of Southern Africa Today*. Braamfontein, African Business Publications, 1979, p. 242.

11 Heribert Adam, Frederik van Zyl Slabbert and Kogila Moodley, *Comrades in Business: Post-Liberation Politics in South Africa*. Cape Town, Tafelberg, 1998, pp. 166–7.

12 Simon Robinson, 'Welcome to the club', *Time Europe*, 29 May 2005. Ironically *Time* itself makes just the same insinuation by entitling its article 'Welcome to the club' and then reflecting on how a handful of black business people are enjoying the delights of the Rand Club which was built by the sweat of African mineworkers. Ramaphosa was quick to inform the reporter that he had let his membership of the Rand Club lapse.

13 Lybon Mabasa, author's interview, Rosebank, Johannesburg, 17 August 2006.

14 Clive Thompson, personal communication with author, 1 January 2007.

15 Cyril Ramaphosa interview with Padraig O'Malley, 26 May 1994.

16 Frans Baleni, author's interview, Boksburg, Johannesburg, 25 October 2006.

17 Matthew 6. 24.

18 Matthew 6. 25–30.

19 Robinson, 'Welcome to the club'.

20 'Ramaphosa sees red over Maybach', *Business Report*, 26 January 2005.

21 'Ramaphosa denies ever seeing a Maybach', *South African Press Association*, 26 January 2005.

22 Donne Cooney, author's interview.

23 'Cyril joins ANC race', *City Press*, 23 July 2006.

24 The Foundation is explained on the Shanduka website at <www.shanduka.co.za>.

25 Griffith Zabala, author's interview, Kyalami Estate, 15 August 2006.

26 Henry Dolowitz, author's interview, Orange Grove, Johannesburg, 30 August 2006.

27 Ndoda Madalane, author's interview, Morningside, Johannesburg, 22 November 2006.

28 The source asked to remain anonymous.

29 Peter Bruce, author's interview, Rosebank, Johannesburg, 11 September 2006; Ann Bernstein, author's interview, Cape Town, 5 April 2007.
30 Simon Cairns, author's interview, London, 9 January 2007.
31 Henry Dolowitz, author's interview.
32 Peter Phaswani, author's interview, Soweto, Johannesburg, 31 August 2006.
33 Frans Baleni, author's interview.
34 Paul Benjamin, author's interview, Rondebosch, Cape Town, 23 August 2006.
35 The tactic failed and a ticket was issued. One of the passengers was Vic Allen, author's interview, Keighley, Yorkshire, 15 July 2006.
36 Fred Phaswana, author's interview, Constantia, Cape Town, 10 October 2006.
37 Vic Allen, author's interview.
38 Ibid.
39 Ishmael Mkhabela, author's interview, Braamfontein, Johannesburg, 15 August 2006.
40 Frank Chikane, author's interview, Tuynhuys, Cape Town, 2 November 2006; Caesar Molebatsi, author's interview, Johannesburg CBD, 5 October 2006.
41 The interviewee requested anonymity.
42 Vic Allen, personal communication, 15 July 2006.
43 Reuel Khoza, *Let Africa Lead: African Transformational Leadership for 21st Century Business*. Sunninghill, Vezubuntu Publishing, 2005, pp. 2, 24–5.
44 Reuel Khoza, author's interview, Sandton, Johannesburg, 26 October 2006.
45 Kader Asmal, author's interview, Parliament, Cape Town, 13 December 2006.
46 Frene Ginwala, personal communication with author, 25 May 2007.
47 Bernard Ngoepe, author's interview, Church Square, Pretoria, 24 November 2006.
48 Rick Menell, author's interview, Main Street, Johannesburg, 25 October 2006.
49 Saki Macozoma, author's interview, Melrose Arch, Johannesburg, 21 November 2006.
50 Kader Asmal, author's interview, Parliament, Cape Town, 13 December 2006.
51 Saths Cooper, author's interview, Killarney, Johannesburg, 17 August 2006.
52 Ishmael Mkhabela, author's interview.
53 Bantu Holomisa, author's interview, Parliament, Cape Town, 5 September 2006.
54 Rams Ramashia, author's interview, Waterfront, Cape Town, 31 October 2006.
55 Caesar Molebatsi, author's interview.
56 Phiroshaw Camay, author's interview Rosebank, Johannesburg, 17 August 2006.
57 Vic Allen, author's interview.
58 Marcel Golding, author's interview, Cape Town, 20 October 2006.

INDEX

A

Ackerman, Raymond, 100
Adams, Gerry, 368, 369
Adopt-a-School Foundation, 389, 390
AFL/CIO, 164, 177
African Mining Group (AMG), 335
African National Congress (ANC)
  liberation struggle, 2, 8, 11, 15, 25, 45,
    49, 67, 75, 83, 84, 85, 100, 130, 136,
    143, 186, 188, 203, 210–41, 245–8,
    252–64, 269–71, 278–82, 284–330,
    355, 357, 360, 362, 363, 367, 368, 369,
    370, 373–81, 383, 384–90, 396
  Lusaka, xi, 98, 186, 210, 222, 223, 224,
    226, 227, 228, 229, 230, 232, 234, 235,
    239, 240, 247, 251, 253, 255, 269, 279,
    286, 319, 321, 353, 383
  Robben Island, 64, 66, 99, 226, 227,
    228, 231, 245, 247, 250, 252, 279, 314,
    321, 335
  Umkhonto weSizwe (MK), 212, 225,
    230, 250, 251, 253, 260, 277, 278
  Women's League, 253, 318
  Youth League, 2, 8, 92, 240, 253, 318,
    329
  see also SACP, Operation Vula
Afrikaans Medium Decree, 72–3
Afrikaner Weerstandsbeweging (AWB),
  236
Agnew, Rudolf, 270
Ahtisaari, Martti, 367, 369
AIDS see HIV/AIDS
Alexander, Peter, xv
Alexander Forbes, 347, 363
Allen, Vic, xv, 116, 139, 140, 146, 157, 163,
  190, 203, 221, 255, 256, 257
All-Union Central Council of Trade
  Unions of the Soviet Union, 173
Amnesty International, 94
ANC see African National Congress

Anglo American Corporation (AAC),
  5, 91, 97, 98, 99, 103–7, 116–29, 130,
  132, 135–7, 141, 143, 144, 146–54, 157,
  164–6, 180, 181, 183, 185, 186, 187, 190,
  191, 191–205, 236, 242, 273, 274, 277,
  284, 286, 309, 311, 320, 333, 334, 335,
  341, 342, 363
Anglo Transvaal Mines Consolidated
  (Anglovaal), 90, 95, 115, 136, 183
apartheid, 2, 5, 6, 11, 13, 14, 16, 23, 36,
  38, 41, 48, 51, 54, 71, 82, 93, 108, 126,
  127, 147, 148, 184, 203, 209–17, 233,
  269, 273, 300, 323, 341, 354, 357, 359,
  383, 384
Argus Group, 341
Arniston, 325, 368
Asmal, Kader, xv, 252, 300, 303, 324, 326,
  327, 373, 395
Associated Chambers of Commerce, 273
Atong, Diamond, xv, 79, 80, 87
Atorama Construction, 87
Ayob, Ismail, 213
Azanian People's Organisation (Azapo),
  67, 219, 322

B

Badela, Mono, 168
Baleni, Andeya, xv, 173, 177
Baleni, Frans, xv, 160, 202, 205, 320
Ball, Chris, 274
Ball, Joanna, 214
Bam, Fikile, 99
bantustans, 4, 5, 12, 14, 28, 30, 35, 44, 45,
  47, 77, 97, 108, 269, 296, 301, 311, 375
Barayi, Elijah, 143, 171, 176, 220, 221, 223
Barclays Bank SA, 95, 104, 274
Barlow Rand, 104
Barnard, Niel, 268–73, 274, 281, 284, 301
Barrell, Howard, 210
BDFM, 341, 342

Beckett, Denis, xv, 37, 91, 98, 396
Benjamin, Paul, xv, 160, 161, 163, 171
Bernstein, Ann, xv
Bidvest Group, 363
biographical form, xi–xvi
Biko, Steve, 25, 26, 48, 72, 79, 108
Bisho, 296, 297
Bizos, George, 212, 269, 274
black consciousness, 20, 24–7, 32, 45, 48,
    51, 52, 54, 57–8, 61–2, 64, 66, 67, 70, 72,
    73, 74, 76, 79, 83, 85, 86, 108, 113, 125,
    126–8, 130, 163, 211, 216, 218–21, 223,
    252, 271, 320, 382
black economic empowerment (BEE),
    276, 329, 333–5, 337–9, 347–50, 351–63,
    364, 378, 379, 380
Black People's Convention (BPC), 32, 56
Blair, Tony, 365, 368
Blanke Veiligheid, 236
Bloom, Tony, 186
Blue Train, 285
Bock, Anthony, 345
Boesak, Allan, 211
Boipatong, 295, 301
Bold Evangelical Christian Organisation
    (BECO), 34, 52
Bolger, James, 366
Boraine, Alex, 123, 124
Boshoff, JL, 48
Botha, Fanie, 124
Botha, PW, 33, 95, 123, 169, 187, 196, 229,
    233, 242–6, 270, 281, 283, 284, 286
Botswana, 14, 48
Brassey, Martin, 161
Brenthurst, 284
Brenthurst Group, 287
British Petroleum, 104
Broederstroom, 275
Bruce, Peter, xv, 343, 344
Brutus, Dennis, 71
Bundy, Colin, xvi
Bushbuckridge, xiii
Business Day, 337, 341, 342, 344
Business Leadership South Africa
    (BLSA), 364
Buthelezi, Mangosuthu, 15, 96, 97, 99,
    105, 269, 297, 301, 302, 311, 315

C
Cachalia, Azhar, 240, 274, 275
Cairns, Simon, xv, 365, 391

Camay, Phiroshaw, xv, 127, 129, 131, 134,
    135, 136, 142, 220, 222, 232
Cameron, Robert, xvi
Cape Town trip, 40–2
Carey, Kate, xv
Carolus, Cheryl, 249, 251, 259, 261, 262
Carrington, Lord, 311
cars, 88, 387, 388, 392–3
Castro, Fidel, 255, 369, 370
cattle, 386–7
Caxton, 336
Centre for Applied Legal Studies, 160
Chalker, Lynda, 365
Chapman, Neal, 274
Charnley, Irene, xv, 174, 175, 176
Chaskalson, Arthur, 161
Chamber of Mines, 115, 133, 182, 190,
    192, 195, 200, 236
Cheadle, Halton, 134, 160, 161
Cheadle, Thompson & Haysom, 160, 166,
    171
Chetty, Shun, 61
Chiawelo see Tshiawelo
Chikane, Frank, xiii, xv, 39, 46, 50, 51, 52,
    53, 54, 61, 69, 72, 85, 86, 91, 107, 108,
    240, 246
churches see religion
Christianity see religion
Ciskei, 296
Clarke, Kenneth, 96
CNA Gallo, 336
Cobbett, Billy, 301
Coca-Cola Advisory Board, 365
Codesa I, 263, 291–2
Codesa II, 293–4, 295–300
Coetzee, General Johann, 98
Coetzee, Kobie, 269
Cohen, Tim, 267
Committee of Ten, 92, 99, 100, 102, 327,
    329
Commonwealth Business Council (CBC),
    365–6
Concerned South Africans Group
    (Cosag), 302, 306
Conference for a Democratic Future, 241
Congress of South African Trade Unions
    (Cosatu), 166, 209–21, 222, 224–9, 241,
    245, 247, 248, 254, 259, 275, 295, 296,
    314, 321, 355, 374, 396
constitution, 51, 54, 80, 87, 93, 141, 143,
    228, 257, 260, 268, 289–311, 280, 281,
    287, 322–4

Constitutional Assembly, 293, 294, 302, 303, 308, 323, 376, 384
Consultative Business Movement (CBM), 122, 276, 277, 304, 306
Cooney, Donne, xv, 264, 390
Cooper, Saths, xv, 57, 62, 64, 66, 252
Coovadia, Cas, 275
Copelyn, Johnny, 218, 328, 338, 339, 340
Council for Scientific and Industrial Research (CSIR), 4
Council of Unions of South Africa (Cusa), 127, 129, 130–6, 137, 139, 141, 142, 160, 161, 216, 218, 219, 220, 225, 232, 383, 396
Cronin, Jeremy, 286, 360, 362
Cuito Cuanavale, 268

D
DaimlerChrysler Maybach, 389
Damelin College, 84, 128
Darragh House, 189
De Beer, Zach, 97–8, 99, 123, 186, 274
De Beers, 104, 105, 116, 118, 119, 203
De Klerk FW, xv, 210, 211, 243–4, 245, 246, 263, 267, 270, 271, 272, 273, 277, 278, 280, 281, 287, 289, 290, 291, 294, 295, 296, 297–301, 302, 307, 308, 309, 310, 311, 313, 315, 326, 343, 391
De Kock, Eugene, 189
De Villiers, Dawie, 243, 310
Dederen, Godfried, xv
Deedes, Bill, 105
Delmas Treason Trial, 240
Delport, Tertius, xv, 268, 272, 280, 291, 294, 295, 308, 310, 316
Democratic Party (DP), 305
Dermont, Nick, 99
detention, 57, 59–70, 75, 76, 77, 78, 79, 80, 83, 85, 94, 125, 163, 179, 216, 218, 271, 322, 383, 393, 396
Diepkloof, 5
Dipico, Manne, 361
Dlamini, Chris, 219
Dlamini, Zanele, 271
Dolowitz, Henry, xv, 80–2, 106, 110, 391
Du Toit, André, xvi, 98
Du Toit, Christiaan, 124, 125
Du Plessis, Barend, 283, 284
Du Plessis, Pietie, 191
Dube, 5, 7, 30, 87
Durnacol, 158

E
East Rand Proprietary Mine, 179
Ebrahim, Hassan, 301, 324
EFK Tucker, 106, 128
Eglin, Colin, 305
Elias Motsoaledi, 5
Eloff, Theuns, xv, 304, 305, 306
Elster, Jon, 289
Erasmus, Major JS, 57
Erasmus, Nicholas, 188
Erwin, Alec, 217, 218
Eskom, 117
Esterhuyse, Willie, 98, 270
ethnicity, 3, 4–6, 12–14, 315, 316; see also apartheid, race
Evans, Gareth, xv

F
Farisani, Tshenuwani, xv, 14, 19, 22, 32, 33, 34, 35, 36, 37, 43, 59, 60, 61, 67, 68, 83, 85
Farnham Castle, 271
farming, 385–6, 394
Federated Chamber of Industries, 273
Federation of South African Trade Unions (Fosatu), 126, 131, 134, 135, 136, 160, 161, 169, 170, 216, 217, 219, 220, 221, 225
Fela, Albert, 40
Financial Mail, 99, 341, 342, 343, 344
Financial Times, 268, 341
First National Bank (FNB), 95
First Rand Group, 347
Fist, 127–8
Fletcher, GC, 118
fly fishing, 282, 283, 325, 368, 386, 387
Food and Allied Workers' Union, 225
Ford, 104
Foster, Don, xv
Foster, Joe, 219
Frankel, Sidney, xv, 281, 282, 283–5
Frankel Pollak, 283, 284
Frederikse, Julie, xvi
Front for the Liberation of Mozambique (Frelimo), 55
Furniture and Allied Workers' Union, 128

G
Gama, Paul, 329
Gelb, Stephen, 354

Gencor, 115, 116, 120, 200
Ginwala, Frene, xv
Godsell, Bobby, xv, 98, 103, 116, 124, 125, 130, 132, 133, 136, 137, 164, 180, 185, 186, 187, 190, 191, 192, 196, 197, 198, 199, 200, 281, 320
Gold Fields, 115, 116, 135, 149
Golding, Marcel, xv, 153, 164, 169, 170, 175, 193, 196, 256, 257, 338, 339, 340
Gorbachev, Mikhail, 243
Gordhan, Pravin, 126, 231, 251, 290, 304
Gordimer, Nadine, 212
Gomomo, John, 219, 296
Gould, William B, 144
Gouws, Rudolf, 97
Gqozo, Oupa, 296, 302
Gqubule, Duma, xv
Green, Pippa, xv
Green Book, 215, 218
Growth, Employment and Redistribution (Gear) strategy, 355, 356, 377, 379
Grantham, Richard, 345
Groote Schuur Minute, 262, 277
Gumede, William, xii, 256
Gundelfinger, Billy, 385
Gush, Peter, 119, 190, 191, 198, 200, 202, 203
Gwala, Harry, 229, 231, 235, 250, 259, 260, 313

H
Hani, Chris, 225, 253, 256, 259, 261, 269, 271, 296, 306, 324, 346
Harvard Negotiation Project, 283
Havelock Trout Farm, 281
Hersov, Basil, 95–6
Hersov, Bob, 95
Heunis, Chris, 279
Heseltine, Michael, 96
HIV/AIDS, 204, 318, 366, 369, 373, 377, 380
Hlaele, Lebohang, 177
Hoffa, Jimmy, 127
Holbrooke, Richard, 364–5
Holomisa, Bantu, 54, 290, 314, 316, 321, 328, 343, 379
Hosken Consolidated Investments (HCI), 338, 339, 340
Hutchings, Gillian, xv, 305, 306
homelands see bantustans

I
Immorality Act, 2
Independent Newspapers, 341
Industrial Workers' Union (FNV), 135, 173
International Commission on Intervention and State Sovereignty, 367
International Confederation of Free Trade Unions (ICFTU), 163, 173
International Defence Aid Fund (Idaf), 163
International Miners' Organisation (IMO), 173
Investec, 339, 347
Irish Liberation Army (IRA), 367
Ismael, Solly, 57

J
Jacobs, Bheki, xv
Janson, Punt, 72
JCI, 115, 149, 183, 200, 333, 334, 335
Jewison, Norman, 127
Johannesburg Philharmonic Orchestra, 390
Johannesburg Stock Exchange (JSE), 283, 337
John Vorster Square, 77, 78
Johnson, Shaun, 98
Johnnic, 98, 333–40, 341, 342, 343, 344, 349
Jolobe, Zweli, xvi
Jordan, Pallo, 259, 262, 286, 328
Judicial Services Commission, 307
June 16, 1976, 71–7, 84, 192

K
Kathrada, Ahmed, 245
Kasrils, Ronnie, 231, 259, 261, 296
Kaunda, Kenneth, 314
Kerzner, Sol, 328
Keys, Derek, 97
Kgotsile, Baleka, 304
Khalavha, 7, 17
Khoza, Reuel, xv, 32, 47, 50, 54, 69, 394
Khumalo, Mzi, 335
King, Mervyn, 274
Kinross, 162, 183
Kissinger, Henry, 122, 311
Klaaste, Aggrey, 91
Klerksdorp, 142

Kliptown, 2, 5, 22, 100
Kloof gold mine, 135, 142, 166, 199, 311
Koekemoer, Cornelius, 56
Kraai, Vella, 92
Kruger, Jimmy, 56
Kruger, Paul, 285
Kuzwayo, Ellen, 60, 73, 77, 92, 93, 99, 100, 102

L
Latimer, CA, xiii
Lebowa, 48
Leipzig option, 295, 297
Lekota, Mosiuoa 'Terror', 57, 240, 260, 261, 274, 319
Lekton House, 165
Lesotho, 14, 40, 86, 139, 140, 141, 200, 202, 207
Liberty Life, 118, 347
Liebenberg, Johann, xv, 137, 138, 144, 150, 152, 154, 155, 190, 191, 193, 196
Lipton, Merle, 273
Louw, Mike, 268, 269, 271
Louw, Raymond, 98
Lutheran Church *see* religion

M
Mabandla, Oyama, xv
Mabasa, Lybon, xv, 19, 26, 53, 54, 55, 60, 63, 69, 70, 72, 85, 88, 322, 393
Mabitlane Primary School, 3
Macozoma, Saki, xv, 108, 222, 239, 240, 246, 314, 347, 348, 350
Macun, Ian, 148
Madalane, Ndoda, xv, 340, 349, 350, 364
Madikizela-Mandela, Winnie, 91, 188, 212, 213, 239, 240, 248, 306, 317, 318, 396
Maduna, Penuell, xiv, xv, 262, 277, 290, 301, 315, 346
Madzena, Captain, 30
Maharaj, Mac, xiv, xv, 85, 99, 224, 230, 231, 232, 234, 235, 246, 247, 249, 250, 251, 255, 258, 259, 261, 262, 263, 264, 278, 279, 286, 290, 291, 301, 304, 313, 319, 347, 368
Mail & Guardian, 344
Makihara, Ben, 365
Malan, Magnus, 278
Malaysia, 356

Maluleke, George, 80
Mandela, Nelson, 2, 8, 44, 66, 67, 92, 95, 122, 213, 224, 227, 228, 229, 231, 240, 245, 248, 249, 250, 252, 253, 254, 261, 262, 263, 269, 271, 274, 277, 278, 279, 286, 289, 295, 301, 310, 314, 317, 327, 329, 353, 368, 370, 374, 388, 391
Mandela Crisis Committee, 240, 282
Mangope, Lucas, 269
Mankweng Police Station, 60
Mantashe, Gwede, 257
Manthatha, Tom, xv, 23, 26, 61, 64, 66, 92
Manuel, Trevor, 249, 251, 259, 260, 261, 262, 286, 319, 328, 357
Martindale, 4
Masondo, Amos, 130
Mass Democratic Movement (MDM), 216, 241, 246
Matthews, James, 214–15
Mayekiso, Moses, 134, 137
Mayibuye Centre, xvi
Mbeki, Govan, 4, 224, 227, 228, 230, 231, 232, 233, 234, 235, 249, 250, 255, 297, 354, 356
Mbeki, Thabo, xii, 227, 230, 250, 253, 254, 256, 259, 261, 262, 269, 270, 271, 277, 286, 290, 304, 311, 315, 316, 317, 318, 322, 328, 341, 342, 346, 352, 356, 365, 369, 370, 378, 384
McBride, Robert, 302
Meadowlands, 4
Meadowlands High School, 70
Menell, Clive, 90, 94, 95, 96, 97, 98, 99, 102, 105, 109, 136
Menell, Irene, xv, 94, 95, 96, 97, 99, 102, 105, 121, 174, 175
Menell, Rick, xv, 94, 95, 105, 106, 316
Menell, Slip, 96
Mentz Committee, 4
Metal and Allied Workers' Union (Mawu), 134
Metropolitan Life, 349
Meyer, Roelf, xv, 196, 268, 272, 273, 279, 280, 281, 282, 283, 285, 287, 288, 290, 294, 295, 300, 301, 303, 305, 308, 309, 310, 316, 317, 320, 324, 325, 326, 343, 368, 379
Mhlaba, Raymond, 229, 245
Mkhabela, Ishmael, xv, 19, 20, 23, 26, 53, 54, 60, 61, 63, 68, 69, 76, 83, 85, 126, 223
Middelbult Colliery, 162
Mills, C Wright, 121

Miners International Federation (MIF), 173
mineworkers, 2, 130–41, 146–9, 162–3; see also NUM
Mittal, Lakshmi, 366
Mlabatheki, Thenjiwe, xvi
Modise, Joe, 96, 230
Mokaba Peter, 228, 306, 317, 318, 388
Mokoape, Keith, 49
Mokoena, Aubrey, 49, 57
Molebatsi, Caesar, xv, 9, 84, 86, 87
Molefe, Popo, 240, 255, 260, 261, 274, 319, 361
Molope Group, 344–5
Mompati, Ruth, 277
Moodie, T Dunbar, 140, 141, 199
Moodley, Strini, 57
Moosa, Valli, 227, 234, 235, 240, 241, 259, 261, 262, 263, 264, 275, 278, 279, 290, 301, 313, 324, 361, 368
Morales, Evo, 370
Morobe, Murphy, 212, 240, 274, 275
Moseneke, Dikgang, 329, 342, 343
Mostert, Anton, 274
Motlana, Nthato, xv, 3, 91, 92, 96, 97, 99, 107, 316, 327, 329, 330, 333, 334, 341, 343, 348, 349, 350
Motlanthe, Kgalema, 228, 229, 230, 231, 234, 250, 255, 369, 375
Motlatsi, James, xv, 140–1, 143, 145, 150, 151, 153, 154, 155, 156, 171, 175, 176, 177, 178, 179, 185, 193, 194, 196, 200, 201, 202, 203, 219, 236, 237, 252, 255, 256, 321, 347, 350, 383
Motsepe, Patrice, 348
Motsepe, Tshepo, 385
Motumi, Margaret, 106
movies, 22–3, 54, 127–8
Mphahlele, Alfred, 140
Mphaphuli High School, 27, 29, 46, 60, 88
Mpofu, Dali, 240
MTN, 337, 349, 350, 363
Mtshali, Oswald, 1
Mtshotshisa, Nomazizi, 174, 282, 316, 322
Mudau, Baldwin, 30–2
Mudau, Hope Mukondeleli, 30–2, 58, 88, 322, 383, 387
Mufamadi, Sydney, 96, 134, 221, 225, 261, 275, 320
Mugabe, Robert, 342
Mulaudzi, Lufuno, xv

Multi-Party Negotiating Process (MPNP), 279, 304, 307, 323, 324
Muofhe, Tshifhiwa, 77
Museveni, Yoweri, 386
Myburgh, Tertius, 187
Myburgh, James, 314–15

N
Naidoo, Jay, xv, 126, 219, 220, 225, 226, 228, 234, 235, 236, 275, 328
Naidoo, Sagree, xvi
Nanise, Simphiwe, xv, 172, 204, 264
National Archives, xvi
National Empowerment Consortium (NEC), 334, 335, 341, 342
National Intelligence Service (NIS), 235, 262, 268, 305
National Party (NP), 2, 4, 5, 30, 43, 119, 120, 209, 210, 233, 242, 244, 245, 246, 263, 267, 268, 269, 276, 277, 280, 281, 287, 288, 290, 291, 293, 294, 300, 301, 302, 303, 308, 311, 313, 315, 323, 326, 328, 341, 343, 352, 356
National Security Management System (NSMS), 195, 272
National Union of Mineworkers (NUM)
Amabutho, 177–8
collective bargaining, 150–9
formation, 130–40
growth, 145, 146, 148–9
launch, 141–2
legal strategy, 160–8
management, 171–6
media, 168–71
NUM News, 170
strike of 1987, 182–205
National Union of South African Students (Nusas), 45
nationalisation, 120, 249, 270, 284, 286, 353, 379
Naudé, Beyers, 76
Ncube, Don, xv, 197
Ndlovu, Duma, xv, 21
necklace, 212–15
Nedbank, 47, 104
Nefolovhodwe, Pandelani, xv, 56, 58, 62
Nel, Christo, xv, 273, 274, 275, 276, 277
Netshitenzhe, Joel, 261
New Africa Investments Limited (Nail), 327, 329, 330, 333–6, 341–4, 348, 349, 350

New Partnership for Africa's
  Development (Nepad), 366, 369
Newclare, 4
Ngakane, Morris, 76
Ngoepe, Bernard, xv, 307, 395
Ngubane, Ben, 279
Nhlanhla, Joe, 261, 271, 346
Nicol, Martin, xv, 158
Norwood Police Station, 78
Nuclear Fuels Corporation (Nufcor),
  154, 155
Nqakula, Charles, 231
Ntsandeni, JS, xv
Ntshilinga, Percy, xv
Nkobi, Thomas, 253
Ntsebeza, Lungisile, xvi
Nyanda, Siphiwe, 231, 232
Nyerere, Julius, 314
Nzo, Alfred, 214, 247, 254, 262, 277, 314

O
Oil Producing and Exporting Countries
  (Opec), 55, 114
Okumu, Washington, 311
Olaf Palme Prize, 390
Old Mutual, 118
O'Malley, Padraig, xv, xvi, 282, 388
Omar, Dullah, 234
Omni Media, 336
Operation Vula, 230, 231, 232, 235, 247,
  250, 251, 258, 262, 269, 278, 279, 304
Oppenheimer, Ernest, 5, 117, 122, 186
Oppenheimer, Harry, 91, 98, 99, 100–5,
  116, 117, 118, 120, 121, 122, 123, 124,
  125, 132, 184, 186, 187, 198, 202, 284,
  285, 286, 287, 341
Oppenheimer, Mary, 118
Oppenheimer, Nicky, 118, 120, 287
Oppenheimer, Philip, 118
Orange Book, 124
O'Reilly, Tony, 341,
Orlando, 5, 50, 73, 75, 78
Oxford, 120, 190

P
Pahad, Aziz, 270
Pahad, Essop, 286
Paisley, Ian, 368
Pakendorf, Harald, 186
Pan Africanist Congress (PAC), 130

parliament, 121, 122, 170–1, 310, 319, 339,
  376,
Patel, Dipak, 231
Paulus, Arrie, 113, 138
Pearsons, 341, 344
Phaswana, Fred, xv, 102, 109, 110
Phaswani, Peter, xv, 88
Phosa, Mathews, 262, 290
Pick 'n Pay, 104
Picker, Liz, 225
Pieterson, Hector, 73
Pillay, Ivan, 230, 231
Pillay, Kuben, xv, 153, 164, 165, 166, 167,
  175, 180, 196
Pimville, 5, 89
Pinder, Rodney, 288
Pityana, Barney, xv, 49, 52, 56, 57, 96, 107,
  223
Pollsmoor Prison, 213
Population Registration Act, 2
Power Park, 5
Premier Foods, 336
Pretoria Central Prison, 62
Pretoria Minute, 278
Progressive Party, 94
Project Free Enterprise, 274
Protea Glen, 5

Q
Qoboza, Percy, 91, 92, 93, 102

R
racism, 2, 12, 24–5, 46, 51, 219, 298, 305;
  see also apartheid
Raine, Sheryl, 168, 169
Ramaphosa, Andile, 385
Ramaphosa, Cyril
  African National Congress, 222–41,
    247–8, 252–65
  black consciousness, 24–7, 48–58
  black economic empowerment, 329–35,
    337–9, 351–63
  business, 329–50, 363–6
  detention, 59–69, 77–8
  early years, 1–18
  family, 3, 6–11, 75–7
  high school, 19–42
  leadership, 378–81, 382–96
  negotiator, 278–93, 293–312, 322–7
  Northern Ireland, 367–9

religion, 16–18, 32–7, 50–3, 86–9
trade unionism, 127–9, 151–9, 162–8,
   170–4, 182–205, 218–21
university, 43–58, 69–70
Ramaphosa, Douglas, xv, 3, 8, 9, 10–11,
   383
Ramaphosa, Erdmuthe, 1, 3, 9–10, 248,
   249
Ramaphosa, Ivy, 3
Ramaphosa, Samuel, 1, 3, 7–8, 322
Ramashia, Rams, xv, 8, 84
Ramon, Christine, 338
Ramphele, Mamphela, 385
Ramutumbu, TA, xv
Rand Daily Mail, 23, 169
Rand Mines, 183
Randall, Christine, xv
Reagan, Ronald, 367
Reception Committee, 224, 246, 252
Reconstruction and Development
   Programme (RDP), 328
Record of Understanding, 301, 302, 303,
   304
Reddy, Thiven, xvi
Reis, Robert, 200
religion
   evangelism, 16, 24, 29, 32, 34–8, 50, 51,
      53, 84, 382, 392–3
   Lutheranism, 9, 10, 16, 17, 23, 32, 33,
      34, 36, 392
   politics, 23, 25, 26, 27, 36, 50, 52, 382,
      384, 392
Relly, Gavin, 98, 100, 118, 119, 186, 187,
   193, 198, 200, 202, 242, 274, 277, 286,
   353
Rembrandt Group, 104
Rhodes, Cecil, 120
Rhodes Scholarships, 120
Riekert Commission, 124
Rivonia, 229
Roberts, Ronald Suresh, xvi, 212–14
Robben Island see African National
   Congress
Rockville, 89
Rugby School, 95
Ruggiero, Renato, 365
Rupert, Anton, 97, 100, 101, 102, 104, 187

S
Saaiplaas, 173
Sabi Sabi, 285

Sachs, Albie, 292
Salae, Puseletso, 139
Sampson, Anthony, 213
Sanders, James, xvi, 251, 268, 271
Sandler, Jonty, 330, 334, 343, 349, 350
Sanlam, 120
Sasol, 117, 285
Saunders, Chris, xvi
Scargill, Arthur, 255, 370
Schoon, Willem, 188
Sedibe, Gabriel, 58
Sekano-Ntoane High School, 19–27, 38,
   75, 84, 169
Seegers, Annette, xvi
Seekings, Jeremy, 25
Selebi, Jackie, 57
separate development see apartheid
Serote, Wally, 41–2
Sexwale, Tokyo, 328, 346, 369
Shaik, Mo, 231
Shanduka, 340, 347, 348, 349, 350, 351,
   390
Shanduka Foundation, 389, 390
Sharpeville, 11
Shell, 104
Shope, Max, 225
Siala, Eddie, 91, 92
Sibasa, 7, 27, 28, 30, 34, 35, 37, 47, 53, 84
Sigcau, Stella, 328
Sikhakhane, Jabulani, xv, 345
Simons, Mary, xvi
Sinn Fein, 367, 368, 369
Sisulu, Albertina, 274, 275
Sisulu, Zwelakhe, 342
Sisulu, Walter, xi, 2, 92, 227, 229, 245, 247,
   249, 253, 314
six-pack agreement, 307, 310, 326
Sizani, Gerald, 78
Slabbert, Frederik van Zyl, xv, 96, 97, 98,
   239, 256, 270, 275, 284, 285
Slack, Hank, 118
Slovo, Joe, 85, 224, 225, 230, 247, 250,
   251, 256, 258, 259, 261, 262, 263, 277,
   278, 286, 290, 301, 303, 304, 305, 313,
   314, 315, 319, 353, 391
Smith, Howard, xvi
Sobukwe, Robert, 53
Socialist Party of Azania (Sopa), 26
Solomon, Hassan, xv
Solomon Mahlangu Freedom College,
   84, 85
Sonn, Franklin, 99, 100, 329

Sonn, Julian, 99
Sophiatown, 3, 4
South Africa Foundation (SAF), 104, 105, 121, 187, 277, 364
South African Institute for International Affairs (SAIIA), 122
South African Breweries (SABMiller), 117, 333, 336, 364
South African Chamber of Business (Sacob), 352
South African Communist Party (SACP), xiv, 108, 204, 216, 221, 224, 225, 226, 228, 229, 231, 232, 243, 250, 251, 255–9, 262, 269, 277, 279, 295–7, 314, 353, 360, 362, 374, 384
South African Confederation of Trade Unions (Sactu), 113, 136, 215, 217, 225, 232
South African Council of Churches (SACC), 164
South African Labour Bulletin (SALB), 169
South African Native National Congress *see* African National Congress
South African Students' Movement (SASM), 48, 73
South African Students' Organisation (Saso), 45, 48, 49, 51, 52, 54, 56, 57, 58, 62, 67, 125
Soviet Union (USSR), 11, 85, 173, 209, 210, 353
Soweto, 5–7, 10, 11, 12, 15, 233, 237–40, 254, 260, 284, 286, 311, 383
Soweto People's Delegation, 237
Soweto Students' Representative Council, 71, 75
Spaarwater, Maritz, 268
Sparks, Allister, xv, 281, 282, 283, 284, 317
Spicer, Michael, xv, 132, 187, 193, 277, 286, 335, 350, 363, 379
St Helena, 162
Stallone, Sylvester, 127
Stanford University, 144
Standard Bank, 104, 347–8, 363
State Security Council (SSC), 270
Steyn, Jan, xv, 91, 101, 102, 103, 104, 105, 109, 110
Stofile, Makhenkesi, 54
Strelitz, Jill, xv
Steward, Dave, xv, 245, 295, 297, 311, 316
Strand, Per, xvi
Stratcom, 272

Strydom, Major Sarel, 58
Student Christian Association (SCA), 51
Student Christian Movement (SCM), 23, 26, 29, 34, 37, 50, 51, 53, 54, 56, 76, 80, 86
sufficient consensus, 292–3
Sunday Times, 187, 306, 337, 344
Suttner, Raymond, xv, 25, 60, 65, 267, 297
Suzman, Helen, 95, 121
Swaziland, 14
Synthesis, 97–8

T
Tambo, Oliver, xi, 2, 83, 92, 99, 209, 210, 213, 223, 225, 227, 230, 232, 233, 235, 240, 249, 250, 253, 254, 269, 270, 271, 278, 286, 314, 315
Tanzania, 85
Taylor, Rupert, xvi
Teamsters, 127
Timol, Ahmed, 77, 78
Thabong, 157
Thatcher, Dennis, 105
Thatcher, Margaret, 105, 351, 367
Thokoane, Strike, xv
Thompson, Clive, xv, 161, 163, 179
Thompson, Julian Ogilvie, 98, 118, 119, 187
Thulo, Ishmaele, 143
Times Media Limited (TML), 341
Tiro, Onkgopotse Ramothibi, 46–8
Titus, Zam, 304
Toyota SA, 333
Trade Union Council of South Africa (Tucsa), 128, 129
Transitional Executive Council, 304, 306, 310
Transkei, 141, 143, 290, 304
Trollope, Anthony, xiii
tribalism *see* ethnicity
Truth and Reconciliation Commission (TRC), 212, 299, 380
Tshiawelo, 6, 10, 11, 16, 126, 127, 248, 322, 382, 389, 392
Tshikovhele, MS, xv
Tshilidzi Primary School, 16, 389
Tshwete, Steve, 260
Tsogo Investment Holdings, 338
Tsvangirai, Morgan, 370
Tucker, Bob, xv, 106, 107, 109, 128, 129, 178

Tutu, Desmond, 96, 97, 212
Turfloop *see* University of the North

U
Umkhonto weSizwe (MK) *see* African
  National Congress
Unilever, 104
United Democratic Front (UDF), 184,
  211, 212, 217, 222, 226, 227, 234, 237,
  238, 239, 240, 241, 245, 246, 247, 249,
  250, 251, 252, 255, 259, 260, 261, 262,
  269, 274, 275, 276, 283, 284, 314, 319,
  384
United Democratic Movement (UDM),
  343
University Christian Movement (UCM),
  51
University of Durban-Westville (UDW),
  43, 126
University of Fort Hare, 44
University of South Africa (Unisa), 45,
  70, 106
University of the North, 43, 44
University of the Western Cape (UWC),
  43
University of Zululand, 44
Unwin, Nigel, xv, 164, 165, 166, 180, 191,
  197, 199
Urban Foundation (UF), 88, 91, 99, 103–
  10, 121, 127, 178, 273, 277, 353, 354
Urban Training Project (UTP), 129

V
Vaal Reefs, 191
Vaderland, 187
Van der Colf, Callie, 200
Van der Merwe, Fanie, xv, 268, 269, 271,
  272, 273, 279, 289, 291, 293, 301, 304
Van der Merwe, Johannes, 188
Van Ryneveld, Tony, xv
Van Wyk, Freddie, 99
Van Zyl, Colonel FAJ, 105
Vavi, Zwelinzima, xiii
Venda Independence Party (VIP), 31
Verwoerd, Hendrik, 120
Victor Verster Prison, 247, 248
Vilakazi, Eugene, 40
Vilakazi, Helbron, xv
Viljoen, Constand, 244

Viljoen, Gerrit, 272, 279, 280, 281, 283,
  288, 290, 294
Vlakplaas, 188, 189
Vlok, Adriaan, 188, 236, 237, 278

W
Waldmeir, Patti, xv, xvi, 268
Weekly Mail, 183
Welkom, 157, 236
Wessels, Leon, 323
Western Deep Levels, 115, 140, 141
Western Native Township, xiv, 1, 3, 4, 5,
  6, 9, 11, 12, 13, 89, 329
Westonaria, 322
Wiehahn, Nic, 124
Wiehahn Commission, 124, 125, 130, 131,
  132, 137, 148, 160, 180, 216
Wilson, Francis, 148
Wilson, John, 274
Witbank, 156, 338
Wits United, 390
Woodhouse, John, 94
Woodhouse Sarah, 94

Y
Young, Michael, 270
Young Ambassadors, 23, 69
Youth Alive, 86, 394

Z
Zabala, Griffith, xv, 19, 20, 39, 53, 60, 61,
  63, 69, 83
Zedillo, Ernesto, 365
Zimbabwe, 342, 346, 369
Zuma, Jacob, 254, 258, 262, 263, 270, 271,
  277, 290, 301, 314, 315, 320, 328, 346,
  376, 378, 379